Thank you to all the Manhattan New School students and alumni, along with their fine teachers, who helped me discover that writing can be thought of as a way to honor and preserve our students' childhoods.

Featured on the cover, spanning their childhood years at the Manhattan New School, are the kindergarten and fifth-grade photos of Maia, Antoniel, Isabelle, Patrick, Laura, Kyla, Aundrelyn, and Riri. On the inside front cover, meet Alejandra, Alex, Daniella, Dominique, and Elisa. And on the inside back cover, you'll find Jun, Ronnie, and Suzannah.

Inside this book, discover for yourself how the delight, wonder, and messiness of writing through childhood grows from kindergarten to fifth grade.

WRITING
THROUGH CHILDHOOD
Rethinking Process and Product

SHELLEY HARWAYNE

HEINEMANN
Portsmouth, NH

Heinemann
A division of Reed Elsevier Inc.
361 Hanover Street
Portsmouth, NH 03801–3912
www.heinemann.com

Offices and agents throughout the world

The author and publisher wish to thank those who have generously given permission to reprint borrowed material:

"I Never Hear" from *All Together* by Dorothy Aldis. Copyright © 1925–1928, 1934, 1939, 1952, renewed 1953, © 1954–1956, 1962 by Dorothy Aldis, © 1967 by Roy E. Porter, renewed. Used by permission of G.P. Putnam's Sons, an imprint of Penguin Putnam Books for Young Readers, a division of Penguin Putnam, Inc.

Excerpt from *My Father's Hands* by Joanne Ryder. Copyright © 1994 by Joanne Ryder. Used by permission of HarperCollins Publishers.

Excerpts from *Only the Moon and Me* by Richard J. Margolis. Copyright © 1969 by Richard Margolis. Used by permission of HarperCollins Publishers.

Credits continue on p. 411.

Library of Congress Cataloging-in-Publication Data
Harwayne, Shelley.
    Writing through childhood : rethinking process and product / Shelley Harwayne.
        p.   cm.
    Includes bibliographical references and index.
    ISBN 0-325-00290-8
    1. English language—Composition and exercises—Study and teaching (Elementary).
    I. Title.
    LB1576.H29 2001
    372.62'3044—dc21
                                                                    2001042427

Editor: Lois Bridges
Production service: Patricia Adams
Production coordination: Abigail M. Heim
Interior photographs: Shelley Harwayne, Joanne Hindley Salch, and Herb Shapiro
Cover design: Catherine Hawkes, Cat and Mouse Design
Cover design coordination: Renée Le Verrier
Manufacturing: Louise Richardson

Printed in the United States of America on acid-free paper
05   04   03   02   01   RRD   1   2   3   4   5

In memory of
my brother
Allen Perner,
who so appreciated
the joys of childhood

and in tribute to
Joanne Hindley Salch
and
Judy Davis,
exquisite teachers of writing
who for so long
graciously
shared with me
their students,
their expertise,
and
their passion for
the teaching of writing

CONTENTS

Acknowledgments   xi

Introduction   xiv

1. MEET SOME CHILDHOOD WRITERS   1

   Benefits of Letting Kids Be Kids   4
   Putting a Premium on Playfulness   19

2. DESIGNING WRITING WORKSHOPS WITH
   CHILDREN IN MIND   21

   Childhood Behaviors and Needs   23
   Childhood Descriptors and Children's Writing   40

3. REVISING OUR USE OF THE WRITER'S NOTEBOOK   41

   Getting Started with Writer's Notebooks   43
   Supporting Notebook Writing   50
   Planting Deep Roots   68
   Setting Realistic Goals   70
   Using Writer's Notebooks with Elementary
      Students: A Summary   78
   Afterword   79

4. RESPONDING TO STUDENT WRITING   81

   The Basics   84
   Conference Guidelines   87
   Writing Conference Transcripts   92
   Improving Our Skills as Conference Partners   106

5. READING TO INFORM YOUR WRITING   111

   Kinds of Reading-Writing Connections   113

   A Closer Look at Assessment-Driven Reading-Writing
     Connections   114

   A Closer Look at Text-Driven Reading-Writing
     Connections   128

   A Closer Look at Student-Driven Reading-Writing
     Connections   145

   A Closer Look at Course-of-Study-Driven Reading-
     Writing Connections   149

   Learning to Talk with Confidence and Competence About
     Quality Texts   150

   Reading-Writing Connections: That's What It's All About   154

6. WORKING WITH OUR YOUNGEST WRITERS   157

   Extending the First Invitation to Write   161

   Whole-Class Gatherings for Young Writers   162

   Conferring in the Early-Childhood Workshop   167

   Special Share Meetings in the Early-Childhood
     Workshop   182

   The Reading-Writing Connection   183

   Providing Early-Childhood Students with Many Reasons
     to Write   191

   Grade Two—What's New?   193

7. SPELLING: AN ESSENTIAL INGREDIENT IN THE
   EARLY-CHILDHOOD WRITING WORKSHOP   209

   The Teaching of Spelling in Minilessons   211

   The Teaching of Spelling in Writing Conferences   215

   Spelling Researcher Routines   221

   Other Spelling Rituals   225

   Informing Parents   226

   The Teaching of Spelling as We Move Up in the Grades   227

   Spellers in Literature   234

8. THE WRITING WORKSHOP: A PLACE TO EXPERIMENT, IMPROVISE, AND INVENT 235

Maintaining the Researcher's Stance in the Teaching of Writing 238
From Small Suggestions to Well-Developed Practice 240
Adding Special Events to the Writing Workshop 243
Other Arenas for Experimenting, Improvising, and Inventing 285

9. FOCUSING ON PARTICULAR GENRES: POETRY 287

Zooming in on Poetry 290
Doing What Comes Naturally: Writing Poetry in Kindergarten 290
These Are a Few of Our Favorite Things: Writing Poetry in Grade One 293
Lean on Me: Writing Poetry in Grade Two 300
Making the Leap: Writing Poetry in Grade Three 305
Going Deeper: Writing Poetry in Grade Four 311
Reaching Out: Writing Poetry in Grade Five 316
When Principals Are Willing to Write Poems 318
Childhood Poets 321

10. EDITING, PUBLISHING, AND OTHER WAYS TO MAKE PARENTS SMILE 323

An Explanation of the Chapter Title 326
The Teaching of Editing 326
Publishing in the Life of a School 328
Informing Families About the Teaching of Writing 341
Send Home Significant Parent Newsletters 355
Keep Parents Smiling 358

CONCLUSION 359

APPENDICES 361

Bibliography 363

Worksheet on School-Wide Rites of Passage in
the Teaching of Writing 376

Questionnaire on Carving Out Time for a
Regularly Scheduled Writing Workshop 377

Worksheet on Implications for
Broad Goals 378

Joanne Hindley Salch's Worksheet for Learning
from Conferences 379

Conference Practice Sheets—Our Youngest
Writers 380

Matthew's Writing Folder—Illustrating Variety
of First-Grade Genres 385

Editing/Publishing Checklist 394

Blank Spelling Study Sheet 395

Professional Development Scenarios in the
Teaching of Writing 396

Calendar Project Directions and Planning
Sheets 398

Index 399

ACKNOWLEDGMENTS

It has taken me five years to complete a trilogy about my experiences at the Manhattan New School. All the while I have been working full-time, as a principal, deputy superintendent, and now superintendent of schools. That has meant being glued to my desk at home on every weekend, holiday, summer vacation, and the few snow days that come our way. So my first thank-you belongs to my husband, Neil, my son, Michael, my daughter, J.J., and her husband, David—I am grateful for your patience, encouragement, and genuine interest in the work I do. With the publication of this book, I am hoping for a long period of writer's block. I look forward to leisurely weekends, family get-togethers, and vacation getaways. I do know what I have been missing.

I am grateful as well to all my colleagues at the Manhattan New School. The elegance with which they run their beautiful classrooms gave me the peace of mind and white space in which to think new thoughts about our beloved children. The brilliance and boldness with which they teach inspired me to generate new thoughts about the teaching of writing. Each time I visit, I remain in awe of their expertise, integrity, and humanity.

To the children and their families I must say thank you, gracias, merci, todah, grazie, danke, tak, eucharisto, shukran, spasibo, dou-jia, obrigado, salamatpo, asante, polla, pale manderit, dekujeme vam, and so on, in all the dozens of other languages that graced our schoolhouse. Thank you for leaving your writing in my mailbox, on my desk, and taped to my office walls. Thank you for being so honest, clever, hardworking, and appreciative. Thank you for asking for advice, taking advice, and offering advice. Thank you for keeping in touch and for sending me copies of your latest short stories, poems, letters to the editor, bat mitzvah speeches, and college essays. Thank you for being proud of me. I am as ever proud of you.

I am likewise grateful to my colleagues at the Central Board of Education. When Al Gore campaigned in our city, he noted, "Just because New York City schools are labeled P.S. doesn't mean they can be an afterthought." Here's to all those dedicated folks who make it possible for one city to educate more than 1.1 million public school children. I am especially thankful for my colleagues in District 2. Someone once suggested to me that becoming superintendent of this district was like being asked to teach the honors class. Indeed, it is an honor and a privilege to work with such smart, decent, and hardworking people. My heartfelt thanks extend to my deputy superintendents, cabinet members, and all the principals, assistant principals, teachers, staff developers, school board members, and district office staff in Community School District 2. My work is continually fed by the classrooms you create, the questions you ask, and the conversations we have.

To all my friends at Heinemann, thank you for your wisdom, caring, and know-how. It has always been comforting to know that you can lift your magic wands and turn thick wads of loose white sheets into beautifully bound books. A special thank you to Lois Bridges, my editor, who not only supports my writing with unconditional love and a keen eye, she also supports my everyday role as superintendent with her confidence, camaraderie, and all those phone calls and electronic communications that give me the courage to keep doing the right thing for children and their teachers. Thank you as well to Leigh Peake, editorial director, who cares so much that our New York City stories of public education get told and told well. I am also grateful to Renée Le Verrier, Maura Sullivan, and Patty Adams, who add joy and expertise to the completion of my books.

And finally, a golden thank-you to all the brilliant researchers, master teachers, and exceptional writers who have paved the way for children to make writing a part of their lives. Your work has revolutionized our understanding of what it means to be literate. You have enriched our schools and the lives of our students and their teachers. We are forever in your debt.

INTRODUCTION

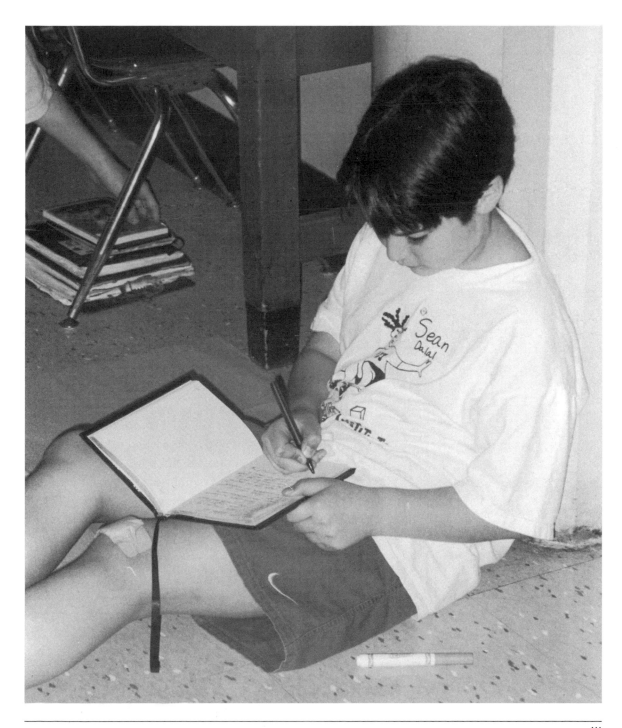

This book stands on the shoulders of all the writing researchers who have so brilliantly built a solid foundation upon which all of us are creating reading and writing classrooms, schoolhouses, and school districts. This particular story is also grounded in two previous publications, *Going Public: Priorities and Practice at The Manhattan New School* and *Lifetime Guarantees: Toward Ambitious Literacy Teaching.* The first book offers a behind-the-scenes description of the elementary school that provides the setting for all the literacy work presented in the second book. In this volume, the last in the trilogy, I provide a close-up look at the teaching of writing, the subject that has always touched me deepest. As a former teacher of teachers in the area of writing, I held on tightly to this subject area when I became a principal, much the way many kindergartners cling to their parents during the first week of school. Only, I never made the separation; I kept on clinging. And this was probably one of the best decisions I made as principal, because knowing my students as writers has added richness to all the other roles a principal has to play.

During the eight years I spent as the instructional leader of the Manhattan New School, a public elementary school in the heart of New York City, I passed many, many hours reading and responding to student writing as well as talking to teachers about their students' efforts and their own. With the turn of every page, I discovered my students' interests and fears, their achievements and frustrations, their friends and enemies. I found out about their family lives, their homelands, their immigration stories, their fantasies, and their dreams. I learned about their tastes as readers, sports enthusiasts, artists, and musicians. I read their opinions about teachers, field trips, bus rides, homework assignments, and life on the playground. I became aware of children who needed to talk to guidance counselors, therapists, and medical doctors.

Working in classrooms during writing workshops also enabled me to fine-tune my teaching abilities. I discovered ways to help children find a place of honor for writing in their lives, to discover accessible genres that best support their content, and new ways to use literature to inform their own writing. I also discovered ways to help students to use their writing to strengthen their skills as readers, ways to use their writing to enrich the quality of life in our school and in our community, and ways to offer deliberate writing challenges that would help students improve the quality of their work. In short, knowing my students as writers enabled me to become a better instructional leader, social director, parent educator, and so on.

Most of all, I discovered that writing could be thought of as a way to honor and preserve our students' childhoods. Which brings me to the title of this book, *Writing Through Childhood.* When we opened our schoolhouse in the fall of 1991, I came prepared to shower my students with many years of writing process know-how. I did not expect to learn so many new things about the teaching of writing. After all, I had been a teacher of teachers. I understood the writing process and workshop approaches, or so I thought. What I didn't understand, or had forgotten, was that writing during your child-hood years is necessarily different from writing during your adult years.

Carey Dunne was a fifth grader at the Manhattan New School when she wrote a letter of complaint to all the shoe manufacturers in our city. The long letter ended with the following passages:

> *Where I live in New York, people have so much choice. They can eat McDonalds, or they can eat Indian. They can live in apartments or they can live in houses. They can walk or they can take a trip on a city bus. But they have no choice in what kind of shoes to wear. It's either big ugly boot with heels, big ugly boot with heels, or big ugly boot with heels. Girls are growing up in 2 seconds. If anyone can change that, it's the people who make it happen. The people who make kids' makeup, kids' clothes, and kids' shoes. It's the people who make money by designing uncomfortable trash that goes on your feet. You are giving us a big push over 8, 9, 10, 11, 12, 13, and 14. While we could be playing, running around, and having fun, we are spending our childhoods doing makeovers! If you would just give us a chance to be kids, think of how many girls' lives would be basically saved. It's not just the heels; it's the effect that the heels give. The effect that somehow changes a girl into a woman faster than a toddler will bite into a lollipop. We have plenty of time to be grown-ups later, but unfortunately only about 11 years to be kids.*
>
> *You can do New York a favor. You can let us be kids. Think of it this way: if people started designing adult shoes with hearts and Barbies and pink flashing lights all over them, how would you feel? You would feel like the world was forcing you to look like a dopey kid, like a baby. Well, I feel like the world is forcing me to look like a nerdy fashion-nut adult. It feels like I am being sucked into this fad of clunky heels. It is like I am not allowed to look like a kid. I hope you realize how hard it is to be a 10-year-old living in 1999 that is not allowed to wear heels. And I am going to ask you one of the biggest favors I have ever asked: please stop making us look like miniature adults with boats on our feet and please start making some shoes using sense. Thank you greatly.*
>
> *Sincerely,*
> *Carey Dunne*

Carey is concerned about young people looking like miniature adults. I'm also concerned about them being treated like miniature adults, particularly in their writing classrooms. Just as I don't want to dress up young girls and send them down the runway as beauty queens who look seventeen when they are seven, I don't want to ask elementary school children to conduct themselves in unnatural and inappropriate ways when they are asked to select topics, genres, writing tools, and techniques.

The Martha Stewart catalog boasts a Snoballer, a plastic handheld device for making perfectly round snowballs. Our students don't need such an adult invention. They don't need to make perfectly round snowballs. Children need to delight in making snowballs as best they can, filled with the wonder and messiness of it all. They need to take pride, when through lots of practice and some adult guidance, their snowballs get rounder, firmer, and grander. Likewise, in our writing workshops, we must look through the lens of childhood, making sure we don't eliminate all the delight, wonder, and messiness that is associated with children at work and at play.

It is my hope then, that this book serves as an acknowledgment that elementary school children are in the Little League of writing, not yet ready for Yankee Stadium. This book also serves as a thank-you to all the Manhattan New School students and alumni, along with their fine teachers, who continue to remind me to always let children be children.

CHAPTER 1

MEET SOME CHILDHOOD WRITERS

*When you end your notebook, you'll probably take one look at it and say,
"Okay, now what am I supposed to do with this?" And you'll stand there, mind
blank and puzzled, doing nothing. Well, what are you supposed to do with it?
Whatever you want. But don't throw it out. It's your childhood, your life . . .*

—Carey and Annie, age 8

Key Writing Lessons

1. We must create writing workshops uniquely designed for children.
2. We want the writing of children to sound like children, not like adults.
3. There are many benefits to allowing children to write like children.
4. Children can write especially well about "childish" topics.
5. Children's writing provides students with a means of preserving their childhood memories.
6. We can actively promote childhood play by elevating these moments when they appear naturally in children's writing.
7. We can actively foster the needed play of childhood by turning children's ideas into projects.
8. Writing offers children a means of exploring and sharing their dreams, as well as their imaginary and fantasy lives.
9. Children who know how to play approach writing with the required openness it takes to craft quality work.
10. School basics need to include play, projects, and messy work.
11. There is a fine line between work and play in our school and young writers reap the rewards of such an attitude.
12. Children who are allowed and encouraged to be children see potential topics everywhere and are able to take full advantage of the writer's workshop.

The pioneers of the writing process approach took their cue from professional writers. Before the groundbreaking studies of such brilliant researchers as Donald Graves, Janet Emig, and Nancie Atwell, it hadn't occurred to most of us to ask young children to select their own writing topics. No, the children simply wrote about whatever topic we assigned. We then corrected their prescribed writing in the prescribed format, the children copied their work over, and we used this work to decorate the monthly bulletin boards. The journey from "assigning" writing to "teaching" writing has been an exhilarating one for many educators, who were able to extend the insights gained from this new way of thinking to many other aspects of school life. Children's voices were now heard throughout the curriculum and throughout the corridors. Tapping into what we were learning about professional writers' processes, we invited children to engage in prewriting activities, prepare first drafts, receive feedback on their writing, revise their language and meaning, take lessons from the texts they were reading, and publish their work.

My eight years at the Manhattan New School helped me see that I initially took these brilliant kernel ideas of the writing process approach to a bit of an extreme. During the course of several years, I read many authors' memoirs, eager to share their insights and ways of working with my students. I reflected on my own writing process and shared my techniques and thought processes with students. I read many professional books on the teaching of writing and attempted to bring the latest ideas to our young students. I met regularly with my colleagues, each of us eager to share the most moving, layered, and brilliant pieces of writing we could find, to push our children's development. Somehow, I had become driven to invite children to do *all* the things that adult writers could do. In retrospect, before opening the Manhattan New School, I didn't stop to sift through these ideas, eliminating ones that were too sophisticated, too adult. I realize now that I had begun to teach the notes I was taking on the books I was reading, the workshops I was attending, and the conversations with colleagues with whom I was collaborating, instead of teaching the children in front of me. And I fear that I was not alone.

All around the city, teachers were inviting seven-year-olds to write their memoirs. Eight-year-olds were being asked to look for new truths about themselves. Nine-year-olds were being asked to name the seminal issues of their lives. Just what were we thinking? It's true that our students love to hear about the work and life stories of E. B. White, Cynthia Rylant, and Eloise Greenfield, but that didn't mean they could *do* what these prolific, talented, and accomplished writers could do.

My eight years as principal of a jubilant and successful elementary school taught me that children don't need to live writerly lives, they need to live lives that are as joyous, playful, and interesting as the grown-ups who care for them can provide. I wholeheartedly agree with progressive educator Deborah Meier, who in a recent interview in *Newsweek* magazine commented, "The most powerful thing you can do for kids is get them into something interesting, help them imagine a life doing interesting things." I would add that the invitations we extend to our children to do interesting things need to take into account the age of our children.

We all know too many children who are growing up too fast, children who have serious looks on their faces and serious concerns in their hearts, real concerns. Children don't need an hour a day to dig deeper, they need an hour a day to be surrounded with child-size concerns, projects, and dreams. For some children, that hour a day of writing workshop can provide an escape from all the sorrow, pain, and turbulence in their lives. Teachers need not judge the success of their writing workshop by the quantity of therapeutic and moving pieces that are produced. Yes, children will write heartfelt pieces, pieces that make the blood rush to the cheeks of their teachers, but we must not be relentless in our pursuit of those. It is more than okay for children to write in ways that are wondrously childish.

Perhaps not surprisingly, the one aspect of the writing process that remained child-size in our schools was publishing. After all, we couldn't hook up our eight-year-olds with agents and editors. We couldn't talk royalties and contracts. Instead, we slapped a thick strip of red bookbinding tape on the edge of a kindergartner's "All About . . ." book and we congratulated her for "publishing" her work. We toasted our students' first picture books by lifting small paper cups filled with orange juice, congratulating the author, and adding the eight-page marker-and-crayon creation to our basket labeled "published work." It was all so simple and so childlike.

Now after eight years of pulling in close to work with young writers across the curriculum and throughout the school day, I am clear in my intention to create writing workshops uniquely designed for children, not for adults, just as those groundbreaking researchers originally intended us to do. I am determined to bring realistic and pint-size goals to all that we ask young writers to do. And I am certain that when we do this, the rewards will be great.

Benefits of Letting Kids Be Kids

We want children to sound like children. We are not interested in helping nine-year-olds write like nineteen-year-olds. In Bonnie Nardi and Vicki O'Day's important book, *Information Ecologies: Using Technology with Heart,* the authors, in presenting the concept of "affordances," suggest,

> Refrigerators are designed to keep things cool, but they also have a well-known affordance of providing a magnetic surface for hanging up notes, children's artwork, cartoons, and other family information. An industry of refrigerator magnet accessories has sprung up around the "extra" affordance—which is no less real than the affordance of cooling food. (p. 29)

Inviting elementary students to write in unadulterated ways does more in a school than teach children an important means of communication. One of the fringe benefits of hosting a writing workshop for young people is the opportunity to see the world through their wide eyes. I've often thought that this is a real perk for teachers, reminding them what a privilege and a gift it is to spend so much time with young people.

Louise Borden's historical fiction tale *Sleds on Boston Common* takes place during colonial times. In addition to being a compelling story of hardship in Boston during the winter of 1774, it also serves as a powerful example of how children look at the world. British soldiers had closed Boston Harbor and had encamped on Boston Common, the site of the best hills in town. Although the grown-ups had more serious concerns, nine-year-old Henry was determined to use his new birthday sled and was relentless in reclaiming the hills of Boston Common for the simple joys of childhood. Children do look at the world differently from adults and have different priorities and sensibilities.

I think of notebook entries like the one written by Lauren in Figure 1.1 as the educator's version of the year-end corporate bonus. After reading something like this, I go home proud of the work I do, eager to share what I received, and feeling a great deal richer.

When we encourage young writers to select grown-up topics and craft them in adult ways, we are denying ourselves a grand opportunity to see the world through their eyes. More importantly, children reap rewards when we teach writing with our students' ages, unique strengths, and interests in mind.

Children Can Write Expertly on "Childish" Topics

One year, Renay Sadis, our second/third multigrade teacher, took ill and was absent from school for several weeks. She asked that I run her writing workshop. "Do something special with the kids," she suggested. I gladly honored her request, eager to have my own writing class for a while. I designed a writing challenge inspired by a teacher who so missed being around her children.

I offered rather simple instructions to the students, but the results had a surprisingly profound influence on my thinking about the teaching of writing at the elementary

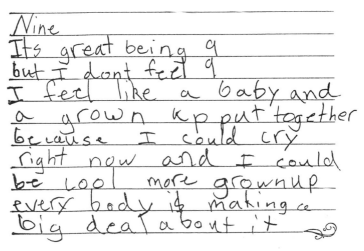

Figure 1.1

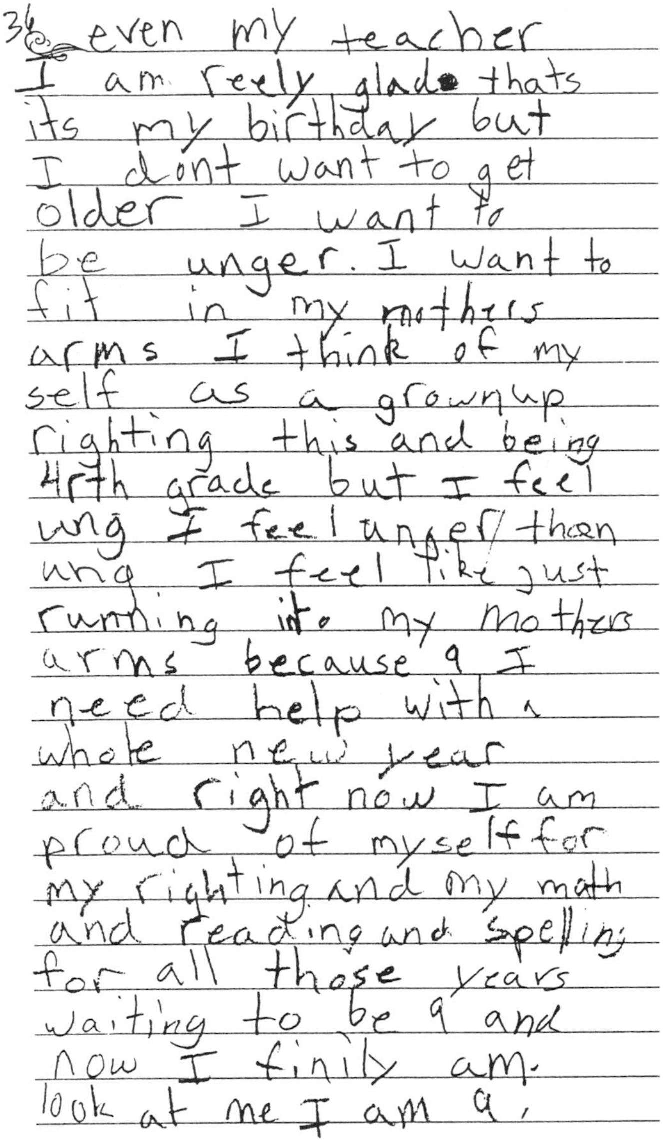

36. even my teacher
I am reely glad thats
its my birthday but
I dont want to get
older I want to
be unger. I want to
fit in my mothers
arms I think of my
self as a grownup
righting this and being
4rth grade but I feel
ung I feel unger/than
uno I feel like just
running into my mother
arms because 9 I
need help with a
whole new year
and right now I am
proud of myself for
my righting and my math
and reading and spelling
for all those years
waiting to be 9 and
now I finily am.
look at me I am 9.

Figure 1.1 (*continued*)

level. I gathered the children in the meeting area and read aloud Jonathan London's picture book *Puddles*. I explained to the students that one reason I love this book is that the author is so good at capturing childhood. He is so good at remembering how much children love to jump in rain puddles. (A colleague, Linda Trifon, recently gave me a copy of a very old children's book titled *The Chatterlings in Wordland*, written and illustrated by Michael Lipman in 1928. The dedication of this book reads in part, "to folk whose feet prefer puddles to pavements." He, of course, was lovingly and admiringly dedicating his book to the children who played on his street.)

After discussing the author's unique talent, I challenged the children to use their writing time to write about topics they believed *only* children could write about well. In fact, I encouraged children to write about those things that most adults could probably *not* write about well (unless of course they were a most talented adult writer like Jonathan London). I then suggested that the children attempt to write with as much quality as they could muster, as we would organize the finished collection into a class anthology to be used as a get-well present for their teacher. If Renay missed being around her children no doubt their words would satisfy her hunger for their company. (One of the big ideas that informs all that I do in the teaching of writing relates to always giving children a reason to do their best. See page 91 for additional information on having real reasons to write and to write well.)

The children seemed delighted with the challenge, as if I had honored the club of childhood to which they all belong. Their writing helped me to pay close attention to this prestigious social order. They wrote enthusiastically, easily, and most of all expertly about topics most of them had never considered writing about before. I not only invited Renay's students to meet this simple challenge but also offered it to children in second-through fifth-grade classes throughout the school. The topics they came up with included the following categories and examples:

Joyful experiences, including skipping down the block, jumping on the bed, pretending to be a rock star, having pillow fights, cooling off in the spray of a fire hydrant, selling lemonade on the street corner, being read bedtime stories, playing with an imaginary friend, and sitting on grandpa's lap.

Rites of passage, including learning to make breakfast, losing a tooth, giving up a security blanket, growing tall enough to reach the kitchen cupboards, and getting an allowance. (See the need for rites of passage in the teaching of writing on page 29).

Childlike behavior, including playing the recorder with your nose, getting gum all over your face, blowing bubbles in your milk, chewing on your hair, and making funny noises with your body.

Bittersweet times, including sharing a bedroom with a new baby brother, getting your own room when your sister leaves home, and getting promoted but realizing your best friend will not be in your class.

More painful experiences, including having to get braces, listening to grown-ups fight, being teased in the playground, having to get used to a new baby-sitter, having to leave a school in the middle of the year, and having to decorate two bedrooms because your parents split up.

A few sample pieces are included here. (In Leo Tolstoy's famous essay, "Are the Peasant Children to Learn to Write from Us, or Are We to Learn from the Peasant Children?" he concludes, "Give the children children's work to read, and give them only children's work as models, for children's compositions are always more correct, more artistic, and morally truer than adults' work." Although I don't believe that children should exclusively read work by other children, I have included many samples of children's work throughout this text, both to make my meaning clear and to serve as material that teachers can share with young students.)

When it snows me and my brother wait for hot cocoa and warm pancakes. When it snows we race like a cheetah racing for its prey, except it's our coats we're racing for. When it snows the snow looks like golden crystals hung from the trees. I love when it snows.

> —Hallie, second grade

"One scoop of ice cream please," I say to the person who's waiting on me. She gives it to me and I say, "Thank you!" I take my ice cream cone to the hot sticky month of June. I start licking it right away. But just then it starts to melt. "Ahh!" I say. "Please mom, will you get me a mountain of napkins?" Just as my mom leaves I start to drown in it. And I think to myself, "Please hurry up mom, it's a hurricane of chocolate!" My mom comes just then, and I paste myself with napkins. When we get home, mom says, "Well, I guess you can't wear that shirt anymore." "Yes I can, I'll just get my brown marker and turn it into the brown shirt I've been wanting!"

> —Johannah, third grade

I have the house all to myself. I am going to eat candy and chocolate and all the other things my mom doesn't let me eat before dinner. And I'm going to turn the music louder than I usually do and have a party with my cat.

> —Lauren, fourth grade

I sit patiently at my Grandma's feet, like a dog waiting to be scratched. She looks down, pats her knees and says, "Come on up." I climb up to the top of her lap and she strokes my knotty black hair. Her lap is soft and warm like a pile of freshly washed laundry. As she rocks me back and forth, I talk, talk and talk, till I run out of breath. I stroke her hazelnut hair, stiff from too much hairspray. I tuck loose gray strands behind her ear.

All too soon, she says, "Munchkin, I need to work in the kitchen." Sadly, I leap off her lap, my body now cold, and follow her into the kitchen, where she is busy and I tug at her apron and ask to help. I help throw carrots and celery into the soup, chop nuts for the cookies and set out plates and silverware for the table.

Grandma and I are like two peas in a pod.

> —Vickie, fifth grade

I had heard the dentist tightens them until they more than hurt. The first time I got my braces tightened, I did not believe it. The second time was a different experience. It was a war between me, my braces and my teeth. My teeth were strangled by the braces and my gums were starting to get sore. My teeth were trying to run in all of the directions possible and trying to flip and spin like gymnasts. I was waiting for them to burst out of my mouth and run. My mouth was trying not to break in half. My braces came closer and closer to my teeth every time they got tightened that visit. First, the right side of my mouth elevated and the left side descended and then they switched so the left side of my mouth was higher just like a see-saw. Now I remembered all of the shiny, glittery, bright colors of rubber bands to choose from. I picked 6 new colors and thought that they were worth the wild war. The dentist frowned and told me that I had to pick only 4. I went home with my new train tracks and clean teeth that would not stop leaning against the railing. Later I felt like an uneven train track. It felt like a sharp plant. It is time to go back to the dentist!

—Joseph, fifth grade

I was delighted to discover the pieces above, as well as dozens of others that I collected as a result of what has come to be called the Puddles Challenge. I wondered why I had inspired so many pieces filled with voice. As an experienced teacher of writing, I was used to every once in a while finding a piece of student work that made me marvel at children's ability to write well. But it was rather rare to simultaneously discover so many memorable works.

On this occasion, I think our students wrote well for a number of reasons. They relished the challenge. They owned the turf. They trusted that they had important things to say. They breathed the details. They delighted in the audience response.

Additionally, students chose issues or events that stood out over time in their childhoods. Having shared Jonathan London's *Puddles*, in which the main characters share the thrill of jumping in rain puddles, it was no surprise that our students wrote about things that happen frequently during their childhood rather than narratives about special isolated events. In other words, one gets the feeling that Hallie can recall many splendid snowy days, Johannah has dripped more than one dessert, Lauren has frequently relished being home alone, Vickie knows very well the comforts of her grandma's lap, and Joseph has many memories of visiting the orthodontist. The cumulativeness of their experiences seemed to make it easier for them to write well about these topics. It is as if they were not merely recalling any one day, but a feeling gathered from many days.

What began as a simple writing challenge in one classroom became a lens through which I began thinking about all our elementary students and their writing. What began as one simple minilesson, challenging students to select topics that really belonged to them, became a filter through which I examined all that we were doing in our workshops. I became determined that everything in our writing workshop demonstrated a deep respect for childhood, capitalized on children's unique strengths and interests, and acknowledged that writing during childhood is markedly different from writing as an adult. (See Chapter 2, "Designing Writing Workshops with Childhood in Mind.")

As building principal, I realized that my main criteria for evaluating the success of a writing workshop was quite simple. I asked myself, "Is the children's writing true to the spirit of childhood?" When I walk about a writing workshop, I expect to be touched by young people's insights, observations, and opinions about the world. I expect to sigh, smile, and occasionally be reminded of my own childhood.

Childrens' Writing Is a Way of Preserving Their Childhood Memories

When we put a premium on topics that are considered meaty, deep, or significant to adult eyes *and* we ask students to probe these issues with sophisticated techniques, we are denying children the opportunity to capture their childhoods through childish eyes. We are also denying them the written texts that will preserve their memories of themselves as children. I recently saw the movie *The Disney Kid,* in which a forty-year-old man is visited by his eight-year-old self. What an experience, what a "This can only happen on the silver screen" experience. Most of us have great difficulty in remembering what we were like when we were children. Oh, how I wish someone had asked me to capture my honest notions about the world when I was eight or nine years old. What was I like? What did I think about? What was important to me? What made me happy? How did I handle friendships, loss, and separation? I simply can't remember.

Bruce Coville, in Paula W. Graham's *Speaking of Journals*, comments on journal keeping as a means of preserving childhood memories. He notes on page 191, "If I'm with a group of fifth graders I'll say, 'There's probably not one of you here who can tell me in detail what happened your first day of first grade, a very important day in your life, but it's all recorded in your under brain. It's all registered there, and there is a way to save it and that's by keeping a journal. Journal keeping is a way of saving your life, saving yourself for yourself, a gift you give yourself, a gift you give yourself ten years later.' I tell them about keeping a journal and using it like a fishhook to pull up images."

The realization that I have meager memories of myself as a child fed my thinking when I wrote a letter to Manhattan New School graduates. In part, the letter read,

> Do all that you can to guarantee that you will remember your childhood years. As hard as it may be to imagine right now, you can forget what you were like as children at the Manhattan New School.

> Write comments on the back of your school photographs and favorite family photographs and put them in a safe place. When you look back on them someday, the scenes and your words will help you to reminisce about your "good old days."

> Gather all of your writer's notebooks and published pieces of writing and store them in a beautiful box tied with a pretty ribbon. What you thought about when you were a child will become precious to you one day.

> Invite your closest friends over and videotape the gathering. Someday you will have an elementary school reunion and that old tape will make you laugh and make you cry.

> Collect copies of your favorite books. They will serve to remind you of what your interests were and if you become a parent one day you will want to share them with your own children.

> Create your own personal Manhattan New School time capsule. Fill it with school pencils, folders, T-shirts, and baseball caps, all with our school logo. Gather your favorite works of art, self-assessments, souvenirs from class trips, invitations to school celebrations, and any other artifacts that will remind you of your very first alma mater.

I think it is essential to remind children that writing will provide them with a significant means of looking back on their childhoods, and I often include this message on the very first day of school when I first invite students to write. (See launching the writing workshop on page 43).

When Wells is grown she can look back on her playground thoughts as a seven-year-old, Angelina will be able to recall her delight in dressing up in her mother's clothes, and Lauren will recall her favorite pet.

> When I go to the playground, I feel like doing everything at once.
>
> Finally, I pick one and do it. Usually I pretend while I'm doing something. For instance, when I am going down the tower made of tires, I pretend that it is a tunnel and when I go on the rickety ladder I pretend it's a net. Other times, like when I'm swinging on the swing or sliding down a slide, I close my eyes and stretch out my arms and sort of float. Playgrounds are fun.
>
> —Wells, age seven

> It's my hamster's birthday. Today is his real birthday, not the day I got him, his real one. He is going to be 1 year old. My baby is 1 year old. Teddy's first birthday. I think I am going to make a hat for him and a cake covered with seed and give him a chewing toy. That will make him happy.
>
> —Lauren, age nine

> A pile of my mother's clothes lie in a laundry basket. My small short arms try to drag it to my room. It bumps left and right on the walls. I shout out, "Next stop, Angie's room!" Sitting on my bed, I put on a long dress then pull it down. I dip my feet into a large pair of pantyhose. I pull the left side then the right side, left, right, left, right. I keep on pulling till it reaches the top of my stomach. I roll them all the way to my hips. I run to my mom's closet. I can't choose from all the color shoes. Finally, I pick black. I slip my little feet inside them. As I run back to my room, the shoes slide off. I stop when I spot a black hat with a rosie rose on it. I reach to get it, slip it on my head. Suddenly, I'm dressed up. I go to our big long mirror. I walk up and down pretending that I was a model.
>
> —Angelina, age ten

We can encourage students to write for and about their brothers and sisters as a means of preserving their siblings' childhoods. When Joanne Hindley Salch was conferring with eight-year-old Eliza, she noted that the third grader had written a great deal about her younger sister Suzannah. Joanne suggested she turn her collage of anecdotes about her sister's younger years into a letter for Suzannah. Eliza followed her teacher's advice and began her soon-to-be "family treasure" with the words, "I am writing this letter to you because I hope that you will keep it for a long time and when you grow up you can remember when you were little." Eliza then wove together stories about Suzannah's hair, primitive way of drawing, the mysterious concoctions she made in the kitchen, her misuse of words, and other such sisterly observations. She ended her letter with the words, "I hope that you will keep this letter for a long time, so long that your children will get to see it and will get to see how you looked, what you did, and how you did things differently from most other people when you were younger."

I recently drove past a shop that specialized in beautifully designed front doors. The store was called Elegant Entries. Notebook entries are not necessarily elegant, but if we teach students how to capture their honest thinking, observations, and reactions, their notebook entries will serve to open doors into their childhood memories.

Children's Writing Can Help Them Appreciate the Joys of Childhood

Not only do we encourage children to honor their childhoods by inviting them to capture those moments in writing, we also promote childhood interests by elevating those moments when they occur naturally in children's writing. For example, when we discover that Luda's writing is filled with such topics as making a cardboard castle out of a refrigerator box, magical chocolate chip cookies she shares with a friend, and the dolls she plans to make, we deliberately ask this third grader to read her writing aloud in order to turn classroom conversation toward the fun of those wonderful "childish" projects (see Figures 1.2–1.4).

I have a special place too. Actually I have two. One is a dusty warm smelling corner. It is very dark. It is seacret because it is blocked by a soft warm couch and a wooden closet. that spot is quiet and peaceful. The second is a cardboard castle out of a refrigiratoc doxe. It's absow secret because nobedy knows where the doon is. I put a blanket on the floor and it becomes nice soft and warm. inside

Figure 1.2

2-10-97

Yesterday my friend
Goran came to my house.
We climbed ate chocolate candys,
made belive that; If we
eat one side of a choclate
chip cookie we would become-
biger, and if we ate the
other side we would become
smaller, and if we ate
the top we would be faster,
and if we ate the bttom
we would be slower. We
had a lot of fun. I
was sad when Goran
had to leave.

Figure 1.3

After Luda reads her writing aloud, all the teacher need do, to add status to this child's playfulness, is to say, "Aren't those wonderful ideas! How many of you do things like that at home? Who wants to share?"

Similarly, when Andrej shares the piece in Figure 1.5 about his collection of hotel soaps and shampoos, we can remind children that collecting things is part of the fun of being a kid. No doubt a piece such as this one will inspire other students to talk or write about their own interesting collections. (See more on collections in Chapter 2.)

I had the honor of attending a memorial service for the late Leo Lionni, at which family members distributed a copy of a commencement speech the wonderful artist and children's writer had delivered at New York's Cooper Union. The speech was titled, "An Irresistible Urge to Make Things," and referred to the main motivation for his work. The world was blessed because Lionni's urge lasted his lifetime. Educators need to make sure that children's urge to make things lasts at least throughout the elementary years.

12—17—96
Today me and my Grandma went
to the library. I took a book
about Dolls. In the book it said
how to make the bodys, the hair
and the clothing, it alsow. said
how to make different kinds
of dolls. Some of them were.
Pocket dolls, Upside-down dolls,
old fashioned dolls, Angel on
my pillow dolls, and a lot of
other dolls. I liked all the
dolls so much that I decided
to make some of those
dolls. I might bring some
to shool, when I make
them!

Figure 1.4

When talking about cardboard constructions, games of make-believe, playing with dolls, and taking delight in simple collections becomes common practice in our elementary classrooms, more students will be willing to take off their masks of "coolness" and once again "act their age." (Of course, it is up to the grown-ups to make sure that no student is subjected to teasing when childish interests are revealed.) In Marisabina Russo's picture book, *The Big Brown Box*, a young boy turns an empty washing machine carton into a house, then a cave, a boat, and a spaceship. I know that some students in elementary classrooms do likewise and as the leader of a writing workshop I would expect to hear about these playful adventures. My job is to publicize these experiences, make the imaginative spirit that initiates them contagious, to help more children see them as topics for their writing. Student writing is more likely to become memorable when children choose topics through which their honest voices and enthusiasm can be heard.

Soap Collection

When I travel and go to a hotel, I collect mini soaps and shampoos. I've taken them from Holiday Inn, Comfort Inn, and several other places too. I keep them in a shoe box. I have so many they get all stuffed up. Once I collected 15 soaps and shampoos at a hotel in 4 days! That's my record! When I was six, I decided to take the Nike shoe box that my new sneakers came in and made it a soap box. The idea about making a soap box came to me in the car when we were driving to Panama City from The Great Smokey Mountains. When we got home after about 20 days I started the soap box. When I was seven, I decided there was a big mess in the shoe box. So, I got a piece of cardboard that we had in the house and I separated the soaps and shampoos by gluing the cardboard in the middle of the shoe box. I have 43 soaps and shampoos now, and my box is getting stuffed up again. I'm planning to get a bigger shoe box, I even have one in mind.

By Andrej Bidikov

Figure 1.5

Elevating Student Interests into Project Topics Brings Energy and Engagement to the Writing Workshop

Writing can be used to foster the joys of childhood by following students' leads and encouraging them to turn sketchy ideas into major projects. For example, when Kousuke writes about observing the moon with his mother (see Figure 1.6), we can suggest that he begin to keep a daily journal of his observations or organize a collection of Japanese fables to share with his classmates.

When Kousuke writes of his love of playing with a yo-yo (see Figure 1.7), we can ask him to offer yo-yo lessons to his classmates. We can also challenge him to turn his interest in playing with yo-yos into significant writing projects. He could write a timeline of the history of yo-yos, interview other yo-yo players in the school community, create a survey to discover other students' interests in yo-yos, write a how-to book about all

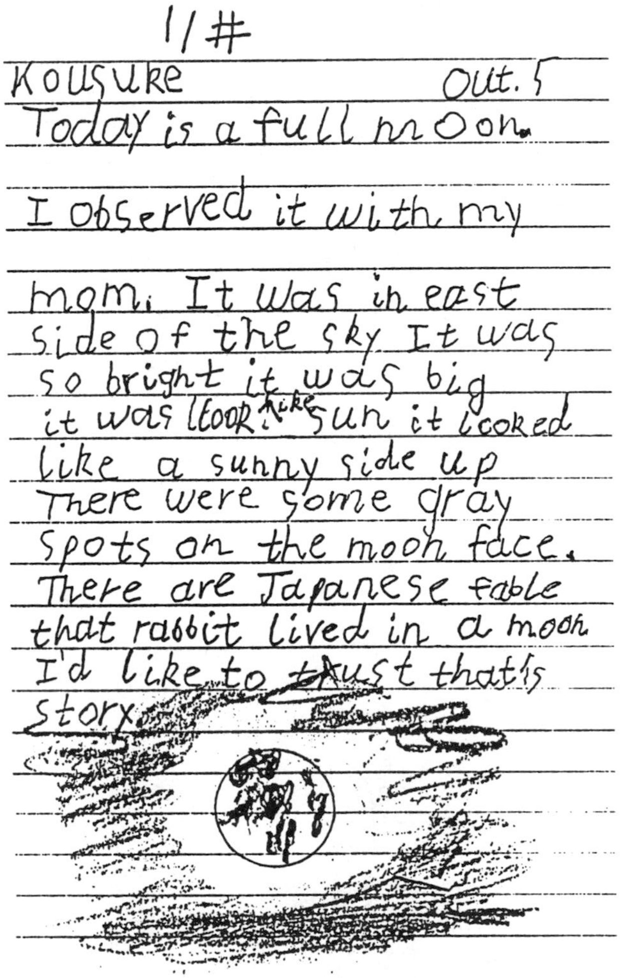
1/#
Kousuke Out. 5
Today is a full moon.
I observed it with my
mom. It was in east
side of the sky It was
so bright it was big
it was look like sun it looked
like a sunny side up
There were some gray
spots on the moon face.
There are Japanese fable
that rabbit lived in a moon
I'd like to ~~thust~~ that's
story.

Figure 1.6

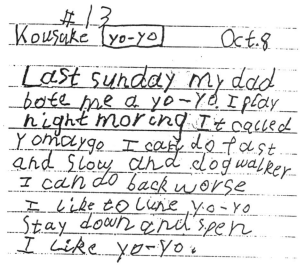

Figure 1.7

the different yo-yo tricks he has mastered, a flier of tips or suggestions for others interested in perfecting their yo-yo talents, or an invitation to join a yo-yo club.

For Kousuke, a second-language learner, putting his English-language learning to real-world uses will additionally increase and support his second-language learning. Through his demonstration and his writing, Kousuke's interest in playing with yo-yos could spread, benefiting the school community. When children share safe outdoor pastimes with one another, recess time becomes more interesting (and easier for the grown-ups on duty).

When Patrick writes of his love of gingerbread houses, we can challenge him to prepare one in class and write up his procedures for class distribution. When Kristina mentions a model of the Statute of Liberty she has created out of Playdoh during her spring vacation, we can ask her to bring the model to class and challenge her to become a curator of a Statute of Liberty museum, inviting others throughout the school to bring in their replicas of the famous lady. We can also brainstorm possible writing projects to enrich and extend Kristina's interest in the legendary statue. When Jeremy reveals that he still likes listening to a tape cassette of songs containing his name that his aunt had given to him as a birthday present when he was younger, we can suggest that with the help of our music teacher he write songs containing the names of his classmates and prepare similar tapes for them.

Writing Enables Children to Explore and Share Their Dreams and Fantasies

Student writing provides a way for children to help us understand their rich imaginative lives. One of our youngest writers eagerly shares such a piece in Figure 1.8.

Figure 1.8

Older elementary students also have rich imaginations that should be feeding their writing. I have learned that Angelina loves to dress up and pretend to be a model and that Luda's cookies have secret powers. Over the years, students have written about numerous fantasy-filled, adventurous moments, including tales of imaginary friends, magical journeys, adaptations of wild computer games or science fiction movies, and poems, picture books, and short stories filled with castles, unicorns, giants, witches, elves, and fairy godmothers.

Their written thoughts serve as an invitation for us to enter their imaginary worlds and remind us once again that we must let our students' childhood needs inform the work we do. (See also section on pretending, on page 23).

Putting a Premium on Playfulness

It strikes me that children who have had lots of experiences designing, cutting, pasting, carving, sketching, painting, decorating, pretending, and otherwise messing around creatively take more readily to the process of writing. Children who know how to play seem to approach writing with the required openness it takes to craft quality work. These fortunate children seem more at ease playing around with words, ideas, images, formats, and the like. The children who can take a ball of Playdoh and turn it into a unicorn and then squash their creation and recast it as a crocodile seem to have a leg up over those children who are less accustomed to imaginative possibility. Children who can imagine their bedroom closet as a forest, a castle, or a secret clubhouse are more likely to be able to imagine their words as a poem, a picture book, or a letter to their grandmother. It comes as no surprise to hear Roland Barth say, "When the playful me shows up, I am ready to be a serious learner. . . . a culture of playfulness is closely related to the capacity to learn."

Some of our students come to school filled with these playful experiences. They have families who enable and encourage them to turn their kitchen tables into labs for mixing magic potions, their pillows and bedspreads into forts, and their empty shoeboxes into museum cabinets to display their seashell, coin, and rock collections. Other students depend on classroom corners and schoolhouse corridors to learn what it means to invent, organize, decorate, and display.

Fortunately, students at the Manhattan New School are in kindergarten rooms in which the dramatic play area is not limited to miniature kitchen cabinets, but filled with all the necessary items to become a travel agency one week, a restaurant the next, and a zoo the next. They are in first-grade rooms in which they can re-create the Thousand Acre Wood, design life-size totem poles, or build a puppet theater from old cardboard boxes. They are in second-grade rooms in which they can count on an inventor's workshop every Friday afternoon, create a clay replica of New Amsterdam, or prepare foods following the recipes of early settlers in our region. And as our students move up in the grades, they continue to "mess around." They create elaborate family trees, invent dance steps to accompany poetry, rock climb in Central Park, seine in the Hudson River, make their own erupting volcanoes, ballroom dance until the boys and the girls are at ease with their arms on one another's shoulders. They attend a school where the basics include play, projects, and messy work. They attend a school where custodians must be requested not to throw out assorted "junk," because children's works in progress require it.

There is a fine line between work and play in our school, and our students reap the rewards of such an attitude. They appear eager to place their original thoughts on paper and they seem predisposed to seeing a project through over time, understanding the notions of drafting and revising, and taking pride in finished work. It's no wonder that children who are allowed and encouraged to indulge in childhood activities are able to see topics everywhere and take full advantage of the writer's workshop.

RELATED READINGS IN COMPANION VOLUMES

Going Public (Heinemann, 1999) is abbreviated as GP. *Lifetime Guarantees* (Heinemann, 2000) is abbreviated as LG.

Children leading joyful lives	**GP:** Ch. 4
Children's voices being heard	**GP:** Ch. 1
Children choosing topics	**LG:** Ch. 2, Ch. 3, Ch. 4, Ch. 5

CHAPTER 2

DESIGNING WRITING WORKSHOPS WITH CHILDREN IN MIND

I think that the key to a good piece is to always have something up your sleeves that keeps your piece interesting. Also, try not to use grown-up language, kids could be reading your piece too.

—Davy, age 10

Finding an idea for writing is like doing an Internet search. Start with a strong feeling or mood and then search for connections.

—Sam, age 10

Key Writing Lessons

1. We must tap the strengths and interests of children in order that our students enthusiastically participate in writing workshops that are effective, productive, and rigorous.
2. Children's natural ability to pretend can facilitate the writing workshop.
3. Children's interest in being collectors can be woven into the writing workshop.
4. Children's interest in rites of passage can become part of the writing workshop.
5. Children's delight in having something over adults can support the writing workshop.
6. Children's growing desire to become independent can further the writing workshop.
7. Children's reliance upon temporary supports has a role in the writing workshop.
8. Children's admiration of older students can inspire structures and projects for the writing workshop.
9. Teachers can invent new ways of working with elementary school writers if they look to children's interests and ways of being as sources of inspiration.

Families that travel with children know when they are in a city or country that is welcoming of young tourists. These places boast museums that invite touching, restaurants that offer crayons to decorate the butcher paper tablecloths, and hotels with safe kiddie pools. Airports in some cities even have special waiting areas set aside for children to play. We need to make sure that we are as supportive and amenable to the children who will be working in our writing workshops as the chambers of commerce are in child-oriented tourist sites.

In *Lifetime Guarantees,* I describe what you might see if you were to enter a writing workshop at the Manhattan New School. I stress that there is no one way to run a writing workshop. They do not come with an owner's manual. Instead, I describe effective variations and innovations on what can be considered traditional workshop components (a short whole-group minilesson, individual writing and conferring time, and small- or whole-group sharing). I also suggest that we value simplicity in the teaching of writing. We are *not* continuously trying to invent new ways to invite children to write. That said, we remain open to improvements in our writing workshops, especially if we are attempting to cater to the particular needs, strengths, and interests of elementary-school-aged children.

Childhood Behaviors and Needs

In order to tease out the implications of designing writing workshops with five-to-ten-year-olds in mind, I began by making a list of childhood descriptors. They included such behaviors as pretending, collecting, looking up to older children, acting silly, and the like. I wondered then about the possibility of allowing each of these childhood behaviors to inspire new ways of thinking about the writing workshop. The trails of my thinking follow.

Please note that I am not intending to think through the issues of childhood in order to make our writing workshops more carefree and less rigorous. I am not trying to add any juvenile, trick-or-treating moments to the writing workshop. Quite the contrary, I am interested in tapping the strengths and interests of children in order that our students are more engaged in writing workshops that are *more* effective, productive, and rigorous at the elementary level.

Pretending

One of my all-time favorite pieces of writing by one of our youngest writers appears in Figure 2.1. It was written by a kindergartner named Maeve, and I remain eternally grateful to her teacher Pam Mayer for not requiring her students to write exclusively "true" stories, as so many teachers do. The "translation" follows Maeve's original words.

It is clear from reading her story that Maeve has been read to. It is clear that she has internalized the shape and sound of the literature she loves. It is clear that making up stories and pretending is what Maeve does in the dramatic-play corner of her

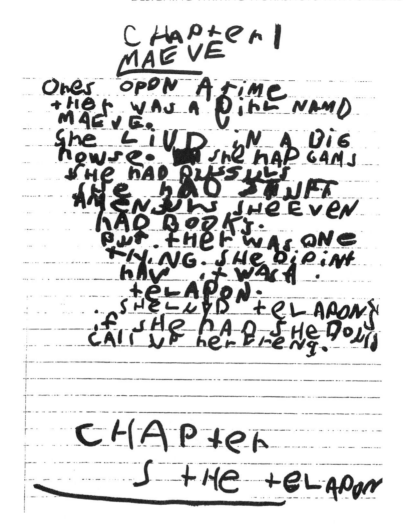

Translation

Chapter 1—Maeve

Once upon a time there was a girl named Maeve. She lived in a big house. She had games. She had puzzles. She had stuffed animals. She even had books. But there was one thing she didn't have. It was a telephone. She loved telephones. If she had one, she would call up her friends.

Figure 2.1

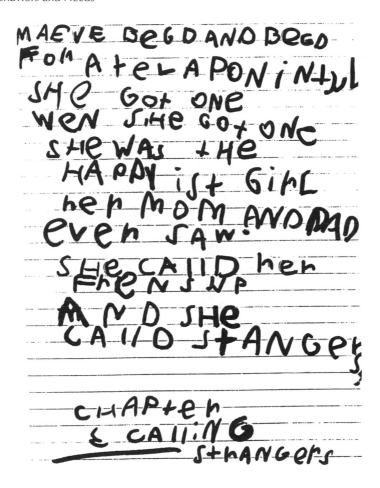

Translation

Chapter 2—The Telephone

Maeve begged and begged for a telephone until she got one. When she got one she was the happiest girl her mom and dad ever saw. She called up her friends and she called strangers.

Figure 2.1 (*continued*)

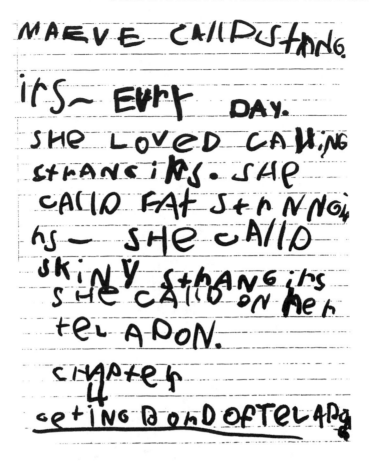

Translation

Chapter 3—Calling Strangers

Maeve called strangers every day. She loved calling strangers. She called fat strangers.
She called skinny strangers. She called on her telephone.

Figure 2.1 (*continued*)

classroom and it is one of the things she does naturally and well during writing workshop time.

When students choose their own topics, might it not be advantageous to support
their "Once upon a time" stories, instead of turning our noses up at passages filled with
pirates, knights, unicorns, and children who, as in Maeve's story, call up fat strangers and
skinny strangers? After all, if we are reading aloud fictional works and talking about fictional
works, our students' attempts at writing fictional works show the power of our teaching.

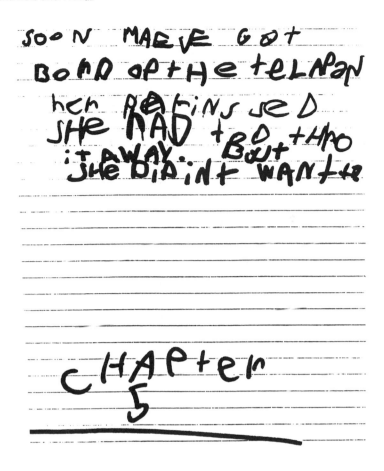

Translation

Chapter 4—Getting Bored of Telephones

Soon Maeve got bored of the telephone. Her parents said she had to throw it away. But she didn't want to.

Figure 2.1 (*continued*)

If children are so at home pretending, should we not capitalize on "pretend" strategies during the writing workshop? There are numerous ways to do this; examples follow.

- When they reread their drafts, suggest, "Pretend you are a stranger reading this for the very first time. . . . What questions would you have?"
- When they reread their finished work, suggest, "Pretend you are a book reviewer reading this text, what would you say about it?"

Translation

Chapter 5

Finally she threw it away. And it was a sad life again.

The End

Figure 2.1 (*continued*)

- When they want to hear something new in their writing, suggest, "Pretend you are your mother and tell this same story from her point of view" or, "Pretend this piece is being written by someone else and tell it in third person instead of first."
- When they read their writing aloud, suggest, "Pretend this is a book in the library. Try reading it the way your teacher reads stories aloud."
- When students are struggling to add authentic dialogue to their stories, suggest, "Pretend *you* are the main character—what would you have said?"

Collecting

Children such as Andrej the soap and shampoo connoisseur are proud of their collections, noting every acquisition with delight, showing patience in organizing and reorganizing their goodies, and thinking cautiously before swapping items. Shouldn't we then be capitalizing on this childhood devotion? Would it not make sense to include the following kinds of activities within our writing workshops?

- Ask students to collect all the books by one writer they admire and take lessons from that writer.
- Ask students to create cards for all their favorite authors and begin collecting them the way they collect baseball cards. (Wouldn't publishers be wise to produce such items for avid readers?)
- Ask students to begin a collection of poems in particular formats. (One child might become known as the collector of shape poems, another of riddle poems, etc.)
- Ask students to collect all the pieces they have written throughout their school career and organize them by genres in an accordion folder.
- Ask students to display a collection of their writing that shows growth over time (from beginning of the year to end, from first grade to fourth, or from first draft to final).
- Ask students to become collectors of something, if they aren't already, and allow that collection to inspire or be the subject of various forms of writing.
- Ask students to search for examples of high-quality writing about people's collections and attempt to borrow techniques as they write about their own.
- Ask students to survey the entire school community about people's unique collections and publish an anthology of findings.
- Ask students to brainstorm formats in which they could write about their collections. For example, can Andrej write letters to hotels asking about the legality of taking those unused minisoaps and shampoos home? Can he do some investigative reporting about how hotel chains select soap and shampoo companies? Can he write a persuasive essay to companies asking them to donate some of their mini-products to people in need, at missions, homeless shelters, and centers for runaway children and pregnant teens? Similarly, children who collect rocks, coins, baseball cards, key chains, and the like can be asked to list all the possible ways that they can use writing to enrich their interest in these items.
- Arrange a day for members of the school community to share their collections. Have students write announcements about the event, invitations, guidebooks, and thank-you notes to participants.

Rites of Passage

Children are always eager to talk about their firsts—the first time they are able to cross the street alone, stay at home without a baby-sitter, or stay up until midnight on New Year's Eve. The question, "Who has a story to tell about finally being allowed to do something that they have long wanted to do?" is a surefire conversation starter in an elementary classroom. Children appreciate rites of passage and take as much pride in them as they do the pencil slashes on their kitchen walls that indicate their growth in inches. This enthusiasm for rites of passage made me wonder if there are equivalent rites of passage within their elementary school writing careers. And if none exist, should we not create them? After all, shouldn't children look forward to school events as much as they do family ones?

At the Manhattan New School, third grade marks a significant writing rite of passage. Second graders long to reach the third grade, because they have heard about the wonderful writer's notebooks the eight-year-olds are lucky enough to carry. Figure 2.2 contains a letter sent to third-grade teachers from a group of second graders at the end of the school year. Perhaps each grade needs its own writing rites of passage, ones all students are aware of and look forward to. (See Appendix 2, "Worksheet on School-Wide Rites of Passage in the Teaching of Writing.") Below are rites-of-passage possibilities in the Manhattan New School community.

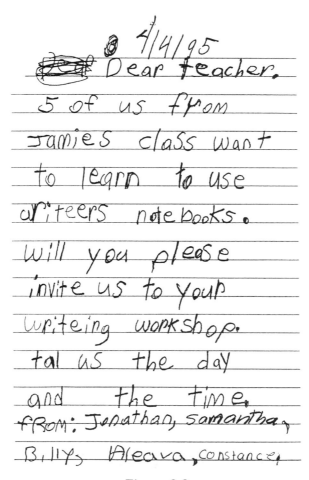

Figure 2.2

Kindergarten

Merely entering kindergarten is a tremendous rite of passage, but then we put markers in our students' hands and ask them to write. Perhaps this is the biggest rite of passage of their entire writing career. Of course, being trusted to spell words as best they can is a monumental close second. Our kindergartners would likely be proud to announce, "This is the year you learn how to write!"

First Grade

Perhaps some of the biggest changes include being asked to write in pencil, not marker, on wide-lined paper with dotted guiding lines for improved penmanship. That's a big deal for six-year-olds. So is the first time they realize that they can write without rehearsing through drawing. Moreover, we ask them to write for many different reasons, and their writing leaves the four walls of their classroom. Our first graders would likely be proud to announce, "This is the year you get to send letters, label your paintings, hang signs in the hallway, deliver invitations, perform your poems, sing your songs" and so on. (See Chapter 6 for more information on early-childhood writers.)

Second Grade

Children begin the year writing freely about a multitude of topics in a multitude of genres and for the first time we introduce the notion of writing templates. In other words, we begin to scaffold their writing by providing accessible formats found in literature. For example, second graders might be seen writing a good news/bad news picture book, and taking great delight in it because it "sounds like a book in the library!" Revision often means adding missing pieces, or removing extraneous ones, in order to get closer to the desired shape and meaning. Our second graders would likely be proud to announce, "This is the year you get to borrow ideas from poems and books you love!" (See additional information on second-grade writers on pages 193–206.)

Third Grade

Children look forward to learning to play the recorder and, as previously noted, third graders feel that they have reached an important milestone when they are finally asked to fill the bound, blank books known as writer's notebooks. After being invited to closely study the design of texts in second grade, third graders are surprised by the freedom the writer's notebook affords. Eventually they realize that the structures, patterns, and shapes of the texts they studied in second grade can come in handy as they shape notebook entries into finished works. Revision usually means gently shaping rich entries into a wide range of purposeful genres. (See Chapter 3 for details on the use of the writer's notebook at the elementary level.) Our third graders would likely be proud to announce, "This is the year you get to carry around whatever kind of writer's notebooks you like!" (See additional information on third-grade writers on page 70.)

Fourth Grade

In our school, fourth grade is known as the year you learn to rock climb in Central Park, the year you dance with Jacques d'Amboise and the National Dance Institute, and have a sleepover at an environmental camp. It is also the year that they learn to use the writer's notebook toward the formal study of several short genres and develop mentor relationships with favorite writers within those genres. Revision requires students to recast their works as they learn to pay more attention to such elements as language, design, pace, and point of view. In addition, fourth graders begin to discover topics that they return to time and again. Our fourth graders would likely be proud to announce, "This is the year you get to study poetry for a long time and take lessons from your favorite poet" or, "This is the year you get to study nonfiction picture book writing and apprentice yourself to your favorite writer." (See additional information on fourth grade on page 71.)

Fifth Grade

During this senior year, perhaps the greatest rite of passage that our students look forward to is being allowed to leave the school on Fridays to eat lunch in the local restaurants. This is a privilege they talk about all through the fall semester, knowing that permission won't be granted until the spring. This rite is so popular, along with ballroom dancing lessons, that our students would truly understand why Natalie Babbitt calls fifth grade "the last, best, greatest year of childhood." In regard to writing, our students are used to keeping a writer's notebook, often developing their own idiosyncratic uses. It is at this time, when they appear so comfortable using their notebooks independently at home and in school, that we add new challenges by asking students to do quick free-writes in response to various prompts, engage in bigger writing projects that take place over time, and begin to finally grapple with the kind of revisions that might look familiar to an adult writer. This is also the year in which many students find topics that they want to stick with for long periods. Our fifth graders would likely be proud to announce, "This is the year you get to write many pieces about one topic that really matters to you" or, "This is the year you are asked to create a poetry anthology over the course of the entire school year." (See additional information on fifth grade on page 75.)

Other Rites of Passage

At workshops and summer institutes when I have asked teachers to brainstorm possible writing rites of passage within their own school communities, their ideas have included the following, in response to the stated prompt:

> **This is the year you get to . . .**
> write for the school newspaper
> develop a pen-pal relationship
> keep a dialogue journal
> write an original play and perform it
> establish an e-mail correspondence with a favorite writer
> create an anthology around a topic of interest

share your writing with a former teacher

produce photographic essays

become a writing buddy with children in another grade

study how writing is used by members of the community

keep a class log of significant happenings

use desktop publishing

When teachers do pull together to decide on possible writing rites of passage attached to different grade levels within their school, the results of their discussion can serve as important information for family members who want to understand the writing curriculum in any one school. (See Chapter 10 for additional information on communicating with families).

Having Something Over Adults

I recently saw a television commercial for a popular cereal. A little girl and her mother are both eating the same dry cereal and the box stands on the table between them. The little girl looks at the picture of a child on the box and announces that her picture should be on the box since she is a kid that loves this cereal. To that, the mother suggests that her picture could also be on the box, since she loves the cereal as well. The child grimaces and cautions, "No you can't because you're a grown-up!" To the little girl playing a role in this television commercial—and probably to most children—the world of dry cereals belongs to children.

Although there are many adults who love to eat dry cereal, ride on merry-go-rounds, or build sand castles at the beach, these activities seem to be generally associated with children. And the children know it and delight in having something that they feel is exclusively their own. In *Going Public* I share a note written by Madeline, an eight-year-old determined to begin a club to raise funds for endangered animals. In her campaign to recruit members, she posts an announcement that boasts, "Remember, teachers nor any other grown-up has *anything* to do with the club!" Madeline's club is attractive to children because it is kid-initiated and kid-run. It is the clubhouse with the secret password. It is the fun-house ride with the sign, "Occupants must be four feet or under." It is the carnival with the regulation, "Grown-ups must be accompanied by a child!"

Children love the occasional opportunity to have something over adults, to know something they don't know and be able to do something they can't do. In Chapter 1, I described the Puddles Challenge I offered our students. Part of its success was that the children thought they had something over me. They were being invited to do something that they could do better than I could do *because* they were children. How powerful and proud they felt.

Occasions with childhood advantage rarely exist in the world of the writing workshop. Not unless we create the kind of rituals, structures, and activities that enable children to understand how the "child can be father to the man." Simply adding choices like the following may be all that it takes to capitalize on children's enthusiasm for things that appear off-limits to adults.

- Label special classroom binders for topics that seem to reoccur in the class, ones that satisfy children's delight in having that "I know something you don't know" feeling. Anthologies might include "Moments with Grandparents," "Connected to Toys," "Playground Thoughts," "Imaginary Friends," "Changing Schools," and "Bedtime Rituals." No doubt, these would become popular reading materials.

- Provide students with opportunities to teach their teachers and their parents the words to the songs they sing, including jump-rope rhymes, hand-clapping chants, camp songs, and pop-chart hits.

- Provide students with opportunities to record and share with teachers and parents information about their favorite playground, board, and card games.

- Provide frequent occasions for children to read aloud jokes, riddles, and story puzzles, thereby satisfying their desire to stump the grown-ups. Invite children to craft original brainteasers.

- Allow children opportunities to write and share reviews of the television shows they watch and movies they view.

- Encourage children to prepare such useful family handouts as "Child-Friendly Sites in the City to Visit," "Top-Ten Birthday Party Activities," and "Restaurants with the Best Kid Menus."

- Encourage children to conduct inquiry studies on topics of particular interest to them. These might include such issues as safety requirements of playground equipment, the patenting procedure for new-toy inventions, and the history of computer games. Of course, students will need time to share what they are learning with their peers. A panel of children could present at a faculty meeting, demonstrating that they know important things that the grown-ups might not.

- Ask children to identify poems and picture books that, according to their discerning eyes, capture the spirit of childhood. Children can try to explain how adults could have written so well about childhood.

- Celebrate and publicize writing formats invented by children. Last year in Joanne Hindley Salch's third-grade room, children began composing newspapers to distribute throughout their apartment buildings and began writing original songs at lunch to be shared with their classmates after the lunch hour. These new writing genres became very popular because they were by kids and primarily for kids.

Moments of Independence

One Sunday morning I received a call from a parent with concerns that her daughter had left the play area at lunchtime and gone shopping. (We acquire a play area by setting up police barricades and closing our Manhattan street to traffic during the lunch hour.) Actually, the child hadn't wandered very far. Right next door to our school is a hair salon, and the owner began peddling his wares by rolling out a cart filled with the latest in hair accessories. Little plastic butterfly clips were the rage at the time, and it seems that some of our girls couldn't resist the urge to make purchases when they took a quick break from jumping rope and playing hopscotch. The school aides on duty hadn't noticed that the girls were actually making purchases as they played on the sidewalk adjacent to the school. The parents were reassured that their children had never left the secure area, but they couldn't believe that their children were bringing money to school and that they had access to retailers during school hours. Of course, we put an end to this "shop while you hop" practice, and the parents reprimanded their daughters for bringing money to school without permission. When I spoke to the girls, however, they didn't think that they had done anything wrong (except for those who "borrowed" money from their mothers' wallets). In fact, they expressed absolute joy in being able to buy "stuff" without asking their parents' permission. They took pleasure in being able to do things on their own.

Children relish moments of independence, especially as they move up in the grades. Writing workshop leaders should thus ask themselves, "What can the students do without me in the writing workshop? How do I create moments of independence for young writers?" It's true that our students select their own topics, make decisions about content, language, and stylistic techniques, and frequently make choices in genre. It's no wonder then that children enjoy writing workshop. It's probably the school subject that affords the most ownership and independence for young children. And yet, those children aren't totally independent. They ask for conferences with their teachers and response from their peers in order to revise and edit their pieces. They still ask for permission to publish, to use the word processor, to illustrate their work. They are often given deadlines, homework assignments, and teacher evaluations.

The following "underground" writing structures are intended for children to handle with minimal adult interference. In other words, teachers need not get involved in these pieces of writing that can be done during recess breaks, lunch hours, or other appropriate times.

advice columns

entries for suggestion boxes

private notes

private diaries (these are different from writer's notebooks; see Chapter 3)

letter writing and e-mail correspondence

petition writing

sports scoreboards

lost-and-found postings

original board game designs to be used during recess

announcements for student-run bulletin boards

paper fortune-telling games, with words hidden under flaps

top-ten lists

book swaps (a system for trading used books from home collections)

club-related rules, invitations, announcements, or newsletters

paper-and-pencil games (e.g., Mad-libs)

Training Wheels

Daniel Meier, then a second grader, handed me a stapled stack of papers, neatly and carefully typed using a big, boldface font. The title simply read, "Meier," and was followed by several pages of clever dialogue broken into scenes and modeled after the television sitcom *Seinfeld.* In other words, Daniel had used a popular television show as a template for creating his own script. Scene 1, in fact, contains the brief explanation, "At the playground on 77th St. and Amsterdam Avenue—this will be like the restaurant in *Seinfeld*—we'll see the four main characters there from time to time." In addition to using his last name as the title, having a regular meeting place, and relying on four main characters, Daniel also attempted to make clever remarks about everyday occurrences. In other words, he had gotten the essence of the *Seinfeld* show.

As noted earlier, using templates—borrowing structures and techniques from other published works—seems to have become a second-grade rite of passage, usually introduced toward the spring of second grade. (Of course, in many kindergarten and first-grade rooms, teachers invite children to compose their own versions of favorite predictable texts or add original stanzas to familiar songs and poems. These activities can be considered as providing templates, but they are usually whole-class collaborative events, with the teacher serving as scribe. Here, I am referring to second-grade teachers who deliberately and thoughtfully read aloud texts that could provide accessible structures for their seven-year-olds to borrow. See Chapter 6 for additional information about our very youngest writers.) After two and a half years of free-form writing during kindergarten, first grade, and the first half of second grade, children seem ready to take on this new challenge, and in fact seem to make great strides as writers because they realize that they can, on their own, deliberately shape their text. They delight in announcing, "I get what that author is doing and I can do that too!" They become the young bicycle riders whose training wheels give them confidence. Those temporary supports allow them to *feel like* bicycle riders, so that they can go on to *actually become* bicycle riders.

Of course, it's not just second graders who need training wheels. All writers, at times, need the kind of supports that give them a leg up, that help them hear new things in their writing, that help them take risks and accept new challenges. I described several of these supports in *Lifetime Guarantees: Toward Ambitious Literacy Teaching*, including those for second-language learners, at-risk students, and for students just beginning to write informational reports. Throughout the pages of this book I will include additional moves that teachers might make as children progress through the grades. These various supports could be labeled templates, deliberate challenges, exercises, or borrowing author techniques (see pages 198–203). Note that these supports are *not* intended to take away ownership but simply to allow students to feel more successful as they are learning the additional skills needed to produce high-quality writing. Most teachers, in fact, present these as options, enabling more independent writers to disregard these supports.

Looking Up to Older Kids

It is fairly easy at schools, even those without multigrade classrooms, to find demonstrations of admiration for the upper grades. At the Manhattan New School, kindergartners love being read to by their third-grade story partners, first graders love sharing the cafeteria at lunchtime with fourth graders, second graders love sitting alongside fifth graders at our student council meetings. The little guys longingly look up to the big guys, feeling privileged to hang out with their youthful heroes. (Older students also benefit from spending time with younger children, appreciating the freshness of their language, the gusto attached to their problem solving, the blurring of lines between work and play, as well as the need to carry themselves with gentleness and calm in the younger ones' presence.) It makes sense then to orchestrate opportunities for children to learn from one another during writing workshop.

The activities described here are designed to bring differing age groups together within the writing workshop in order to enrich the writing of younger and older children alike.

Writing Buddies

Just as children meet weekly with their story partners or book buddies in order for different-aged children to pore over picture books together, children of different grades can be paired to regularly meet to share their writing. The younger children will gleefully share their writing and take gentle advice from their older friends. The older children should be encouraged to share only those pieces appropriate for younger listeners.

Cross-Grade Special Projects

In Chapter 8 I describe a fifth-grade and second-grade author study I conducted at the Manhattan New School. I highly recommend such collaborations, as in addition to the children learning so much from one another, it gives teachers a chance to spend big blocks of time together. In addition to joint author studies, I can also imagine teachers working together to produce a multigrade literary magazine, publish a school newspaper, create a school handbook, or study a genre.

Joint Genre Studies

Imagine adding energy to the writing workshop by arranging for a second-grade class and a fourth-grade class to study the writing of poetry together for several weeks. What literature would be read aloud? What poetic techniques would be taught? What response structures would be put in place? What new ways of publishing would be invented? Similarly, I could imagine designing a cross-grade study on writing informational picture books, interviews, or letters.

Cross-Grade Writing Workshops

I am not referring to any special event or course of study here, but to the regular, everyday writing workshop. Children benefit from having new audiences for their works in progress. I can easily imagine a group of third graders and a group of fifth graders gathering every Friday to share their work. No doubt, the youngsters will work just a little bit harder to impress the students they look up to or the ones that look up to them. This structure would also enable teachers to pull together to study conferring techniques.

Writing with a Younger Audience in Mind

When children are writing for real reasons, they understand the value attached to working hard to make their meaning clear, writing with a specific audience in mind, using their best handwriting, and correcting their spelling so that others can appreciate their writing. It becomes very helpful, therefore, to ask older students to produce writing that will be added to the libraries of the lower-grade classrooms. In so doing, the younger children get to hang out with their older friends as they suggest topics of interest, respond to drafts, and celebrate finished work.

Joint Share Meetings and Celebrations

Imagine a monthly whole-school gathering in which children come up to the microphone in the school auditorium and share the writing they are most proud of. Early-childhood children read aloud in front of upper-grade students and get responses from them. Upper-grade students carefully select pieces to share in front of this mixed audience and likewise receive feedback from their younger schoolmates. Having been moved and impressed by the work of the older students, how many younger children will apprentice themselves to older students, attempting to do what these accomplished poets, nonfiction reporters, and picture book writers have done?

Sibling Invitations

As principal of the Manhattan New School, I was once asked by kindergartner Alex if he could visit his third-grade brother Jeremy's class during writing time. Of course the teachers involved agreed with this novel plan, and in walked the five-year-old, writing folder in hand, to work alongside his brother on their individual pieces of writing. No doubt Alex asked for spelling help and his big brother obliged. No doubt Alex felt comfortable in this upper-grade classroom as his kindergarten teacher took a similar approach to writing workshop in her classroom. Alex's idea caught on and other siblings made the same request. In fact, children without brothers or sisters in the school asked for equal time, requesting that friends from their school bus route or after-school programs be invited to visit during writing time.

Reading-Partner Collaborations

In *Lifetime Guarantees*, I describe several multigrade writing collaborations produced as end-of-the-year celebrations of book-buddy partnerships. Kindergartners and their upper-grade partners worked together to produce carefully designed finished works, ones that incorporated the writing abilities of students of differing ages. These included poetry anthologies and question-and-answer books (see *Lifetime Guarantees*, Chapter 1).

Paired Dialogue Journals

Imagine if every upper-grade student was assigned to keep a dialogue journal with a lower-grade child. Time could be set aside weekly for the pairs to write to each other and ceremoniously exchange journals. Teachers could help the younger children read their older friends' letters and support them as they wrote their responses. Teachers of older students could make suggestions as to how to extend their younger friends' thinking, push their risk taking as spellers, and add to the youngsters' general fluency as writers.

Of course, the grown-ups in the school can also keep dialogue journals with children. It is our hope that children will look up to us as well. See Figure 2.3 for a page from a journal I kept with first-grader Chelsea.

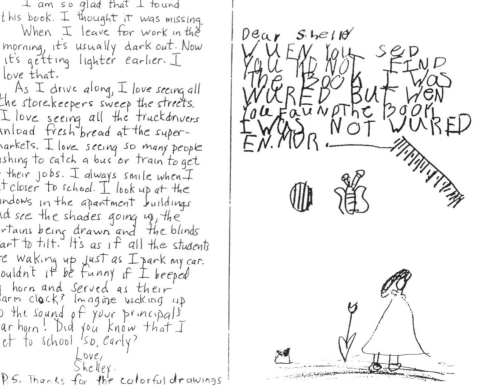

Figure 2.3

Although Chelsea only responded to a bit of my letter, I know that she asked for help in reading all of it. I always try to serve as a model for students, filling all of my writing with engaging ideas, interesting observations, and rich sensory detail.

Childhood Descriptors and Children's Writing

At staff meetings, colleagues might be asked to brainstorm descriptors that acknowledge the unique tastes, interests, and strengths of children and then be challenged to tease out the implications for the teaching of writing. Certainly, new teaching ideas will be born if teachers include such possibilities as "Being Silly" (the place of humor in the writing workshop), "Making Messes" (the role of ongoing, hands-on projects attached to writing), or "Love of Toys, Candy, Playgrounds, and Magic Tricks" (orchestrating long-term research writing connected to childlike interests).

Teachers might set aside time to explore the unique needs of childhood, including following Yetta Goodman's advice to take "kid-watching" seriously, reading some of the books cited in the bibliography in Appendix 1E, and spending time talking to children about the times at school when they feel most engaged, empowered, and enthusiastic. Finally, teachers might be asked to reflect on their current writing workshops through the lens of childhood in order to fully appreciate how children who write differ from adults who write.

RELATED READINGS IN COMPANION VOLUMES

Going Public (Heinemann, 1999) is abbreviated as GP. *Lifetime Guarantees* (Heinemann, 2000) is abbreviated as LG.

Writing workshop components	**LG:** Ch. 2
Rites of passage	**LG:** Ch. 3
Genre courses of study	**LG:** Ch. 3, Ch. 4, Ch. 5
Supports for young writers	**LG:** Ch. 4, Ch. 5, Ch. 10
Multigrade collaborations	**GP:** Ch. 4
	LG: Ch. 1
Keeping dialogue journals	**LG:** Ch. 10

CHAPTER 3

REVISING OUR USE OF THE WRITER'S NOTEBOOK

I love the smell of a new page. Like wheat, that wheat down by the old farm in Vermont. It smells clean and white. . . . It's silent, unlike other pages that scream to be written on. I wonder if it tastes like it smells. Like delicious things. The smell and taste of something wonderful. My body shivers slightly when I turn to a new page. I just love new, fresh pages.

—Kate, age 10

Key Writing Lessons

1. The writer's notebook is our main tool for helping children remain attentive and observant and use their insights when they craft text.
2. These bound, blank books are particularly helpful to young writers, because they are portable and help children see the potential for writing everywhere. They also demonstrate that not everything you write need be a story. Additionally, they have the potential to become a lifelong habit.
3. Young writers need easier ways to understand and use this sophisticated writer's tool.
4. Teachers can shift the kind of writing children do in their writer's notebooks by:
   - sharing their own adult notebooks and tapping into read-alouds that resonate
   - demonstrating in school the value of a portable tool
   - inviting children to take the scientist's inquisitive stance and assigning at-home writing exercises
   - capitalizing on firsthand experiences and keeping dialogue journals with a few students
   - demonstrating notebook writing in front of students
   - using poetry to help students understand notebook writing
5. We must have realistic goals concerning the use of writer's notebooks. Their use changes as children move from grade three to four to five.
6. Our goals are based on the teaching and learning discoveries which follow:
   - The use of the writer's notebook is different for young writers and changes throughout the grades.
   - If teachers spend abundant time helping children take in their world, they will need to spend less time helping children fix up drafts.
   - Very short, clear genres are magical at the elementary level and big blocks of time are needed to reach goals.
   - Good writing is not something that you save for revision and students' writing needs to do good work in the world.

For my birthday one year, my son sent me a copy of Jill Krementz' calendar titled *The Writer's Desk.* One of my favorite pages contains a gorgeous black-and-white photograph of Susan Sontag at her writer's desk. Sontag's words accompanying the photograph read in part, "I like to go out. I like to talk. I like to listen. I like to look and to watch. Maybe I have Attention Surplus Disorder. The easiest thing in the world for me to do is pay attention." Educators, throughout the grades, probably wish that this were true for all of their students.

Our students *do* pay attention—at least most of them do most of the time. Sometimes they pay attention to things other than what we expect. Instead of listening to the teacher present her minilesson on the importance of including details in their writing, they might be studying the little piece of spinach stuck in their teacher's tooth or thinking about how the fresh stain of spaghetti sauce on their friend's T-shirt is shaped like Texas. In their own way, they have discovered the power of detail.

Ann Turner's poem "Look Up!" in her classic collection *Street Talk* suggests that children pay more attention to the world around them than do grown-ups, who never look up when they walk down the street. It's rather surprising, then, to meet children who say that they don't have topics to write about, can't think of any details to add, or don't have any opinions to share or observations to make. Often these reluctant or bland writers have come to think of writing as getting down a story, any story, making sure it has a beginning, middle, and an end. One wonders if these children aren't paying attention to the world around them or if they have just never realized that writing is so much more than cranking out a formulaic story.

We want children to notice, pay attention, marvel, and be fascinated with the world around them, both at school and outside of school. We also want them to appreciate that what captures their hearts, tickles their senses, and fills their minds belongs in their writing. Our main tool for encouraging children, in grades three through five, to always lead attentive and observant lives is the writer's notebook. Simply stated, these bound, blank portable books are intended to help students see that the potential for writing lies everywhere. They are the child-size version of the daybook Don Murray has so eloquently described. Their use and effectiveness with children was researched and confirmed by many Manhattan New School staff members who had once been connected to the Teachers College Writing Project.

Getting Started with Writer's Notebooks

Our third graders enter class in September, bursting to begin filling their writer's notebooks. Since it is public knowledge that this is a third-grade rite of passage, some children even arrive with a beautiful blank book tucked into their backpacks with their other new school supplies. Teachers often ask to display these new books, along with others that they have collected. The display inspires students to shop for their own, according to their own personal tastes. Teachers post a due date for blank-book ownership on the class calendar and suggest shops in the neighborhood that carry a large variety of these books. Of course, we provide for any child who is unable to secure a book on their own. Until the red-letter day arrives, children talk, plan, imagine, dream, share, and otherwise long for the time when they are invited to put pen to paper in their very first writer's notebook. Teachers know the importance of getting notebooks started well and so are willing to resist the urge to have students fill them immediately. Waiting for the big day to arrive adds drama to the event and quality to the eventual writing.

Years ago many of us fell in love with Jean Little's classic, *Hey World, Here I Am!,* a book that offers young readers a chance to get to know a committed and fresh-thinking notebook keeper. I still adore the contents of this book, but I have come to realize that the title is just as significant as the messages inside. When we put blank notebooks in children's hands, we hope that they too will announce to the world, "Hey World, Here I Am!" In other words, the notebook provides a place for children to record their take on the world, to record who they were when they were eight, nine, ten, and eleven years old. In fact, whenever I have the opportunity to introduce writer's notebooks to children, I begin by suggesting, "Imagine doing the kind of writing that you will want to save for a lifetime. When you are twenty, fifty, or eighty, you will still keep these beautiful bound books in a special place because you will always want to recall what kind of kid you were, what you paid attention to, and what you thought about the world when you were young." Sometimes I carry with me Gina Willner-Pardo's picture book *What I'll Remember When I Am a Grown-Up.* This beautiful story helps children understand the difference between all the things that happen in your life and those moments that are worth holding on to. It also demonstrates that seemingly trivial observations can be significant.

In reviewing James Stevenson's poetry anthology *Popcorn,* the *School Library Journal* commented, "Through Stevenson's vision, the ordinary everyday world—summer storms, lemonade stands, rental bikes—is made extraordinary. A book to savor." My hope when I introduce writer's notebooks to elementary-age children is that the same will be said about their completed notebooks. I suggest to children that they too will be doing the kind of writing where the everyday world is made extraordinary; they too will create books worthy of savoring. I go on to explain that what they choose to record in their notebooks will eventually be used to craft important pieces of writing, the kind of writing that they will be proud to put their names on.

Students benefit from seeing how others have used writer's notebooks. In addition to inviting fourth graders into our third-grade classrooms to show their beginners' notebooks, teachers also display pages from student notebook pages that they have copied over the years. These carefully selected models show a wide range of writing formats, including questions, observations, memories, family stories, overheard conversations, favorite words, street scene descriptions, clippings, character sketches, found poetry, lists, and the like.

Teachers (and principal) share their own notebook pages, providing a few accessible models. (Teachers must be very careful in choosing such entries to read aloud, taking into account the needs of their young writers. Teachers should not be demonstrating how they searched for significant threads in their writing or probed entries to get to the "story behind the story." There will be plenty of time for this type of development when children move on to adolescence and adulthood.) Teachers demonstrate to students all the ways their notebooks came in handy and the range of writing they chose to include. They present the writer's notebook as a children's opportunity to take advantage of "literate occasions," as Don Graves has inspired so many teachers to do.

High Hopes

When we first opened our school, we were a kindergarten through third-grade building. We would grow by moving up in the grades with our children. We were interested in introducing writer's notebooks to our third graders, our seniors, for the reasons listed below. (We have never invited our kindergarten through second-grade children to keep writer's notebooks in a wholesale way. For a complete description of our work with our five-, six-, and seven-year-olds, and a discussion of introducing writer's notebooks to these students in individual and limited ways, see Chapter 6, "Working with Our Youngest Writers").

• We were after a way for children to notice more, respond more, think new thoughts, hear more, and so on. Notebooks are portable. You carry them everywhere because you never know when something significant or appealing will take place. You witness an intriguing scene, you overhear a captivating conversation, you recall a haunting memory, a random thought crosses your mind, and so on. Writer's notebooks help children discover the topics and issues they really care about, so of course their writing improves. (By the way, despite my inclusion of it above, I have learned to avoid using the word *haunt* when I invite children to recall images. The word invariably elicits Halloween stories!)

• We were after a dramatic way for children to appreciate that not everything they write needs to be a story with a beginning, middle, and end. We also wanted our students to understand that not everything they write deserves to be drafted and revised. Not all writing deserves equal attention. Many students had the idea that no matter what popped into their heads, they had to add a sharp lead, some telling details and a clever ending.

• We were interested in school structures, rituals, and activities that had the potential to last a lifetime. Notebook keeping felt like one of those habits that could make a difference in students' lives in the long run. Much like reading the newspaper, letter writing, and public speaking, keeping a writer's notebook could enrich our students' lives forever. Besides, it is one of those school-initiated activities that can easily and preferably take place outside of school, with no teacher assistance required. We love when learning continues to take place when teachers are *not* there.

I envisioned our third graders joyously running into school to share entries from their writer's notebook, much the way they greet me with, "Shelley, I learned a new move in gymnastics. Do you want to see it?" Or the way they tell me that they learned a new magic trick, card game, or piece on the piano. I expected our children to be bubbling over with pride, eager to share, and in possession of entries *worth* sharing. That was the plan, at least.

Rethinking Expectations

Needless to say, hopes for the writer's notebook were not initially met during the first year of our school's existence. Our problems were probably not very different from those that teachers admit to me as I travel to school districts around this country. The children were using their writer's notebooks to record the kinds of school writing they had gotten used to doing, those half-page "The day I . . ." stories.

I could argue that we were too busy getting a new school established to give writing our all. Or I could point out that our rites of passage had not been established or publicized, and therefore our children didn't arrive excited about this new venture. Or I could claim that our first students did not have the Manhattan New School writing experiences that our students now entering third grade have received. I could point out that we didn't have fourth graders to inspire third-grade writers. None of these excuses come close to the real reason our early attempts at notebooks were disappointing. Above all, we learned during that very first year that our thinking about writer's notebooks was much too sophisticated for our then "seniors," children who had only been on this planet eight years. This admission demands deeper explanation.

David was a third grader who entered our school in the fall of 1991, our first year. After much explanation and information, David was asked to carry a writer's notebook. Since our incoming third graders had not attended schools where the use of a writer's notebook was encouraged, this was a new tool for our students. Rather than writing on loose sheets of draft paper, we were trying to give David the message that *not* everything he records will become a draft. The collections of entries would give him an array of possibilities, and he would only work on (revise, edit, then publish) things that really mattered. We were also trying to give David the message that he no longer had to think "story" every time he wrote. Rather, he would be able to do all kinds of jottings—quick one-liners, lists, random thoughts, lingering images, overheard conversations, striking observations, poems, and responses to literature. There were no rules, no absolutes, no "thou shalts." We were looking for raw material that David could eventually develop and turn into finished works. We would help him collect this raw material and teach him how to discover the potential for his words to be shaped into appropriate genres and eventually do good work in the world.

And then it happened—we looked at his notebook. Figures 3.1 and 3.2 represent the kind of writing that David (and many of his classmates) was doing. As is evident, David was using the pages of his writer's notebook to record daily events in very short

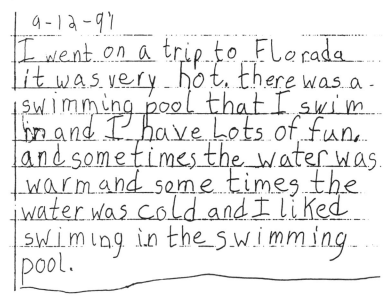

Figure 3.1

narrative passages. When we spoke to David we didn't even sense that he was personally connected to any of his entries. His teacher asked him to write and he did, easily. Probably too easily. He wrote about any old thing that popped into his mind. He was writing in a way that brings to mind the phrase *a sow's ear*. He was writing in a way that did not result in raw material to be shaped later into important published work. No silk purse happening here.

This kind of writing was very humbling for the teachers on staff. After all, we had been teachers of teachers. We had been traveling around the city introducing this "revolutionary" writing tool to teachers and children in all the boroughs. And here we were unable to make it work in our own school. We felt frustrated at the time, but in retrospect, the students' disappointing use of their writer's notebooks forced us to do some serious reflection and rethinking of what had become the "given" for us in the teaching of writing in the upper grades.

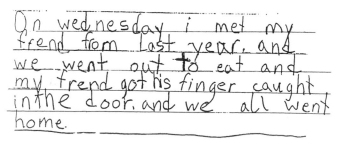

Figure 3.2

Most important of all, we realized that third graders were *not* upper graders. At the university, we had always divided our workshop presentations into kindergarten through second grade, third through sixth grade, coupling middle and high school as secondary. I suppose we had imagined that our third graders, our oldest students, could do all the things we had seen work so well with older students. It was clearly a rude awakening for us to realize that third graders, particularly in the fall, are still early-childhood students. We realized that it was educationally unsound and inappropriate for us to ask or expect these very young writers to use their first writer's notebooks in the same ways that more fluent and sophisticated writers use theirs.

When we see clusters of children build with blocks in kindergarten and then we cross the hall and observe fourth graders building with blocks, we expect the block building in the two rooms to differ in complexity. We also have come to expect that the conversations that accompany the activity will be different. As children get older, their attention spans increase, their negotiation skills improve, and their imaginations develop.

The same expectation of growth over time holds true with various yearly activities. We expect children's abilities to design a pattern or draw a self-portrait to become more sophisticated as children move up through the grades. Similarly, if a kindergarten teacher wants to teach children about Martin Luther King Jr., the meaning of the Thanksgiving holiday, or how eggs hatch in an incubator, we expect that her content would be different from that of the sixth-grade teacher who is exploring the same issues. We expect change in schools, and the elementary level affords us the widest screen to watch these changes occur. It comes as no surprise, then, that we had to discover a more child-like vision for the writer's notebook when working with our eight-year-olds.

In the early years of our school, we took a very hard look at the use of the writer's notebook at the third-grade level. What we discovered was that we had the right students. We had the right tool. We just had the wrong image in mind of how best to use this tool. We had to think "beginning writer," not "sophisticated craftsperson." We had to devise a more transitional use of this very important writer's tool. We had to begin by thinking of the notebook as a tool to help children who didn't seem to pay attention to the world around them. For those eight-year-olds who seem to naturally take in and respond to their surroundings, the notebook had to become a container in which they could save and savor their observations and ideas. When these goals are clear in the minds of teachers, the use of a writer's notebook can make sense for young children.

(One reason that our five- and six-year-olds don't need this writer's tool is because they have no problem paying attention to the world around them. They seem to notice everything. Many children somewhere toward the end of grade two begin to feel self-conscious and worry if they are doing things the right way, the way their friends are doing things. They seem to become conformist thinkers, losing the surprising ways they used to talk and interact with the world. As they enter grade three, the notebook encourages them to keep on honoring the fresh thoughts that pop into their mind. See related information in Chapter 6, "Working with Our Youngest Writers.")

Above all, in researching the use of notebooks with third graders, we learned that good writing need not always be a result of revision. Writing is not a matter of squeezing a skeletal draft out of a child, then asking just the right questions to get the child to add the good stuff, the engaging lead and a few telling details. No, good writing need *not* be reserved for revision time. Children can learn to pay attention and take in their worlds. Children can do quick first-draft jottings that take your breath away. They can write poignant, powerful, important entries that are filled with observational truths and language worth savoring. If children begin with good raw material in their notebooks, revision becomes a matter of gently reshaping their thoughts and making decisions about language, genre, and structure. Children can then learn to read their notebooks, looking for picture-book-shaped entries, poetry-shaped entries, and so on.

Our ways of working with writer's notebooks with young writers became less sophisticated, and at the same time much more effective and powerful.

Figure 3.3 is a sample from David's notebook from March of that same school year. He is still writing about Florida, but he has changed as a writer.

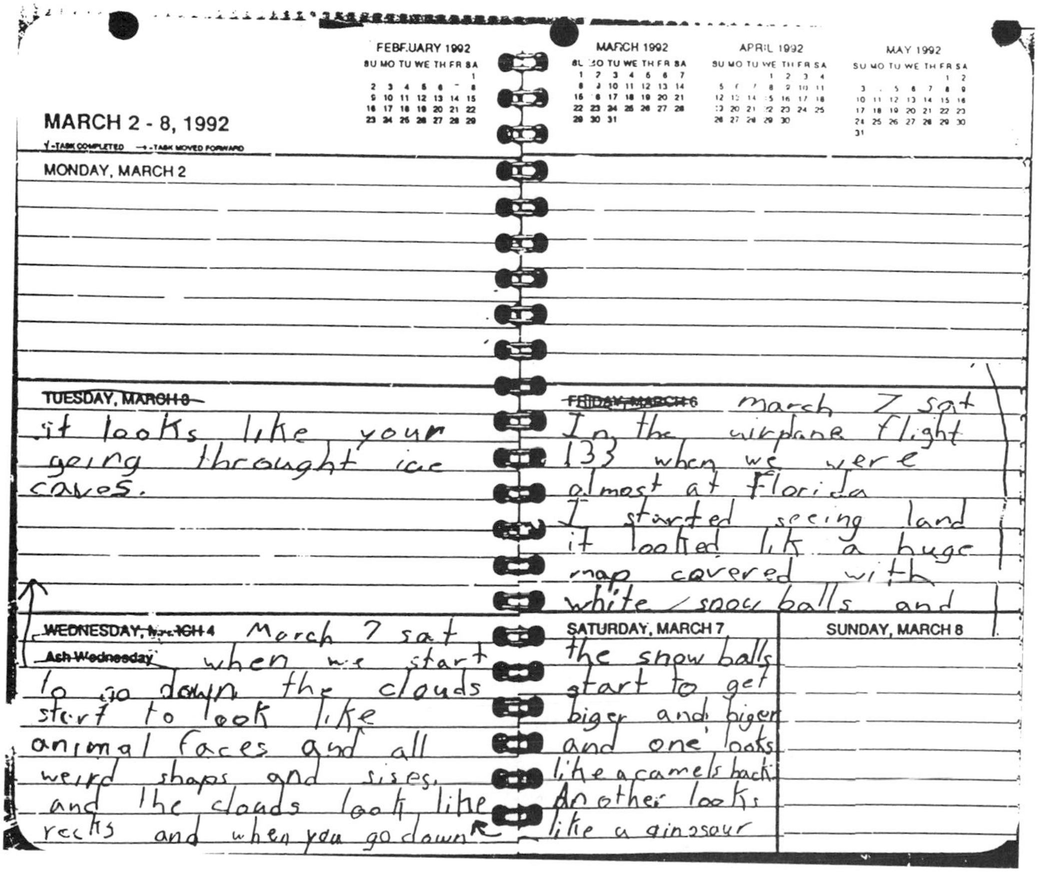
MARCH 2 - 8, 1992

MONDAY, MARCH 2

~~TUESDAY, MARCH 3~~

it looks like your going throught ice caves.

~~WEDNESDAY, MARCH 4~~

~~Ash Wednesday~~

March 7 sat when we start to go down the clouds start to look like animal faces and all weird shaps and sises. and the clouds look like rocks and when you go down

~~FRIDAY, MARCH 6~~ march 7 sat In the airplane flight 133 when we were almost at Florida I started seeing land it looked like a huge map covered with white snow balls and

SATURDAY, MARCH 7

the snow balls start to get biger and biger and one looks like a camels back Another looks like a dinosour

SUNDAY, MARCH 8

Figure 3.3

David's writing has become much more reflective, filled with sensory details and strong imagery. He is no longer writing plot alone. He is no longer treating the pages of his writer's notebook as if they were pages in a ship captain's log filled with bed-to-bed daily happenings. In fact, you could easily imagine this eight-year-old's jottings being reshaped into poetic forms.

One major reason for the shift in the quality of David's writing has to do with tense. He is no longer writing retrospectively, looking back and trying to recall what the view from the airplane was like. Instead, he is writing onboard the plane, on a Saturday. He is writing about something as it is unfolding before his eyes, yielding entries much richer than his earlier attempts.

Supporting Notebook Writing

David's teacher wanted all her students to do what David had done, taking full advantage of this portable writing tool. We therefore invited students to use their notebooks throughout the school day and across the curriculum. We trusted that if children began turning to their notebooks whenever a thought took hold *inside* of school, there was more of a likelihood that they would use their notebooks in a similarly effective way *outside* of school. In addition to encouraging students to carry their notebooks everywhere in order to write about unfolding events, several other classroom supports were put in place that pushed David and the other young writers in his class to show signs of having what Sontag called Attention Surplus Syndrome. These are discussed below.

Teacher Demonstrations

In addition to sharing notebook entries written at home, we also wrote alongside our students, demonstrating how writers can be moved by things in their immediate environments. For example, one day Alexandra wore a funky hat to class and I explained to the children how noticing her hat got me thinking about something that was important to me. I wrote and then shared the following notebook entry:

> Alexandra's black hat brings back lots of memories of my daughter. She really got into hats in high school. Big black ones with wide brims, dark green velvet ones, even very old-fashioned ones with veils, feathers, and sequins. She liked to stop and browse in every secondhand clothing store and every antique store we passed. Now the hat rack at home is empty. J.J. is at college and I miss her.

Inviting Children to Take the Scientist's Stance

We shared with our older students some of the very reflective and rich writing that younger first graders were doing, particularly during science class, as a means of giving them an alternate image of notebook writing. We talked to our older students about what made the simple observations in Figures 3.4–3.7 effective.

A six-year-old studying a shoebox filled with seashells wrote, "The shells are nice and they smell like candy. I love candy. And inside the shells the color is like seaweed" (Figure 3.4). A six-year-old observing a twisted tree branch wrote, "The whole wood is very nice, but I don't like brown. I wish I had long hair because I could braid it just like them. It looks like a tree" (Figure 3.5). A first grader examines a cactus and writes, "The cactus are very nice but they hurt us. I just hurt my finger and it hurts it really does. Never mind, I'll put a bandage on it" (Figure 3.6).

Our third graders understood that these pieces were filled with strong voices and strong imagery because the budding scientists really wanted their readers to understand what they were discovering. Their younger classmates weren't afraid to ask questions, voice opinions, jump to connected images and thoughts. We explained to the older students that they need not be in science class to take this same researcher's stance. When they visit their grandma, look out their bedroom windows, or baby-sit their little sisters, they could include honest wonderings, close observations, and insightful metaphors. We sensed that our students did wonder why their grandma's hands looked different from their mother's, did notice the wall of stripes the street lamp created when it shone

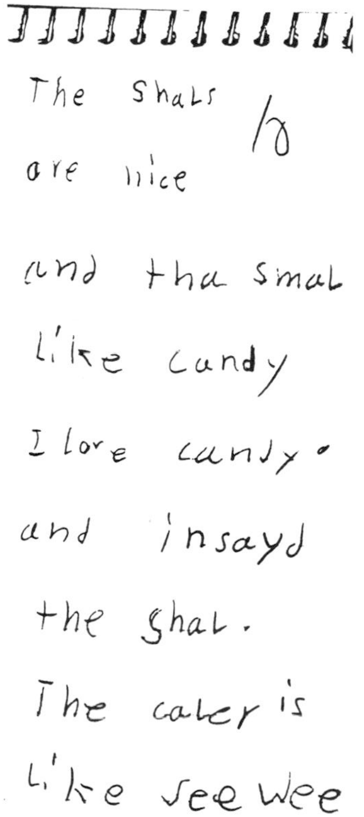

The Shals
are niice

and tha Smal
like candy
I lore candy.
and insayd
the ghal.
The caler is
Like see wee

Figure 3.4

the hol 6
wod are
vary nice
But I dont like
Brun I wish
I had long
hav because
I cad Bradit
Jast Like
tham. it
looks Like
a tree.

Figure 3.5

through their bedroom blinds, and did think their baby sister's hair felt like the silky strands they pulled off cobs of corn. Our students just didn't know that these kinds of comments were effective ways to enrich their writing. They came to our school from classrooms all over the city, and many of them were constrained by a narrow under-standing of writing. We simply had to liberate them.

Tapping into Read-Alouds That Resonate
Teachers began to think of their everyday read-alouds as prime opportunities for children to write in their writer's notebooks. They taught children to quickly jot down any ideas that came to mind during read-aloud, and to think of those phrases as bookmarks to be

The caktis7
are vary
nice But tha
hrt ows
I Gast hrt
my tiger
and it hrs
it rely das.
naver maynd
I'l Pot a
Banday on it.

Figure 3.6

returned to later. In other words, children didn't stop listening to the text being read aloud. Instead, they learned to keep their notebooks opened on their laps and quickly record moments of interest. (See more in Chapter 5, "Reading to Inform Your Writing").

Capitalizing on Firsthand Experiences

We provided lots of firsthand experiences, deliberately designed to get children writing as things were happening around them. Joan Backer, then a third-grade teacher, and I took advantage of eight- and nine-year-olds' boundless spirit of adventure. For example, we took the children on a walking tour of the neighborhood, notebooks in hand. Thomas stood on the corner of Second Avenue and wrote the entry that appears in Figure 3.7.

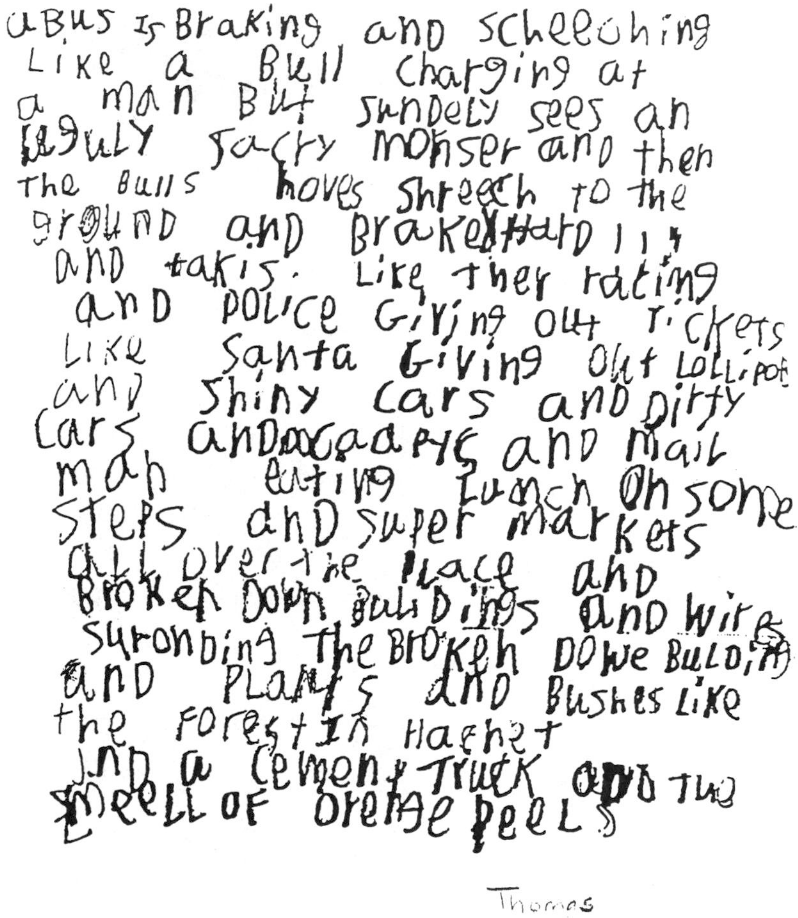

a Bus is Braking and schleeohing
Like a Bull charging at
a man But sundely sees an
ugly Jacty mohser and then
The Bulls hoves shreech to the
ground and Brakes Hard 1 1 1
and takis. Like ther rating
and Police Giving out Tickets
Like Santa Giving out LOLLiPoe
and Shiny cars and Ditty
cars and Garbage and mail
man euting Lunch On some
steps and super markets
all over the place and
Broken Down Buildings and Wirs
Suronbing The Broken DOWe Buldin
and Plants and Bushes Like
the Forest In Hachet
and a Cement Truck and The
smell of orenge peels

Thomas

Figure 3.7

Once, we put Danny's weekend find of forty salamanders into containers and placed them center stage in the middle of the meeting area. I began by talking about looking hard at things. I was trying to encourage students to do the kind of observing that suggests the intensity of Su Dong Po, the Chinese artist. He writes, "Before you can paint a bamboo, the bamboo must have grown deep inside you. It is then that, brush in hand gazing intently, you will see the vision rise up before you. Capture the vision at once by the strokes of your brush, for it may vanish as suddenly as a hare at the approach of the hunter."

After our chat about the difference between simply glancing and really seeing, everyone, including the teacher, student teacher, and myself attempted to capture the image of salamanders floating in clear plastic bowls. We shared our favorite lines, then students talked about which ones best captured the image before us. Our third graders particularly liked the following descriptions:

His tail looks wiggly and squishy like Jello.

I could just imagine that he was praying for food.

It's just floating around looking through blurry eyes at the huge giants, us.

When it's just laying there it reminds me of when I'm watching TV, laying still, not moving.

His tail is waving like a windshield wiper, wiping the glass.

The salamander is green like it's seasick, has spots like chicken pox, and a tail that looks like a big car ran over it. It looks like it had a bad day.

I then read aloud descriptive excerpts from Jean Craighead George's *The Moon of the Salamanders*, and we marveled at how professional writers use language to capture scenes. We all agreed that this author knew what the children's writer Leon Garfield meant when he said, "While it is the business of the scientist to make the marvelous commonplace, it is the business of the artist to make the commonplace marvelous."

We also sent clusters of children out to walk the halls of our school, capturing scenes that caught their attention. Students then shared their writing, and we talked about the passages that were particularly effective. A few examples follow.

A Music Class

The children are having music with Maxine. Bells are ringing and tambourines are shaking. Maxine has her legs crossed and is sitting in the rocking chair like a queen.

A Kindergarten Room

The kindergarten kids are talking all at once like a baby squeaking a hundred squeak toys all at once. Some are sucking their thumbs like two-year-olds. Some are trying to read their favorite books and some are raising their hands like polite children.

In the Office

Someone is working the copy machine and when she opens it a flash of green glows on her shirt. A boy is making a book using neon colors. They were shiny like the sun. His hat has neon colors too. I think people love shiny neon.

Once, we took advantage of a severe thunderstorm and asked the children to capture the feel of listening and watching the storm from the safety of their classroom. One student began, "The rain is banging on our window, begging to come in."

One time, I asked children to capture the feel of the classroom when Joan was absent and a substitute teacher took her place. "Write so that Joan will really understand what your day was like," I suggested. Dana wrote the entry in Figure 3.8. I like to think that this student was exaggerating just a bit, although I do recall sending the unfortunate sub home by midmorning and covering the class myself.

These invitations to write about shared experiences were extended in a playful spirit of fun and camaraderie. We wanted our students to discover the joy in effectively capturing their thoughts on paper. The students were able to do a good job because they

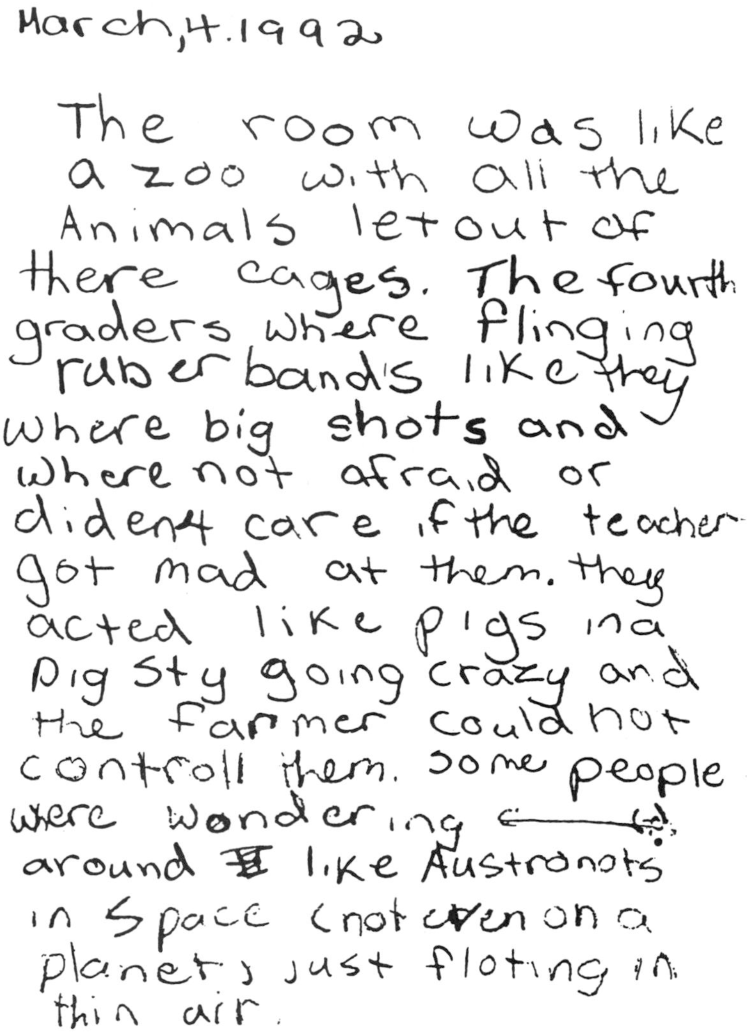

March,4.1992

The room was like a zoo with all the Animals let out of there cages. The fourth graders where flinging ruber bands like they where big shots and where not afraid or diden't care if the teacher got mad at them. they acted like pigs in a pig sty going crazy and the farmer could not controll them. Some people were wondering around ⊞ like Austronots in space (not even on a planet) just floting in thin air.

Figure 3.8

were engaged in the experiences and were writing during or very close to the event. They were also able to respond well to one another's efforts because they had actually been there. It was as if they had all lived through the first draft. They knew when they or a classmate had effectively captured an experience on paper.

Assigning At-Home Writing Exercises

In class we prepared students to take part in some deliberate writing challenges, exercises that would push them to use their writer's notebooks in new ways. When the writer's notebook is thought of as a friendly neighborhood playground, it becomes the perfect place for writing "exercises," challenges that invite children to stretch their skills, learn from peers and mentors, take new risks, and safely and confidently show off their latest accomplishments. For example, we read aloud short, poignant character descriptions, and then asked children to attempt one at home. I began with this passage from Claire Nicolas White's memoir, *Fragments of Stained Glass*. Although very much a piece of adult writing, the third graders were able to offer their observations of why it was a good description. This led to helpful conversations about noticing things, and what kinds of details can help a reader to really get to know a person.

> She ate her chicken with jam, her ham with pineapple slices. Her nose was sharp and long as a blade, her forehead high and knobby, her tongue too big for her mouth so that she held onto it with her teeth. Her long hair was always flapping against her nose like a sail against a mast. She was the color of a wet beach on a gray day and spoke very slowly in a voice that was always on the verge of laughter . . .

That night, many children chose to capture their mothers on paper. One student wrote,

> My mom has sharp green eyes, pale peach lipstick, thin nose, and her legs are always crossed. She's wearing Guess jeans, a dark blue turtleneck, black suede pumps, and Calvin Klein stockings. She has a long neck, emerald green framed glasses and very sharp facial features.

(Interestingly, one classmate asked the writer, "How did you know what kind of stockings your mom was wearing? You couldn't tell that just from observing her!")

Another student shared this description:

> My mother wears her engagement ring all the time. She's always talking about wedding this and wedding that. She always wears red lipstick that smells like cherry. She gets her hair cut every time it grows back. She wears her hair curly all the time.

The children discussed which descriptions were most revealing, noting the differences between ones that contained only visual details and ones that included actions or words spoken. They also noted the difference between ones that captured their family members at a particular point in time and ones that referred to their usual ways of being.

We also asked students to find one sentence in their notebook and work on it till it could move an audience. Children shared such strong one-liners as:

> My cat Rosie has white booties, a black fur coat, and bits of gold dust scattered across her back.
>
> The sun was warming up the flowers like moms warming up their babies.
>
> I watched the slithery, sticky honey drip against its plastic bottle as it slid onto my plate.
>
> As I walked into the lonely auditorium, I started to wonder if ghosts were entertaining other ghosts.

We also asked children to capture authentic at-home dialogue that would truly represent their family life. Of course, we insisted that they record only those conversations that would be acceptable to their families for sharing.

One third grader wrote about a conversation his teenage brother had with his mother:

B: Has anyone seen my sneakers? I thought I left them in the living room.

M: Did you look under the recliner? I think I saw them sticking out.

B: No, those were Daddy's. I wasn't sitting near that chair.

M: Well, keep looking. They've got to be somewhere. They didn't walk away.

B: They didn't walk away? Why do you always say that? It's so ridiculous. Of course they didn't walk away.

M: Well, you don't have to be rude, just keep looking.

Doing these kinds of exercises is like practicing scales on the piano. The children were trying new things, hearing new voices, and delighting in become better writers. To this day, we still offer writing challenges when student writing seems to have reached a plateau. (For a fuller explanation of the role of exercises, see "When Mentors Really Matter" in *Lasting Impressions: Weaving Literature into the Writing Workshop*, Heinemann, 1992.)

It's important to point out that none of the above invitations, challenges, or exercises were ever collected, corrected, revised, edited, or published. They were not the traditional "story starters" that took ownership away from students. No, they were simply seen by the teachers and the students as a way to practice paying close attention. Notebook pages were the perfect place for young writers to practice their skills and to hone their craft. The writer's notebook gave us a perfect place to experiment and play with our writing.

Keeping Dialogue Journals

Over the years, I've kept dialogue journals with many students, some of them in kindergarten through second grade. These correspondences served many functions including deepening our relationship, promoting students' risk taking as spellers, and inspiring youngsters to read what the principal wrote just to them. When I began writing to third graders, children who had begun to keep writer's notebooks, letter writing also served to promote their notebook keeping. I tried to write engaging letters filled with detailed observations and honest insights, the kind of content you might expect to find in a writer's notebook. I never kept journals with more than three or four children in any one season. I didn't want this important activity to turn into drudgery. I also took a full day to respond, not pressuring myself to write back immediately. Children usually took the journals home to write to me and then left them on my desk the next morning. I wrote back to the children that evening and they picked the journals up the following morning. Although only a few children kept these dialogue journals at any one time, you can be sure they shared my responses with one another. (Keeping dialogue journals is a wonderful way to get to know a few children particularly well. It's also a practice that can be taken up by other people in the school—teachers, volunteers, parents who care about writing and can spare a few minutes each night.)

Dana was a third grader when we began keeping a dialogue journal together. She began by responding to my content and then learned to initiate topics, as is evident in the journal pages that appear in Figures 3.9–3.11.

My original invitation read as follows:

Dear Dana,

I've started journals with children in kindergarten, first, and second grade. Every day I write to them and they write back. I realized I needed a third grader. Would you be willing? I leave the books on my desk. Whenever you have time you can pick this one up.

We can write about anything. Right now I 'm thinking about my mom. She's not feeling well, so I'm trying to figure out how I can visit her more often. Isn't it hard to believe that when you grow up, you usually don't live with your parents? She used to take care of me, now I'm taking care of her. That reminds me of a book called A Special Trade. Have you read it? It also reminds me of the work your mom does. Doesn't she help older people? I hope you write back.

Love,
Shelley

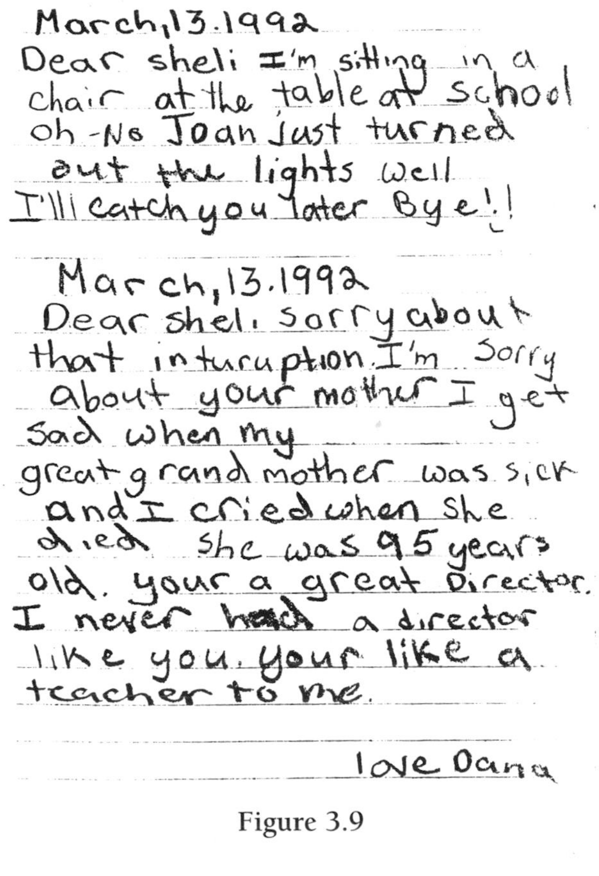

> March,13.1992
> Dear sheli I'm sitting in a
> chair at the table at school
> Oh -No Joan just turned
> out the lights well
> I'll catch you later Bye!!
>
> March,13.1992
> Dear shel. sorry about
> that inturuption I'm sorry
> about your mother I get
> sad when my
> great grand mother was sick
> and I cried when she
> died she was 95 years
> old. your a great Director.
> I never had a director
> like you. your like a
> teacher to me.
>
> love Dana

Figure 3.9

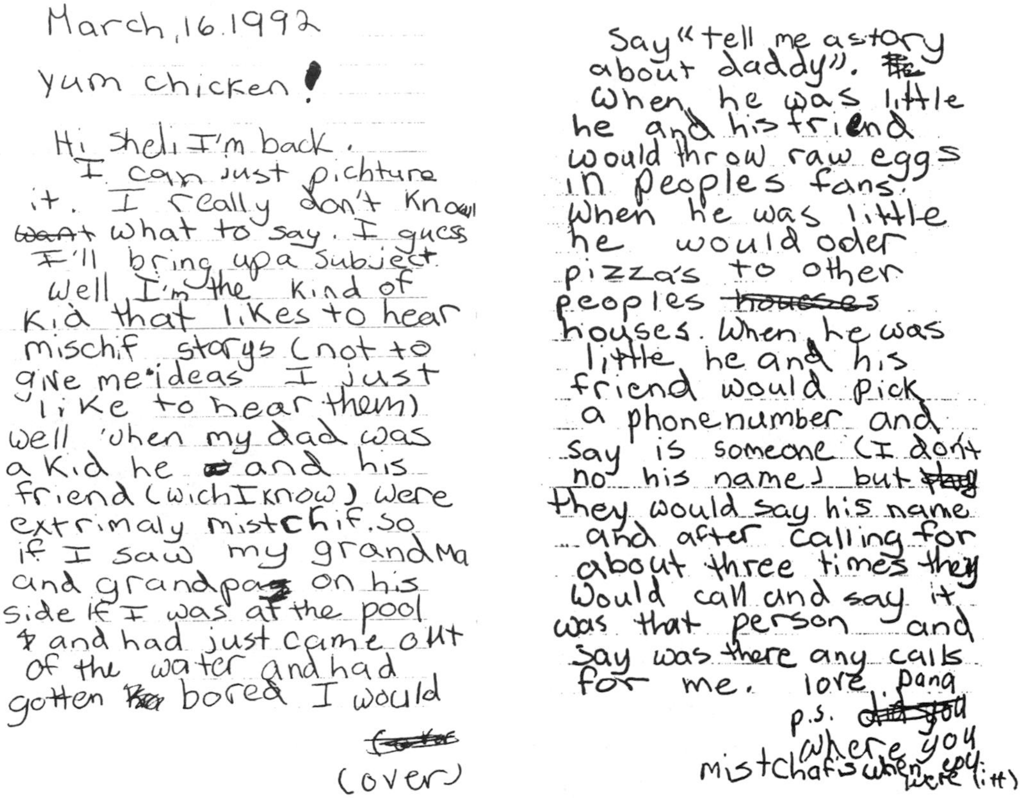

March, 16.1992

yum chicken!

Hi sheli I'm back.
I can just pichture
it. I really don't Know
want what to say. I gues
I'll bring up a Subject.
Well I'm the kind of
kid that likes to hear
mischif storys (not to
give me ideas I just
like to hear them)
well when my dad was
a kid he and his
friend (wich I know) were
extrimaly mistchif. So
if I saw my grandma
and grandpa on his
side if I was at the pool
& and had just came out
of the water and had
gotten bored I would

(over)

Say "tell me a story
about daddy". They
When he was little
he and his friend
would throw raw eggs
in peoples fans.
When he was little
he would oder
pizza's to other
peoples houses
houses. When he was
little he and his
friend would pick
a phone number and
say is someone (I don't
no his name) but stay
they would say his name
and after calling for
about three times they
would call and say it
was that person and
say was there any calls
for me. love, Dana
p.s. did you
where you
mistchaf's when you
here (it)

Figure 3.10

After reading Dana's first letter (Figure 3.10), I wrote the following in response:

Dear Dana,

*Thanks for your two-part letter. I think you're a fine writer. Your writing sounds so honest—
just like you.*

*It's Saturday night. My husband just barbecued chicken for dinner. Even in the winter we
use our barbecue. It's on the back porch, right off the kitchen, so it's easy to get to. Sometimes
it's really windy and cold so my husband has to wear his jacket and gloves. What a funny
sight to watch him cook in stormy weather. We live right on the beach so it gets really cold
and windy in the winter.*

*Later, we're going to work on the bibliography of my new book. Do you know what that is?
I have to make a list of all the books I mentioned in my book. Then I have to put them in
alphabetical order. I hope to finish this job on Sunday.*

See you Monday, Shelley

Dana's response in Figure 3.10 demonstrates how dialogue journals can help students discover important topics and realize that they have significant things to say about

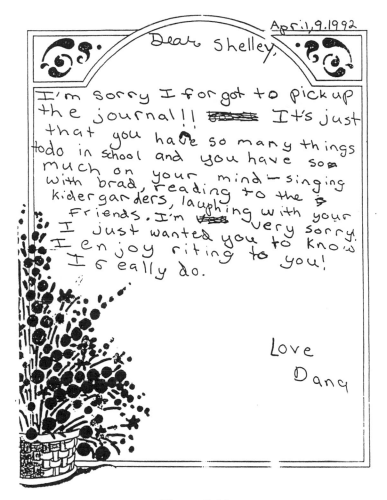

April,9.1992

Dear Shelley,

I'm sorry I forgot to pickup the journal!! ~~It's~~ It's just that you have so many things todo in school and you have so much on your mind — singing with brad, reading to the kidergarders, laughing with your friends. I'm ~~very~~ very sorry. I just wanted you to know I enjoy riting to you! I really do.

Love
Dana

Figure 3.11

those topics. Keeping dialogue journals with particularly reticent writers can be a way to help them get a leg up in their writing. When they become more at ease putting pen to paper, they are more likely to continue writing without the presence of a dialogue partner.

Figure 3.11 is an apology note Dana sent me when she forgot one day to pick up our dialogue journal. I loved reading about what was keeping her so busy. Her apology was easily accepted.

Using Poetry

In *Lasting Impressions: Weaving Literature into the Writing Workshop*, I devote an entire chapter to "Literature and the Writer's Notebook." I discuss ways to use literature to launch and enrich the keeping of writer's notebooks. I list books in which the main character keeps a notebook and books in which the main character leads a wide-awake life. I suggest books that serve as a metaphor for notebook keeping and explore the possibilities of sharing published writers' notebooks with children. I include the memoirs and biographies of professional writers, as well as discuss the use of their speeches, profiles, interviews, and promotional material. I also list books published in diary and journal formats. If I were writing that book today I would devote prime attention to yet another category of literature, a select kind of poetry that can help young writers appreciate what's possible when they are just beginning to keep writer's notebooks.

Many years ago I was speaking at a conference in New York City; my topic was "Improving the Quality of Student Writing." I began by asking the audience to listen to a few excerpts from a student's notebook and then talk about what they might say to this young writer. I then read the following passages:

> I never hear my mother come
> Into my room late late at night.
> She says she has to look and see
> If I'm still tucked exactly right
> Nor do I feel her kissing me.
> She says she does, though,
> Every night.

> Now I'm stretched out on my stomach,
> Watching things walking in the grass.
> Most of the things I see are small—
> Like ants. There's an anthill nearby,
> And I like best to put crumbs down
> And watch the ants take them back home.
> Sometimes I stop them with a stick,
> But mostly I just watch them go.
> It must be very hard, I think,
> To carry a crumb
> When you're hardly as big as one.

Several of my colleagues from the Manhattan New School were in the audience that day, and when I read these pieces, I overheard these teachers asking one another, "Who wrote that? Is that one of your students?" When I heard these responses, I knew I was on to something big.

I had been having a bit of fun with my audience. The "entries" I had read and presented as having been written by children in our school were in fact published poems written by accomplished, published poets. The first is entitled "I Never Hear" and was written by Dorothy Aldis; the second is "Watching Things," by Marci Ridlon. The teachers present believed that these pieces were written by children from our school. And why shouldn't they have believed me? Aside from the fact that speakers usually tell the truth, these poems sound like children could have written them. Children *would* wonder if their mothers really kiss them when they're asleep at night. Anthills are endlessly fascinating to kids. In other words, these poems are true to the spirit of childhood in topic, in tone, in language.

Of course, it meant a lot to me that I could convince the colleagues that know our students best that a child in our school *could have* written texts like these. I knew I was on to something powerful. I began collecting literally hundreds of similar poems, primarily in free verse. (I've discovered that free verse sounds to children as if the author wrote it with ease, as opposed to rhyming poems, which children sense take considerable time and effort. I was sharing these poems as if they were notebook jottings and therefore wanted to give children the feel of someone capturing reactions, observations, and thoughts.)

In addition to the poems being free verse, they had to sound like a child could have written them. I was amazed how easy it was to discover poets who knew how to capture the voice of a child. I began sharing these poems with Joanne Hindley Salch and her third graders. The children at first thought I was sharing entries written by students in other classes. (That's how true to the spirit of childhood these poets were. In addition, I had copied all these poems into a blank notebook and so the students didn't see the published anthology I had discovered them in. It wasn't very surprising that at first they thought I was reading material written by children in the school.) I always told the children that those words were not written by students but by grown-ups who either remember what it was like to be young or have lots of contact with children in their current lives.

The poems worked wonders in many of our classrooms. It was as if the children were saying, "I can do that. I have ideas like that." Joanne added additional poems that she had been using and we spent one weekend categorizing the entire collection, in the hopes of one day putting an anthology together. (Categories are described on page 64.) The anthology is still on our "to do" list.

By the way, we didn't emphasize that we were reading *poems*. It was more of a, "Hey, listen to this . . ." experience. We didn't want children to think we expected them to write poems in their writer's notebooks. In fact, we were simply using these poems, which had a notebook sound and feel, to invite our children into a new way of writing and get them out of the "story ruts" they were often in. We didn't even count on the poems for possible topic choice connections, which of course many children naturally made.

I shouldn't have been at all surprised that these poems worked wonders. I explained a similar phenomenon when I describe the parents' writing workshop in *Going Public*. There, I included poems that made the adults say, "I could do that!" The adults not only believed that they could produce writing of such high quality, they were able to imagine how the poets came to write such pieces. They could imagine the creator of "Morning Strangers," a poem filled with observations about passengers the poet meets on the bus each morning, sitting with a little memo pad in hand, taking notes on the human scene.

They could imagine the grandmother who wrote "New Neighbors Across the Street" look-ing out her window each day and recording her observations. This was also true of our children. When they heard the following poems, written by Richard Margolies in his col-lection *Only the Moon and Me,* they could easily imagine a child jotting down his thoughts after a run-in with a bully at the playground or in bed at night, listening to all the sounds his body makes and recording them in the pad he keeps on his night table.

> If you're afraid
> of a big dog
> he'll smell it
> and bite you.
> If you're afraid
> of a bully
> he'll see it
> and beat you up.
> Bullies and big dogs have a lot in common.

> My stomach growls.
> My throat gurgles.
> My teeth click.
> My fingers crack.
> My toes thump.
> My nose sniffs.
> My lips pop.
> Even my blinks make a sound.
> I'm really very noisy,
> in a quiet way.

We surrounded students with many, many poems with this type of voice, spirit, and outlook. Many were written by such prominent poets as Nikki Giovanni, Lee Ben-nett Hopkins, Siv Widerberg, Michael Rosen, Myra Cohn Livingston, Jean Little, Lucille Clifton, and of course Richard Margolies. All dealt with topics that would come naturally and easily to a young person. And all were free verse, although written in a variety of for-mats. Some were in the form of a series of questions, others were built on language play, some contained lists. Others could be imagined as having been written by a child engaged in close observation, recalling a scene from his mind's eye, or writing about something as it was happening (e.g., Marci Ridlon's "Watching Things"). We also shared poems that reminded our students that they could write about things that happened every day as opposed to special events (e.g., Dorothy Aldis' "I Never Hear," in which the child thinks about the mother coming in to kiss her while she is asleep each night). Young writers need the option to write about noticings over time, the little yet significant things that happen day after day.

Poems that fill the categories described above are *not* hard to find. I've held many staff development workshops in school libraries in which participants searched through the poetry shelves for accessible and appropriate poems to share with their young notebook keepers. The categories are not nearly as important as whether the poem answers in the affirmative the question, "Could you convince your colleagues that a child in your class wrote it?" If so, the poem will probably inspire other young notebook keepers.

Although explaining that poems fit into different categories is not essential, for some children, determining formats helps them branch out in their own writing. Third graders often get caught up in writing one type of narrative, so that "The Day I Went to Disney World," follows "The Day I Got My New Bike" and "The Day I Learned How to Surf the Internet." Realizing that thoughts in the form of questions, lists, or firsthand observations qualify as writing inspires children to try new ways of responding to the world and new ways of recording their thoughts in their notebooks.

After spending several weeks at the beginning of the year filling children with these entry-like poems, our students' writing did markedly change. (For the titles of anthologies filled with these kinds of poems, see the bibliography in Appendix 1.) Students were looking at the world through wondrous eyes and writing toward this new image of what writing could be. Several third-grade students' notebook entries appear in Figures 3.12–3.15

The Cloud
The Cloud was big
and white sitting
still and low over
the tall New york
city night. the steam
was rising up to it
but still it was big,
broad, and stubborn.

Figure 3.12 Billy's Entry

PaPa   4/2/93

You no when PaPa ~~holts~~ holds
You in his ~~of~~ arms

But When You get
maryd some ~~e~~ One
els will have you in
There arms

But not PaPa,

Figure 3.13   Gina's Entry

Sari writes:

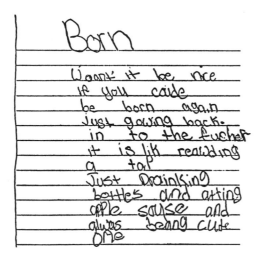

Born

Woont it be nice
if you cade
be born again
Just going back.
in to the fucher
it is lik reawlding
a tap
Just Drainking
bottles and atting
aple souse and
alwas being cute
one

Translation of Born

Wouldn't it be nice
if you could be born again
just going back in to the future
it is like rewinding a tape
just drinking bottles and eating
apple sauce and always being
the cute one?

Figure 3.14   Sari's Entry

These children were in Joanne Hindley Salch's third-grade class and their writing demonstrates that these carefully selected poems served as a change agent, directly influencing the way students viewed the world and the way they chose to record their thinking. (See Joanne's book *In the Company of Children* for other ways she lifted the quality of her students' writing.)

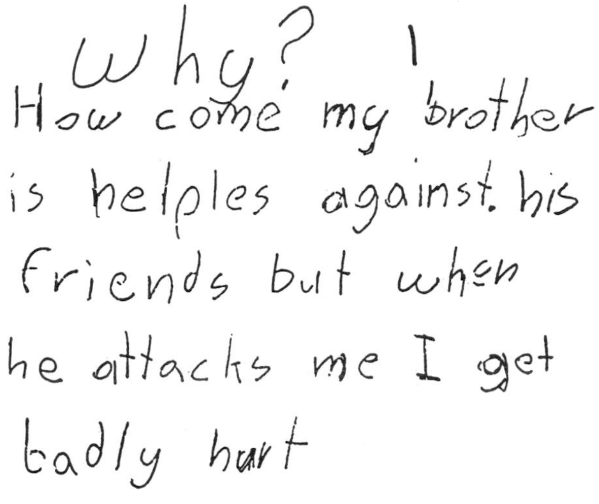

Why?
How come my brother
is helples against his
friends but when
he attacks me I get
badly hurt

Figure 3.15   Alexei's Entry

Their words bring to mind Grace Paley's comment, "Poetry is the school I went to, to learn to write prose." They also recall these words of John Ciardi: "The good poet cannot fail to shame us, for he proves instantly that we have never learned to touch, smell, taste, hear and see." When children take lessons from wonderful poets, lessons that can enrich all their writing, not just their writing of poetry, we start to understand the words of Diane Ackerman from her essay "White Lanterns." She writes, "The best poems are rich with observational truths. Above all, we ask the poet to teach us a way of seeing, lest one spend a lifetime on this planet without noticing how green light flares up as the setting sun rolls under, or the gauzy spread of the Milky Way on a star loaded summer night." She goes on to say, "The poet refuses to let things merge, lie low, succumb to visual habit. Instead she hoists things out of their routine, and lays them out on a white papery beach to be fumbled and explored."

It's no surprise that so many of the students' entries appear to be simple, publishable poems. After all, we had surrounded students with so many short, free verse poems. Frank Smith has reminded us that "the problem may not be that children don't learn in school but that they learn all the time. And . . they will learn exactly what is demonstrated." Even though our young students' beginning attempts were rather short, they were a far cry from what David and his classmates had done at the beginning of that very first year.

Because their teachers and their peers responded so favorably to these short poetic pieces, third graders were eager to publish them as is, with just a hint of gentle reshaping into better poetic form. As children got older and more used to keeping a writer's notebook, they were no longer in such a hurry to quickly publish these short thoughts in poetic form. Instead, their initial short entries became longer and often led to bigger projects in a multitude of genres.

Planting Deep Roots

Inviting young writers to take part in all the interactions described above, including providing powerful demonstrations, capitalizing on shared firsthand experiences, and using poetry as models, gets students off to a good start as notebook keepers and shifts them away from using their notebooks in bland, uninspired ways. They become alert, active, and aggressive as they take in their world. Third-grade teachers often treat notebook writing as a genre unto itself, and postpone publishing until class members understand the reasons for keeping a notebook and their pages filled with rich raw material that has publishing potential. Then, as the children move up through the grades, their use of this writer's tool changes.

The entries included here illustrate how fourth graders tend to write lengthier pieces rich in detail and develop a topic of importance, using their writer's notebook as a place to experiment with various ways of presenting that topic. They also use their notebook as a place to experiment within the genre courses of study that their teachers have presented.

At the Manhattan New School, we had many children who wrote about their "home countries," including Serbo-Croatia, Albania, the Dominican Republic, Korea, and dozens more. Some of our city kids wrote about their "country homes," weekend getaways often a few hours outside the city. In Figure 3.16 fourth grader Sofia writes about her beloved country place. (See writing about a place on pages 266–286.)

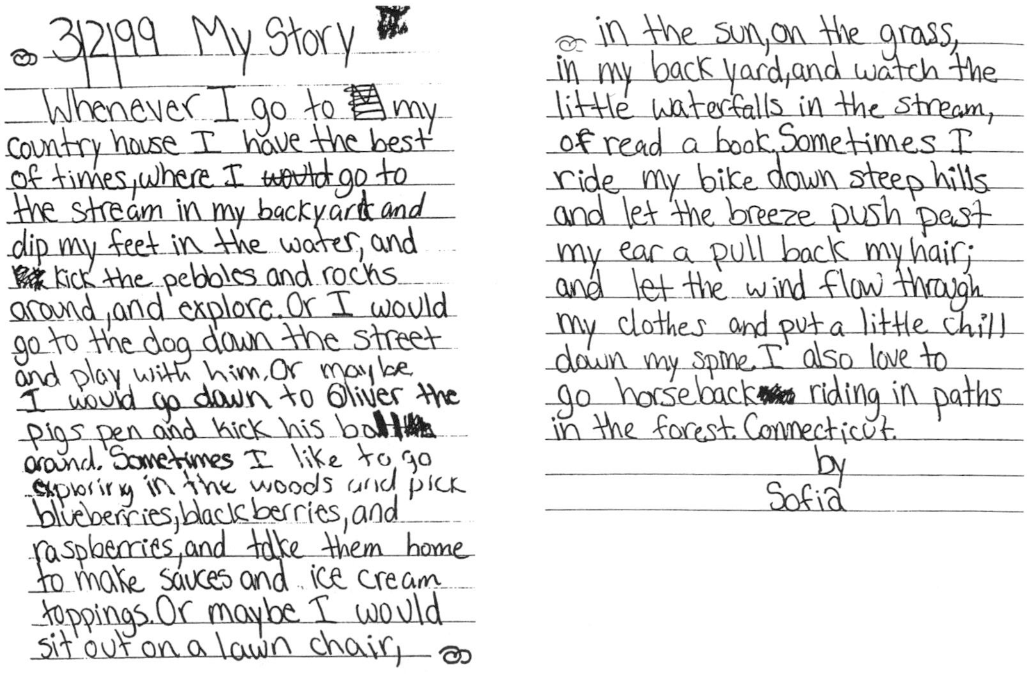

3/2/99 My Story

Whenever I go to my country house I have the best of times, where I would go to the stream in my backyard and dip my feet in the water, and kick the pebbles and rocks around, and explore. Or I would go to the dog down the street and play with him. Or maybe I would go down to Oliver the pigs pen and kick his ball around. Sometimes I like to go exploring in the woods and pick blueberries, blackberries, and raspberries, and take them home to make sauces and ice cream toppings. Or maybe I would sit out on a lawn chair, in the sun, on the grass, in my back yard, and watch the little waterfalls in the stream, of read a book. Sometimes I ride my bike down steep hills and let the breeze push past my ear a pull back my hair; and let the wind flow through my clothes and put a little chill down my spine. I also love to go horseback riding in paths in the forest. Connecticut.

by
Sofia

Figure 3.16

In Figures 3.17–3.19, fourth grader Lauren writes breathlessly and at length about her cat Lily. As the following unedited notebook entries illustrate, her writing remains true to the spirit of childhood, filled with the voice of a nine-year-old. Choosing to write in many different ways about her cat (including in the voice of her cat!) Lauren has given herself a challenge that fifth-grade teachers often assign their students (see page 75).

Riri, also a fourth grader, has many poems in her writer's notebook, as her teacher David spent several weeks teaching a poetry course of study (see Figures 3.20–3.25).

Fifth graders are encouraged to continue writing longer, meatier entries, filled with sensory detail. Their notebook pages brim with possibilities. When we stop to confer with students in a fifth-grade writing workshop and read pieces like those by Cara in Figures 3.22 and 3.23 you are likely to hear teachers suggest the kind of strategies listed on page 75. Just as composers use the piano to sketch out their works, so too our oldest student begin to use their notebook pages to sketch out their works.

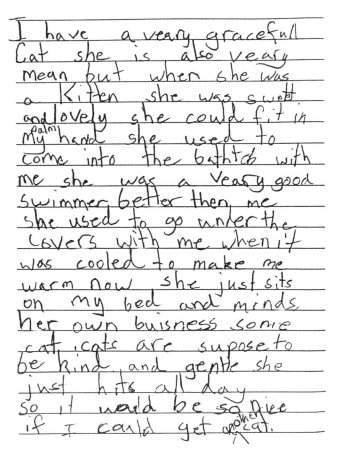

Figure 3.17

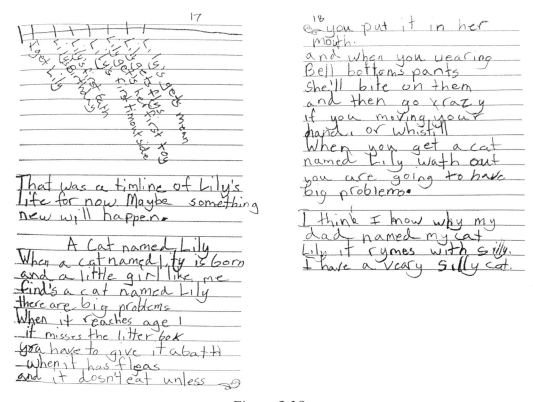

17

18

you put it in her
mouth.
and when you wearing
Bell bottoms pants
she'll bite on them
and then go crazy
if you moving your
hand. or whistill
When you get a cat
named Lily wath out
you are going to have
big problems.

I think I know why my
dad named my cat
Lily it rymes with silly.
I have a veary silly cat.

That was a timline of Lily's
life for now. Maybe something
new will happen.

A Cat named Lily
When a cat named Lily is born
and a little girl like me
find's a cat named Lily
there are big problems
When it reaches age 1
it misses the litter box
you have to give it a bath
when it has fleas
and it dosn't eat unless

Figure 3.18

Setting Realistic Goals

The following grade-level descriptions offer a school-wide perspective on the use of writer's notebooks. Of course, grade-level expectations are never carved in stone. Teachers assign and innovate on their use based on the needs, interests, and strengths of their students. Additionally, when children in a school are asked to use the same tool, year after year, their consistent use builds effectiveness and expertise. It is much easier for fifth-grade teachers to help their students produce moving pieces of writing if those children have, for several years, been seeing the potential for writing everywhere.

Grade Three (Our Eight-Year-Olds)

As stated previously, we invite all our third-grade students to keep writer's notebooks. We want these early experiences to be joyful and celebratory. (Rakheli told Joanne Hindley Salch, her third-grade teacher, that the disappointing part of her celebration of Yom Kippur, the Jewish holiday known as the Day of Atonement during which observers fast, was not that she couldn't eat but that she couldn't write.) We continually tell children what we see in them as writers. We work very hard at the beginning of the year, for as long as it takes, to ensure that the quality of children's original jottings is high. (This goal

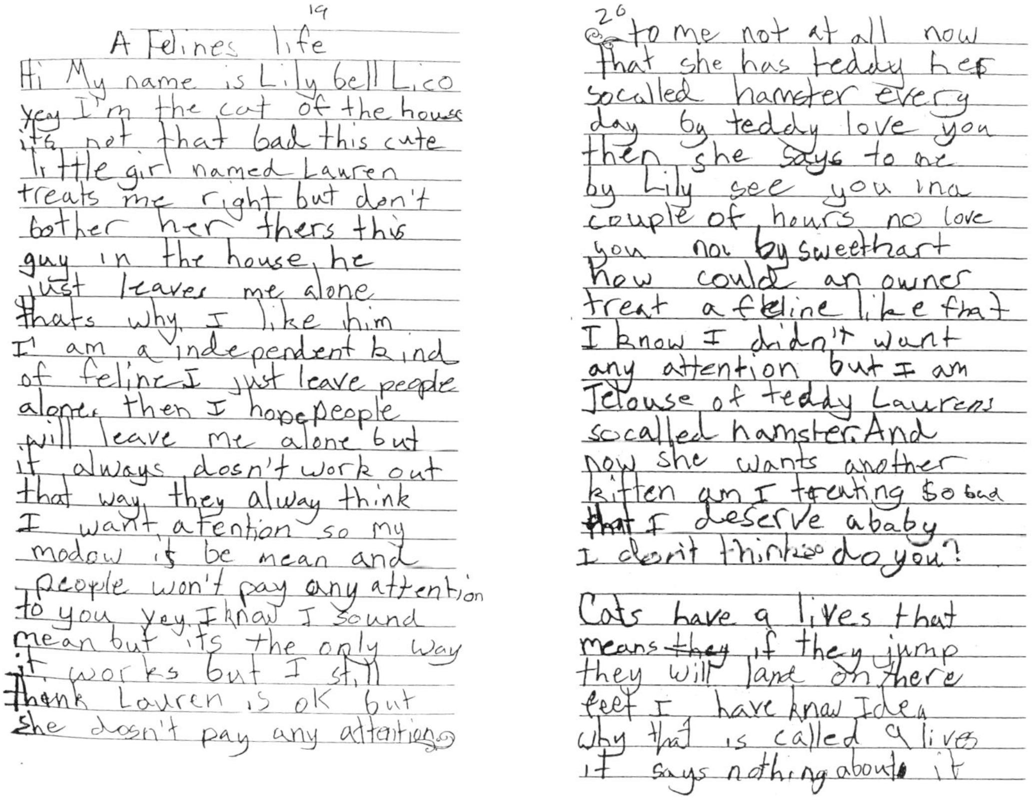

Figure 3.19

is mainly achieved through the various challenges, exercises, and sharing of carefully chosen literature as previously described; such activities are designed to catapult students into an alert way of life.) As previously noted, keeping a writer's notebook is almost a genre unto itself. We are willing to devote big blocks of time to getting the notebooks started on the right track, because once that happens, the rest comes easy. We can do all kinds of publishing if the children have good ongoing raw material. Publishing usually means gently shaping the entries that they care most about into short, manageable formats. Occasionally teachers will lead a whole-class genre study, but only occasionally. For the most part, our eight-year-olds choose the genres that best suit their notebook entries. They understand that form must support content.

Grade Four (Our Nine-Year-Olds)

In grade four we begin the year by making sure that our students still find keeping a writer's notebook a joyous pastime. We ask if they have written in their notebooks during the summer months when we were apart. We postpone publishing until we are sure notebooks are valued and children are attentive and responsive to the events of their lives and to their surroundings. When students use their notebooks regularly and almost

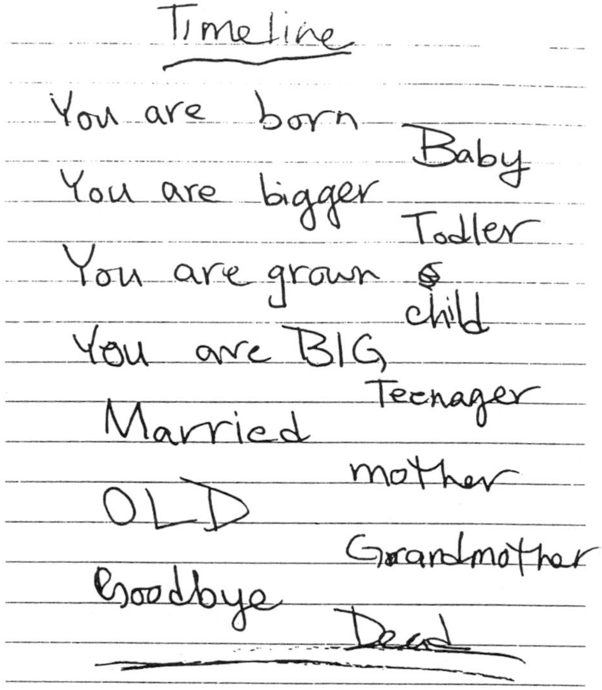

Timeline

You are born — Baby

You are bigger — Todler

You are grown & child

You are BIG

Married — Teenager

OLD — mother

Goodbye — Grandmother

Dead

Figure 3.20

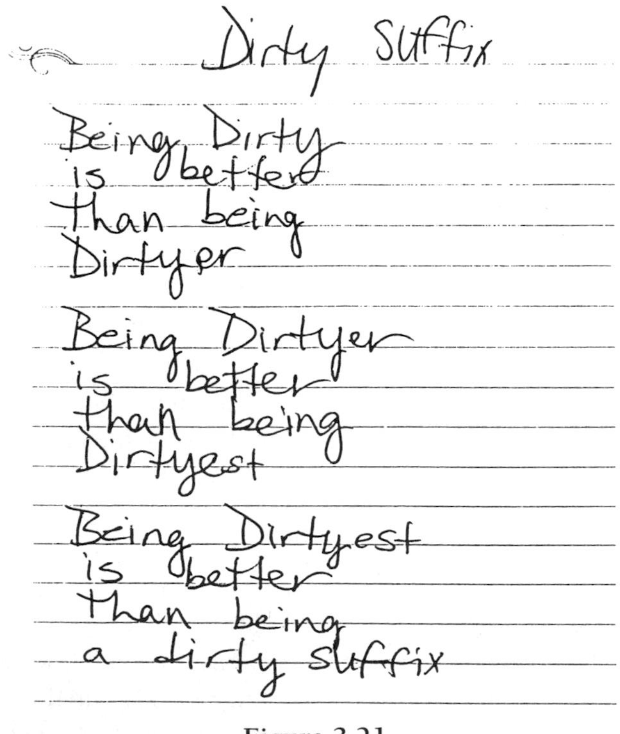

Dirty Suffix

Being Dirty
is better
than being
Dirtyer

Being Dirtyer
is better
than being
Dirtyest

Being Dirtyest
is better
than being
a dirty suffix

Figure 3.21

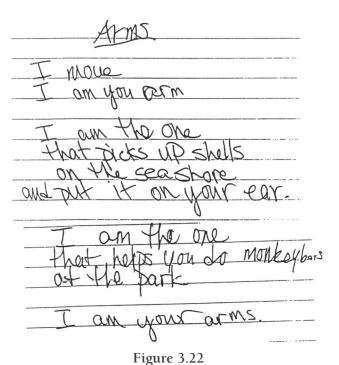

Arms

I move
I am your arm

I am the one
that picks up shells
on the seashore
and put it on your ear.

I am the one
that helps you do monkeybars
at the park

I am your arms.

Figure 3.22

When I was little
I would sit, and
on the big swivel chair
at my dads
desk. I would turn around
and around. I would
push away from the
desk and suddenly I
would have no
way to spin around.
I would get up and
pull the chair by
its back to the desk.
I would pick up
the phone and pretend
I was some important
person, like Martha Clark.
I would take out a
piece of notepaper
and doodle on it and
pretend to write

script. I would take more
papers and try to hold
the phone between my
ear and my shoulder.
I would hang up the
phone, open one of
desks and pretend to
look for some papers.
I would close the
drawers and look for
some more in another
door. Then my days
as legal woman would
end. I became
a preschooler again.

Figure 3.23

I remember visiting my grandpa when I was 4 or 5. I remember sitting on his lap while he was holding out a tray of wafer cookies. I would eat the chocolate, and he would eat the vanilla. He would read me my favorite book. I remember sitting on a leather lounge chair on the patio. I remember leaving. I remember walking down steps and saying good bye.

I don't remember whether I liked him, though. I can't even remember his hair color. I wonder why he never visited me?

Every summer my Aunt Mildred comes to visit. She's like a grandma to me. Each summer she takes me shopping and spoils me like a grandma would. When I was little we would watch

the Price is Right. She would yell, "lower, lower", at the T.V. Then, we would go to the pool and I would play with my friends and she would play cards with their moms. Today we still go to the pool except I can't stand the Price is Right.

Cara Freed

Figure 3.24

automatically and their pages are filled with rich entries, we know it's time for publishing to begin.

We frequently ask experienced students to explain writer's notebooks to new students in the grade. Fourth graders are often asked to serve as guest speakers introducing the writer's notebook to third-grade classes. On occasion, representatives from a third-grade class visit a fourth-grade writing workshop and report back to their classmates on the use of writer's notebooks.

When the fourth-grade class seems ready, we add more formal genre studies. These are usually more frequent than in the third grade, but don't begin until the teachers know their students well, the class routines are clearly in place, and most important, the children are writing significant entries and are as comfortable sharing them as they are showing off their stickers, baseball cards, and key chain collections.

We have no required genres at designated grade levels, although standardized assessments at the fourth-grade level do influence teachers' choice of genre. In other words, in New York City, fourth graders are assessed on their abilities to compose responses to literature, narrative accounts, informative reports, and sets of procedures. These genres are therefore woven into the fourth-grade year. Teachers might also carve out units of study on such short genres as poetry or picture books, or allow students to study the works of favorite authors representing a wide range of accessible and appropriate genres.

Grade Five (Our Ten-Year-Olds)

In grade five, the sky is the limit. Students have been keeping writer's notebooks for over two years and are ready to use them in some of the ways their teachers might use theirs. We usually see students using their notebooks to make longer commitments to fewer topics and favorite genres. Students at this age, our ten-year-old seniors, also become known as specialists. Clara is the class poet; Adar, the class commentator on world events; Julianna, the social activist writer. Each has learned to use their writer's notebook in the ways that work best for them.

Some students in the fifth grade seem ready to use their notebook in especially sophisticated ways. They reread their notebooks noticing important issues, gaining new insights, lingering to gather more information, and inventing bigger writing challenges.

These older students began pushing their thinking by using some of the following strategies:

- asking themselves questions about entries that stood out
- making connections between entries
- talking to family members to gain additional insights and perspectives
- doing outside research on related entry topics
- connecting ideas in their notebook pages with their reading of newspapers, novels, and poetry
- sharing selected entries with classmates and letting the follow-up conversations inspire additional writing
- revising significant entries based on techniques learned from studying a literature excerpt or gleaned from in-depth study of one author

Eventually these richer entries are crafted into a wide range of genres, including family vignettes, letters to friends, picture books, photographic essays, articles for school publications, and so on. Once again, students, with help from their teachers, select the genres that best support their content. When things are going well, you can find a multitude of genres in any fifth-grade writing workshop.

Alexandra crafted the family vignette in Figure 3.25 after conferring with Judy Davis, her fifth-grade teacher. Abby, one of Judy's sixth-grade students, combined several notebook entries and revised several drafts to create the surprising tribute to her city and her father that appears in Figure 3.26.

Similar to their third- and fourth-grade colleagues, fifth-grade teachers don't rush whole-class formal studies of genre. They know how crucial it is as children move from third to fourth to fifth grade to begin each school year with a renewed commitment to keeping a writers' notebook, especially if interest waned during the summer holidays. Fifth-grade teachers also know how important it is to help students discover more sophisticated uses of their writer's notebooks before asking them to work toward any one by Alex Viola   grade 5

Christmas Tree Shopping / 12/7/98
I walk down the winter-fresh streets
stumbling because of my heavy boots.
Small puffs of frozen breath scurry
out of my mouth as I shiver while
gazing into a "Hot & Crusty" store. Its
drifting fragrance of fresh bagels
float around me. Holding   my mother's
hand tightly, I stare at all the evergreens,
bushy and spikey leaning against store
windows. The smell of pine clings to my
nose as a memory of tightly wrapped
presents fills my mind. The pom-pom
on my colorful hat bobs up and down
as I run towards one tall tree perfectly
bushy standing by itself. I yell out,
"This is the one!" While pushing my
way through the crowd my green eyes
light up, imagining how the tree would
look with red and green lights cascading
down every side. My mother and father
stride over to the salesman and point
to the tree that I was fixed on. After
awhile, the salesman wraps the tree
up in net-like string and walks away
smiling at his bills. My dad and mom
steadily pick up the large tree as I
bounce ahead, full of christmas.

Figure 3.25

particular genre. For example, fifth graders who have used the pages of their writer's
notebook to make their language more precise, try out different perspectives, understand
the shape of pieces of writing, experiment with slowing down and speeding up their
prose, and use telling details to create setting are more likely to take full advantage of and
excel in a course of study on picture book writing. Formal genre studies later in the

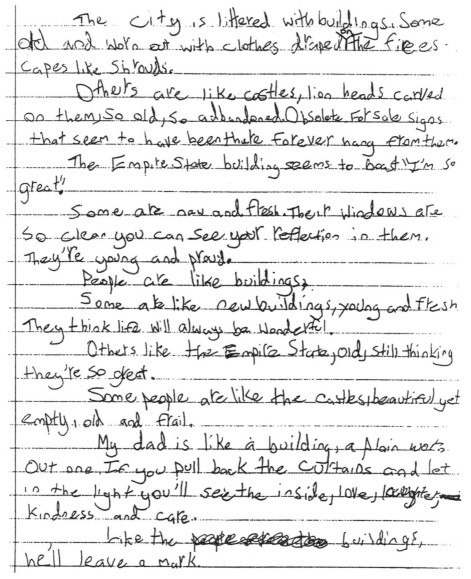

The city is littered with buildings. Some old and worn out with clothes draped on the fires. Capes like shrouds.

Others are like castles, lion heads carved on them. So old, so abandoned. Obsolete For sale signs that seem to have been there forever hang from them.

The Empire State building seems to boast "I'm so great!"

Some are new and fresh. Their windows are so clear you can see your reflection in them. They're young and proud.

People are like buildings.

Some are like new buildings, young and fresh. They think life will always be wonderful.

Others like the Empire State, old, still thinking they're so great.

Some people are like the castles, beautiful yet empty, old and frail.

My dad is like a building, a plain worn out one. If you pull back the curtains and let in the light you'll see the inside, love, laughter, kindness and care.

Like the ~~people and the~~ buildings, he'll leave a mark.

Figure 3.26

school year offer students platforms to show off the fine-tuned techniques they have been experimenting with earlier in the year.

When postponed a few months, these studies can also serve as energy boosters, adding drama and a renewed interest in and enthusiasm for the writing workshop. Teachers add sparkle to the school corridors by displaying students' picture books and mounting their poems, essays, and nonfiction. Postponing formal genre studies also gives teachers and students who are new to the school a chance to ease into the rigors and routines of the writing workshop.

Using Writer's Notebooks with Elementary Students:
A Summary

The simple, realistic goals outlined above are based on the teaching and learning discoveries that we have made over the last eight years. These can be summarized as follows.

- **The use of the writer's notebook is different for young writers and changes as they move through the grades.** It is said that adults write to discover new truths about themselves; when young children write well, when they are encouraged to pay attention, form and voice opinions, and when they know that their thoughts will be heard and respected, they often let us in on truths they have already discovered. The writer's notebook enables wide-awake children to let us know what is really on their minds. In addition, children can learn to use their notebooks in more and more sophisticated ways as they move through the grades.

- **If teachers spend time—abundant time—helping children take in their world, they will need to spend less time helping young children fix up drafts.** As noted in *Lifetime Guarantees*, "When the first is in place, the second becomes much easier." It is therefore not surprising for third-grade teachers to spend a great deal of time at the beginning of the year ensuring that students understand the reasons to keep a writer's notebook and have ample strategies for filling these blank books with rich observations, memories, ideas, reflections, and so on. Fourth- and fifth-grade teachers profit from children's familiarity with this writer's tool, but begin each year making sure that all students understand the purposes and uses of keeping a writer's notebook.

- **Very short, clear genres are magical at the elementary level.** Certain forms of free verse, letters, simple picture books, vignettes, toasts, brochures, interviews, how-to pieces, newsletter articles, songs, posters, personal essays, and photographic essays are some of our most popular formats. This has implications for classroom library collections. We need to model texts in all these various forms. An additional benefit to the privileging of short genres in our classrooms is the potential for publishing to occur more frequently—with more frequent publishing comes more opportunities to teach the mechanics. We do care about punctuation, grammar, spelling, handwriting, and the like (see Chapters 7 and 10). Genre studies are postponed each year until the teacher feels confident that the students are enthusiastic and thriving notebook keepers.

- **Good writing is *not* something you save for revision.** Young writers can do first-draft writing that is powerful and memorable. We no longer have to roam the classroom sucking out details. Students often begin writing with a detail that has caught their eye. When students have rich entries, it is no longer a complicated leap from keeping a writer's notebook to crafting a beautifully revised and edited finished work. When students write from an abundance of high-quality raw material, they more easily revise by making decisions about focus, structure, genre, meaning, and language.

- **To reach our goals we need big blocks of uninterrupted time.** This can't be said often enough. Students do need time for inspiration, information, and conversation, but most of all they need time to write. (See *Lifetime Guarantees* for additional information about such basics as time, structures, routines, and rituals in the writing workshop.)
- **Students' finished work needs to do good work in the world.** Students will not keep writing if their words are merely hung high on a bulletin board or stuffed into a folder or portfolio. Students need real-world response to their words. (See Chapter 10, "Editing, Publishing, and Other Ways to Make Parents Smile.")

Afterword

Although we continue to have confidence in the writer's notebook as an important tool for students and this entire chapter has been devoted to rethinking its effective use with elementary school children, readers should not see the writer's notebook as some new orthodoxy. I am sure there are many fine teachers of writing who have discovered other ways to ensure that their students lead attentive and observant lives. Similarly, there are many writing teachers who have experimented with the writer's notebook and have designed their own ways to modify, adapt, and otherwise make this potentially very useful tool work effectively for the students they know best. Their stories need to be told so that their know-how and expertise can be added to our professional conversations.

RELATED READINGS IN COMPANION VOLUMES

Going Public (Heinemann, 1999) is abbreviated as GP. *Lifetime Guarantees* (Heinemann, 2000) is abbreviated as LG.

Lifelong habits	**LG:** Ch. 1
Adult literacy demonstrations	**GP:** Ch. 2
	LG: Ch. 1
Dialogue journals	**GP:** Ch. 2
	LG: Ch.1, Ch. 10
Capitalizing on firsthand experiences	**GP:** Ch. 6
	LG: Ch. 10
Using poetry to inspire notebook keeping	**GP:** Ch. 5
	LG: Ch. 5
The value of big blocks of time	**GP:** Ch. 1
	LG: Ch. 2
Students' writing doing good work in the world	**GP:** Ch. 4
	LG: Ch. 3, Ch. 10
Tapping into read-alouds that resonate	**GP:** Ch. 2
	LG: Ch. 1

CHAPTER 4

RESPONDING TO STUDENT WRITING

Getting stuck isn't having nothing to write about, getting stuck is not knowing how to write about that thing.

—Carey, age 8

I think that to be a writer you have to have that power, that spirit, the medal that you hold inside to fight for that freedom to write. And to ride out of those city walls to escape the writer's block soldiers. And to ride out to a very, very far away land and right there find that magical place inside your heart.

—Aaron, age 8

Key Writing Lessons

1. Conferring is a crucial component of the writing workshop and the element that is the most dramatically different from traditional ways of teaching writing at the elementary level.
2. Classroom teachers have many questions about the content as well as the process of conferring individually with students.
3. Conferring becomes easier when workshop "basics" are in place.
   - When teachers have clear and consistent routines, conferences become a regular part of the classroom environment and children know what is expected of them.
   - When classrooms have accessible and abundant materials and supplies, students are less likely to interrupt conferences.
   - When schools have supportive school-wide structures and beliefs, conferring becomes easier because all members of the community value such essentials as talk, options, assessment-driven instruction, and realistic goals.
   - When teachers are well-informed about writing, conferences become easier and more effective because teachers can offer valuable information to students.
   - When a climate of trust exists, teachers and students can tend to the work at hand.
4. It is helpful to have a framework in mind when conferring with students.
5. There are practical ways that educators get answers to the inquiries above.
6. Educators can become better at conferring by processing other people's conferences and by studying their own.

As hard as I try, I simply cannot recall ever having a one-on-one meeting with a teacher in elementary, middle, or high school, to talk about my own writing. That kind of school activity was nonexistent in the 1950s and 1960s when I attended New York City public schools. My own children, who attended New York City public schools in the late 1970s and 1980s, probably had just a few sporadic opportunities to meet individually with a teacher to talk about their writing. Things are certainly different today in classrooms around the city and around the country.

Having a conference with the teacher is common practice in writing as well as reading workshops. Conferences, in fact, constitute an essential component of the literacy workshop and this non-negotiable structure necessarily has strong implications for many aspects of classroom life.

Although the content of whole-group gatherings during minilessons and share meetings may be markedly different from traditional ways of talking to children about writing, those gatherings somehow seem manageable, even to a teacher who has been reluctant to engage in a workshop approach to teaching. After all, the children are all doing the same thing at the same time, except instead of being seated at their desks, they are usually gathered in a meeting area. Whole-group gatherings may seem doable, but the one-on-one conference often startles the first-time observer.

I cannot remember the first time I witnessed a teacher attempt to confer with one child while thirty other students carried on their regular classroom lives, but I have seen the look on the faces of novice student teachers, new parents to our school, and visiting educators from other countries. This classroom structure does stand out and first-timers are filled with curiosity and questions. For example, they want to know:

- What are the other children doing while the teacher is busy with one student?
- How do you keep the volume so low?
- How can the children work without interrupting the teacher?
- How does the teacher decide which child needs a conference?
- How long does the teacher stay with any one child?
- How many children does the teacher get to on any one day?
- What are they talking about, anyway?
- How does the teacher know what to say?

Thankfully, there are many resources I can suggest to these newcomers in order to begin to answer their questions. I can show them the bookshelves in my office, filled with practical professional reading (see bibliography in Appendix 1). I can arrange for them to spend big blocks of time in classrooms in order to learn the answers to many of these questions. In addition, I can and often do offer a few of my own general comments. I suggest that worthwhile conferring can occur when several basic conditions are in place.

The Basics

In *Lifetime Guarantees*, I describe the basics that enable our teachers to spend their time helping children become better writers. In this section, I repeat those basics in order to describe what role they have in enabling teachers to confer one-on-one with children while the rest of the class carries on in a peaceful and scholarly fashion. Since honest and purposeful conferring is one of the major ways teachers help students lift the quality of their work, it is essential that teachers are able to respond to students thoughtfully in the conference setting.

Clear and Consistent Routines

When teachers have clear and consistent routines in their writing workshops, children know what is expected of them. They don't have to interrupt conferences in order to ask what to do next, where to put their work, or how to edit. These procedures have been taught clearly and consistently. Children also understand that when a teacher is conferring with another student, they have very clear options. They can write, and keep on writing. (See the passage that follows on the well-informed teacher, who knows how to keep children engaged in writing.) They can quietly and respectfully ask a classmate for help. They can read to solve their writing problems. They can listen in on the teacher's conference with another student (unless for some very special reason it is deemed a private one). They also know that there are consequences for being disrespectful during a writing workshop (or for that matter during any time in the school day). Each teacher has his or her own way of handling children who act inappropriately, but none let the issue slide.

Accessible and Abundant Materials and Supplies

When teachers have accessible and abundant materials and supplies in their classrooms, students need not interrupt a conference every time they need a sheet of paper or a staple gun. When abundant supplies include a plentiful and powerful library of well-written text, teachers can enrich their conferences by easily referring to books read. (See conference transcripts, beginning on page 92 as well as Chapter 5, "Reading to Inform Your Writing.")

Supportive School-Wide Structures and Beliefs

When teachers work in schools that have supportive school-wide structures and beliefs, they are more likely to have effective conferences for the following reasons:

• Supportive schools work hard to eliminate interruptions and keep special programs to a minimum. It is very hard to really listen to children when your classroom door keeps opening and closing and children keep walking in and out for seemingly endless reasons.

- Supportive schools have realistic curriculum demands. In other words, teachers can set aside the time it takes to create the kind of writing workshops that allow for regular and meaningful conferences.
- Supportive schools value talk. It is much easier to engage students in meaningful writing conferences when children feel comfortable talking to adults. Children who are used to being silenced and constantly reprimanded are unlikely to talk comfortably about the birth of their new sister, the death of their grandfather, or their hopes of becoming a basketball star.
- Supportive schools value interactive classrooms. In other words, no administrator, parent, or colleague would wonder why a teacher is talking to one child while the rest of the class is engaged in various independent activities. The school does not think of children as empty containers waiting to be filled by a teacher who has all the answers.
- Supportive schools appreciate the process nature of learning. Students understand rough drafts and revisions in their work in dance, art, sports, science mathematics, and reading, as well as writing. Our students are as open to suggestions from their classroom teachers for making their writing better as they are to suggestions from our physical education instructor for improving their dribbling. They have learned not to expect to get everything right the first time out.
- Supportive schools privilege options. In other words, our teachers and their students have learned that there are many ways to solve any one problem. Conferences are less stressful when students are open to thinking through their writing struggles as well as possible ways to improve their work in progress.
- Supportive schools understand the importance of assessment-driven instruction. Although workshops differ in many ways, all teachers believe in the importance of listening individually to students. We listen when students read aloud books, poems, and articles, and when they talk about their reading. Similarly, we listen when students read aloud their own writing and talk about it. How else would we discover what students need and want to learn? One-on-one conferring provides teachers with a rich opportunity to take notes on individual students' needs. Our students, throughout the grades, are so used to conferences, they would probably think something was missing if teachers didn't stop to chat with them about their work.

Well-Informed Teachers

When teachers are well-informed, with rich background knowledge and a deep understanding of the writing process approach, they are prepared to teach students how to work independently. They share essential and effective strategies that enable students to write for sustained periods of time. They are also able to inspire children to *want* to spend time writing, because they have helped students to understand what writing is for. It comes as no surprise that our students take full advantage of the time set aside for writing. When students are eager to send finished work into the world, they do not waste precious writing time. (See related information in *Lifetime Guarantees*, Chapter 3, "Discovering Real-World Reasons to Write," and Chapter 10 of this book, "Editing, Publishing, and Other Ways to Make Parents Smile.")

When teachers are well prepared to teach writing, it shows in their conferring. When students receive helpful and practical advice from teachers during writing conferences, they come to understand just how important these one-on-one moments are. Because of this, they are more likely to honor their teachers' requests to never interrupt a writing conference and to use soft voices during workshop time.

A Climate of Honesty, Trust, and Respect

Those new student teachers, prospective parents, and visiting educators often ask me about discipline problems. "Don't you have any?" they ask. The children seem so well behaved during their writing workshops, and in fact they are. Of course, we have students who act out, particularly in the lunchroom or playground, when fooling around can get out of hand, but our children rarely act out in the classroom. They are not fooling around in the coat closet, whining for drinks of water, or needling their classmates during writing time. They're engaged in their work and they have a lot of work to do. There is no time for fooling around. In addition to rigorous work schedules and experienced teachers who know how to engage children as well as manage classrooms effectively and fairly, a climate of trust permeates these rooms and keeps disciplinary action down to a bare minimum.

If teachers are to really listen to one student while all the others are working in the classroom, this climate of trust must exist. The teacher must trust that the conversations students are having around the room during workshop time are important and respectful ones. The teacher must trust that the suggestions agreed upon in her last conference with a student will be acted upon when the student walks away. The teacher must trust that students will take care of all materials and supplies in appropriate ways. Likewise, students must trust that teachers will respond honestly and compassionately to their writing. Students must trust that teachers will not share their writing publicly without their permission. Students must trust that they will have ample time and help to make their writing the best it can be. Students must trust that teachers will appreciate the hard work of *all* student writers, not privilege the work of a few.

In *Going Public* I write about how crucial a classroom climate of honesty, trust, and respect is to the success of a writing workshop. Those words bear repeating here. I note, "It doesn't matter how brilliant our minilessons are or how clever our conferences are if children make fun of each other's handwriting, dialect, or choice of topic. These things don't matter at all if the really important stuff isn't in place. Children will not share significant stories, take risks as spellers, or accept new challenges if the classroom is not secure or supportive. The tone of the classroom can make or break your writing workshop" (p. 104).

Conference Guidelines

Several of the questions listed on page 83 have not as yet been answered. In particular, I have not addressed the issues of which students the teacher talks to, for how long, and how frequently, as well as the million-dollar question, "What are they talking about, anyway?"

There are of course no carved-in-granite answers to these questions. If a teacher showed me an exact plan for her conferences a week in advance (the way I used to prepare my weekly lessons when I started teaching thirty years ago), I would be concerned about the authenticity of her writing workshop. Yes, a teacher can have a list of children whom she needs to meet with as well as a clear sense of those children's needs as writers (in fact, she should), but the good news and the bad news about the writing workshop brings to mind Don Murray's wonderfully titled book *Expect the Unexpected*. I have found that the teachers I know best, all experienced and successful teachers of writing, don't have any scripts, timetables, or flowcharts for their writing conferences. How could they? They have come to expect the unexpected. And it's often the unexpected that makes the writing workshop the most surprising and thrilling part of a teacher's day.

It's no wonder our teachers have such a difficult time leaving precise conference notes for substitute teachers. How do you leave plans for talking to Alex about taking risks in his spelling? Or Alicia, who has been writing about not making friends easily? Or Rachel, who is attempting to write fantasy and needs to find professional writers she can learn from? How do you tell a substitute teacher how to respond when a student wants to leave class in order to talk to the science teacher because she needs details about guinea pigs to weave into her story? Or another misplaces her notebook and can't hold back the tears? Or another wants information about line breaks for her poem, while another is asking for help with placing red herrings in the mystery she is writing, and yet another wants to know if *The New York Times* will publish letters to the editor written by nine-year-olds?

No, a teacher cannot anticipate all that will occur in any one writing workshop. She can't leave an exact lesson plan for her substitute teacher, nor could she precisely program her own day's conferring. Yes, there will be children she will definitely want to talk to, but there will also be unexpected children who ask for help. But can any teacher of writing say how many minutes she will allot to each student? Or how often she will need to check back with that same child? Or exactly what she will say as she confers with each one? I highly doubt it.

During my eight years as principal, I have conferred with hundreds of children about their writing as I stopped in to visit their classrooms, conduct demonstration lessons, or cover classes for absent or busy teachers. I'm convinced more than ever that responding to student writing is an art, not a science. Even though I know our students fairly well and I'm aware of the courses of study taking place, I tread lightly, knowing there may be information about that young writer and the context of his current work that I am unaware of. Clark Kent being Superman is obvious; knowing exactly what to say in a writing conference is not.

I have found it incredibly helpful, therefore, to carry a simple framework in my head whenever I approach young writers. I have a few conference guidelines in mind, no matter the age of the student. The first two have everything to do with who this student is as a writer; the second two have to do with the piece of writing at hand.

First, I want to find out how the students feel about being asked to write.

Second, I want to know if students take risks as writers.

Third, I want to find out if students understand what writing is for.

Fourth and finally (and something I think about only when the first three conditions are in place), I want to find out if students have strategies for improving the work at hand.

An explanation of each guideline follows.

Finding Out How Students Feel About Being Asked to Write

I want to know if students feel confident and positive about being asked to write. If they are reluctant to write, I want to know why. If they use the pages from their writer's notebook to do math homework or make paper airplanes, I want to know why. If their writer's notebooks are ragged, empty, or constantly misplaced, I want to know why. If writing is the only school subject they *aren't* interested in, I want to know why. That's always where my conference with a new student begins. I can get at the above kinds of information by asking questions such as the following:

- Why do you think your teacher has asked you to keep a writer's notebook?
- Do you find it easier to write in your notebook at home or at school? Why?
- What is the best thing about keeping a writer's notebook? What is the most difficult thing about keeping a writer's notebook?
- Do you ever have trouble writing? If so, what do you do to get going?
- Do you think you will write over the summer vacation? When you graduate? When you are an adult?
- How would you feel about school if writing were not on the daily agenda?

Finding Out If Students Take Risks as Writers

Of course, there are all kinds of ways to take risks. We frequently need to encourage very young children to take risks as spellers. Older students might take risks with respect to choice of topics, experimentation with new genres, and sharing their work with wider audiences. I can figure out if children are taking risks by asking questions such as the following:

- Have you done something in this piece of writing that you have never done before?
- If I looked through your writing folder would I find fairly similar writing (in topic, genre, writing techniques)?
- Have you been thinking about trying something new or different in your writing? Are you ready to go ahead?
- Have you ever heard or read some other topic or technique in another student's writing or in something written professionally that you think would be too difficult to try?
- If a teacher says that a student "plays it safe" in writing, what do you think the teacher means?
- Have you ever chosen a word because it was easier to spell than another one?
- How does it take courage to be a writer?
- Where do you think it is easier to take risks—in the playground, in the cafeteria, in the writing workshop? Can you explain your thinking?

In addition, I can find out if students take risks by skimming through their portfolios or notebooks with the writers at my side. For example, if I discover that a writer does only one kind of writing, I'd want to know if the student is afraid to try something new or lacks the background to try a new genre. We want our students to attempt many forms of poetry, fiction, and nonfiction. There needs to be lots of ways to shine as a writer in any school year, in any writing workshop. The student who struggles with nonfiction may be a fine poet. The student who can't write subjectively may be a fine journalist. (Of course, students may be sticking to one kind of writing because they have found an area of expertise or an area of interest. They should then be expected to take risks within that category.)

Within each of these broad genre areas, as noted earlier, we put our trust in brevity. Short people, short genres. We privilege short forms of poetry, nonfiction, and fiction.

We've also discovered the need to clarify our thinking about risk taking. Taking risks as writers does not mean that students have to write about risky things. There is life beyond the personal narrative. Of course, our students still do narrative writing, but when they write about personal things, we don't cross the line. In the eight years our school has been in existence, we have never had to hide a piece of writing on open-school night. We don't ever play therapist. We never ask children (who have after all been on this planet less than ten years) to spill their guts onto the writing tablet or share their innermost thoughts, fears, or nightmares. That's not to say that in our safe, supportive classrooms, children never bring up heartfelt issues and traumatic moments. Of course they do, and teachers handle these issues professionally, privately, and confidentially, and sometimes by seeking parental or professional intervention.

There are many topics that will move an audience. As noted in an earlier chapter, we delight in pieces that sound like real children wrote them. We're not interested in pushing children to write in such sophisticated or precocious ways that readers can't believe that children did the writing. Yes, we want our children to write in powerful ways, but at the elementary level that does not require complicated genres, layered meanings, symbolism, or heart-wrenching topics. Childhood is short enough.

Enjoy seven-year-old Haden's narrative "The Dress Up Disaster," in Figure 4.1. We consider it a powerful piece of personal narrative writing.

Finding Out If Students Understand What Writing Is For

I worry when students have never put their writing to real-world uses. (See more on this in *Lifetime Guarantees*, Chapter 3, "Discovering Real-World Reasons to Write.") I often ask students the following types of questions, all variations on the same theme:

- Who might you give this to?
- Where might you send this?
- Who would benefit from reading this?
- How can you go public with this?
- How can this piece improve the quality of our lives at school or your life at home?
- Where in the real world does this piece of writing belong?

Finding Out If Students Know How to Improve Their Writing

My fourth and final guideline, and the one I think about only when the first three conditions are in place, involves finding out if students have strategies for improving the work at hand. In other words, if students don't feel good about being asked to write, if they don't take risks or put their writing to real-world uses, it's highly unlikely that I'll fret about whether they know how to lift the quality of their work. When the first three conditions are in place, I feel fine talking to young children about issues of crafting, revising, and editing their work.

It is at this point that I can remind the student that the point is to write well, to try and move an audience, to pitch as if it were the last out in the bottom of the ninth. Any of the following questions might direct my conference:

- What questions might your classmates have if they hear this piece?
- What do you want your readers to think about (feel, realize) when they hear your writing?
- What kind of additional material might you need to do the best job possible?
- How can you describe the shape of your writing (the architecture of the piece)? Does it feel well-balanced and complete?
- Have you been fussy enough about your choice of language?

The Dress Up Disaster
by Haden Minifie

My sister and I were playing
dress up. Colby wore a pink tutu
with buttons shaped like hearts
and a beautiful cape with lots of
different designs and beautiful colors
like red, green, pink, purple, and blue.
They were the kind of designs that
were very much like the windows
in a church. The cape was tied
around her neck. I was wearing a
long veil that was like a skirt. The
shirt I wore showed my belly
button when I picked my arms up.
Colby and I got the clothes from
the cabinet next to my bed. I
pretended to go to work so I
grabbed a purse, slipped it over
my head and onto my shoulders,
and slowly walked out the door.
As I was fixing my hair, Colby
shut the door with a BANG!
and my hand got stuck in it.

I screamed and burst into tears.
Finally, Colby pulled opened the
door. She ran to get Daddy
while the tears came out of my
eyes like shooting stars. When
I saw Daddy, I felt safer and
knew that my hand would get
better soon.

THE END

Figure 4.1

- What lessons are you learning from the literature you are reading? Are there specific techniques that your favorite writers use that you might consider trying in this piece? (See Chapter 5, "Reading to Inform your Writing").
- How can I help you to make this the best piece ever?

Most of these questions serve to turn passive writers into active ones, much the way strategy talk in the reading workshop is intended to turn passive readers into active ones. Many of these teaching/learning interactions will be illustrated in the transcripts of the writing conferences that follow.

(It should be noted that the guidelines listed on page 88 not only inform the conferences I have with children, they also serve as guidelines when I launch writing classes, design minilessons, carve out courses of study, and so on. See Appendix 4, "Worksheet on Implications for Broad Goals.)

Writing Conference Transcripts

Several years ago our superintendent asked me to speak at a principal's meeting about improving the quality of student writing. I asked if I could demonstrate the work we do in our school rather than talk about it. I asked Joanne Hindley Salch and Judy Davis to attend the principal's meeting along with a few students who we thought wouldn't be afraid to share their writing and confer in front of a roomful of principals. The following are transcripts of some of the conferences that took place that day.

(It's important to keep in mind that these were public demonstrations aimed at highlighting conference essentials. As the writing teacher, I probably spoke more than usual in order to teach the educators in the audience in addition to the young writers at my side. I also needed to be a bit more talkative so that the children didn't freeze up in front of the onlookers. It's also important to point out that regular classroom conferences would no doubt have referred more frequently to materials, events, and people in the classrooms and in the school. Despite their limitations, these transcripts do highlight several conference essentials.)

Conference with James

James was a sixth grader in Judy Davis' class. I knew James well and was confident that he thought of himself as an accomplished writer, that he took risks as a writer, and that he understood ways to put his writing to real uses for real audiences. Although I needed to begin by reminding him of his intended audience, the focus of the following conference was primarily on lifting the quality of his work. I visited his writing workshop on the day prior to this very public conference. James was taking part in a classwide challenge. Judy had invited the students to create original picture books to be read by young children in our school. The students had been reading many picture books intended for young audiences and discussing their features. James looked through his writer's note-

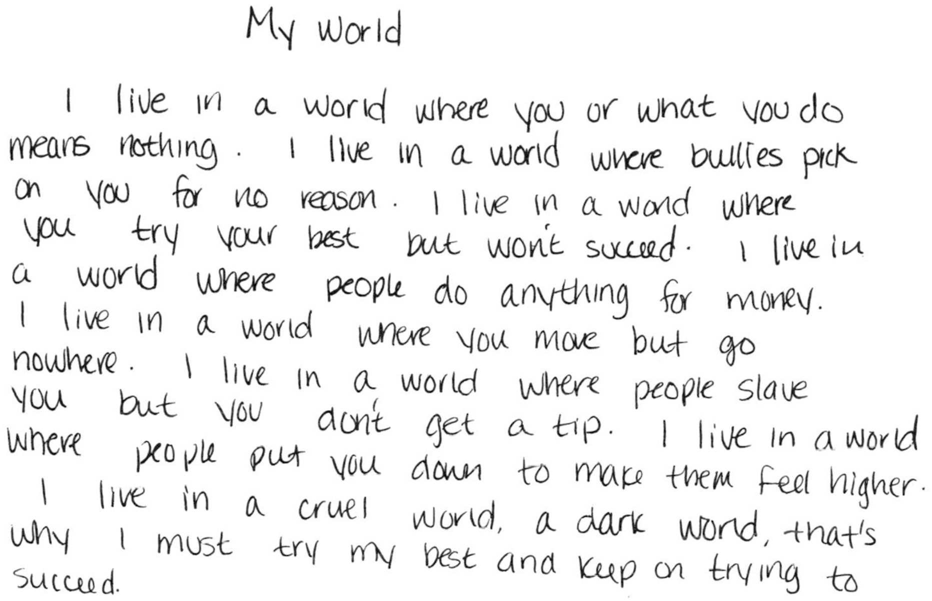

My World

I live in a world where you or what you do means nothing. I live in a world where bullies pick on you for no reason. I live in a world where you try your best but won't succeed. I live in a world where people do anything for money. I live in a world where you move but go nowhere. I live in a world where people slave you but you don't get a tip. I live in a world where people put you down to make them feel higher. I live in a cruel world, a dark world, that's why I must try my best and keep on trying to succeed.

Figure 4.2

book for entries that had potential to become picture books. Unfortunately, James forgot who the audience would be for this project and chose an entry about how life can be cruel and dark, filled with bullies and greedy people, shown in Figure 4.2.

I reminded James about the purpose of this project, asking him to reevaluate his decision to turn such a heavy piece into a picture book for young children. He needed to ask himself, "Is this an appropriate topic for young children? Is this an appropriate topic for the picture book genre?" James rethought his decision and chose another idea for his picture book project. He began thinking of the possibilities attached to a short entry dealing with the boredom and seeming endlessness of waiting in a doctor's waiting room. Because he didn't think he had enough ideas to warrant turning the pages in to a picture book, I suggested he interview other children in the school. I arranged for James to speak to some third graders who had strong opinions attached to waiting room experiences. This public conference began with my invitation to James to read aloud his new draft titled "Waiting for the Doctor."

Shelley: James, why don't you read your new draft aloud and I'll try to help you make this the best picture book possible?

[James reads the draft in Figure 4.3. The audience of principals applauds and laughs when he finishes.]

Shelley: James, you can tell from everyone's reaction that you have written a wonderful piece. The thing that strikes me most of all is that it has a gorgeous shape. It feels whole. I can imagine the pages turning. And that ending is just too good to be true. It's perfect. Did you have the ending in mind when you started writing?

Waiting for the Doctor

As me and my dad enter the clinic I tell him
"I hope this doesn't take long." "In and out" he says.
We go to the front desk and sign in then we sit
down and wait. People go in and out while me and
my dad wait and wait and wait. Kids cry out
to their parents while me and my dad wait
and wait. Doctors call to their paitions but not me.
Still me and my dad wait and wait and wait.
I go to read a magazine and then I finish.
I still wait and wait and wait.
People watch tv shows while I wait and wait
and wait. Kids wander around while we wait
and wait and wait. Parents dig in their pockets
trying to find a quater for the pay phone. While
they hund we wait and wait and wait. I beg
my dad for some money for the Snack Bar he
said 'no' so I just sit their and wait and wait
and wait. The doctor finally calls me into the room.
the phone rings he answers and leaves leaving me
and my dad to wait and wait and wait.
then he enters he's holding three needles
in his hand and tells me to roll up my sleeve.
then he puts the needle halfway to my arm
I tell the doctor can't this wait."

Figure 4.3

James: I did. You see, I'm like a joker and I wanted to end it funny so little kids wouldn't be nervous when they went to the doctor.

Shelley: So you had your audience in mind. Good for you. I do have a suggestion for making this a really memorable book. Why don't you take a blank book like this and figure out where the pages will turn. Parcel the words out. Section them off. Your image is to have a page for each of the little scenes, isn't it?

James: Yes, I think so.

Shelley: Well, your job is to make sure that every page is as good as the page before. When I read your draft to myself I read it faster than you read it aloud. You read it slower, because I think the reader needs to feel the slowness of waiting. You also read it slower, I think, because the reader needs time between that wonderful refrain of "wait and wait and wait." Sometimes those words come up too quickly, one after the other. Some parts of your writing are stronger than others because you give us just a little bit more of the scene. You added just a fraction more to some of the ways you passed the time. In fact, the moments that have *you* in them, like the part where you are asking your dad for money for snacks, or you're sleeping in the uncomfortable chair, those parts are more effective than some of the others. Don't be in such a rush, James. Make each page the best you can by adding the details that will really help the reader understand the agony of waiting. Does that sound like a good plan?

The conference ended here with James accepting the challenge. Joanne was then asked to evaluate the conference for the principals in attendance. She commented on the following things:

- It was important for James to have a sense of audience and knowledge of genres. How else could he have decided if his first choice of topic was inappropriate for a younger child's picture book?
- James' writing community gave him a world of writer's tools and strategies. He kept a writer's notebook, he freewrote about waiting rooms, he had access to blank draft books to support the shaping of his words, and he interviewed other members of the community when he needed more information.

I can't stress enough that in conferences, children should be encouraged to take full advantage of the school community. Children should be sent off to talk to other writing experts—other children who have crafted successful picture books, for example, or other topic experts, in this case children who have thoughts about waiting rooms. In addition, people who confer in a school setting, whenever possible and appropriate should refer to school publishing outlets and/or ways that students' writing can enrich or improve the life of the school. (See more on this in *Lifetime Guarantees*, Chapter 3, "Discovering Real-World Reasons to Write" and Chapter 10 of this book, "Editing, Publishing, and Other Ways to Make Parents Smile.")

Joanne continued her processing by commenting on the strengths of my conferring. She highlighted the following:

- It is important to ask honest questions, not ones you know the answers to.
- It is important to use the writer's strengths to help him mentor himself.
- It is important to have a good working relationship between the writer and the conference partner.

James wasn't writing to please me as a teacher but as a genuine reader of his writing. In my work with James, I relied primarily on helping him gather more raw material and see the structure of his piece more clearly.

Waiting for the Doctor

1. As me and my dad enter the clinic, I tell him "I hope this doesn't take long." In and out," he says "In and out."

2. We go to the front desk and sign in. We sit down and wait.

3. I hear kids cry out to their parents, trying to escape the pain. While they cry, my dad and I wait and wait and wait.

4. People walk in and out of the clinic impatiently. They seem to be nervous. While they pace back and foorth, my dad and I wait and wait and wait

5. I watch parents check for wet diapers while the kids look at sesame street on the chic's tv. while the toddlers watch tv and parents check for wet diapers, my dad and I: wait and wait and wait.

6. I flip through a sports magazine. Michael Jordan is on the cover. He's going to take the Championship, After I finish reading the article, my dad and I wait.

Figure 4.4

When he returned to his classroom writing workshop, James began his revision by placing slash marks at those places in his draft where he wanted to begin in a new page. He transferred each piece to the pages of a blank draft book and with the continued support of his teacher Judy Davis, he eventually completed the work shown in Figure 4.4.

James' words are now worthy of publishing in picture book format. This is a memorable text, as effective as some of the published books that come across our desks. (Of course, we must help him to understand the grammatically correct way to refer to himself and his father!)

7. A lady hunts in her purse for some change for the payphone but she only has singles. While she keeps hunting, my dad and I wait and wait and wait

8. The doctor calls his patients. He calls the blonde toddler, the kid with the sore throat and the baby with the fever. But not me. So I go to the doctor and say "When is it my turn?" "Soon," he says. So, I sit down and my dad and I wait and wait and wait.

9. I get hungry so I beg my dad to buy me a Snickers, the caramel covered with peanuts would sure ease the pain of waiting. He says, "NO." Still, me and my dad wait and wait and wait.

10. I sleep uncomfortably, my head nods back and hits the chair. I wake up in pain. I have a stiff neck and my leg has fallen asleep. Still, my dad and I wait and wait and wait.

11. The doctor finally calls me in. I sit on the examining table. The paper russles when I move around. The phone rings. The doctor answers, then leaves. So my dad and I wait and wait and wait.

He enters with three needles in his hand. He tells me to roll up my sleeve. I roll slowly, one cuff at a time. He puts the needle halfway to my arm. I tell the doctor, "Can't this wait!"

Figure 4.4 (*continued*)

Conference with Mehmet

Mehmet is also a sixth-grade student in Judy Davis' class. He speaks Turkish as well as English and has been attending our school for four years. (See more on his early years in *Lifetime Guarantees*, Chapter 10, "On Loving and Learning Language.") I distributed several pieces of Mehmet's writing to the principals gathered prior to this public conference, so they would get a feel for the range and quality of his texts. Figures 4.5 and 4.6 are representative of the pieces included in this packet.

I didn't know Mehmet as a writer as well as I knew James. Therefore, in the conference that follows, I first attempted to figure out if Mehmet realized his potential as a writer. I then acknowledged what an English-language risk taker he had become, and then I probed his understanding of putting writing to real-world uses. Once I was clear on these three issues, I encouraged him to continue a project he had started, one with a clear purpose in mind.

Shelley: Mehmet, I read through many of the notebook entries and published pieces that your teacher pulled together for today's conference and I was really struck by the "Mix Berries" piece. Do you know why?

MiXBerries

As I throw some of the sour balls in my mouth one by one, my teeth start to crush them, and the blueberry flavor spreads around my mouth. Once again my mouth is joyful. I start with the raspberrys then to blackberries, and the blueberries. Once I have all these flavors in my mouth, I notice that there's mixed berries in there. Every berry has it's own flavor. As I bite in-to them, they pop like ballons and my mouth is filled with all the delicious and colorful juices

Figure 4.5

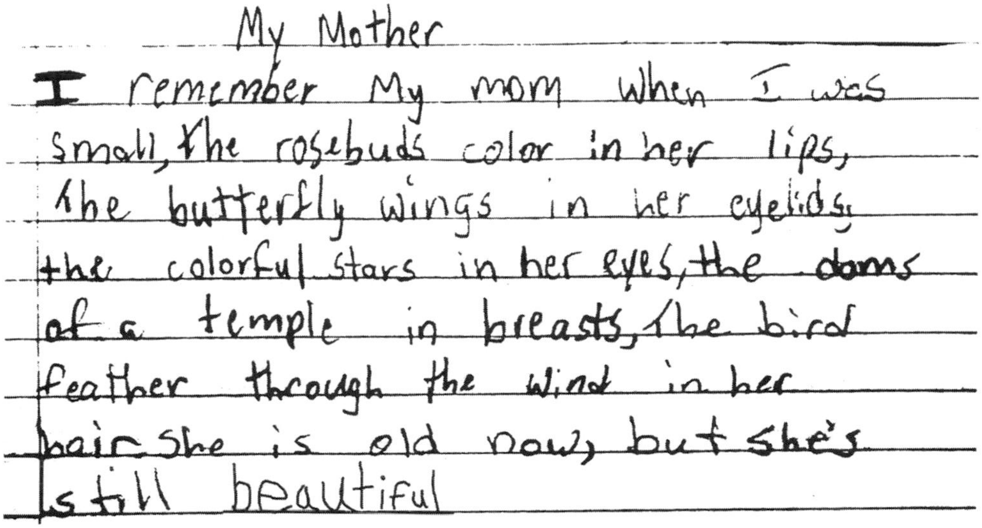

My Mother

I remember My mom when I was
small, the rosebuds color in her lips,
the butterfly wings in her eyelids,
the colorful stars in her eyes, the doms
of a temple in breasts, the bird
feather through the wind in her
hair she is old now, but she's
still beautiful

Figure 4.6

Mehmet: Not really.

Shelley: Well, I'm happy to tell you. I think it's the most surprising thing in the world to even think of writing a piece about the feel of mixing candy flavors in your mouth. I don't think anyone in the whole wide world has ever thought to write such a piece. Good writers are always trying to surprise their readers—with their ideas or their choice of words or the forms they choose to write in. It really is breathtaking to see such honesty in your writing too. And I'm blown away by how much English you've learned in these few years. I don't think I would have learned as much Turkish if I had moved to your country. Many of the folks who read your work today told me how poetic you are. Do you know what they mean?

Mehmet: No.

Shelley: I think they hear poetry when they read your words. Like that piece about your mother. It's hard for us to imagine how you learned to write with such metaphors. You certainly take a lot of risks when you write. Do you know how I can help you today?

Mehmet: Not really.

Shelley: Well, whenever I see your writing I wonder how to help you publish your work in real ways. I think your words need to do good work in the world. Do you know what I mean?

Mehmet: Not really.

Shelley: Well, yesterday when you showed me your latest work, I started to think about how your words could feed the world. How your words could make a difference to real people in the real world. Could you read this short entry aloud?

Mehmet: Sure. [Mehmet reads the following lines aloud.]

> Life is a game. Play it.
> Life is a song. Sing it.
> Life is a change. Spend it.

Shelley: When I heard that, I imagined it as a big inspirational poster to hang in the school hallway. Just as when I heard the entry about your mother I thought it would have made an incredible Mother's Day card for your mom.

Mehmet: Well, what I did . . . My mom doesn't speak good English so I translated it into Turkish.

Shelley: How perfect. Good for you. It would have been too bad if it hadn't been read by the right person. In the same way, when I look at all your writing, I ask myself, "What might he do with this?" That's why I thought when you are finished with your collection of "Life is . . ." sayings, you might think of presenting them on a large sheet of oak tag and hanging it for all to see, the way other posters inspire us at school. Or if that doesn't sound right, perhaps you can think of another way to go public. Does that make sense?

Mehmet: Sure.

Shelley: Now you need to think about the thoughts you've put down. Are you satisfied with the ones you have or do you want to experiment with a few more?

Mehmet: I think I have some more.

Shelley: Are you ready to share them?

Mehmet: Not yet.

Shelley: Okay then, keep going. And come see me when you'd like to share any others.

When Joanne invited the principals to comment on the conferences with Mehmet and James, it was evident that a clear message had come across to the observers—"Don't be afraid to teach." Lesley Gordon, a colleague, commented, "I realize that celebration alone doesn't do it. Whether the students are proficient or not, they can be encouraged in a way that they don't want to refuse the offer." Anna Switzer, another principal colleague with a critical eye, suggested, "Shelley was like a locomotive. She had something instructional to say, but there was room for the children to say no. It was not a touchy-feely approach. You need a lot of knowledge and I respect that. You can't teach from a foundation of nothing. It's okay to have something floating around your head. There are standards you are reaching for and goals in mind." Anna's insightful comments bring to mind how crucial professional development is in teachers' lives. I only have information to share because I remain a student of literacy learning.

As I look back over the last transcript, it is clear that I wanted to be sure that Mehmet understood what writing is for. When he revealed that he translated his tribute to his mother into Turkish, I knew he understood how to put his writing to real uses. In this conference, I was also thinking about English-language learners. Mehmet's piece about his mother might be viewed as being filled with too many exaggerated comparisons, but we need to appreciate that Mehmet is pushing the frontiers of his thinking. He is taking risks. He is, no doubt, learning from the texts he is reading. Mehmet is also surrounded by many proficient speakers of English and many proficient writers. All the children in that room need to know what it means to move an audience. Mehmet is learning a great deal of English by writing frequently and he will keep on writing if he receives feedback and he feels he is growing as a writer and user of English. As teachers, we need to make sure that he publishes along with his classmates and that we discover many unique opportunities for him to make his words count.

Conference with Aleava

Aleava is a third grader who willingly and enthusiastically writes in her writer's notebook, yet does not publish as frequently as her teacher Joanne Hindley Salch would expect. On the day prior to our demonstration conference, Aleava decided to pull an entry she had written about friends and use it as the basis of some sort of writing project. (Students use the word "project" when they have decided to take entries from their notebook and shape, craft, or revise those ideas into a publishable finished work.) Her entry appears in Figure 4.7.

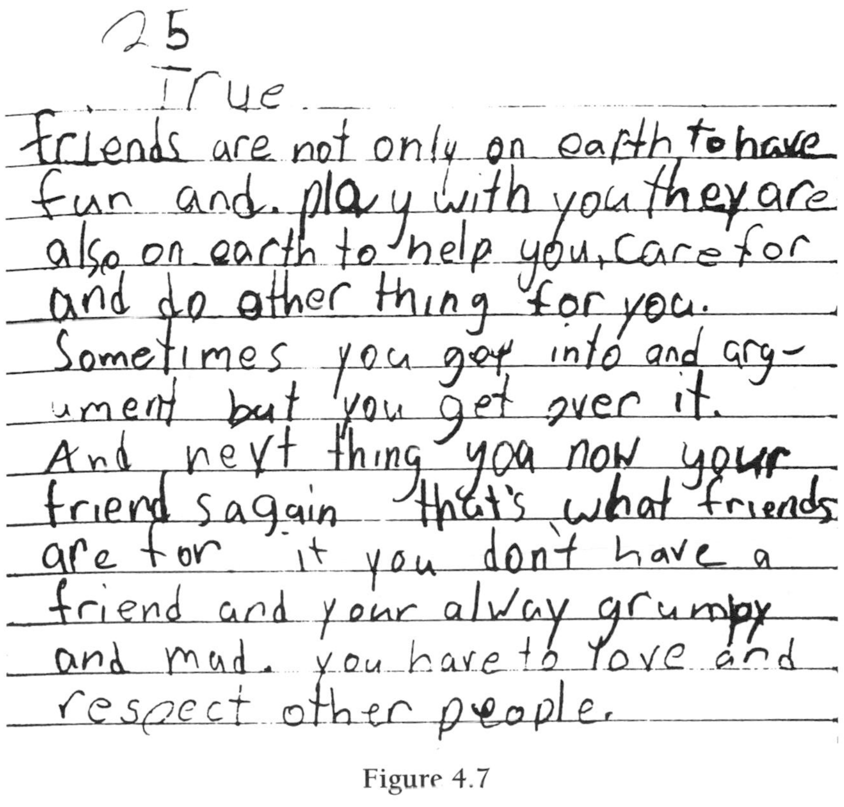

25

True

Friends are not only on earth to have fun and. play with you they are also on earth to help you, care for and do other thing for you. Sometimes you get into and argument but you get over it. And next thing you now your friend s again that's what friends are for it you don't have a friend and your alway grumpy and mad. you have to love and respect other people.

Figure 4.7

In this conference, Aleava reveals that she is about to do something new, to write about something serious instead of her usual light, funny pieces. My intention was to help her do the best job possible.

Shelley: Aleava, you look like you're lost in thought.

Aleava: Well, I want to work on this "Friends" entry and turn it into something.

Shelley: Do you know why you've chosen this one?

Aleava: Well, every day it sits in my notebook and I just keep passing it by.

Shelley: So it just stands out to you? I did read that entry and I also read several of your other entries and a few of your finished works. Do you need any help right now?

Aleava: Yeah. I'm not sure what to do with it.

Shelley: May I tell you something I noticed? This entry sounds very different from the others because in most of the other pages of your notebook I see people on the page. Like the entry about how your daddy taught you not to talk to strangers and the one about loving horses when you were really little. Those pages are filled with real people doing real things. You really captured those experiences. And now you have to learn to do the same, even when your topic is not just one particular thing that happened on one particular day.

Aleava: But friends are people.

Shelley: Of course friends are people, but writing can be so much better when you write about particular people doing real things. You have such big important ideas in the entry about how important friends are and why they are on this planet, but I guess I expected to see some examples. I was waiting for stories of real people.

Aleava: I wanted to write something important. I used to do just funny, now I wanted serious and important.

Shelley: Well, if you want to write something really important and feel proud to put your name on it, you have to ask yourself, "Can I move my audience with my words?" And my suggestion is to add examples so your readers really understand your big ideas. It's hard to imagine what you mean without some real stories. Do you have any?

Aleava: Well, last year there was this girl named Constance. We were friends. Then we had an argument, but we made up. But I forgot what the argument was about or exactly how we fought and made up.

Shelley: Sure, everyone forgets things. Do you know what writers do? They make up the truth. You have that right as the writer. Sometimes I write about my childhood and I can't remember exactly what happened, so I invent what I think probably happened.

Aleava, if you read your entry over I think you'll find places to add the stories or moments you remember, even if you have to add a little fiction to those moments. Have you ever seen a really flat balloon with no air in it? I think there are places in your writing that are like little flat balloons and you need to add life to those place by pumping in some stories. Can you look your writing over and find places where you might add some life?

Aleava: Like here where it says that friends "are also on Earth to help you, care for you, and do other things for you."

Shelley: How might you add some real-life examples of what you mean there?

Aleava: Like, last year when my markers fell, Constance helped me to pick them up.

Shelley: Aleava, so far both your examples are about Constance. Do you think this whole piece is going to turn out to be about Constance or do you think you'll be talking about other people?

Aleava: I think I'll stick to Constance.

Shelley: Well, that's a very different commitment you are making. Good for you for having realized that.

Aleava: I'm not sure I remember so much.

Shelley: Well, some of the stuff you can fudge, and just invent like we said before, but you can also do what James did. Were you listening to what I asked James to do when he ran out of ideas for the waiting room?

Aleava: Uh-huh.

Shelley: Well, you too can talk to other students and see what they remember about Constance. Their stories will probably remind you of true moments you've forgotten. And after you've gathered more, you can decide if any of them will help your readers understand all the big things you have to say about friendship.

When Joanne processed this conference, she noted the following:

- It's very helpful to use child-friendly metaphors. Aleava understood filling up a flat balloon.

- It is valuable to have the student reread in order to identify the places that lacked specificity. That's a strategy she can use with all her pieces, not just this one.

- Again, the student was encouraged to take advantage of the community in which she worked. She could interview others students about Constance, a child who had moved away. She need not think of her writing as an entirely solitary act.

- Other pieces of her writing were used as counterpoint to her current piece. If she could put people on the page in one, she could do it in another.

Conference with Caroline

Caroline is also a third grader in Joanne's class. She is a prolific writer, eager to fill her writer's notebook. She has become particularly interested in making sure her readers can picture what she is writing about. She therefore spends a great deal of time setting scenes with lots of close observations. She is also an avid reader, easily becoming hooked on a series of novels or on the works of favorite authors. Joanne thinks of her as a child in fast-forward, her mind always racing ahead to what she can do next. When I spoke to her the day before our demonstration work, I asked if she were ready for a big writing challenge, one she couldn't speed through. Caroline, a strong, confident writer, is certainly ready to focus on lifting the quality of her work.

Shelley: I've been rereading some of your writing and I've noticed something interesting. I noticed that there is a big difference in your writing when you write short pieces than when you write long pieces. Do you know what I mean?

Caroline: No.

Shelley: Well, I'll tell you. Let's look at "My Day Friday."

[Caroline laughs.]

Shelley: Why are you laughing?

Caroline: It took two weeks to write and it's eighteen pages long.

Shelley: It sounds like you recorded every minute of that day. We even know what your teacher ate for lunch. Do you have any idea why you decided to do this?

Caroline: Not really. I thought it would be a good idea at first but after a while I got bored.

Shelley: Well, Caroline, you are just an incredible observer. You don't miss a thing. You are able to record the tiniest details. And I know that you read really long chapter books. And your writing often sounds like the start of a really long book. It sounds like the start of a really big writing project. But you don't go very far with it. You just write this kind of introductory piece and I find myself wondering, "What is she getting at?" Like the one about the family dinner or spending the day with your mom. Even though this writing is filled with gorgeous images, I'm not sure I know what your meaning is. As a reader I'm not sure I know why you are bothering to set all these scenes. Yet when you write short pieces, I get your meaning rather easily. Can you read some of these aloud?

[Caroline reads the following entry aloud.]

A House

My house is a huge house
made of bricks.
Its windows are big
just like big eyes looking out on a field.
The living room will be made of wood.
The fireplace will be burning hot
while I read my book.
My room will be big and beautiful and
full of toys and everything.
My house—
But when will I ever get one?

Shelley: It's only eleven lines long, Caroline, but we really understand what it's like to be a child who dreams of living in a house. When you finished reading it, there was no question in my mind of why you wrote it. Would you like to read another of these short ones?

[Caroline reads another entry aloud.]

Rain

The sky turns dark.
The clouds move closer.
Drops fall in front of my face.
Soon it is raining.
I look out my window
Happy I'm inside.

Shelley: You're so good at including those zingers at the end that really help us understand your point. So do you understand what I mean when I say your writing is very different when you write short than when you write long?

Caroline: Yes.

Shelley: So what can you do?

Caroline: Write short.

Shelley: Well of course you could choose to keep writing short, but if I were going to really challenge you as a writer, I'd like to see you bring your two strengths together. You are great at crafting these long, flowing images, and you do know how to make your meaning clear. You just have to bring both these gifts to the same piece of writing, to write long with meaning. Earlier you said you got bored with that long piece, "My Day Friday." I think your boredom as a writer shows up in your writing. Listen to the beginning of this piece you wrote: "When I wake up on a Saturday morning my mind asks me, 'What shall I do today?' Soon I'm so curious about that question, so I ask my mom. She says, 'I thought we'd spend the day together, go shopping and stuff like that.'" It's such a lovely beginning and then you go on to explain the day, but then I expect something to happen. But you just give a glimmer of your life and I begin to wonder what you want your readers to really understand about your life or the life of your characters.

I think the time has come for you to write to please your taste as a reader. You need to find a mentor, someone you can learn from, a writer you admire, who writes long but knows how to make her meaning clear. You need to push yourself to find the right topic and attempt to write the kind of longer piece you love to read, but in a way that is powerful. Do you have any writers in mind?

Caroline: Donald Graves or Laura Lee Hope?

[At this point, the sixth-grade teacher interrupted with an offer.]

Judy Davis: Caroline, there are lots of sixth graders in my class who have learned to do what you'll be attempting to do. I think it might be good for you to visit with us during writing workshop time.

Shelley: The message is clear Caroline—we're going to help you find mentors who can show you how to accept this big writing challenge.

In the postconference discussion, Joanne and the principals talked about the need to know a student's history. You can't say something about the student as a writer unless you've read more than the work at hand. How else can you begin an observation with, "Here's what I noticed about you as a writer"? As I look back at the transcript of this conference, I am reminded once again that our job is to teach. Even when children are successful writers, we need to have goals in mind. Helping students connect what they read to what they write is always a secure path.

(See section on conferring with early-childhood students in Chapter 6, "Working with Our Youngest Writers." See Joanne Hindley Salch's Worksheet for Learning from Conferences in Appendix 5.)

Improving Our Skills as Conference Partners

Judy, Joanne, the students, and I received a great round of applause for our willingness to confer and process those conferences so publicly that day. Joanne's comments helped to identify what she considered my strengths as a conference partner. In addition, since the conferences were videotaped that day, I have viewed them on numerous subsequent occasions. Each time I watch them, I tease out additional observations about conferring with children. (Multiple viewings have also made obvious my weaknesses as a conference partner. Above all, I tend to so enthusiastically and quickly suggest a possible format for the student's work that it is hard for the child to disagree. Mea culpa! In general, I need to postpone offering suggestions until I have found out if the student has his or her own intentions.)

I can summarize my learning as follows:

- Children aren't always aware of what they are good at. It helps to begin by highlighting their strengths, telling them what you see in them as writers.
- Children don't need an overdose of directions. Keep suggestions to a minimum and present each clearly and explicitly.
- Children don't always seek clarification. If you're not sure they're with you, don't hesitate to ask, "Do you know what I mean?"
- Children respond to friendly chatter. Don't try to formalize or formulize conference responses.
- Children usually don't need very lengthy conferences. Get them interacting with your suggestions as quickly as possible.
- Children usually agree with their teacher's suggestions. Find out if children have plans of their own before you offer yours, even if yours are sensible ones presented in a tentative voice.

- Children need child-size projects. Make sure genres are appropriate to the age of the child.

- Children see the world differently from adults. Remember to marvel at their ideas, interests, and observations.

- Children learn what is demonstrated. When they confer with their peers, you will have been their role model. Take the responsibility seriously.

Today, whenever I am in a position to demonstrate writing conferences, in addition to explaining what I am hoping to teach I try to share what I have learned from having taught. That's the major way I keep on growing as a writing-conference partner and help others to improve their practice. (Of course, I also grow by watching others confer, reading professional books about conferring, and talking to other writing teachers about conferring.) All the resources I rely upon confirm that no two writing conferences are ever the same. There is no script to follow, no steps to memorize. Even the guidelines I have in mind as I confer remain just a tentative framework, never a definitive procedure. It is therefore essential to always look back and then look ahead. Videotaping your conferences helps, audiotaping and transcribing your conferences helps, taking notes as you confer and collecting samples of the students' writing to accompany them also helps.

I recently spent a few hours with some upper-grade teachers at an elementary school in our district. We gathered in their staff room to talk about the concerns they had for the young writers in their classes. Each teacher presented the story of one child in his or her class, and then I met with that child in a public conference. That evening, I attempted to recall each conference, rereading copies of the students' work and studying my hastily jotted notes. I then wrote a letter to the staff including what I had learned that day about conferring. Part of that letter appears here:

Below please find a few key ideas that rose to the top when I reflected on our two hours together.

- *The more you know about a child, the easier and more effective a conference can be. Thank you for providing those brief histories of your children.*

- *When children don't respond to a question immediately, there is no need to fill the silence. Waiting time is so important.*

- *I can't confer without the right tools handy. I've often thought that I should wear a carpenter's apron, filling my pockets with different kinds of paper, scissors, tape, literature excerpts, and so on.*

- *I am always searching for metaphors and similes that resonate for children in order to make my meaning clear. ("I'm going to read it like a newspaper editor who has to make a column shorter. Can you guess what I omitted?" "These scenes are like flat balloons. You need to puff air into them." "Have you ever gone into an elevator and stood next to a person who is wearing too much perfume? It's much better when there is just a hint of fragrance in the air. So too, when you use a new writing technique. You need to use it like it's expensive perfume—use it sparingly so that the technique doesn't overwhelm the reader.")*

- *Children need lots of ways to excel at writing. (The five children represented letter writing as response to literature, historical fiction, personal narrative, newsletter sportswriting, and "memoir" writing.)*

- *When children learn to do something new, provide opportunities for them to do it again. (When Faith spotted the first vague line in her historical fiction letter, she needed to be asked to find other places to do the same. Then she will own the technique and, in fact, be able to teach it to others.)*

- *It often helps to get children talking and then give them back their words, especially if their writing lacks the rich voice of their conversation. (Evan needed to get his energy up and be challenged to weave that into his text. Sarah needed to switch those summaries of camp life to the sensory scenes she so eloquently described when prodded.)*

- *If children don't seem to have real energy for a piece, it's next to impossible to "force" revision. Time and again, I must remember the old notion that revision must not be seen as punishment but as a compliment. We must believe wholeheartedly and convey to our students that the better the piece is, the more it deserves revision.*

- *Reading aloud a student's work often helps the writer to know what is needed. (I wonder how many times I either read or reread the student's work back to them.)*

- *Being able to confer in such a luxuriously quiet setting reminded me that in the usual classroom writing workshop, it is essential that everyone use hushed and respectful tones so that we can really listen to children and they can really listen to us. Classroom management does count.*

- *Writing from memories can be made more childlike. For example, students can be asked to write vignettes to accompany pages in their family photo albums, or to create annotated timelines concerning some aspect of their childhood, or very simple picture books that stitch together a collection of related memories in order to have a way to remember what they cared about when they were young, and so on.*

- *It's always important to tell children what you see in them as writers. Sometimes they accidentally stumble on an effective technique, unaware of what they have done. If we name the technique for the writer, they are more likely to deliberately return to this technique when they want to create the same effect. (For example, Phoebe needs to know that leaking out the information at the beginning of her haunted house piece created a suspenseful mood.)*

- *Containers for authentic publishing help children to understand what writing is for and inspire them to lift the quality of their work. (Evan wants to make his arm-wrestling announcement the best it can be. After all, it will appear in the monthly class newsletter. He knows that writing is not for bulletin boards and portfolios alone.)*

Reflecting upon my conferring helped crystallize my beliefs about responding to students' writing and enabled me to share those learnings with others. I realized, however, that as a guest speaker working with a few children in the staff room of a school, I faced several handicaps. I didn't have a personal relationship with these children. They had no reason to trust my advice or openly share their concerns. I didn't have a deep understanding of their histories as writers, only the brief summary presented by their teachers. But perhaps my greatest obstacle to successfully conferring was not knowing the books in those children's classrooms. I didn't know the books they had read and those they were currently reading. I didn't know which books had become dog-eared and which authors had become unknowing collaborators. I didn't know which genres they had studied and which authors were potential mentors. Such reading-writing connections as these are so essential to the success of a writing workshop, they form the subject of the next chapter.

RELATED READINGS IN COMPANION VOLUMES

Going Public (Heinemann, 1999) is abbreviated as GP. *Lifetime Guarantees* (Heinemann, 2000) is abbreviated as LG.

Writing workshop basics	**LG**: Ch. 2
Students' writing put to real-world uses	**LG**: Ch. 3
Social tone of classrooms	**GP**: Ch. 4
Working with second-language learners	**LG**: Ch. 10

CHAPTER 5

READING TO INFORM YOUR WRITING

You will find that you get jealous of other people's writing. You will struggle not being able to bear the thought that they are better writers than you. There is a secret to that. The way to get that stuff out of your head is to try to write like them instead of giving up.

—Carey and Annie, age 8

Key Writing Lessons

1. Reading-writing connections can be divided into four major categories: those that are assessment-driven, text-driven, student-driven, and course-of-study-driven.
2. Assessment-driven reading-writing connections imply that the teacher has noticed a felt need and is acting upon it in order to help students improve their writing.
3. Teachers can create archives or minilesson scrapbooks to document their teaching.
4. Teachers can create a shelf of their favorite literary resources for teaching students about writing.
5. Text-driven reading-writing connections can add energy to the writing workshop and inspire students to lift the quality of their work.
6. Carefully selected literature can inspire students to attempt new formats.
7. Newspapers contain a wide range of lessons for young writers.
8. Autobiographical information about authors can be selected or adapted with young writers in mind.
9. Students can learn a great deal from work written by members of the school community.
10. Classroom interactions can be designed to encourage more students to make student-driven reading-writing connections.
11. Students and teachers must learn to talk about good writing with confidence and competence.

Walking from class to class it becomes very clear that teachers and students at the Manhattan New School expect to take lessons from the writers they admire. Classroom charts, posters, and blank big books sport such love-of-good-writing labels as:

Lines We Love

Memorable Passages

Book We Wish We Had Written

Excerpts to Save and Savor

Mentors on Our Mind

Literary Excerpts We Are Envious Of

The world of reading-writing connections is alive, well, and growing in our school. In fact, in regard to improving the quality of student writing, helping children take lessons from well-crafted texts is equally as significant as encouraging children to be responsive to all that surrounds them (the point of keeping a writer's notebook) and providing students with teachers who know how to respond thoughtfully to their work (the point of continually improving our writing conferences).

Recently, while holding a student's black marble composition book, I flipped to the inside back cover and was amused to discover that it still contains the material labeled "Useful Information." I don't think that information has changed since I was an elementary student holding the very same kind of notebook. It includes multiplication and measurement conversion tables. I wonder if students ever refer to these "useful" charts. If their notebooks are used for writing, they require a very different kind of useful information. Much of that information is rooted in how authors craft quality literature.

Kinds of Reading-Writing Connections

The possibilities attached to making reading-writing connections are so extensive that I have divided them into the following categories in order to present the breadth and depth of each.

Assessment-Driven Connections

In this case, the teacher notices something happening in student work and deliberately chooses a text that illustrates something specific the children need to learn. In other words, the text chosen for the classroom read-aloud, the writing workshop minilesson, as reference during a writing conference, or as part of a homework assignment is not random or arbitrary; rather, it clearly supports the teacher's effort to teach needed content. The teacher has used her reading of students' writing and her reading of a wide range of literature to inform her teaching of writing. She will ask students to read (or listen to) and respond to carefully selected texts in order that the students' reading can inform their writing.

Text-Driven Connections

When reading or browsing literature, the teacher discovers a particular text that inspires her to think about something she would not otherwise have thought about. The teacher connects her reading to her students' writing and uses this connection to help further those of her students. In other words, the text pushes the teacher to think new thoughts, devise new challenges, and otherwise lift the quality of student work. Once again, the teacher shares the chosen literature with students in order that their reading and discussion of the text informs their writing.

Student-Driven Connections

Students, on their own, enter into apprenticeship relationships with their favorite texts, authors, and genres. In other words, they borrow a wide range of elements from the books they are reading, including topics, stylistic devices, characters, language, and overall design structures. Students embed these elements into original works and are not always aware that they have borrowed them from authors they admire. These authors, by the way, can include fellow classmates. Some students deliberately and knowingly lift elements from the works they are reading and usually consider this act a compliment, not a crime. Taking lessons from the writers they admire should be as satisfying to children as having ice-cream money in their pockets.

Course-of-Study-Driven Connections

The teacher invites students to engage in long-term studies that revolve around reading-writing connections. Required finished products, complete with due dates, are usually attached to these whole-class studies. The idea for these studies can come from student interests, teacher expertise, curriculum demands, or school-wide or community events. These studies can also originate from the assessment-, text-, and student-driven reading-writing connections described above. In other words, some connections can become so successful that the teacher builds a long-term study around them. Examples of study-driven reading-writing connections include author and genre studies.

A Closer Look at Assessment-Driven Reading-Writing Connections

Teenagers are often incredulous when they observe their parents engaged in what they consider to be inappropriate, authoritarian, or old-fashioned acts. They then ask, with as much sarcasm as they can muster, "And the reason you're doing that is . . . ?" That question, without the superior sneer, is actually a very fine question for educators to ask of one another. In schools, it can take such respectful forms as, "Help me understand why you've chosen to read that book aloud today" or, "Why have you decided to go on that field trip at this time?" or, "Why have you brought that particular group of children together today?" These questions are not insinuations of wrongdoing. New teachers would benefit from posting a reminder in their classroom containing the simple word "Why?" All educators need to know that what they choose to teach should not be random. We can't afford to take the attitude demonstrated by the less-than-enthusiastic teenage remark "Whatever." Teaching is based on assessed needs, not on whatever we seem to be in the mood to do. Educators need to be continually asking themselves, "Why are we doing what we are doing?"

Assessment-driven reading-writing connections imply that the teacher has noticed a felt need and is acting upon it. Whether the teacher has chosen a literature selection to share in a writing workshop minilesson or as a classroom read-aloud or individually with a child during a writing conference, the teacher should be able to begin by saying, "The reason I've chosen this book is . . ." And the teacher's reason should be clearly connected to the work being done by the students. In a book review column for *The New Advocate*, I wrote, "When teachers pay close attention to the needs of young writers in their writing workshops, they discover areas that need strengthening. Teachers then search for literature that will help them demonstrate the needed quality, effect or technique" (p. 260).

Needs-Based Minilessons

In the last twenty years, I am sure that I have taught hundreds of writing workshop minilessons. Year after year, I created lesson after lesson based on the needs of my students. Some of those lessons were no doubt very effective, others less so. The truth is, I can't remember most of them. In retrospect, I wish I had kept records of those lessons, a sort of minilesson scrapbook. By now, I would have dozens of scrapbooks brimming with teaching interactions. I envision these scrapbooks as beautifully bound, large blank books. On the left-hand page, I would have taped in a duplicated copy of the literature sample I had shared, complete with the comments I made. (Although I can't remember the specifics of most of the lessons, I am quite sure that most involved sharing a piece of writing, either my own, another student's, or a selection from the classroom library.) And on the right-hand side, I would have included examples of student work that demonstrated that students benefited from the minilesson taught. Imagine having such a collection. Absent students could find out what they missed. Teachers could refer back to past lessons, benefiting from a reference book spanning the entire school year. ("Remember what we said about Cynthia Rylant's style . . . ?") Substitute teachers could get a feel for what the students have been studying. Principals could place current lessons in context. Teachers would have useful data on their teaching, being able to reflect on what they had or had not accomplished.

Today, I highly recommend to all the teachers that I work with that they begin creating just such an archive. Although I don't have my own cumulative body of work to share, I do have some current favorite minilessons based on assessed needs. Before sharing these, some general comments about the use of children's literature are in order. In *Lasting Impressions* I talk about the value of having a few well-worn books on your classroom shelf and I make several suggestions as to their use. First, read these books aloud in their entirety before carving out any teaching moments. Remember, authors didn't write these books so that educators could use them for minilessons. Second, books are unlimited storehouses. You can highlight many different aspects of any one book. You never use up a well-crafted text. And third, time to talk about these texts is crucial. There are no shortcuts to helping students appreciate good writing. Finally, after presenting a new idea in a minilesson, it makes sense to refer back to it when you walk about the room conferring with writers, and to have students who have put this new idea to good use share their work at the close of the writing workshop. (See *Lifetime Guarantees* for more information about structuring the writing workshop.)

Having said all this, I can now refer to my most dog-eared texts. I keep these books on a separate shelf in my office and I reach for them whenever I want to address a specific need in a writing workshop. I store transparencies of selected pages in the books so I can display them on an overhead projector, and I try to talk about these texts in natural ways. I choose elementary words over technical ones. I create child-friendly metaphors rather than sophisticated ones to make my meaning clear. And I avoid writing process buzzwords and language arts textbook clichés with as much determination as I avoid mosquitoes carrying the West Nile virus. Periodically, I add new books to the needs-based categories described below as well as create new categories based on the students and their writing.

Below are some minilessons based on assessed needs and the books I've used to address them, along with accompanying teaching interactions.

To Encourage Students to Pay More Attention to Their Surroundings

Whenever I read aloud Stephen Krensky's *My Teacher's Secret Life,* I suggest that if the main character were a real live student in our school, he'd be a great writer. The children talk about how he pays careful attention to everything in his environment and how he has a great imagination. He wants things to add up. After reading this book I often ask the children to share the small telling details they have noticed about me and about their teacher. (I make sure the students understand that these are to be gracious observations.) The children usually come up with their favorite mannerisms, language expressions, and gestures.

To Reinforce the Value of Notebook Keeping
and Eliminate Children's Spelling Fears

I read aloud James Stevenson's *The Pattaconk Brook,* in which Sidney the frog keeps a writer's notebook. In addition to exposing students to the poignant relationship between the frog and his friend Sherry the snail, this book can lead to valuable talk about lyrical language and the role of spelling in keeping a writer's notebook. Sherry, who has ideas for Sidney's notebook but doesn't pay attention to how words are spelled, says, "I'm a listener, not a speller."

To Add to the Class Repertoire of Writing Strategies

Roni Schotter's *Nothing Ever Happens on 90th Street* is a madcap city adventure brimming with suggestions for young writers. The minilessons are even highlighted on the back jacket. They include, "Write about what you know"; "Observe carefully and don't neglect the details"; "Find the poetry: a new way with old words"; "Use your imagination"; "Ask what if?"; and "Add a little action." Students also come to realize that if you pay attention, there is always something happening on any street.

To Expand Students' Notions of Recording Observations

Betsy Lewin's *Walk a Green Path* is filled with the kind of jottings we hope children will make about their own environments. I usually highlight the three kinds of ways the author has chosen to record her observations. On every double-page spread, the reader finds a painting, a poem, and (in italics) some precise nonfiction information about the plant that is the subject of the painting and the source of the poetic tribute. This book can lead to all kinds of talk about the role of sketching in keeping a writer's notebook, as well as opening the possibility of doing some nature writing. In addition, students will have strong models for making poetic observations accompanied by factual background data.

To Put Children's Senses to Work
and Help Them Craft Short, Lyrical Scenes

Rosemary Wells' *Night Sounds, Morning Colors* is the kind of book I would choose if I were asked one of those annoying desert-island survival questions: "If you could have only one children's book to teach writing on a desert island, which would you choose?" This book, about a young child going about her everyday business as the seasons change around her, has it all for me—a child's attention to detail, point of view, language, ideas, and metaphors. In addition, the picture book is broken up into very short, separately titled vignettes, models of manageable length for young writers. (Wells' *Lucy Comes to Stay*, a collection of very short stories about a young girl and the arrival of her new puppy, can serve as a similar model.)

To Encourage Detailed Observations Using Precise Language

My Father's Hands by Joanne Ryder is one of my most well-worn books. It begins, "My father's hands are big and strong, scooping up earth and lifting sacks of seeds. Thin cracks run down my father's fingers. Dirt fills every line and edges each nail black." After sharing this book, classroom talk usually centers on the powers of close observation needed by fine writers. Sometimes I ask children to flip through the pages of their writer's notebook to look for places where they could have zoomed in to notice more.

To Help Students Savor Lines They Love

Ralph Fletcher's *Twilight Comes Twice*, with illustrations by Kate Kiesler, deserves to be read many times. Students are quick to call out their favorite lines from this story of a child's observations of dawn and dusk. One of the most oft-quoted reads, "With invisible arms dawn erases the stars from the blackboard of night." Students wonder how the author thinks such thoughts, chooses such language. I suggest children get in the habit of recording favorite lines from literature in their writer's notebooks so they can return to them and study them. I also ask them to find lyrical lines in their own writing that they could imagine Ralph Fletcher placing in his notebook.

To Shows Students That Language Can Be Used in Surprising Ways

Each time I read aloud Jane Yolen's *Nocturne*, I feel privileged to be in the know about children's literature. The evening walk taken by a parent and child is described with poetic language worth saving and savoring. Every child, in kindergarten through fifth grade, senses something magical in the air when I read such lines as,

> In the night,
> in the velvet night
> in the quiltdown quietdown velvet night . . .

Not only do students talk about what makes this language so surprising and memorable, this book also helps them to realize that the little moments in their lives are often worth writing about.

To Demonstrate Presenting Factual Information in Literary Ways

Marion Dane Bauer's *If You Were Born a Kitten* reminds students that nonfiction information can be presented in lyrical ways. The book begins, "If you were born a kitten, you'd slip into the world in a silvery sac," and continues with the births of twelve different animal babies. Each image is delivered with surprising details, strong verbs, and effective metaphors. The text and illustrations are very large, allowing you to engage large groups of children at a time. Don't be surprised if the room fills with stories of their own pets giving birth or the arrival of new brothers and sisters.

To Illustrate the Importance of Simile and Metaphor

You don't have to live in the woods to appreciate Marsha Wilson Chall's *Sugarbush Spring*, about a joint family project of making maple sugar. City kids marvel at the story behind the syrup they love to pour on their waffles and pancakes, and Jim Daly's incredibly lifelike paintings make them feel right at home. Whenever I read this story aloud, I find myself rereading favorite lines several times. Even the youngest listener appreciates hearing about how the two holes in the trees are, "like front and back bellybuttons," or about the boiling sap that makes steam "bath-tub warm, cotton-candy sweet," or the child who "squints [her] eyes into microscopes," and the "ribbons" of syrup that the children enjoy pulling and stretching in the snow. Children leave the gathering area after this read-aloud eager to write in ways that really make the reader smile and say, "I know exactly what the author means!"(For additional information on teaching figurative language, see pages 273–286).

To Demonstrate That Common Topics Can Be Written About in Fresh, Engaging Ways

Sometimes I teach a minilesson by grouping a stack of books together that cumulatively add up to a bigger point. For example, I keep a shelf devoted to topics I often see children write about, including visits to grandparents, getting a new pet, playing sports, moving to a new house or apartment, and the arrival of a new sibling. Inevitably someone in the class has written about these issues, and so my points are especially well received. I can demonstrate that ordinary events can be written about in extraordinary ways. Robert Burleigh has written a poetic account of a basketball game in *Hoops*. The words are quite different from the predictable blow-by-blows most children churn out. Michael Cadnum in *The Lost and Found House* offers a first-person account of moving to a new house from a young child's point of view. The author's choice of details allows us to understand the boy's emotions without the author ever naming them. Young writers can take serious lessons from this text. Laurence Pringle's *Naming the Cat*, with illustrations by Katherine Potter, helps young writers zoom in on just one aspect of their pet's life and tell the story straight and true in an interesting fashion. Children can also understand how developing the character of the people that surround the pets in our lives often adds richness to narratives. We care about the pet because we care about the people in the pet's life.

To Provide Students with a New Way to Generate Rich Memories

In *Letter to the Lake*, written by poet Susan Marie Swanson, with illustrations by Peter Catalanatto, the young female character, on a cold wintry morning, recalls spending her summers on a lake. In her mind she composes a letter to the lake, detailing specific moments. The notion of writing a letter to an inanimate object is surprising to most children, even when they realize that the letter is just in the child's mind. Children are quick to call out things they could write to in order to help recall their past experiences. Some of our students used the technique in their writer's notebook, addressing entries to their old apartments, their baby blanket, their bunk bed at camp, their grandmother's rocking chair, and even a bookmobile they visited when they lived in a rural section of our country.

To Encourage Students to Use Pleasing Sounds and Rhythms in Their Writing

Duke Ellington is quoted as having said, "If it sounds good, it is good." Part of the challenge in the writing workshop is to encourage children to pay attention to the sounds of words and their arrangements and to notice the rhythm in the books they read, not just in poetry but in prose. Then we can encourage children to listen to the sound of their own writing, letting their fine-tuned ears push them to revise their works in progress. Young writers need to trust that "if it sounds good, it is good." *Train* by Charles Temple, with illustrations by Larry Johnson, is one of those books that clearly demonstrates how the writer can deliberately choose and arrange words to create pleasing effects. In a review of the book that I wrote for *The New Advocate* (Winter 1997), I point out that "the reader feels the magic of a long train ride. The author's choice of words and their arrangements, coupled with the gentle repetition and rhythm of the sounds, makes the reader feel the movement of that train." After reading this book aloud and discussing the sounds of the words, I ask children if they have ever changed a word in their writing because it simply didn't sound right.

To Help Students Appreciate Literary Description

Motley the Cat, with words by Susannah Amoore and paintings by Mary Fedden, is a lush adventure story involving a mysterious cat searching for a home. Children quickly fall in love with the "enormous striped-like-a-tiger cat with a scarlet collar, glittering lime-green eyes, and great curves of wiry whiskers springing from either side of the widest nose ever seen on a cat." The author provides long, meandering descriptive sentences that weave the natural setting into the activities of Motley and the human characters that surround him. The paintings are as evocative as the text, inspiring many students to reminisce about their first encounters with their own pets. This book is a principal-on-call's delight. It takes a long period to read aloud, the words and pictures engage even the most aloof students, and the conversations about content and craft it inspires could go on at length.

To Illustrate Recalling Memories in First Person, Present Tense, and Sensory Narratives

Children usually can't imagine using the present tense to tell a story that took place in the past. When I read Sherry Garland's *My Father's Boat* aloud to children, they understand the power of such a deliberate choice. When the main character, a young Vietnamese American, goes fishing with his father, he hears stories about the fisherman grandfather he has never met. After response to the book and the second reading aloud, children can usually explain how the present tense makes the reader think that they are accompanying the boy on the fishing trip and can actually hear the "squishy noises" of the father's rubber boots, taste the cold rice, hear the "slapping waves," smell the "fish and sweat," feel the mist tingling his face, and see the "glowing jellyfish."

To Help Students Appreciate Specialized Vocabulary

Children love animals and they love knowing things about animals that most grown-ups don't know. The following three books can be presented together in order for children to learn that there are specific and precise words for the places different animals live as well as unusual and surprising names for their young: *Armadillos Sleep in Dugouts: and Other Places Animals Live* and *A Pinky Is a Baby Mouse and Other Baby Animal Names,* both written by Pam Munoz Ryan and illustrated by Diane deGroat, and *Kangaroos Have Joeys* by Philippa-Alys Browne. After discussing these books, children can be enticed to research the specific names of different kinds of flowers, colors, houses, boats, and so on, and to talk about how the use of specific terms adds power to their writing.

To Help Children Appreciate Revealing Details

Jeannette Caines' *Window Wishing*, illustrated by Kevin Brooks, is as useful today as it was when it was first published in 1980 and I shared it with youngsters in my very first writing workshop. A young brother and sister spend their vacation with Grandma and through the author's careful choice of telling details, the reader comes to appreciate this nonconforming, free-spirited, full-of-life woman. This sneaker-wearing, worm-raising, kite-building grandmother who doesn't like to cook is a perfect companion for her grandchildren. A natural follow-up with young writers is to ask them to think of those tiny details about people they know well that would help a stranger really get to know the chosen person. I often ask, "What are some of the things that you notice about this person that passersby probably wouldn't?"

To Inspire Children to Use Writing to Improve the Quality of Their Lives

I enjoy reading Doreen Cronin's *Click Clack, Moo: Cows That Type,* with pictures by Betsy Lewin, to children as well as to adults. In it, the cows write protest letters to the farmer, demanding improvements in their living conditions. Other farm creatures join the cows and the farmer faces the threat of his animals going on strike. This terribly funny, tongue-in-cheek story might require some simple explanations of labor and management for the youngest listeners, but eventually all students will understand the power of letters, requests, petitions, signs, and so on to make a difference in one's life. Children easily begin talking about the letters of protest and letters of request that they might write.

To Remind Children of the Power of Saying Things in Surprising Ways

Andrew Clements' book *Workshop,* with magnificent illustrations by David Wisniewski, is as well received by children as by adults, but the children seem even more excited when they realize that each tool that is presented as you move through the book, is being used to build a beautiful carousel that doesn't appear in its entirety until the very last page. When children struggle to find a topic to write about, I often share this book, noting that many areas of expertise, including baseball, Lego constructions, soup making, costume designing, gardening, and so on, can be written about in a way similar to what Clements' has done with carpentry tools. Children can also write short descriptions of the tools of their trade, making them add up to a satisfying whole. Of course, children might also learn from the author's stylistic devices, filling each page with carefully chosen descriptors forming short staccato, listlike descriptions of each tool. I tell students that I will never look at an axe in the very same way after appreciating it as "a chopper, a splitter, a sudden rusher. Axe finds the board that hides in the wood. Axe is the great divider."

To Help Students Appreciate the Sounds of Words and Their Arrangements

The last time I shared April Pulley Sayre's *Home at Last: A Song of Migration* with students, I was reminded of just how flexible teachers must be, always ready to capitalize on the teachable moment. I had intended to share this book in order to illustrate how authors use refrains to add a satisfying shape to their writing as well as to demonstrate how a scientific topic like migration can be written about with literary grace. As I shared it with a group of third graders, I was struck by the lovely sound of the words and their arrangements, particularly when I got to the passage about migrating whales that read, "Once there, he and his family will feast on plankton aplenty. Fat and full . . . they'll be . . . home at last." I couldn't help but announce how joyful it was to pronounce these alliterative phrases. I asked the children if they thought that all those *P* and *F* words were deliberately chosen or just included by chance. The children agreed that the author wanted to make the book sound great and so she picked her words carefully. As the discussion was taking place, I happened to realize that the three girls sitting in front of me were named Maia Montes de Oca, Melissa Medunanjin, and Mia Mazer. I asked the children if they thought their parents worked hard to pick first names that sounded well with their surnames. The children enthusiastically called out the names of additional friends and acquaintances who had alliterative names. One baseball fan proudly added the name Mark McGuire to our list, not to be outdone by another student who then shrieked, "Sammy Sosa!"

To Allow Students to Hear Something New in Their Writing

When students seem bored with their writing or have reached a plateau, I know it is time to give them challenges that will enable them to hear something new in their work. I usually turn to carefully selected short pieces of literature, ones students will envy and ones that contain structures and writing techniques that they will find easy to emulate. The magic lies in finding just the right texts.

I often choose to read aloud and then reread aloud Ruth Brown's short picture book *Toad,* a stunning account of a most unpleasant toad who gets caught in the jaws of a monster. The author writes, "A muddy toad, a mucky toad, a clammy, gooey toad, odorous, oozing, foul and filthy, and dripping with venomous fluid." I talk to children about alliteration, the pleasing rhythmic sounds of the words, the effect of strings of adjectives, and her use of the surprise ending. I then challenge students to try some of the author's techniques in their own notebook writing. But first I share my own attempt. I deliberately choose to write about something totally removed from the world of toads, so children wouldn't think I was asking them to write another slimy tale. In the tribute to mashed potatoes below, I try to use a great deal of alliteration and strings of sensory adjectives.

> I love mashed potatoes,
> Soft mounds of mashed potatoes.
> Buttery, bumps of mashed potatoes.
> I love to run my fork along,
> Making gravy grooves through those mounds.
> I love to scoop those bumps
> With a silvery spoon.
> Oh yes, I love mashed potatoes,
> Especially when
> My throat is sore, so sore.
> How comforting to have
> A soup bowl filled with my mama's
> Mashed potatoes.

An additional benefit to such exercises is that they seem to provide comfort to students who are just learning English. Such students appreciate the leg up offered by a pattern to follow or a technique to borrow.

To Help Students Appreciate the "Gestalt" of Writer's Notebooks

Such books as Amy Hest's *How to Get Famous in Brooklyn* or Marissa Moss' *Amelia's Notebook* are particularly helpful at the beginning of third grade when notebooks are first introduced. They are also helpful to share with any new students who might enter the school in the upper grades. Students learn from these notebook keepers how to use this portable tool to capture their childhood thoughts and experiences. Similarly, the following passage from Lois Lowry's *Anastasia at Your Service* can help notebook keepers understand the eventual shaping of notebook entries into published genres.

> "Dad," asked Anastasia as they ate, "do you have your notebook with you?"
>
> He looked surprised. "Of course I have my notebook. I always have my notebook with me. Every writer does. You never know, if you're a writer, when you might have to take notes on the human scene." He pulled a small leather-bound notebook out of his pocket.
>
> "No kidding. What does that mean: Notes on the human scene?" asked Anastasia.
>
> He thought for a minute. "Well, I eavesdrop and observe people. Then I make notes about what I see and what I overhear. After a while, I use some of that stuff in poems."

To Offer Children More Challenging Structures for Crafting Personal Narratives

Students who write many first-person narratives can become complacent, always writing them in similar, set ways. In order to make sure that children are continuing to grow as writers and willing to accept new challenges, teachers might share a wider variety of personal narratives. The following texts demonstrate alternate ways to structure narratives.

In My Mama's Kitchen by Jerdine Nolen, with illustrations by Colin Bootman, contains several short accounts of significant family happenings that take place throughout the seasons of the year in the kitchen of a young girl's home. Children not only think of their own topics in response to many of the events, including birthday celebrations, wedding preparations, and good-news announcements, they can also take lessons from the structure of the book. After reading the book aloud, and providing time for children to respond to the text, I ask, "Do any of you have places that you know so well, that have such important events or experiences attached to them?" I ask children to jot down the place and list possible events or experiences, suggesting that they might want to put together a collection in the way the author has done.

In *Daddy Played Music for the Cows,* by Maryann Weidt with illustrations by Henri Sorensen, a young child grows up on a dairy farm in rural America. Moments of shared music and play in the barn between a daughter and her parents serve as threads that help the reader appreciate the passage of time and the changes in the young girl. As we watch the child mature, we realize how important the memories of these shared moments are to the young girl. After sharing and discussing this picture book with upper-elementary-grade students, I asked if students could think of one thing that they have kept on doing as they moved from being infants to ten-year-olds. One child suggested he could share all the different birthday parties his parents had thrown him, each with a different decorated ice-cream cake. Another said that every Christmas week his family drives to Virginia and he could write about those car rides and all the different cars his parents have driven.

Ann Turner's *Christmas House* demonstrates to children that it is possible to describe the same memory from many different people's points of view. Kathryn Lasky's *Pond Year* demonstrates how to weave an abundance of factual information into a first-person narrative, as well as how to use the changing seasons to scaffold the passage of time in a narrative.

To Provide Students with an Alternative Resource for Finding Potential Topics

Frequently when I read aloud a picture book, I am struck by our students' enthusiasm for the illustrations. It seems as if some pictures resonate for children as much as the words do. It's not surprising for children to say, while pointing to an illustration, "That reminds me of . . ." It becomes important, therefore, that we select texts with wonderful illustrations and that we give children time to linger over them. It also becomes important, especially when class registers zoom to over thirty students, that we select texts whose illustrations can be seen from the back of the meeting area. Crowded classrooms result in a lot of bobbing heads and a lot of faraway floor spots.

Chris K. Soentpiet's picture book *Around Town* is the story of a young girl and her mother enjoying the weekend sidewalk happenings on the bustling streets of a big city. Many children were inspired to capture the sights of New York after viewing the illustrator's vivid and larger-than-life paintings. The middle entry on Abby's notebook page in Figure 5.1 was written in response to these pictures. Ben, another third grader, wrote the response to this same book that appears in Figure 5.2.

Similarly, Kathy Henderson's *A Year in the City* is one of those books in which the pictures, luxuriously detailed scenes by Paul Howard, are as evocative as the text. Children don't have to be city dwellers to be inspired to tell their own seasonal stories after listening to and looking at the pages of this picture book. (See Chapter 8 for more information about learning to write about the setting you know best.)

To Help Students Realize That Writers Must Engage the Real World

Elisha Cooper's *Ballpark* offers behind-the-scenes information on the preparation of a ballpark before a big game and the actions of the players, spectators, and ground crew during the game. Children quickly sense how much time the author had to spend making ballpark observations. How else would he know that a groundskeeper might taste a few strands of grass, a player touch a ribbon for good luck, or that the ground crew has a snakelike hose? This book also suggests to children that writers are always looking for new ways to approach their topics. The author didn't just write everything he knew about a ballpark. Instead, he chose to focus on the specific actions of all the people involved in a baseball game. Additionally, I ask children, "What kinds of jottings do you think the author made in a reporter's pad or writer's notebook?"

To Help Students Appreciate a Great Title

Sometimes I begin a discussion about the importance of choosing an intriguing title by sharing a news story I viewed on television. It was a segment about a handyman who was having trouble earning money until he started calling his company Rent-A-Husband. Changing the name of his company attracted a lot of attention and a lot of business. "So too," I explain to the children, "the title you select will attract people's attention to your

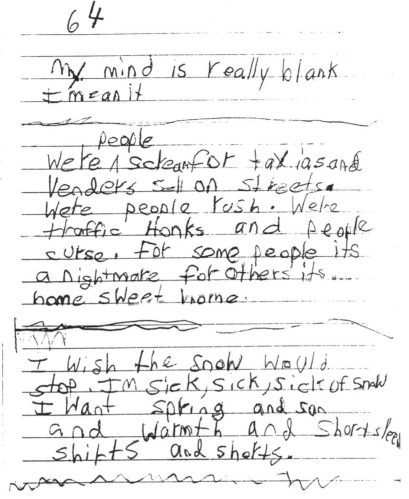

6 4

My mind is really blank.
I mean it

people
We're A scream for taxias and
Venders sell on streets.
Were people rush. We're
traffic Honks and people
curse. For some people its
a nightmare for others its ....
home sweet home.

I wish the snow would
stop. Im sick, sick, sick of snow
I want spring and sun
and warmth and short sleev
shifts and shorts.

Figure 5.1

writing and make them want to read it." Then I usually pull out a stack of books with clever titles, including Jennifer Owings Dewey's *Faces Only a Mother Could Love*, a collection of short nonfiction reports on unusual-looking animals, Joanne Settel's *Exploding Ants: Amazing Facts About How Animals Adapt*, another nonfiction collection filled with fascinating animal stories, and Susan Stockdale's *Nature's Paintbrush: The Patterns and Colors Around You*, a question-and-answer book about living things. We make guesses as to why the authors chose these enticing titles and then I extend the conversation by reading aloud excerpts from all three. Students realize that the authors kept the quality high inside the books as well. Finally, I extend the conversation beyond nonfiction writing. Children leave the meeting area realizing that poems, personal writing, and picture books all deserve carefully composed titles.

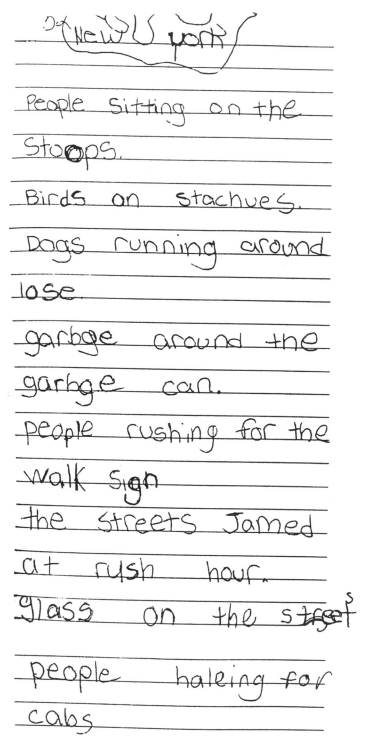

New york

People sitting on the
Stoops.
Birds on stachues.
Dogs running around
lose
garbge around the
garbge can.
people rushing for the
walk sign
the streets Jamed
at rush hour.
glass on the streets
people haleing for
cabs

Figure 5.2

To Help Students Appreciate Choosing Just the Right Verb, and to Introduce Personification

Charlotte F. Otten's *January Rides the Wind: A Book of Months*, with lifelike illustrations by Todd L.W. Doney, is filled with poetic tributes to each month of the year. In addition to sparking great conversations about children's seasonal pastimes, celebrations, and memories, this is an effective book for illustrating how the surprising verb can turn good writing into memorable writing. In it, "January *rides* the wind," "March *eats* the winter," and "September *squeezes* what is left of summer into night-cool cider" (emphasis mine). In addition to using ordinary verbs in surprising ways, the book also contains such glorious verbs as *huddles*, *swaddles*, *smolders*, and *billows*. This book can also be used to teach young writers about the power of personification, as the attributes of each month are presented in human terms. After sharing this book, I often engage students in thinking about the verbs they tend to choose and I challenge them to expand their repertoire. In the spirit of a parlor game, I give students a location and ask them to brainstorm verbs usually associated with this locale. For example, when I suggest "garden," students offer, *dig*, *weed*, *plant*, *prune*, *water*, *spray*, *rake*, and *grow*. I then challenge them to think of ways to use these words in describing our school. A student might suggest, "The teacher weeded the class library, getting rid of the raggedy books" or, "The student was digging in his pencil case to find an eraser." Other locales I might toss out include the kitchen, the baseball field, or the swimming pool.

To Demonstrate That Books Can Be Returned to Again and Again

The minute I opened Kristine O'Connell George's *The Great Frog Race and Other Poems*, wonderfully illustrated by Kate Kiesler, I knew that this book would become an all-time favorite. In the introduction, the late Myra Cohn Livingston points out that these poems are filled with "music, keen observation, fresh metaphor, personification and meaningful flights of fancy." What teacher or student of writing, both of poetry and prose, could ask for anything more? I therefore reach for my well-worn copy whenever I sense that students don't realize that they need to take lessons from the books they are reading. On the very first page, in a poem about pollywogs, the poet describes these creatures as "chubby commas." "What could be more perfect?" I ask my students. "That's the kind of writing I admire. It's the kind of writing I need to study. It's the kind of writing that makes me ask, 'How did the writer do this? What can I try to do that this writer does?' All the poems in this collection make me say, 'I wish I could do that.' " I then suggest that students search for the kind of books that will make them respond likewise.

Discovering Books That Address Student Needs

As teachers read their students' writing and stop to confer with them about their works in progress, they will discover additional writing needs, including such essentials as learning to:

- control the passage of time
- flesh out scenes
- use authentic dialogue
- add satisfying endings
- listen for the satisfying sound of words
- select forms that support content

Teachers will then need to find texts that will become the co-teachers in their writing workshops. These accessible texts, presented well, will invite children to respond, "I get it, I know what she's doing. I could do that too!"

Although the above section contains references to many books, one can be an accomplished teacher of writing without knowing or owning every wonderful book. Instead, writing teachers need to find a manageable number of books they love, ones that are appropriate to meet the needs of the children in their classrooms, and share them wisely again and again. Dozens of cookbooks line my kitchen windowsill, but in truth, I refer to only a select few. I have discovered the ones that feel right, the ones that can teach me what I need to know. Similarly, experienced teachers of writing find themselves referring to a few familiar books that help them get the job done. Although teachers at the Manhattan New School are more than willing to share and swap resources, it became common knowledge that you don't remove Donald Crews' *Big Mama's* from Sharon Hill's room, Jane Aragon's *Salthands* from Karen Ruzzo's, Marilyn Singer's *Turtle in July* from Paula Rogovin's, Julie Brinckloe's *Fireflies* from Joanne Hindley Salch's room, or Aliki's *Those Summers* from Judy Davis'. These are the books our teachers return to time and again. Their writing workshops just wouldn't feel whole without them. (See *Lifetime Guarantees* for additional nonfiction and poetry titles, as well as Manhattan New School book reviews in *The New Advocate* from the winter of 1996 through the spring of 1998.)

A Closer Look at Text-Driven Reading-Writing Connections

Although this category of reading-writing connections does not originate from a felt need followed by a search for appropriate literature, neither does it imply a "Whatever-pops-into-our-heads, let-the-muse-inspire us, what shall we do today?" kind of teaching. Instead, I am referring to those wonderful moments when we're reading a book, a magazine, a newspaper, or even a poster, pamphlet, or brochure, and the reading helps us to realize what's missing from our students' writing, or the reading suggests possible ways to add energy to our writing workshop, or the reading inspires us to provide new child-size ways to help students lift the quality of their writing. In other words, I am referring to those glorious moments in your reading when you find yourself saying, "Hey, my kids could do that!"

Teachers find themselves in this position only if they know their students and their writing well, so although these ideas may be text-driven, they certainly are not disconnected from the students and the writing they are doing.

Introducing New Formats

When I first saw *Stone Bench in an Empty Park*, a poetry anthology put together by noted anthologizer Paul Janeczko, with black-and-white photographs by Henri Silberman, I was reminded of a writing and photography project created by Manhattan New School teacher Renay Sadis. In *Lifetime Guarantees* I include examples of the street scenes taken by Renay's students and the poetic images they wrote to accompany their photographs. This school project took place several years ago. Janeczko's book was published in the year 2000. Certainly, Renay's project was *not* inspired by reading this published book, but the similarities reinforce that students can attempt ambitious projects if the topics are realistic and appropriate.

Whenever I browse in a public library or children's bookstore, I am always pleased to discover a book whose format would be great to throw into the class pot, especially if workshop energy is low, or certain children have not as yet discovered a genre that sparks their interest, or the format is one that would be very supportive of student content, needs, or interests. The first time I spotted the following books I knew that they would serve as helpful models for some of our students and that a contagious, renewed spirit would ripple through the writing workshop.

Snapshots from the Wedding by Gary Soto is a picture book that looks like a photo album, to the credit of illustrator Stephanie Garcia. The author, an accomplished poet, provides well-crafted and lyrical descriptions on each page. The children appreciate that cousin Isaac has "baby teeth, white as Chiclets" and that the bride has "hands, soft as doves." I read it aloud and suggest that children may want to bring in their own family photo albums and carefully compose captions for each picture. This invitation is particularly well-received by English-language learners, whose photo albums are filled with scenes from their home countries. Reluctant writers also appreciate the safety net of such a clear writing challenge.

Pepper's Journal: A Kitten's First Year by Stuart J. Murphy, illustrated by Marsha Winborn, is part of the author's series highlighting mathematical understandings. Although the pages are filled with many references to calendar time, the format of this book can serve as a model for children whose interest in a new pet or a new sibling would lend itself to keeping a topic-specific journal. The left-hand pages contain the highlights of monthly events in Pepper's life, while the right-hand pages contain more reflective thoughts and observations about the kitten.

Pictures of Home by Colin Thompson can be an inspiration for class artists and writers. In it, the artist offers page after page of paintings of different homes, most with a rather magical or mystical mood. Each painting is accompanied by a quote or haiku about home written by an actual child from an English schoolhouse. I can easily imagine the class artist, the one who specializes in dogs, airplanes, or flowers, preparing a set of illustrations and then collecting appropriate quotes or verses from classmates.

River Friendly, River Wild by Jane Kurtz, illustrated by Neil Brennan, is a collection of powerful free-verse poems related to the devastating Red River flood in Grand Forks, North Dakota, in 1997. The poems, told through the eyes of a young girl, present a chronology of the author's experiences as she prepared for the flood, escaped it, and returned to start her life anew. Children living through such memorable experiences as the arrival of a new baby, moving to a new apartment, or changing schools might want to do what this author has done, chronologically recording the experience through an anthology of poems.

A Seaside Alphabet by Donna Grassby, with enticing illustrations by Susan Tooke, is an alphabet book devoted to all things coastal. The author, in addition to playful alliterative sentences describing each seaside scene, provides detailed notes on everything from Atlantic salmon anglers to surfers zigzagging on zephyrs. Very young children often choose to prepare alphabet books, usually to show off their knowledge of words beginning with each letter and to take advantage of this very basic template for student writing. For older students, the alphabet book becomes a more ambitious challenge when, as in this book, each letter is connected to an umbrella topic of interest and background information is provided for each page. (Although children appreciate the alliterations in this book, asking them to craft an entire book of alliterative sentences seems unnecessary as it would no doubt make it difficult for them to make their writing as meaningful as possible.)

Hey, Little Ant by Phillip and Hannah Hoose, with illustrations by Debbie Tilley, began as a song written by the authors, a father and daughter. Children love the book for many reasons including the opportunity it presents to talk about the moral issue related to humans squishing ants. They also love the book because the words can be sung, the illustrations showing the ant's point of view are quite dramatic and surprising, and the text rhymes, making it quite easy for the children to join in on repeated readings. I suggest yet another feature to budding writers. "Imagine," I say, "an entire book written as a conversation between two characters. Can you think of any topic that you could share by just having two characters speak to one another, a topic that lends itself to presenting two points of view?" If any students are interested in trying to use this format, I point out that this is not play or skit writing. There are no stage directions included. I also suggest that students need not make their conversations rhyme, knowing that that challenge might also limit their ability to create a meaningful text. (Some ambitious students do attempt rhyme, hoping that their words can be put to music as well.)

Once again, it is not essential that teachers use the books described above. What is beneficial is that writing teachers read with their antennae out, always asking themselves, "I wonder if I should invite my students to try that?"

The Newspaper as Inspiration

I have long thought that I could lead a productive writing workshop for teachers by simply providing daily newspapers, scissors, a duplicating machine to copy and enlarge clippings, and acetates to create overhead projections. That's how rich a teaching reservoir I consider the newspaper. In addition, I think of the daily reading of a newspaper an essential requirement for educators. How else can we serve as literate models, connect students' learning to the world, and provide needed background information when asked? Then too, the newspaper is often filled with important information for writers as well as samples of quality writing.

Information for Writers Lifted from the Newspaper

One summer day several years ago, while teaching a summer institute in Dublin, Ohio, I returned to my hotel room to find a copy of *USA Today* outside my door. I began my presentation the next morning by talking about all the possible worthwhile lessons I could teach from that one day's paper (July 31, 1997).

There was an article by Bob Minzesheimer about writer Richard Ford, who won the Pulitzer Prize for fiction in 1996 for his book, *Independence Day*. In the article, Ford discusses what he calls the "triggering word," a word he saves in his notebook "because it seems to have a certain fabric to it. . . . *Independence* was a word like that. It kept showing up in my notebook and I thought, 'What's this about?' I could easily imagine sharing this information with students and asking them to search through their notebooks for any words that keep reappearing, asking if they want to spend more time with the topics connected to that word.

The reporter also describes Ford's passion for reading aloud: "He reads aloud everything he writes to test it, listening for the rhythms and pauses, seeing if he can get through the sentences without running out of breath." This information would also serve as a rallying call for the young writers at school to reread their work aloud, listening carefully to the sounds and arrangements they have chosen.

Another article in that same paper suggests that surfing the Internet is still not as popular a pastime as watching television and reading. Certainly this article would lead to some interesting talk about obstacles to having sufficient time in our lives for reading as well as writing.

A third article discusses romance writer Janet Dailey's admission of plagiarizing passages from writer Nora Roberts. Roberts comments, "I believe writing is a discipline. I write every day. Even if I'm not writing well, I write through it. I can fix a bad page. I can't fix a blank one." Plagiarism is always an important issue to discuss with young writers and Roberts' advice would be worth sharing with students.

Another article's headline read, "Bookstores may be on the upswing, but book sales are down." In it, reporter Dierdre Donahue explains how bookstores have become popular hangouts but that most books have a very short shelf life. The article is filled with behind-the-scenes details of publishing books.

The final article that would be worth sharing in an upper-grade writing workshop is a listing of the fifty best-selling books. Students could survey the titles, paying attention to the genres, and then discuss whether all those formats are represented in their classroom.

This one day's newspaper has given me a week's worth of writing workshop mini-lessons.

Newspaper Articles That Illustrate Elements of Quality Writing

In addition to the kind of literacy-related news articles described above, there are abundant articles to clip because they contain the kind of literary qualities we want to share with children. On countless occasions, I discover well-written articles that suggest elements missing from student work. Of course, one must take care not to ask young children to attempt too sophisticated moves in their writing. Once again, selecting articles to share, just as selecting poems and picture books, requires knowing good writing and knowing your students. Teachers need the ability to spot pieces of literature that will resonate for their students and they need to know how and when the authors of those pieces can become mentors for their students.

One year when Joanne Hindley Salch invited her third graders to create cards for Mother's Day and Father's Day, she asked if she could take down an old *New York Times* newspaper announcement I had hung in the staff restroom that honored the Yankees World Series win the previous fall. Joanne shared the page with her students, encouraging them to say thank you in specific and surprising ways. The ad read, "Thank you, Yankees. For making history. For defining the word *team*. For giving us a spring and summer we'll always remember. And an October we'll never forget. For being true heroes to kids (from 5 to 95). For giving New Yorkers another reason to feel proud, go crazy, and have yet another parade. For showing dignity the 125 times you won. But especially the few times you lost." You can be sure that many eight-year-olds wrote very memorable lines to their parents that year.

I frequently find myself lifting one-liners or short excerpts and explaining to students why they stood out for me. For example, when the Rev. Vashti Murphy McKenzie became the first woman bishop of the African Methodist Episcopal Church, she announced, "The stained glass ceiling has been pierced" (*New York Times*, July 12, 2000). "What a strikingly perfect metaphor for a clergywoman," I might explain to children. "Churches have stained glass windows and she has broken through a barrier at the church, so putting the two images together really helps me understand the importance of the occasion."

When the remains of an unknown dinosaur was discovered, the Associated Press recorded, "Scientists have discovered the bones of what could be the largest meat-eating dinosaur ever to walk the earth, a needle-nosed, razor-toothed beast that may have been more terrifying than Tyrannosaurus rex. . . . The dinosaur had a long, narrow skull and a jaw shaped like scissors" (*The New York Times*, March 11, 2000). I might tell students, "The writer used such specific detail, I could probably sketch that dinosaur."

When a severe February snowstorm hit the northeast, Rick Bragg offered the following lead to his article in *The New York Times* (February 12, 1994):

> Because of the snow, so much snow, the miracle of birth had to unfold on a couch in Teaneck, N.J.
>
> Because of the snow, so much snow, a 90-year old man in Port Chester, N.Y. couldn't get a hot meal. But in Manhattan, a delivery man with ice in his eyebrows and terror in his eyes made a suicidal-type run on an out of control bicycle with a $7 order of mooshu pork.
>
> Because of the snow, a man stood waiting for a truckload of roses that never showed, on the one weekend of the year when lovers can't be lovers without something red.

I might suggest to students, "The writer's repetition of those beginning phrases really made me feel just how bad that snowstorm was."

After another long bout with bad weather, an editorial in the *The New York Times* (January 11, 1994) began, "New York has so much of everything—so many subways, skyscrapers, races, creeds, controversies, pizzerias, bodegas and dim sum parlors—that it is only right that it has so much weather." I might suggest to students that the use of a long list in the middle of this sentence effectively added to the feeling of so much choice in our city, so much abundance.

I have gotten in the habit, at the end of each school year, of clipping memorable lines from the college graduation speeches published in the *The New York Times*. One year, political figure, Henry Cisneros, as he advised graduates to stay the course and stick with things, was quoted as saying, "It's like the difference between the shooting star that flashes across the sky and is gone—you're not even sure it was there—and the North star that is there every night, night after night" (May 29, 2000). I might share this line with students, asking them to think of situations in which this metaphorical thinking might apply. Would they use it to describe choosing true friends, giving piano lessons your all, or appreciating their parents? Children often need practice doing things collaboratively and orally before they can be expected to do these things on their own and in writing. (See Chapter 8 for more ideas about teaching students about the use of similes and metaphors. See *Lasting Impressions* for more information on the value of oral exercises.)

When Ted Turner and Jane Fonda announced their plans to divorce, I wonder if any teachers in New York City showed the front page of the *New York Post*, which read, "Ted No Longer Fonda Jane" (January 5, 2000). Playing with language and appreciating other's attempts also belongs in our writing workshops.

Additionally, teachers might spot in the newspaper examples of new formats to introduce to students, including timelines, character sketches, interviews, reviews, photographic essays, field guides, and editorials that serve as authentic persuasive essays. Of course, it's not just headlines, captions, one-liners, and brief passages that can be shared with students. Occasionally, there are entire articles that would be appropriate and beneficial to share, ones that would support students' growth as readers.

As teachers read the newspaper each evening, they need to keep a pair of scissors handy, ever on the lookout for what might be effective and appropriate for their children. In addition to using their discoveries to improve the quality of students' writing, they might also be nurturing a lifelong newspaper reading habit. Students, and perhaps members of their families, will join in on the search, sending in newspaper writing that stands out for them. More importantly, of course, students will begin talking about what's happening in the news, certainly an essential goal for all educators.

Autobiographical Information That Adds Up

In Chapter 1 of this book I explain that, in the past, I read many authors' memoirs, eager to share their insights and ways of working with my students. Today, I still read autobiographies and other bits of biographical information about the authors I admire, but I am very careful to sift them through the lens of childhood, eliminating ideas that are too sophisticated and presenting pint-size versions of these texts to children.

For example, M. E. Kerr's *Blood on the Forehead: What I Know About Writing*, is clearly intended for older students, the young adults who read the author's acclaimed novels. In the author's note that begins the book, Kerr suggests that "there are certain courtesies that the writer should extend to the reader." Although Kerr presents a very fine list of courtesies, they were certainly written with the older student in mind. I just love, however, the notion of writers being courteous. Imagine telling a group of third graders that you heard that writers have to be courteous to their readers. Perhaps I would ask, "We know that we don't say please and thank you to our readers, so how can we be courteous?" Would the children suggest using their best handwriting, checking their spelling, using lovely paper? Would we have to add such strategies as answering the readers' questions, not making the reader seasick by jumping around too much, choosing the best words, or making the ending sound like an ending?

When reading autobiographical material, I am particularly tuned to the authors' childhoods, looking for activities or stances that can easily be shared with children. When sharing such books as *Beatrix Potter* by Alexandra Wallner, a biography of the classic children's writer, it is helpful to ask, "What is it about the way this writer spent her childhood that enabled her to become a successful writer?" (See Appendix 1 for bibliographies of children's authors' life stories.) Students who are learning to take their own writing seriously understand how important it was for Beatrix to capture the things she loved on paper. They appreciate how many hours a day she devoted to her interests and they understand how diary writing, drawing, and following her interests enabled her to become a talented writer.

Some authors offer specific childhood writing activities. In Liz Rosenberg's poetry anthology *The Invisible Ladder*, Linda Pastan, one of the poets, reveals, "In what I think of as my lonely childhood (I had no brothers or sisters) poetry kept me company. I read poems as if they were letters written to me, and I wrote poems back as answers. In a way I've been doing the same ever since." I have shared this quote with students and encouraged response to it. I then read aloud several poems, suggesting children try to do what Linda Pastan does. "Imagine," I say, "that these poems are letters written directly to you. You can write a response to the ones that stand out. You can write poems as letters back to the poets." Writing a response as an imagined letter to the poet did enable several reluctant writers to discover a new way to put pen to paper.

Ducky by Eve Bunting, illustrated by David Wisniewski, is the story of a crate of bathtub toys that washes overboard during a storm, and one feisty yellow plastic duck that floats all the way to shore. When I first read the book, I thought it would be particularly appropriate for our early-childhood students, but then I read the author's note and had that feeling, "Hey our big kids could do that!" In the note, acclaimed and accomplished writer Eve Bunting explains that the story is based on a real event. A crate of plastic bathtub toy animals, en route from Hong Kong to Washington State, did wash overboard, and scientists have been tracking their whereabouts to learn about currents, winds, and tides. The news story inspired the author to create this fictional account. I wondered if our students could do likewise and suggested to our fifth graders that they begin clipping the kind of newspaper articles in which they saw the potential for a children's picture book. Our files filled with such stories as a New York shopkeeper who collects nautical "junk," a Poughkeepsie detective who cares for a family in Mexico, an explanation of how local streets get their names, the death of the man who delivered diphtheria serum by dogsled relay to Nome, Alaska, during the 1925 epidemic, the promise of a tree to any homeowner who requests one, and the life of a man who works as an underwater inspector. Classroom discussions centered on what it would take to turn these newsworthy nuggets into well-developed picture books, aimed at an elementary school audience, complete with satisfying plot, design, and language.

Fifth-grade teacher Judy Davis turned the task into a whole-class assignment based on only one news article, the story of a Manhattan veterinarian who cared for exotic pets and was about to lose the lease on his office. Judy's fifth graders broke into small clusters, each group deciding on how they would let this kernel of an idea become a picture book. One of the most clever of the finished products included a big book involving animal characters from children's literature that needed to visit the veterinarian. Poor Spot had the chicken pox, Corduroy felt itchy, the Cat in the Hat had a stomachache from eating too much "Green Eggs and Ham" and "Chicken Soup with Rice," the Very Hungry Caterpillar lost his appetite, and so on.

Literature That Demonstrates Distinctive Differences in Craft

Many small research projects begin for me when I come across a piece of literature that deals with a kind of topic that many of our students might choose to write about and yet the piece sounds so different from the work that students generally do. I necessarily ask myself, "What makes this sound different? What is this author doing that our students are not doing? Can they learn to do this?"

For example, one day I was reading Beverly and David Fiday's *Time to Go*, the story of a young farm child saying good-bye to the farm his family is leaving. Certainly, many of our students choose to write about their experiences of having to move away from a place they love, be it an apartment in their city neighborhood, another state in our country, or their faraway homelands.

I told our fifth graders that in addition to the very precise and strong choice of words in the book, I was taken by the authors' use of the conditional tense. The book is filled with "I'd like to" thoughts. The child would like to put down fresh straw in the barn, would like to end the blackbirds' noisy squabble, would like to find a lush green pasture for his cow, and so on. He can't do any of these things because of course, as the title suggests, it is time to go. I realized that our older students rarely rethink an experience, an event, or a place by using this grammatical structure and taking such a reflective stance. I challenged the students to use the pages of their notebook to explore something they would like to do, but for some reason can't.

Students found the challenge a fairly easy one. Their topics were varied, but all their pages were studded with the words "I'd like." This structure allowed them to think new thoughts. They wrote of old neighborhoods they would like to live in again, grandparents they would like to spend more time with, younger stages of life they'd like to return to, and family trips they would like to relive. This grammatical challenge enabled the students to produce writing containing hitherto untapped topics, moods, and perspectives.

Kate wrote,

Vermont

I'd love to have stayed
In that warm white house
With trickling streams outside,
And sweet old grandparents inside.

I'd love to have stayed
To learn how to drive that old tractor
And help fix the ancient barn door.

I'd love to have stayed
And eat marshmallow sandwiches
Everyday for lunch,
And walk the dog with grandpa,
And catch frogs at the lake.

I'd love to have stayed
And help on the farm,
And garden some flowers.

I'd love to have stayed
In that warm white house
With those sweet old grandparents
And eat marshmallow sandwiches for lunch.

Playing with this one grammatical structure led to continued study in our upper grades with teachers and students searching for additional literature that contained the "I would" stance. We discovered several different categories of usage, and each pattern inspired the students to try very different types of writing.

William and the Good Old Days by Eloise Greenfield is not filled with "I would *like*" thoughts, but rather with sentences beginning, "I would" or simply, "I'd." The young main character is looking back at an experience and using the phrase to explain what he used to do time and again. When William used to visit his grandmother's restaurant, the author writes, "I'd pick out *any* kind of juice I wanted. And after I drank it, I'd wash my hands and go help Grandma fold the napkins. When we finished, I'd lean over a little bit and hold my stomach." Again, the introduction and elevation of this structure inspired students to choose very new topics. Instead of their usual "One day . . ." accounts, they chose events that took place over and over again in their lives, occurrences that were memorable, familiar, and meaningful.

I even collected picture books that were filled with more fanciful and imaginative "I would" thinking. Lezlie Evans' *If I Were the Wind* is filled with "I would" promises made by a mother to her young child. The author includes such statements as, "If I were a coat I'd protect you from the cold" and, "If I were a book I would tell you a tale." Similarly, Margaret Park Bridges' picture books *If I Were Your Mother* and *If I Were Your Father*, with illustrations by Kady MacDonald Denton, present engaging "If I were . . . I would" conversations between children and parents, based on a reversal of roles. Fred Hiatt's *If I Were Queen of the World*, with illustrations by Mark Graham, contains page after page of plans the young girl would carry out if she were queen. Lindsay Barrett George's *My Bunny and Me* presents a young boy's imagining about what he would be able to do if only the bunny he drew were real. The very simple design provides a supportive structure for students to borrow.

Crescent Dragonwagon's picture book *Diana, Maybe* is also filled with "I would" thoughts as the main character imagines life with a half-sister she has never met. Her thoughts, however, are grounded in reality. She is not imagining something entirely out of reach, she simply wants to have a sister in her life, someone she could tell riddles to, accompany on shopping trips, and borrow clothes from.

Poems can provide similar structures. Zaro Weil's, "If It Were My Birthday," is filled with "I'd" phrases, each introducing a fantastic intention. The structure of Judith Viorst's poem "If I Were in Charge of the World . . ." invites writers to share dreamlike and imaginative thoughts.

What began as a small find in one picture book led to a search for related constructions in others, and on to new challenges for student writers. When teachers are able to make the time to read and respond to children's literature in the company of their colleagues, additional crafting techniques will surface (see list below). Perhaps one teacher will notice how one author stretches small moments of time out and then invites colleagues to search for similar literature examples. Placing these resources side by side will enable teachers to name the techniques used and decide which ones would be appropriate for their students to try if taught, encouraged, and supported to do so. Additionally, if teachers have time to plan their lessons together, deciding on the best ways to convey new writing information to children, the results will be even greater for both children and teachers.

Noting Additional Crafting Techniques

You're reading, and you notice fairly simple techniques and stylistic devices that you have never seen your children use. You sense that your students could learn these techniques and their use would make their writing richer. These might include learning to.

- use repeated refrains
- write endings that circle back to beginnings
- learn to write in satisfying clusters of three (e.g., *From my bedroom window, I can see my grandma's apartment house across the street, the tops of the trees in Central Park, and the lights from the Empire State Building.*)
- switch from generic background information to particular occurrences (e.g., *My apartment building is filled with elderly people. There is no one for me to play with. When I come home from school all I do is watch T.V, play solitaire, read books, do homework, or sit at the computer. It's just me, myself, and I. One day a new neighbor arrived who changed all that.*)
- ask questions in the middle of description or narration (e.g., *My grandma's kitchen is packed with food. There's hardly any space left in the refrigerator. It's hard to find what you are looking for in the cupboards. Even the countertops are covered with boxes, jars, and cans. How does grandma stay so thin?*)

(See Appendix 1 for a bibliography of picture books that support teaching about crafting techniques.)

Sharing the Work of Writers in the Community

Sharing literature to demonstrate crafting options should also include sharing work done by members of the community, grown-ups and children alike.

One day I walked in on Amy Usis, a teacher doing professional development work in our district. (She is actually called a "distinguished teacher," a title given to expert teachers who are challenged to live alongside two teachers in a school with many at-risk youngsters, filling their classrooms with exemplary literacy practice.) Amy was showing a child's piece on the overhead projector (see Figure 5.3), pointing out some of the strengths in a fourth-grade English-language learner's piece of writing.

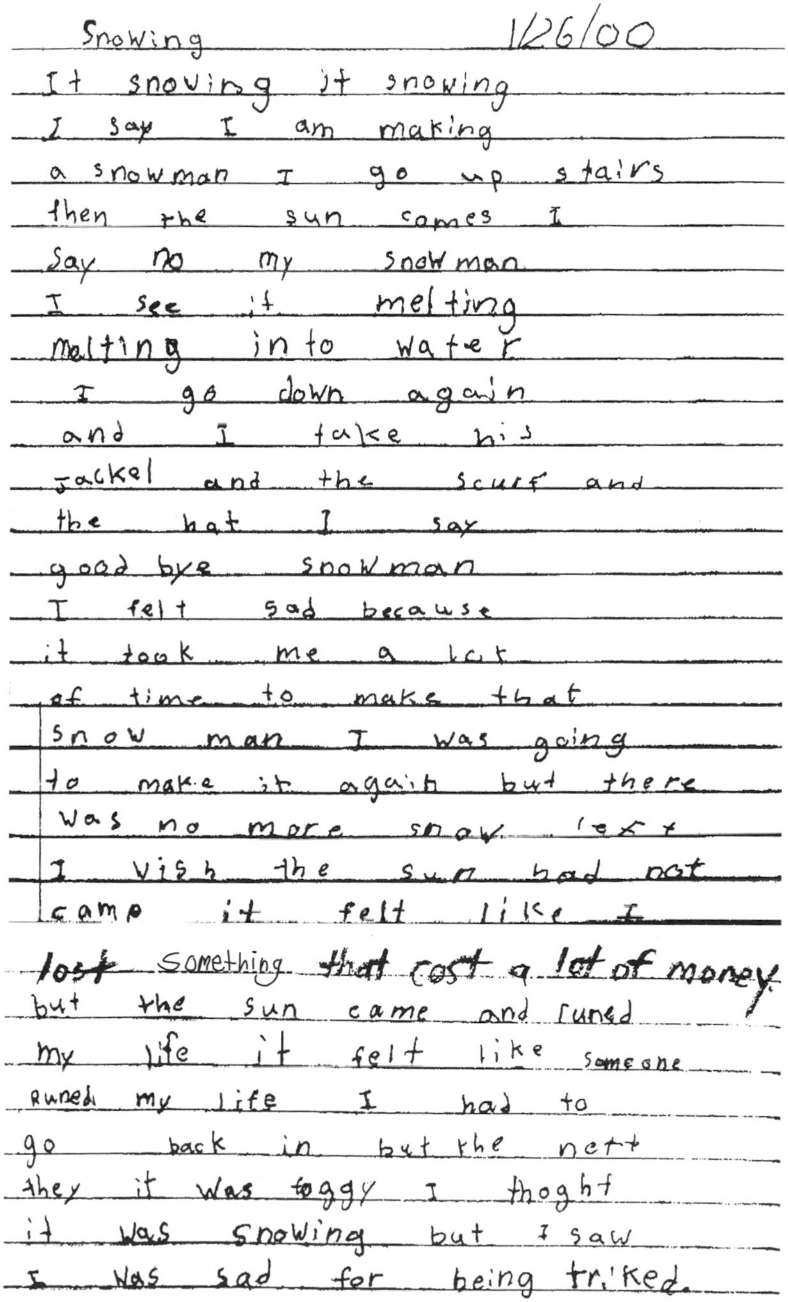

Snowing   1/26/00

It snoving it snowing
I say I am making
a snowman I go up stairs
then the sun comes I
Say no my snow man.
I see it melting
melting into water
I go down again
and I take his
Jackel and the scurf and
the hat I say
good bye snowman
I felt sad because
it took me a lot
of time to make that
snow man I was going
to make it again but there
was no more snow. text
I vish the sun had not
came it felt like I
lost something that cost a lot of money
but the sun came and runed
my life it felt like someone
runed my life I had to
go back in but the nett
they it was foggy I thoght
it was snowing but I saw
I was sad for being triked.

Figure 5.3

I couldn't resist joining the conversation that surrounded this piece of writing. Yes, we could talk to the writer about slowing down as he moved from noticing that it's snowing to building a snowman to going upstairs. Yes, we could talk to the writer about clarifying the last sentence. What did he mean by "I saw I was sad for being tricked?" But more important, we need to do what Amy so wisely did, and begin with this child's strengths as a writer. And we need to talk in such clear and specific ways that everyone in the class can appreciate and attempt, if they so choose, to do what this writer has done.

Amy pointed out that the writer was able to convey strong feelings, and I suggested zooming in to really notice how those feelings were conveyed. For example, the writer used repetition very effectively—"It's snowing, it's snowing . . . I see it melting, melting . . . But the sun came and ruined my life. It felt like someone ruined my life . . ." "Repetition of key words is one way to build feelings," we told the children, "because it says, 'This is really important. This is worth saying twice.'" We also suggested that the writer let us know how he was feeling through his clever use of comparison, as in, "When the snowman melted, he said that it felt like he lost something that cost a lot of money. That idea really helps us to understand how upset he was." Students left the meeting area with two very specific, practical strategies for making their readers feel what they are feeling. In fact, on the very next day, a classmate who was writing about her grandmother's illness, wrote, "My grandmother has cancer, cancer . . ."

Teachers know the pieces that move them, but sometimes struggle with how to describe to students the elements that make those pieces effective. My main suggestion for teachers who struggle is to hang out with teachers who don't. (See learning to talk about good writing on page 145). In my own life, listening to people who talk well about writing is the major way I improve my own ability to talk about good writing, *that* and reading books like those listed in Appendix 1. (Even reading professional books requires time to meet with other teachers to talk about the ideas contained in them. Talking through the ideas of others is the only way I know to allow those ideas to inform one's own work.)

Garth Boomer, the late Australian educator, has suggested that teachers need to cut off the top of their heads and let students look inside. This is true for classroom teachers who share their insights with their students, and it should also be true for people like me who write books for classroom teachers. The following is my attempt to cut off the top of my head and let readers look inside as I talk through what I see in the piece written by Patrick in Figure 5.4. (By the way, I am sure to learn even more if I share this piece of writing with a group of writing teachers, simply by suggesting, "Tell me what you see.")

The standard spelling version of Patrick's piece is as follows:

My cat Hunter is the cat I have always wanted. He is gray and he has green eyes and a white belly, and black stripes and black spots on his belly. He has a pink little nose. When me and my dad were in the process of moving Hunter got lost. He was so scared. He was lost for a very long time. I was worried about him. He was buried behind some shoes in the closet with the door closed. But the way life is we found him. For a minute there, he felt like he had goosebumps. But he did not have goosebumps because he had fur. When I think of brushing my teeth, I get goosebumps and when I think of someone's nails scratching a car I think of goosebumps. Oh and P.S. same thing with a chalkboard.

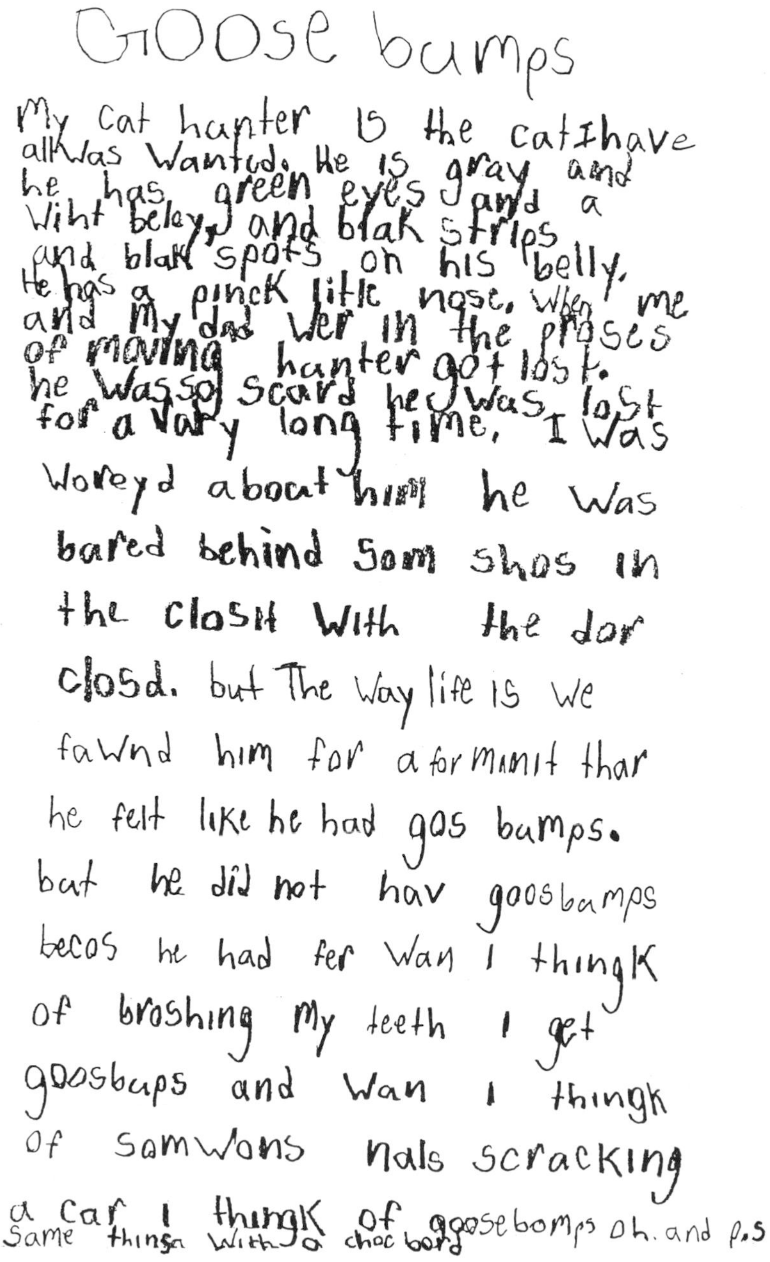

Figure 5.4

I was at first put off by the title of Patrick's piece, thinking it was going to be just a run-of-the-mill retelling of yet another *Goosebumps* story. I was relieved to find a story about real goosebumps. Children's titles can be misleading. I must point out to children that titles do count.

I had to remember to *not* let Patrick's spelling keep me from appreciating how interesting he is and what a good writer he is. That's not to say that I am not concerned about his spelling. Of course I am, and I need to plan for his growth as a speller, but not at the expense of his self-esteem as a writer. I must be sure that Patrick knows what a good writer he is even though he has difficulty using standard spelling.

I love his opening sentence, "My cat Hunter is the cat I have always wanted." It is so different from what children usually write, the very predictable, "I have a cat named Hunter."

I appreciated his description, as well. The repetition of the words *black* and *belly* added to the music of the piece. I also like the unusual "pink little nose," as opposed to the more usual "little pink nose."

I would love to talk to him about that early line, "He was so scared." It seems misplaced. How did he know then that the cat was scared? Doesn't that belong as a comment after he finds him? Or does he mean, "I bet he was so scared"?

Similarly, does the wonderful line about finding him "behind some shoes, in the closet, with the door closed" (great buildup of detail), belong *after* "we found him"?

I adored the, "But the way life is . . ." line, right in the middle of the piece. It was a great and surprising way to shift to the good news.

Patrick's voice comes shining through in this piece. In addition to "But the way life is . . . ," I loved, "For a minute there . . . ," and "Oh and P.S . . ." He has a very comfortable, conversational tone.

I also loved Patrick's willingness to shift to the topic of getting goosebumps, giving such rich sensory details. This section was such a total surprise, even though the title gave a hint of what was to come. It's rare that children juxtapose such contrasting images. Who would expect to read about brushing one's teeth in a piece about a lost cat? That's the magic of this piece for me. As a reader, I just love to be surprised.

I can't stress enough the importance of teachers making copies of those pieces of student writing that, over the years, have appealed to their taste as readers. Teachers need especially to hold onto the ones that contain possible crafting lessons for other students. A three-ring binder filled with these student works, placed on acetates for overhead display, would be as powerful as the minilesson scrapbook described earlier.

In addition to student writing, teachers can share work written by the adult members of the community, including parents, colleagues, and administrators. I was taken by surprise one day to enter David Besancon's fourth-grade class at the Manhattan New School to discover that he was sharing with students a draft of a short article I had recently written for our school's column in *The New Advocate*. (This lead appears in the fall 1998 issue). I was returning to work after a short illness, and decided to use a hand-written note attached to the draft as a way of thanking the teachers for their kindnesses. David made copies for all the students so that they could jot their questions down, write in the margins, and underline parts they wanted to talk about.

I wrote:

Last winter I had a short stay in the hospital. The bag I packed brimmed with books. I tucked in those I hoped to read before the surgery took place and those I hoped to read afterwards. I must admit, reading for me in the hospital turned out to be not reading at all. The room was so sterile, bland and boring. The interruptions were endless—temperature, blood pressure, medication, and loudspeaker announcements. And I was so uncomfortable, anxious and hungry before the surgery, in pain and sleepy afterwards. For me, there was no such thing as curling up with a good book in a hospital. But then I came home.

I felt awful about being away from school. I felt awful about not being able to sit at the computer and work on some chapters for a book that was long overdue. I felt awful about having kept the news of my surgery from my mother. Mostly, I felt awful about the pain that ensued each time I tried to raise or lower my body. But then there were my books.

I didn't want to watch television. I didn't want to listen to music. I didn't even want to talk on the telephone. I didn't want any remotes, headsets, wires or buttons. I wanted no plastic, only paper in my hands. I simply wanted to ease myself onto that familiar couch in my favorite room in the house and get totally lost in other people's worlds. Reading brought me solace, comfort, nourishment and escape. I was in charge of the selection, the pace, the duration and the pictures in my mind's eye. I only heard the wind outside and the pages turning inside. I also had my favorite view out the window whenever the author made me pause to think about my own life or the lives of others.

I learned from Charles Frazier's *Cold Mountain* what it was like to fight for survival during the Civil War. I learned from Doris Lessing's *Love, Again* what it is like to be sixty-five and falling in love. I learned from Doris Kearns Goodwin's memoir *Wait Till Next Year* what it was like to grow up as a passionate Brooklyn Dodgers fan in the 1950's. I learned from Virginia Hamilton Adair's poetry collection, *Ants on the Melon*, to look at the world with new eyes and insights. I learned from Mitch Albom's *Tuesdays with Morrie*, to be ever so grateful to have left the hospital and ready to appreciate each day anew.

Of course, I missed my colleagues and my students, but I was filling my life with other compelling people who had passions, challenges, conflicts, strengths and weaknesses. And the lives of these literary companions would of course inform my role as school principal when I returned to work.

Reading got me through my post-operative pain and for the last three years I have been watching how reading has gotten my daughter through law school. Of course she reads her required legal texts, but at the gym, on long weekends, and her frequent train rides back to New York, my daughter reads the novels I send her way. Will she be a better attorney because she has understood the abused child in Keri Hulme's *The Bone People?*, marital relationships in Carol Shields' *Happenstance?*, family forgiveness in Rebecca Wells' *The Divine Secrets of the YaYa Sisterhood?*, the struggles of a young Japanese woman in Arthur Golden's *Memoirs of a Geisha?*, and religious persecution and bigotry in Pete Hamill's *Snow in August?* Of course she will. She will be a more compassionate daughter, sister, girl-friend, neighbor, colleague, as well as attorney because she lets her life be touched and informed by the people around her, both real and fictional.

And then there are the youngsters in our care. Will reading do for them what it does for me and for my daughter? Will they be better doctors, carpenters, musicians, teachers, bus drivers, librarians, architects, and politicians because they read? Of course they will if we do things right. I couldn't read in a sterile room filled with interruptions, anxiety, hunger and discomfort. Nor can the students in our classrooms. If we expect the students in front of us to look to reading for pleasure and solace in their adult lives, we need to give them the gift of reading today. We need to create beautiful reading rooms with calm, uninterrupted reading hours. Above all we need to fill our bookcases with the best books available. I wouldn't have attempted to read if my bedside didn't boast the best novelists, journalists, historians and poets. When we have the best books, and use them in thoughtful and well-informed ways, our children will need their favorite views out the window. Their reading will inspire them to pause and think deeply about their own lives and the lives of others. Isn't that what reading is for?

I scrawled the following handwritten note at the bottom of the page.

March 9, 1998

Dear friends,

I have nothing to show for my week away except the above few paragraphs and some incisions in my middle. (Of course, the latter are not for show.)

Thanks for all your kind calls, cards, books, etc.

I hope this brief writing gives you a feel for my days in the hospital and at home.

Love,
Shelley

I didn't stay long enough in David's room to hear what the children had to say about my writing. (I was afraid my presence cramped their style. After all, they probably wouldn't critique their principal to her face. Then too, I wasn't sure I even wanted to hear what they liked, knowing that I always think of ways to improve my writing each time I look back and reread.) My guess is that David wanted them to hear the content, the pro-reading stance, as much as he wanted them to look at my writing style. If I were leading the discussion, perhaps I would point out the following very noticeable techniques:

- The last sentence of each paragraph serves as an invitation to read more ("But then I came home" and, "But then there were my books)."

- There are many lists of concrete details within sentences (perhaps too many)— "temperature, blood pressure, medication, and loudspeaker announcements" and "remotes, headsets, wires and buttons." To me, these kind of chock-filled sentences always seem to hit the reader over the head, calling out, "Pay attention to this part!"

- There are many sensory details. I wanted the reader to feel the paper in my hands, hear the sound of the wind outside, and see that view out the window.

- There are several series of sentences beginning with repeated phrases ("I felt awful about," "I didn't want to," and "I learned from"). I think I let my ear do the editing. Those repeated phrases just sound right to me, adding threads to hold the content together.
- My ending circled back to the beginning, repeating, "I couldn't read in a sterile room filled with interruptions, anxiety, hunger and discomfort. Nor can the students in our classrooms."

Teachers in the upper elementary grades will find that studying appropriate works written by adults in the school community carries extra rewards. When I entered David's classroom that day, I sensed that students were totally engaged in this discussion. Their enthusiasm was not because the writing was so powerful, but because their principal had written it and they were interested in knowing what I had to say and how I said it. I also think that they took it as a compliment that David shared with them a note intended for teachers. Later that day, when passing me in the hall, many students acknowledged that they had read my writing. Our fourth graders were committed writers now with the utmost respect for others that took their writing seriously.

Teachers need not be in schoolhouses with published writers in order to share adult writing. At a minimum, principals write letters to the staff, teachers write letters to parents, parents write articles for the school newspaper. If teachers don't think any of these are worthy of sharing with children, then perhaps the conversation needs to turn to the quality of our own writing and the need for adults to do what we ask children to do. How can we ask children to write with grace and attempt to move an audience when we don't think about those things when we write whatever we write?

A Closer Look at Student-Driven Reading-Writing Connections

The point of surrounding students with wonderful literature and engaging them in conversations about what makes those pieces work, is for students to internalize the process and begin making connections on their own.

Children like Maeve, the kindergarten author of the book about telephones on page 24, seem to make these connections early and naturally, without teacher intervention. Maeve is a prime example of a child who has come to school filled with the sound, shape, and feel of literature. Her connections to the books she has been read to show up in her speech and in her play, and then they effortlessly spill out onto paper when she begins to write. Making the literary world part of her everyday world seems to come as naturally to this five-year-old as reaching for her parents' hands when crossing a city street.

Haden, a third grader, wrote "The Rainbow in the Cupboard," an innovation on *The Indian in the Cupboard*. Her eleven-page book began, "Once upon a time there was a medium sized girl who always wanted to help other people." Her parents proudly sent me a copy of the book, which was written for pleasure at home, with the following note attached:

> *Shelley!*
>
> *Haden and I wanted to share this with you. This is all Haden's creation! Bill and I are completely blown away by what she's done! Don't miss the inside of the back book jacket titled "About the Author." It certainly confirms for us your concepts and dreams for Manhattan New School are working!*
>
> *Kempy Minifie*

Of course, not many children choose to spend their free time rewriting their favorite books. For the ones that do, the rewards are great. Today, Haden is a very accomplished writer. In the fall of her senior year at the Manhattan New School, she wrote the family scene that appears in Figure 5.5.

Shelby Wolf and Shirley Brice Heath, in the fall 1998 issue of *The New Advocate*, make a strong case for children learning from the literature they hear and read. They note, "Good writers have important things they want to say and many of these stem from their own life experience and creative imagination. Still, we argue that they will be better equipped to say these things if they are given multiple opportunities to read, discuss, and lean on established texts in creating and recreating their own forms of authorship." (See the use of writing templates in Chapter 6, "Working with Our Youngest Writers," and discussion of borrowing specific elements from authors in Chapter 8, "The Writing Workshop: A Place to Experiment, Improvise, and Invent." Their important research documents the ways two young girls have benefited from "rewriting" both the poetry and prose they have heard or read.

For the majority of our students, who don't seem to automatically connect what they read or hear to what they write, we must design classroom interactions that support such connections. The point of the two previous sections, those describing assessment-driven and text-driven reading-writing connections, has in fact been to help children take such writing lessons from high-quality texts. It is hoped that children will learn from the deliberate moves designed by their teachers and eventually will sit in the driver's seat, reading like writers on their own.

Here, I'd like to explore additional classroom practices that encourage more students to make their own reading-writing connections.

• It almost seems too obvious to note, but more children will take crafting lessons from their reading if we suggest that they do. We need to be upfront with students, perhaps saying such things as, "Whenever you are reading and admire something the author has done, be sure to take notes on it, copy the passage down in your writer's notebook, or ask me to make a copy of the page. Know that it is more than okay for you to try to do what that writer has done."

It was a windy mournful rainy-day. "There's nothing to do" I shouted! I flopped on the couch with an empty brain. Bored; I went into my bedroom and asked my sister if she would play a game with me. "Sure"! "How about make-believe"! "Okay". We opened up the dress-up bins and pulled all the clothes out and dumped them on the floor. "Let's be princesses." Colby said. We both picked out beautiful robes and scarves. Hats dresses gloves, and shoes. Last of all, we picked out our best crowns and gracefully set them on our heads. Then we proceede in the hallway. Walking with our chin up, head high, back straight, and pointed toes. We walked draaintly into the kitchen to my mom who was making dinner. "What's for dinner today cook"? we asked. "Green beans and rice for tonight your majesties". answered mom. "Very very good." said Colby. "We will be sitting in our parlor thrones having tea with our friends! Just remember to have our royal supper on the dinning room table in five minutes"! When we were settled having pretend tea, Colby said to me, "I wish we really were princesses. Living in beautiful castles and having sevents. I could stand in the mirror all day and admire myself". "Well" I said. "I'd love to be a travler who would who would go seeking her future. She would meet new people and have more friends". "I'd love to be a princess one day though". Suddenly, dad called, "Haden and Colby, time to fold laundry"! We gloomily walked over to the living room and folded the shirts, dresses, sweatshirts, and pants. We realized that we were not princesses anymore.

Figure 5.5

- When we confer with students about the books they are reading, we can include questions that probe their reading-writing connections. Of course, *after* discussing the content of the books and their responses to them, we can ask such questions as:

1. What do you think of this author's style?
2. Are there things this author has done that you would like to do?
3. Are there parts in this book you are envious of, wishing you had written them?

4. Are there places you found yourself rereading because the text was so well written?

5. Did you stop to read aloud any lines or sections to your family or friends, or wish someone was around so that you could share these parts?

6. Did you have the urge to copy any parts into your writer's notebook so you could reread and study them?

• Whenever children note that they have learned something about writing from their reading, we need to publicly acknowledge such work and give the students time to tell the story of their connections. We can follow children's leads when they express an interest in a particular author. Would this author be an appropriate choice for an author study attached to the writing workshop? In other words, can children take crafting lessons from this author? We can post students' attempts at imitating, borrowing, and otherwise learning from other writers, including classmates. Student excerpts can sit alongside those of professional writers. Examples can be posted on charts or bound in scrapbooks for future reference.

• We can clear up the difference between plagiarism and learning from other writers. We can also introduce such phrases as "Retold by . . ." or "Inspired by . . ." Remember, children are not carrying around legal contracts when they publish. They are still rookies, not ready for the major leagues.

• When we read aloud parodies, versions, fractured stories, and takeoffs, we can acknowledge that these are kinds of writing that published authors do. We can tell students that although we don't want a steady diet of these, it's okay for students to try them once in a while if they so choose.

• In writing conferences and at share meetings, we can remember to ask students about their sources of inspiration. We can celebrate a wide range of ways that students get ideas for their writing topics and their writing techniques, including literary ones.

• Teachers who make their own reading-writing connections need to serve as models, encouraging students to do likewise.

• When children write in very literary ways and we sense that they have learned much from at-home reading, we can invite family members in to share some of the literature that has made a difference in their children's writing.

• When we speak to students or eavesdrop on their conversations or moments of dramatic play and we hear elements of literary "talk," without making students self-conscious, we can remind them that those qualities can be woven into their writing.

• We can invite children to keep a journal about the connections they make between what they read and what they write.

• We can invite children to keep a writer's practice book, a separate place for them to save all their attempts at learning from writers. Such a container will elevate the practice.

• Whenever student writing, for whatever reason, brings to mind the work of a published writer, we can serve as matchmaker, encouraging students to enter mentor relationships.

A Closer Look at Course-of-Study-Driven Reading-Writing Connections

When teachers sense that a particular quality of good writing is making a big difference in students' writing, they might choose to delve deeper, turning a quick minilesson into a well-thought-out course of study. For example, teachers could decide to devote big blocks of time to studying such issues as the use of precise verbs, authentic dialogue, or telling details. In addition to reading aloud texts that illustrate these qualities, teachers might highlight these elements in read-alouds, inquire about them during individual reading and writing conferences, and assign homework that requires students to keep up the search for additional examples. Teachers might also expect students to apply what they are learning to the finished pieces of writing they are currently producing. (See Appendix 1 for professional literature that supports the teaching of specific writing techniques.)

Other courses of study that rely heavily on reading to inform writing include the very popular author study. Teachers need to search for those authors whose writing demonstrates what is within students' reach. Then they need to extend gracious invitations for students to borrow freely from these silent partners, wrapping students in support as they do so. (See *Lasting Impressions* for more information on conducting author studies. Additionally, in Chapter 8, "The Writing Workshop: A Place to Experiment, Improvise, and Invent," I include an in-depth study of the author Jonathan London. This course of study is included in this later chapter because, perhaps surprisingly, I invited second graders and fifth graders to work *together* to learn from an author.)

Formal genre studies, of course, require immersing children in many examples from literature. In *Lifetime Guarantees*, I present several essential steps in a poetry course of study. These include surrounding students with a wide range of poems, reading them aloud over and over again, inviting students to make their own discoveries, providing structures for students to save and savor their discoveries, helping children find the words to talk about what they admire in poems, helping children form mentor relationships with favorite poets, and providing students with a rich toolbox of poetry techniques.

The above suggestions apply as well to any genre study. Even the study of birthday cards in a kindergarten classroom could involve asking students to study cards they love and attempt to use the techniques employed. (I have seen young children attempt to make birthday cards in the shape of a big 5 or 6, create slots for coins, decorate with sparkles, and add funny rhyming verse.) At the Manhattan New School, in addition to poetry, other popular genre studies include picture books and many formats of nonfiction and real-world writing as described in detail in *Lifetime Guarantees*. (See also Appendix 1 for a listing of picture books in letter format.)

Teachers can also design courses of study related to areas of inquiry. Once again, children's literature plays a central role. For example, when students study water as part of their science curriculum or immigration in social studies, all members of the school community can scan library shelves gathering all the different ways people have written about these topics. In addition to realizing genre options, children will, no doubt, pick up additional content information as well as crafting techniques. Similarly, when children seem to be writing a great deal about grandparents, pets, or new babies in the family, teachers can create study stacks related to these topics.

Learning to Talk with Confidence and Competence About Quality Texts

Teachers of writing need content knowledge, pedagogical know-how, as well as skill in creating scholarly communities. Among the many requisite elements of content knowledge is considerable expertise in knowing what makes for good writing. If school communities are to take pride in their teaching of writing, it is important that all members of the faculty be well informed about the qualities of good writing. The adults in our community are able to select choice literature, present effective minilessons, and make helpful conference suggestions because they study good writing. Caring about students' abilities to make reading-writing connections demands taking care of teachers' own abilities to make connections between the literature they share with students and the literature they coach students to compose.

Imagine how much more powerful writing teachers would be if they had many opportunities to listen to experts talk about texts, especially well-written ones. I believe that my own confidence in talking about writing stems from having had the opportunity to listen to such gifted writers as Georgia Heard, Ralph Fletcher, Dorothy Barnhouse, and Vicki Vinton talk about writing during our days at the Teachers College Writing Project. I listened, learned, marveled, and eventually joined in. I not only learned about elements of good writing but I learned fresh ways of talking about writing and myriad ways of being a critical reader of writing. (That experience was so helpful to me as a writing teacher that I am currently working on a book titled *Great Minds Don't Think Alike: Writers Look at Student Writing*, in which I ask accomplished writers to observe what they see in student work. I think readers will be quite surprised by what different experts notice and how they describe what they see in any one piece of writing.)

Today, I firmly believe that all teachers of writing need similar learning experiences. Teachers of writing need to learn from reading professional books on crafting, from listening to the experts who speak at colleges and conferences, as well as from listening to one another. In other words, teachers need time to pull together to look at texts and discuss what they see. (As a fringe benefit, teachers would become familiar with the resources in their own school that are probably only a few footsteps away from their own classroom door.)

Prompting Staff Members to Talk About Good Writing

Occasionally I come across a wine review in the newspaper. I might have on some occasion even tasted that very wine reviewed. I may have even thought the wine delicious, but there is absolutely no way I could have talked about that wine in the way wine connoisseurs can. I simply can't spot "an intense buttery aroma and a scent of yeast, with a soft, smooth taste, good fruit, and medium body." I'd need a lot more experience in sampling a wide variety of wines. I'd need experts to point out the finest examples. I'd need to hear the words used to describe what I was tasting. I'd need to able to say, "So that's a woody flavor, the plummy scent of cassis, a fleshy body, a long moderate finish, and well-integrated tannins." In other words, I'd need a lot more familiarity with wines, the language used to talk about wines, and confidence in my taste as a consumer of wine. Teachers of writing need the same—not to drink more wine, but to sample, discuss, and refine their tastes as readers of good writing.

If my staff felt ill at ease talking about good writing, I would refer back to my days as a staff developer. In my previous work, I often met with people who felt awkward when asked to talk about good writing. They were insecure about their opinions. They were sure other people had more technical knowledge and more sophisticated tastes as readers. Talking about good writing brought to mind images of their old college days when only the professor had the right answers and understood what made for quality texts.

Through the years, at workshops, conferences, summer institutes, and staff meetings, I've relied on several prompts to free people to talk naturally about what they admire when they read. Some can easily be used with students as well. These are discussed below.

Share Well-Written Literature Excerpts from Surprising Places

This activity could become a ritual at staff meetings. You can open or close meetings by sharing a short, surprising piece. When the pieces don't resemble standard selections from literature, people seem to be less intimidated and more willing to talk about what they admire.

One September I returned to school, eager to share samples of literature I had acquired on my summer travels. One was a daily menu from Mufaletta's, a restaurant in Saint Paul, Minnesota. It was written by the chef, Zach Bredemann, and began as follows:

Today's Soup

Life can be a series of tough decisions. Relax with the knowledge that your soup does not have to be one of those. Enjoy a cup or a bowl of Minnesota-grown chicken and wild rice soup and leave those tough decisions for Monday.

As the menu continued, the chef described the daily special, pasta and fish, with as much voice and vitality as he had the soup.

I also shared the note appearing in Figure 5.6, which Joanne, Judy, and I received in our packet of evaluations after teaching a summer institute in Denver, Colorado. The note was written by Norton Moore, a participant in the institute. Norton's writing is not only very complimentary and clever, it is also filled with strong images and lyrical language.

Evaluation of an Approved Inservice Program

Explain how the workshop did/did not meet your expectations.

Dear Shelley, Joanne and Judy,

I read in the paper that New York City ships its sewage sludge to Colorado. This material is used as fertilizer on our farms. You are a distinct and delightful change from what New York usually sends us. But just like that other bounty, your visit will bring forth a rich harvest on our rocky soil.

Do you have any questions? Would you like a response from the instructor?

— Norton Moore,
Ponderosa School, Cherry Creek

(Optional)   Name _____
              School _____

Other Comments:

Figure 5.6

Judi Klein, our school secretary, brought me the following piece of writing done by her mother-in-law, a poet named Doris Klein, when the local fish-store display caught this grandmother-poet's eye.

Each day as I pass the local fish store, I am treated to an ichthyological feast! /The artist who makes this beautiful window display uses his fish palette according to the gems he has on hand. Yesterday, it looked like this:/ In the center, a shark's head lay open, and from its ivory teeth, small pearl scallops spilled onto the shaved diamond ice. On one side, a large cauliflower with jade leaves was encircled by coral salmon steaks. Fresh shucked oysters, pale as opals, preened against the shimmer of smelts./At the bottom tier, lobsters, bold as rubies, were set into ruffled lettuce dresses. Amber sea urchins, with their whiskers, tickled clams on the half shell./The store? Citarella./The artist? Fernando./The prices? Same as Tiffany's.

Share Published Anthologies from Other Schools

Over the years, many people have sent us copies of their school literary magazines. These are usually filled with their students' best efforts and so it is easy to talk about the pieces that move us. At the same time, there are usually a few pieces that fall short of being as particularly effective as the others. People are usually reluctant to talk about pieces that were written in their colleagues' workshops, particularly if the pieces show any signs of needing improvement. Somehow it's a lot easier to talk about what writers may have done to improve their writing if the people involved are unknown to us.

Pair Student Writing with Published Writing

Every teacher can be asked to bring to a staff meeting one piece of student writing and one piece of published professional writing that share a similar quality. Teachers can explain their choices, trying to use the same language to talk about both pieces.

Think Through Published Adult Writing and Student Writing Alongside Information from Professional Writers

I've shared Don Murray's classic list of qualities of good writing and then asked teachers to think about these qualities as they apply to a popular children's picture book as well as a successful piece of student writing. In *Learning by Teaching: Selected Articles on Writing and Teaching,* Murray talks about the qualities of "meaning, authority, voice, development, design and clarity," which he says apply to fiction, nonfiction, and poetry.

Look at Published Adult Writing and Student Writing Alongside Quotes About Writing from Famous Writers

Similar to the activity described above, teachers can be asked to hold a piece of student writing or a piece of published writing in one hand and a sheet filled with quotable quotes about good writing in the other. They can look for examples of these qualities in the writing selections or places where the writers might have benefited from these bits of advice. The sheet might include such classic gems as:

> "Don't write about man, write about a man." —E. B. White
>
> "No surprise for the writer, no surprise for the reader." —Carl Sandburg
>
> "While it is the business of the scientist to make the marvelous commonplace, it is the business of the artist to make the commonplace marvelous." —Leon Garfield
>
> "Don't say the lady screamed, bring her out and let her scream." —Mark Twain
>
> "The more particular you are, the more specific you are, the more universal you are." —Nancy Hale

Use Standards Vignettes or Writing Samples as a Springboard

Hardly a day goes by when I don't receive an article, envelope, or binder filled with information on yet another standards document. For me, the most interesting and valuable part of these deliveries are the classroom vignettes and student writing samples. Such questions as, "Could this happen here?" "Would we want this kind of work here?" and "How does this differ from our own expectations?" can get staff conversations going.

Read a Piece of Children's Literature Alongside a Published Review of the Work

Reviews make wonderful conversation starters because we often totally disagree with the reviewer or we are pleased with the review but amazed that we didn't notice many of the things that the reviewer did. Well-written reviews also give us new ways to name the qualities we admire. Sometimes we don't realize that the language we are using is becoming predictable, almost trite. It's helpful to hear a new voice talk about writing from a fresh point of view. It's also helpful to ask teachers to write their own reviews. This is a powerful way to help educators feel comfortable talking about good writing. Perhaps staff members can write a review column for the school newsletter, a local newspaper, a neighborhood bookstore, or a professional publication.

Treat a Piece of Student Writing as Literature

Select a strong piece of student writing, then duplicate it (with student permission) and distribute it as reading material. Encourage teachers gathered to respond personally to the piece as they would any piece of literature. After group talk, reread the piece in order to talk about the qualities of good writing it displays. Remind participants to keep their conversations cliché-free. In other words, encourage teachers to talk about their observations without using the overused labels that inhibit our thinking (e.g., "colorful words," "descriptive language").

There are numerous benefits to sharing a piece of student writing with the entire staff. First, student writing reminds us what a joy it is to be around children. We get to see the world through very young eyes. Former teachers delight in noting growth over time for individual writers. Studying one piece for a considerable length of time also affords us the luxury of really paying attention to the student's strengths as a writer, not taking our usual stance of helping the writer improve the piece. Sharing one piece of writing with an entire staff can also be quite eye-opening and for some quite humbling. Not all teachers will see the same things. One person might cite a strength another considers a weakness. Teachers will realize that responding to writing, even quality writing, is an art, not a science. Great minds really do not think alike. (See also response to Patrick's "Goosebumps" piece on page 142).

Reading-Writing Connections: That's What It's All About

While visiting the Hage school in San Diego, I was struck by a very funny sign hanging in the staff restroom. It read, "What if the Hokey Pokey really *is* what it's all about?" Those of us who have been teaching and learning about improving children's writing know better. We would probably agree that making reading-writing connections is really what it's all about. Learning to read like a writer, reading to inform your writing, apprenticing yourself to a favorite writer, feeling envious when you read great writing, feeling confident talking about quality writing—that's what it's all about.

(See *Lasting Impressions: Weaving Literature into the Writing Workshop* for additional information about helping students make significant reading-writing connections, as well as pages 192–193 in this text.)

Related Readings in Companion Volumes

Going Public (Heinemann, 1999) is abbreviated as GP. *Lifetime Guarantees* (Heinemann, 2000) is abbreviated as LG.

Assessment-driven instruction	**GP:** Ch. 6
	LG: Ch. 9
The importance of quality literature	**GP:** Ch. 4
	LG: Ch. 1, Ch. 9
The importance of knowing students well	**GP:** Ch. 2, Ch. 4, Ch. 5
	LG: Ch. 9
Structuring the writing workshop	**LG:** Ch. 2
Nonfiction resources	**LG:** Ch. 4
Poetry resources	**LG:** Ch. 5
Playing with language	**GP:** Ch. 4
	LG. Ch. 10
Adult literacy models	**GP:** Ch. 2
	LG: Ch. 1
Poetry course of study	**LG:** Ch. 5
Teachers learning about literature	**LG:** Ch. 1, Ch. 7

CHAPTER 6

WORKING WITH OUR YOUNGEST WRITERS

I love books. I love books. I love to swallow books.

—Noah, age 6

Key Writing Lessons

1. Early-childhood writing workshops can be described as rigorous comfort zones.
2. The thoughtful launching of the early-childhood writing workshop is crucial to its success.
3. The content of early-childhood writing workshop minilessons changes as the school year progresses.
4. Basic minilesson categories include instruction in handling materials, using soft voices, selecting topics, spelling hard words, completing a piece, sharing work with friends, and other procedural issues.
5. As the year progresses, students benefit from minilessons devoted to improving the quality of student work and finding real audiences for completed work.
6. Conferring in the early-childhood writing workshop requires the teacher to celebrate students' efforts and then extend them.
7. Teachers can use conference moments to offer big reading and writing challenges to students who are ready for them.
8. Share meetings can be adjusted to meet the needs of very young writers.
9. The writing of young students can be used to teach reading in the early-childhood classroom.
10. Using children's literature to lift the quality of student work is an essential component of the early-childhood writing workshop.
11. Teachers can rely on carefully chosen books to develop effective writing workshop minilessons.
12. Teachers need to plan for a variety of writing genres.
13. Second grade is particularly well-suited for reading-writing connections.
14. Writer's notebooks can become a significant rite of passage as students move into third grade.

When I turned fifty, Noah's family left a little gift on my desk. It was a carton filled with fortune cookies with a gracious note wishing me good fortune in the years ahead. It wasn't until later in the day that I realized the fortunes in those cookies were very special. I cracked the first one open and was delighted to discover a fortune about having many years surrounded by fine literature. The next thanked me for giving children a love of school. The next promised that former students would continue to visit me. I realized of course that second grader Noah, together with his brother Adar, a recent graduate, and their mom, Laurel, had created these original fortunes. Noah later explained how they typed the tiny messages and inserted them into the cookies with a tweezer.

Perhaps my favorite fortune in the collection read, "Tough day at the principal's office? Proceed directly to any kindergarten classroom, sit on the floor and play with blocks!" Noah's family didn't know I have been taking that advice for years. Whenever the paperwork gets to me, I head for an early-childhood classroom. Nothing cheers me as quickly as a visit with our five-, six-, and seven-year-olds. I'm not much of a block builder, however. If I'm lucky, the youngsters are writing. As building principal, there is nothing more joyful to me than to enter an early-childhood writing workshop when it is going well. All those big sheets of paper filled with colorful rainbows, flowers, houses, dinosaurs, stick figure family members, and early attempts at sketching favorite toys, pets, vehicles, and action figures. All those eager little hands trying to spell the words they are saying slowly and softly over and over again. All that fuss over the kinds of papers and markers. Something as simple as new blue paper can cause a rush of enthusiasm. All those sweet faces eager to share their writing with whomever walks through the door. And then you read their words and your heart melts. You can fall in love ten times over in a good early-childhood writing workshop.

It's as if I'd hung a sign that reads, "Wanted: teachers who adore young children, are good listeners with lots of patience, have exquisite management skills, and who truly understand early-childhood development, issues of oral and written language acquisition, and the role of drawing in children's communication." Our early-childhood writing workshops run well because we are privileged to have exquisite teachers at their helm.

Our teachers make the writing workshop look so easy. In some ways, it is. Every day, the same routines. Every day, the same materials in the same place. Every day, the teacher sets aside big blocks of time. Every day, the children are eager to participate. Every day, the teacher coaches, nudges, supports, smiles, celebrates, and extends the children's work. Every day, the children groan when it is time to stop.

In many ways the workshop is, of course, not easy at all. The teachers have to be incredibly well prepared. Throughout the workshop, they have to be able to tap into what they know about the writing process approach, developmental issues in spelling, children's literature, and the reading-writing connection. They have to have the pulse of the class as a whole so that they can choose and prepare just the right minilessons. They have to know their children individually and extremely well so that they can coach them appropriately during conferences. Their management routines have to be clear and well established, in order that they can spend quality time conferring with children. They have to know how to finesse a whole-group Author's Chair meeting, so that the soft little voices who are sharing are able to receive kind and helpful response from their classmates. They have to have efficient record-keeping systems so that all that paper winds up neatly and appropriately stored in the right folder or portfolio.

Early-childhood writing workshops should be comfort zones. That doesn't mean that teachers don't teach. Quite the contrary. Perhaps they are best described as *rigorous* comfort zones. The children need to feel good about themselves as writers. They need to know that the workshop is a safe place to take risks. They need to write for many reasons. And at the same time, the grown-ups need to be helping the children become better writers. (Nowhere do my conference guidelines seem clearest than when I'm with our youngest writers. See pages 167–181).

In my years of traveling about the city doing staff development work, I came to appreciate the kinds of things that can go wrong in early-childhood writing workshops. Sometimes the children don't take the workshop time seriously because the setting is *too* casual. The children are munching snacks and their writing papers seem to serve as placemats to catch the cookie crumbs and salt from the pretzel rods. They wander aimlessly about the room, never hunkering down to work.

The children make no attempt to finish anything. They staple together thick wads of paper, not because they have an idea for a book but because they like to staple. They stuff this unused paper into their finished folders, or worse yet, simply dump them into the trash basket. They have never learned what writing is for.

The children form a Pied Piper line waiting to talk to the teacher, or worse yet, they interrupt the teacher as she confers with another student. The children have never learned to be writing teachers themselves, sharing their work with one another.

During share time, the audience doesn't really listen to the writer reading his work aloud. Instead, the children are braiding one another's hair, unraveling the edges of the meeting area rug, running for tissues or drinks of water, or playing with the Velcro tabs on their sneakers. They've never learned that response is sacred to a writer.

In some workshops, children make harsh sounds by shuffling chairs and using their playground voices. They make marks on other children's work or, worse yet, destroy other children's creations. They've never learned to respect the work and the workplace of other writers.

All this is of course unacceptable. We need those beginning workshops to be nurturing as well as scholarly. Early-childhood teachers make our gardens grow. We count on them to nourish the attitudes and skills that will allow children to flourish as they make their way through the grades.

In the following sections, I share what I have been learning in the last eight years about creating fertile ground for writers in our kindergarten and first- and second-grade classrooms.

Extending the First Invitation to Write

This book was begun during a summer break, in which our school was undergoing major renovations. I learned all about asbestos abatement, masonry restoration, roof replacements, waterproofing, and the like. Our school was filled with tile layers, air monitors, scaffold builders, electricians, roofers, contractors, subcontractors, project managers, architects, plasterers, inspectors, and more. My head was swimming with construction progress schedules, anticipated delays, security and safety precautions. At the end of the summer, with the majority of the work left undone, my final words to all these workers were "hasta luego."

I asked them to leave. "See ya' later. Take a break. Leave us alone." And I was quite serious. I asked the general contractor to vacate the building until the school year had gotten off to a calm beginning. We can't have workers in the school when we are building new relationships, establishing routines and setting classroom tones. "Come back in a few weeks," I requested. "Our whole school year depends on how we get started."

Certainly the success of our writing workshops depends on how we get started. I've always believed that the way to begin is to decide what you value. If I want very young children to feel joyous about writing, take risks, and understand the many reasons people write, then my launch should support these beliefs. My favorite first-day plan always involves a tour of the classroom or of the school.

Imagine narrating a walking tour of writing possibilities. I'd show children all the reasons to write in the classroom, and how the kind of paper we choose matches our intentions. First stop, the guinea pig cage. We have clipboards nearby, filled with pads to make observations. Next stop, the piano with music paper for writing songs, melodies, and lyrics. At the block corner we have a basket filled with oak tag strips in case students have to make neighborhood signs. In dramatic play, all kinds of paper, depending on what world the children are creating. Restaurants, travel agencies, spaceships, and supermarkets all have different writing requirements. We use different kinds of paper when we write menus, take orders, plan itineraries, issue tickets, record data, label foods, print fliers, and offer coupons. I'd point out the empty bulletin boards, informing children that this is where we hang announcements. (Later when a child writes, "My mom is going to have a baby," I will resist the urge to necessarily turn the statement into a story. Instead I will say, "That's a good news announcement. We need to hang it on our board.") When I get to the library corner, I'd announce quite dramatically that this is a place for a very different kind of writing. Here we will use blank books to write the kinds of materials that the teacher might share during read-aloud time. I might even offer a few suggestions. "You might want to try and write some story books, alphabet books, information books, how-to books, or counting books."

After filling the children up with all these irresistible options, I'd then talk to them about how drawing can help them make their meaning clear and about spelling as best they can, stretching words out to hear as many sounds as possible. We'd try a few words together, just for the fun of it and to prove to the children that I'll be able to read their writing because, "That's just how five- and six-year-olds spell!" (See more spelling information in Chapter 7.) That would be the end of my first invitation to write and from then on I'd watch very carefully, letting the children teach me what else they need to know.

Whole-Class Gatherings for Young Writers

First Minilessons

In the first few weeks of school, I'd continue supporting the beginning writers' efforts, with short whole-class gatherings (minilessons). Many of the following issues will likely arise.

How to Use Materials Well

My best advice is not to assume anything. Teachers of five- and six-year-olds might find themselves saying, "We don't need to put fifteen staples in a booklet when only two will hold the pages together." "If we don't cover our markers, they'll become as dry as a desert." "When you use lined paper, the lines go across the page, not up and down. The lines are like the sidewalk and the words are supposed to sit on the lines." (Metaphors and similes help. See more information on their use in Chapter 8.)

How to Use Soft Voices and Be Respectful

Demonstrate. Demonstrate. Demonstrate. "When I want to talk to you, I won't shout out across the room. I'll walk over, bend down, and speak to you softly. I expect you to do the same." "If you are talking to a friend, I won't start talking to you right smack in the middle of your conversation. I hope you notice that I'll be waiting my turn." "Writers work real hard on their writing and they are so proud of their work, so I won't ever write or draw on someone else's work and I expect neither will you."

How to Think of Topics

Topic choice for very young children is rarely as complicated as it can be for older students or adults. Early in the school year, kindergartners and most first graders start drawing, and their drawing helps them decide what they will be writing about. ("It looks like a lion. I'm going to write a story about the zoo!") Writing workshops proceed extremely well when, coupled with the ease with which most uninhibited youngsters put marker to paper, it is clear to them that writers write for many reasons. When children know that they can write birthday cards, shopping lists, lost-and-found signs, announcements, thank-you notes, how-to books, "Once upon a time" stories, and so on, they usually behave as they do in a hands-on children's museum, wanting to do it all, not knowing what to do first.

How to Spell Hard Words

I frequently hear teachers telling young children that they have to stretch words out like a rubberband. This thought needs to be accompanied by frequent whole-class demonstrations, otherwise the teacher will find herself endlessly walking about the room slowly enunciating words. (See better uses for conferring beginning on page 167.) Teachers who advise children to stretch out words must remember to tell them why this strategy will help their spelling: "When you say words slowly, you hear more of the sounds in the words." (I imagine there are teachers who play records at a slower speed, to help children understand what it means to say a word slowly!) This issue of spelling is so essential to the success of an early-childhood writing workshop that it is tended to separately in Chapter 7, "Spelling: An Essential Ingredient in the Early-Childhood Writing Workshop."

What to Do When You Finish a Piece

Teachers need to be very clear about how you know when your piece is really finished and what container it goes into once done, otherwise youngsters can whip off several pieces within any writing workshop and their writing folders become sloppy, stuffed, and unwieldy. On the other hand, some children will finish one piece and not know to start another, thereby becoming idle or feisty during the remainder of the workshop.

It's important that teachers help children to slow down, making sure that they have done their best with each piece that they slip into the "finished box." (It is helpful to have such a container for completed work so that writing folders contain only current pieces. Otherwise, young children can spend ten minutes fumbling through their stack deciding which piece to work on.) I can imagine telling our youngest writers, "Putting a piece of writing into the finished box is like mailing a letter to your best friend. You really want her to appreciate it. Before you slip that letter into the mailbox, make sure your name and date are on every piece. Make sure you read your work over. Did you complete your drawings? Did you spell as best you can? Remember, you want your best friend to really understand what you are trying to say." (See additional information about editing and publishing in Chapter 10.)

How to Share Your Work with Friends

Teachers might, in the early weeks of school, suggest that students read their writing to a friend or two before slipping it into the finished box. Minilessons directed at introducing sharing might include information about finding a quiet space, being a careful listener, saying kind things, and asking real questions. Young children need to know that it is more than okay to move about the classroom during a writing workshop, and that talking—talking in hushed tones—is expected. Teachers might want to ask two children to demonstrate sharing a piece of writing. In addition to receiving minilesson advice on how to share well, students will get better at responding respectfully to one another's work by eavesdropping on teacher conferences and by participating in share meetings. These whole-group meetings held at the end of writing workshops enable individual children to receive feedback from the whole class on work in progress and finished work, all under the direction of the teacher. (See section on whole-class shares in Chapter 2, "Reflecting on the Teaching of Writing" in *Lifetime Guarantees*, as well as discussion of special share meetings in the early-childhood workshop on page 182 of this book.)

Other Procedural Issues

Teachers who keep a keen eye on their classroom will discover many other procedural issues that need clarification. These might include such basics as the following:

- how to distribute and collect writing folders (Come up with an orderly system, preferably relying on student helpers, and stick to it.)
- how to find and use such necessary tools as markers, scissors, and staplers (Keep them in consistent locations and don't assume children know how to use them. Demonstrate, demonstrate, demonstrate!)
- what to do if you want to make changes in your writing (Teach children how to cross out, cut and paste, etc.)
- what to do if you run out of space (Use carets, add pages, make asterisks, etc.)
- what to do if you need a conference (Have clear procedures for asking peers for help and asking teachers for help.)
- how to edit your writing (Be clear on editing procedures. Teach children how to check for specific items and how to use any simple checklist you devise.)

Eventually, once the room is humming and children know what is expected of them, I would turn my minilesson efforts toward lifting the quality of student work.

Minilessons That Lift the Quality of Children's Work

Briefly described below are some of my favorite minilessons used in early-childhood writing workshops. They are the tried-and-true lessons, ones I have been teaching in one form or another for almost twenty years. Most are aimed at such goals as developing fluency, adding clarity, including specific detail, answering the readers' questions, and finding real audiences for student work. (See pages 187–191 for additional minilessons that tap into excerpts from literature, a major resource for improving the quality of children's writing, as well as spelling minilessons on page 211.)

To Help Children Recognize When Their Writing Is Too Sparse

"A funny thing happened to me last night," I say. "I took your writing home and read all your pieces as my bedtime reading. And to my great surprise, as I was reading some of your writing, I got so hungry. Some of your pieces made me feel very full and satisfied, but some of your writing made me hungry! And I didn't get hungry for apples, or chips, or cookies. No, I got hungry for information." I then share a few bare-bones pieces, demonstrating why I got so hungry. Finally, I ask children to reread their work and tell me if I was probably full of information or starving for more.

To Help Children Expand on Their Writing

"There's a line from a song in *Grease* that keeps playing in my head when I read your work," I say. "It goes, 'Tell me more, tell me more!' As I read this work aloud, can you guess the places where I started to sing, 'Tell me more, tell me more!'?" Children love singing this refrain, with its rhythmic beat. Of course, I can't share the actual lines that follow from the song "Summer Loving." They're too suggestive; but I can invent my own. How about, "Tell me more, tell me more, when I tap on the floor"? When a piece of student writing is read aloud during share meeting, a student listener can be asked to tap gently on the floor when they hear places in which the writer needs to add more. (See page 182 for additional ways to enrich share meetings.)

To Show Children How Their Writing Can Be Put to Good Use

I often play a "Words Can Make a Difference in the World" game. I list on a chart many of the pieces currently being written in the class and then ask children to match these with possible authentic publishing ideas. For example, I might list the following:

A Poem About Your Grandma's Cooking

A Thank-You Note for a Gift from Your Aunt

A Funny Story about Going to the Dentist

A Labeled Drawing of Your Favorite Animals

A List of Friends to Invite to a Party

An Informational Book About Koala Bears

Directions for Playing Go Fish

I then ask children to match publishing ideas with the pieces of writing. These might include:

Put It in a Frame and Give It as a Gift

Add It to the Class Library

Share It with Your Family

Mail It to the Person Mentioned

Collect Other Pieces About the Same Topic

Hang It on the Refrigerator Door

Share It with Another Class

Of course, there is no one right answer, and children learn a great deal from trying to explain their choices. They are also reminded of possibilities of topic, format, and publishing.

To Help Children Use Descriptive Language

I ask students questions like the following:

- Which sentence better helps you understand: "I had a great dessert last night" or "I had two scoops of Rocky Road ice cream in a waffle cone with chocolate sprinkles on top"?

- Which is easier for you to picture inside your head: "My mom is nice to me" or "My mom always tucks me into bed, reads me two or three stories, kisses me good-night, leaves a glass of water on my night table, and turns on my night light"?
- Which would help the reader really appreciate what you are trying to say: "I like snow" or "I like how snow gives children a whole new way to play outdoors, covers everything with a pretty white blanket, and sometimes when it comes down heavy gives children extra vacation days"?

I then explain the difference between general and specific information, suggesting that whenever possible children be more specific. (Inevitably children say, "I'm being more pacific!")

To Make Better Use of Verbs

A similar issue pertains to the use of verbs. Many of our youngest writers may not have heard the word *verb*, but they can certainly understand that certain action words give more information to the reader. For example, they can tell you that, "I jogged to school" gives more information than, "I went to school," or "I gulped down my lunch" gives more information than "I ate my lunch." Second graders seem to take great delight in choosing just the right verbs.

To Incorporate Various Materials into Their Writing Process

Early-childhood students seem to delight in using a wide variety of writing materials. "Today boys and girls, I'm going to show you many different kinds of paper. Your job is to help decide why certain kinds of paper might be better for certain kinds of writing." I then very dramatically lift more than a dozen kinds of paper from my tote bag—including beautiful stationery, adding-machine tape, yellow legal pads, preprepared blank draft books, art sketch pads, long sentence strip paper, blank recipe cards, index cards, a diary, small notepads, oak tag sheets, blank name-tags, stick-on papers, blank transparencies, and music paper. Children are eager to suggest how these kinds of materials could be used and the new material adds energy to the class.

To Elicit Sensory Responses in Their Writing

"I know that you learn about the five senses when you study science," I might say, "but today I want to talk about our senses when we study writing. Your job when you write is to make your readers use some of their senses. Today I am going to read aloud some of the writing done by children in this class and I want you to tell me if the authors put any of your senses to work. In other words, have your friends made you see, hear, smell, feel, or taste anything with the words they have chosen to include in their writing?" I then read aloud some student work and talk about their effect on the listeners.

To Appreciate Surprising Elements in Their Writing

"Yesterday during writing workshop, I felt like I was attending a few surprise parties. (Those are parties that you don't expect. Someone plans them and doesn't tell you about them, so they are a surprise. You've probably seen people jump up and yell, 'Surprise!' when the guest of honor opens the door.) As I walked around the room, so many of you surprised me with your writing. So today, I'm going to begin our writing workshop by telling you about all the wonderful surprising things I discovered in your writing because all good writers want to surprise their readers." I then share unusual topics, clever formats, interesting choices of words, and so on.

Serving as Model

In addition to offering minilessons to start the writing hour, I would take care every time I write for the children. In other words, I would make sure that every agenda, letter home, classroom sign, and class news story is as well written as possible. Sometimes, when teachers worry that their students' writing is bland, I ask them to reflect on the quality of the writing that they do in front of their children. We can jazz up those morning messages. Instead of, "Today is Wednesday. It is raining," we can begin, "I can't believe I forgot my umbrella on this dreary, wet morning." Remember, children will learn what we demonstrate.

Conferring in the Early-Childhood Workshop

After these whole-class gatherings, children usually leave the meeting area to work individually on their writing. The teachers I know best then begin moving about the room, stopping to confer with children. When I join in, I carry the same guidelines in my mind as I do when I confer with older students (see pages 88–92.) If I don't know the young writer at all, I talk with the classroom teacher, look through the student's portfolio, and watch the child at work, before I begin my conference. I want to know what the child thinks of this writing business.

Does he seem comfortable with marker in hand?

Does he think there is a difference between writing and drawing?

Does he understand that writers pick letters deliberately so the reader can understand his words?

Is he is a risk taker? Does he attempt new spellings?

Does he realize that there are different kinds of writing? Does he try any of these genres?

Does he understand why his teacher has invited him to write?

Does he realize that writing is meant to be read by real people?

Of course, there is no lockstep way to get this information. I want our conversations to be natural. I talk to the children in the same way I would chat with neighborhood children sitting on my front porch.

What's uppermost in my mind, however, is my role as a teacher. Years ago I learned that the job of a writing teacher, in the primary classroom especially, is to celebrate and extend. Most of us have gotten really good at celebrating our students' efforts. We all need to become good at extending children's efforts. We can't be afraid to teach, even if our students are first-year writers.

Classroom teachers and principals who know their students and the teaching of writing well are in a prime position to approach young writers with seriousness of purpose. We are not merely window-shopping when we walk around those classrooms. Our job is to make a difference, not just to make children feel good. We need to be productive and feel accomplished, and so do the children.

(When I served as principal of the Manhattan New School, I always looked forward to conferring with young students and I trusted that my responses to their work would help them grow as young writers. After all, I had spent many years studying children's writing and writing workshop instructional techniques. Elementary school principals who do not have a rich background in the teaching of writing still need to bend down low when they visit early-childhood classrooms. They need not serve as conference partners, but as interested visitors. If they cannot offer suggestions for improving student work, they can acknowledge the importance of learning to write well. They can inquire about how the writing workshop runs. They can talk about their own writing. They can ask if reading helps students to write. And although I previously noted that the teacher's job is not to just make children feel good, principals can serve a sort of proud grandparent role, simply asking children to read their writing aloud and marveling at what children *can* do. When administrators talk to children about their writing, there are fringe benefits. They learn so much about their school community and child development, as well as individual children's interests, questions, problems, and abilities.)

I often begin early-childhood conferring workshops with the piece in Figure 6.1, written by a five-year-old named Joseph. I then ask the participants how they might respond to this young writer. I stop them as soon as the room fills with lively talk, suggesting that they shouldn't be making any teaching decisions until they request, "Shelley, tell us something about Joseph." We are not teaching the list of colors, we are teaching Joseph, a five-year-old with attitudes, skills, interests, and a history as a writer and a reader. Teachers must know their young students as writers as well as new parents know their infants as eaters. Mothers and fathers can go on at length about their babies' likes and dislikes, what digests well and what doesn't, what new foods they're ready for and what they are not ready for. Similarly, teachers must rely on all they know about their students in order to support and facilitate their growth as writers.

I then add the following background information. "Joseph is a shy, soft-spoken child who only speaks when spoken to. He rarely draws and spends his writing time copying print off charts in the classroom. It's apparent that Joseph knows a handful of initial consonant sounds as he makes appropriate guesses during shared reading time.

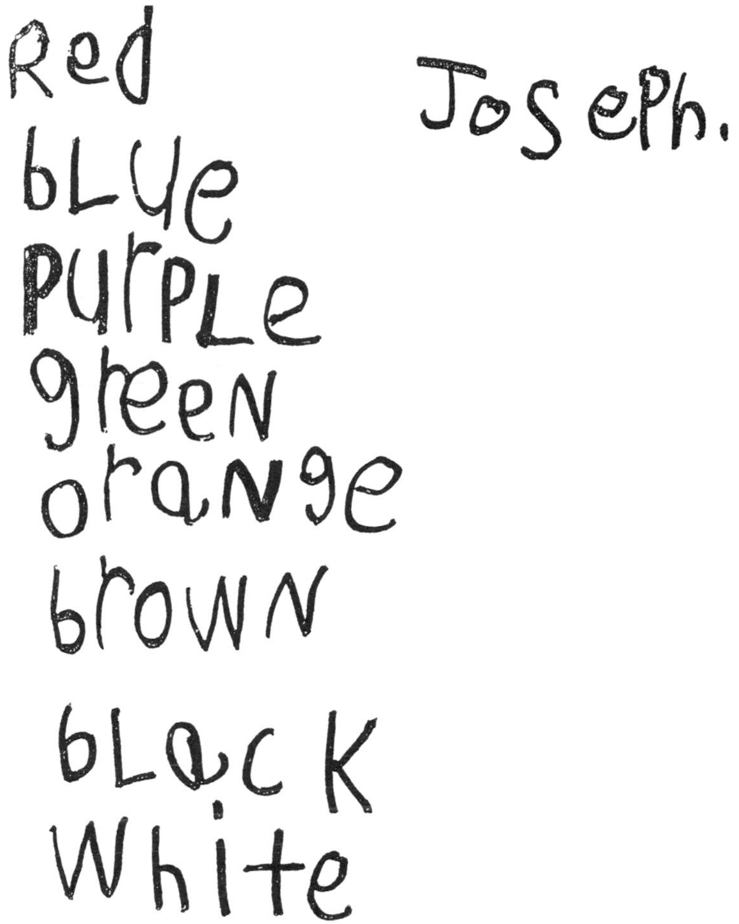

Red
bLue
PurPLe
green
orange
brown

bLacK
White

Joseph.

Figure 6.1

You are not surprised to see this list of paint colors copied off the paint chart hanging on a back wall."

Then I suggest, "Before you decide what you are going to say to Joseph, try and verbalize what your goal for Joseph is as a writer. Imagine if his mother was coming to school for a meeting and you wanted to tell her what you are working on. Think big. Don't think about the piece in front of you. Think about Joseph."

It is helpful to postpone making suggestions until you know where you are headed and can articulate that direction. For example, if you make the decision that the most important thing for Joseph right now is to make him feel good about being a writer, the real teaching part of your conference might sound something like this:

> Joseph you are *so* good at copying those words perfectly off the paint chart. I wonder if you wouldn't like to make a real paint chart as a gift for Ms. Harris next door. I could give you a big sheet of oak tag and you could make a real chart for her classroom.

I've not only made Joseph feel good about what he has written, I've also taught him what writing is for.

On the other hand, you could make the executive decision that above all what Joseph needs is to take risks as a speller. You know he knows a few initial consonant sounds and you have a hunch he can be successful at invented spelling. Your conference, therefore, would take a very different path. The teaching part might sound something like this:

> Joseph, when I look at all the pieces in your writing folder, I notice that you spend a lot of workshop time copying words off the classroom walls. I have a hunch that you do this because you want to spell like the grown-ups. I could help you learn how to write the words you really want to use.

When words like these are spoken in a supportive, kindly manner, not in a "I caught you," punitive way, children usually respond quite honestly. They are grateful for the help. They appreciate having the tools needed to write about what is really on their minds.

You could have also decided that above all what Joseph needs is to talk more, or to use drawing more. Your conferences then would have taken very different directions. Joseph could have surprised you by speaking passionately about becoming a house painter like his father when he grows up, and he might have led you into entirely different territory. Again, responding to student writing is an art, not a science. We can hope to be helpful only if we act thoughtfully, not whimsically. (See Appendix 6 for additional practice material aimed at strengthening teachers' abilities to decide on appropriate goals based on student histories and to think through how to best convey needed information to students.)

When prospective candidates hope to secure principal jobs in our district, they are asked to assess classrooms as part of the interview process. At these school visits, they are asked to say what they saw, make recommendations for improved instruction, and then discuss how they would reach those goals. In the writing workshop, teachers are actually doing the same thing every time they stop to confer with a child. They take into account what they know about this writer and see in their current work, they think of one important recommendation, and then they provide the child with strategies to act upon that suggestion. The big difference between the principal candidate and the teacher at work is that the teacher is not just saying what she would do, she is doing it, thoughtfully and effectively as she weaves about the classroom.

My best advice to a new teacher of primary-age children is to get to know your students well. Let them know how much you care. Read great books about the primary writing workshop. Visit with great teachers of writing. Think about each of your students and the big goals you have in mind for them. Make your decisions. Keep them simple. Don't teach too many things at once. Find the words to convey your information in a way that young children can understand. Watch what happens. Enjoy the power of your teaching.

If early-childhood students are ready to reread their work and question whether it is the best they can do, I might lead them down the very same paths as those directed by the questions listed on page 91. I might ask them to do any or all of the following:

- anticipate the audience's response
- gather more information
- rethink the shape, format, or purpose of the piece
- use literature as a model

These four strategies serve me well, even with very young writers. The following examples illustrate these possibilities.

Luke, an enthusiastic first-grade writer, has whipped off the following:

My mom buys me presents. My mom buys me food.

My mom lets me play. My mom lets me play video games.

And that stuff is fun.

I know Luke is ready to think about making his writing even better. I ask him to imagine sitting in the Author's Chair. "What questions do you think the children will ask you?" Luke understands. "They'll ask me what kind of presents does my mom buy and what kind of food, too." I remind Luke that his job is to answer the readers' questions. Luke adds on to his piece and turns it into the following poem, to be given to his mother as a gift.

My Mom

My mom buys me presents
Toys, like cars and transformers
Food, like strawberries and carrots
My mom lets me play
She plays board games with me
We play the Allowance Game with fake money
We play Operation with little fake bones
We play Candyland with little people.

Adam, a six-year-old, writes enthusiastically about building snowmen in Central Park. His piece is only three sentences long, filled with charming spelling inventions. He wants to write more about building with snow, but doesn't know what else to say. I hand him a small notepad, suggesting he could live like a reporter, interviewing his classmates and members of his family to gather more information. "Come see me when you fill this pad," I say, "and I'll show you how you might use this information to make your piece even better." Adam follows through and together we turn his writing into a how-to book on building snow people, to be added to a basket of nonfiction books. Someday, Adam will be very ready to understand what keeping a writer's notebook is all about.

In a conference with Matthew, I use a piece of literature to help him think about the shape of his piece. When I visit his classroom, the first grader eagerly shares his writing. On a sheet of storybook paper (the kind with space for drawing at the top and lines for writing at the bottom), he has written, "Today the mail is here. Sometimes I get packages. Sometimes magazines. Sometimes I get letters." I tell him that his writing sounds like the kind of books that are used to teach young children how to read. We look at a few in his classroom. I point out how each page has one simple line, repeating many of the same words. I call his attention to the illustrations that help young children guess the new words. I also point out how the last page is usually just a little bit different, sometimes having a bit of a surprise. "Endings should sound like endings," I tell him, "People should know they're on the last page."

I ask Matthew if he'd like to turn his idea into a book that children can use to learn to read. He agrees and takes a blank book. He copies each line he has already written onto a separate page, inserting the missing words "I get" to the magazine page, "so the children who are learning to read get to see the same words over and over." He then adds one more page-turner: "Sometimes for my birthday I get presents *and* cards." And then he adds his big ending, "I LOVE THE MAIL!"

When visiting P.S. 183, a neighboring school to the Manhattan New School, I pulled alongside Ali, a first grader, who was writing about her grandfather, her poppy, who had passed away. She had a few kind thoughts already down when I approached. I asked what she might do with the piece when she was done. She wasn't quite sure, but one suggestion I threw out caught her attention. She could slip all her memories into a small photograph album, one of those little brag books, adding an appropriate family photograph to accompany each one. Ali would then give this album to her mother on her birthday, as a tribute to her mother's father. A few days later, Ali sent me the thank-you note that appears in Figure 6.2.

Ali worked very hard on her big publishing idea. After all, this would be a gift for her mother on her birthday as well as a tribute to her grandfather. Having a real purpose in mind is strong motivation for children to make their writing their best.

Throughout all these simple conferences, similar elements appear. In each, I wasn't afraid to make explicit suggestions. In each, I helped children find ways for their writing to do good work in the world. In each, I was trying to offer these very young students practical ways to lift the quality of their work. It's no wonder I enjoy conferring with young children. I know that I'm not simply window-shopping. I feel productive. I feel as if I've made much needed purchases and can now cross these items off my shopping list.

The day that I visited Ali's classroom, I also visited several other early-childhood writing workshops in her school. When I returned home, I reflected on the day and sent the letter below to the teachers.

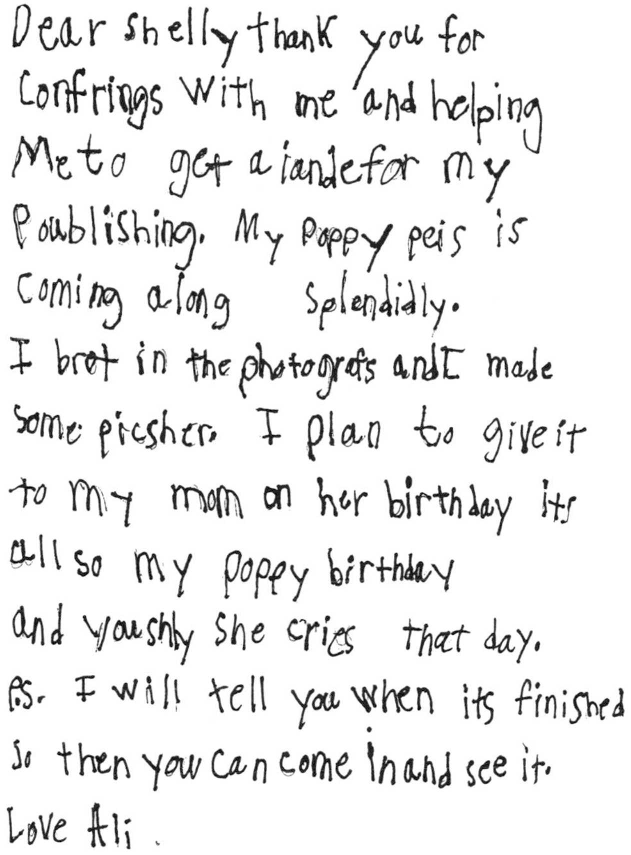

Dear shelly thank you for
Confrings With me and helping
Me to get a iandefor my
Poublishing. My Poppy peis is
Coming along   Splendidly.
I bret in the photogrfs andI made
Some picshers. I plan to give it
to my mom on her birthday its
allso my poppy birthday
and yaushly She cries that day.
P.s. I will tell you when its finished
So then you Can come in and see it.
Love Ali .

Figure 6.2

March 23, 2000

Dear P.S. 183 teachers,

What a treat it was for me to confer with children in your writing workshops. I have many memorable images in mind. I can't believe that a young boy wore a black velvet bow tie because I was coming. I can't believe that children could learn about effective similes from watching David Letterman. Does "Cracked me open like a lobster" qualify as beautiful language? I can't believe that Charlotte had mice in her dishwasher and that she used the letters in her name to help her write di<u>ch</u>wa<u>ch</u>er. I can't believe that a young writer would say, "New York is like an angry clock that never stops ticking." I can't believe that children actually get to go bowling and eat dinner with Knicks players if their families contribute enough money to charity. I can't believe that a teacher could wink at her children to calmly and individually send them off to write. Most of all I can't believe how much I learned that day.

When I returned home I reread my quick jottings and then tried to distill what I learned about the teaching of writing, conferring, and my own tendencies as a teacher of writing. If I didn't reflect on what I did and what I learned, the events of the day would merely wash over me. Instead, what I did and learned on that one day can now inform my work with other students on other days. Stopping to try and name what's important and identifying any big ideas or areas of further inquiry are what keep me alive professionally. What I've done below is not very different from asking a child, when he has revised a piece of writing successfully, "What have you done in this piece of writing that can help you in another piece of writing?" This reflection on our work in order to improve tomorrow's practice reminds me of the old saying about the difference between giving your friend a fish or teaching her how to fish. I'm interested in ways of teaching that make a difference in the long run, for students, teachers and myself.

• It was easy to confer in your early-childhood classrooms because the rooms were calm, the environments carefully designed, and the blocks of time unhurried. In addition, the children were eager to share, respectful of one another, willing to take suggestions, proud of their work, and most of all these very young writers seemed to be deliberately trying to write well. Congratulations! You have created very fertile ground for children to become competent and enthusiastic writers. These qualities serve to remind me of what to look for when I visit other classrooms.

• Time and again my conferences required children to imagine what they might do with their piece of writing. If they had no idea, I was happy to offer suggestions. "Do you think you might want to turn this into a family heirloom (photos with vignettes), a thank-you letter to your grandmother for the special coin she gave you on that 'not-so-okay' day, a 'gift of story' for your dentist to hang in his office?" In other words, I am determined to demonstrate to children that writing can make a difference in the world. Writing is not really for bulletin boards, portfolios, and file folders. These containers are for copies. The real ones should go out into the real world.

• I was limited in my resources because I didn't know your children or their classrooms. In other words, had I been their regular conference partner, I would have referred more frequently to literature, to their past histories as writers, and to other writing lessons that had been taught. (A minilesson scrapbook would really be a valuable tool, an archive of all lessons taught, complete with excerpts from literature, children's attempts to try techniques, and even words spoken. Children could return to these pages and guests could browse to get a sense of what has come before. Teachers could also reread the accumulated minilessons to prompt their own reflections on their teaching of writing.)

• I often reread children's pieces back to them so they can hear the power of their words (or the lack of clarity, energy, or voice in their work). Sometimes I also reread when children are sharing with the whole class so that the children can really appreciate the content. It can be hard to respond to too soft voices. (I usually sit near the writer who is sharing so that I can reread aloud if necessary. "Would you mind if I read this aloud? I want you to listen along with your classmates. Besides, good writing should always be read more than once.") I visited a school in Tampa and all the early-childhood classrooms had wonderful portable microphones so that all voices could be heard. Not a bad idea!

• It's important to maintain the teacher stance. In other words, don't be afraid to teach.
    If shared meeting responses are taking children away from the task at hand, don't be afraid to intervene. If children hesitate to work hard to make their writing better, don't be afraid to require them to do so. If students' writing doesn't make sense, don't be afraid to tell them so in the clearest and kindest way possible. If children go on and on in a conference, don't be afraid to give explicit instructions and make a polite exit. Once you know your chil-

dren well and have established caring relationships, you can expect a lot from them and they will deliver because it is safe to take risks in all your classrooms.

• *I can't confer without pen in hand. Not only do I have notes about every child and their writing, but I often ask children to attempt things right on my slip of paper. For example, they are often very willing to try a spelling in my "grown-up" pad. Then too, I often write down the exact words children say and give them to the children to get them started on their writing. Or I map out their pieces. Or I cut their pieces up (with permission, or copies of their pieces), and tape down sections on a slip of my paper. Or I take research notes (like when I asked that young boy to name all the different kinds of writing that filled his notebook pages. Remember, I was trying to get him away from the "everything that happened to me today" kind of entries). Or I record the memorable lines when they read aloud to me so I can tell them what they are good at as writers.*

• *I am welcoming of bystanders and attempt to pull them into other children's conferences when it is appropriate, especially if they are eavesdropping, could serve as additional audience, or the point is so valuable that I sense many children need to understand it. This is also an effective management technique as more children feel touched by the teacher's presence.*

• *You might consider having a wider variety of paper in the early-childhood writing workshop. Children love to choose appropriate paper—long slips of paper for lists, oak tag sheets for signs and posters, stationery for letters, preprepared blank books for picture books, and so on.*

• *When teaching is clear and powerful, there is evidence in the children's work. It was obvious that you have been stressing beautiful language in many of the classrooms. I'd suggest that you broaden the definition of this term so that in addition to the use of similes, children realize that carefully chosen, precise verbs and specific nouns can also make the reader say, "That piece is so beautifully written." So can carefully crafted descriptions and well-placed repetitive lines. Remember, the young poet's line, "The green grass, the spiky green grass"? That was beautiful language without any similes.*

• *Children are not as fragile as they sometimes seem. (Of course, some are, and you know who they are and how far you can gently nudge them.) For the most part, children love to try new things, craft a memorable piece of writing, and move an audience. With the right tone of voice, you can help children become used to taking out parts that don't build meaning, adding clarification, and otherwise gently revising pieces so that they are proud to put their names on them. (Michael was willing to omit parts that didn't build meaning in his "Becoming Famous" piece. Jennifer was willing to eliminate the red juice from her dinosaur piece.)*

• *Poetry becomes easier for children when they can cut, move around, and then paste the lines they love. Those blank magnets would have come in very handy when I conferred with the young girl on her "Monkey Tree" poem. Do order those blank magnets. They are much cheaper than Xerox machines, although one of those would really come in handy. (A chicken in every pot, a Xerox machine in every classroom! Too bad they are so expensive.)*

• *When children have made an incredible leap in their writing, try and arrange for them to repeat the performance. For example, the child who selected her notebook entry about the park and said it could be a poem (she was absolutely on target, don't you think?) should be asked to look through her notebook for another entry that contained a "poetry-shaped idea." Can she do on her own what she just did with my help? (Lift the most powerful lines, rearrange them to form a poem, add additional thoughts, etc.) Can she then teach a friend to do likewise?*

    • *I was delighted that the children were not being asked to do any too-sophisticated genres. Your goals for the young writers in your early-childhood workshops felt very appropriate. No doubt, they could publish many worthwhile pieces in a year. Do you have certain genre courses of study, selected for each grade level, so that occasionally you are teaching all children to write in one format at the same time? That seems like another important conversation we could have.*

    • *I was equally delighted that your principal shadowed me for the entire day. How fortunate you are that Eric is so interested in the teaching of writing and appreciates the importance of writing in children's lives as well as the importance of professional growth in the teaching of writing in teachers' lives.*

Thanks for a great visit. To many more important professional conversations.

Respectfully,
Shelley

When we give ourselves the gift of reflection time, we realize that we have learned as much as we have taught.

Special Conference Challenges

When I visit early-childhood writing workshops I often spot young children who whip off several pieces in the space of a short time. Many of these children seem to have reached a plateau, always satisfied in the writing they produce, never discovering real important writing projects, ones that rise above the others. Teachers of these complacent students often ask, "What else is there to do? Are there different challenges I should be suggesting? Are there more-demanding projects that would make sense for this writer, at this time?" Over the years I have asked younger students to participate in any or all of the following tasks aimed at slowing down young writers in order that they create pieces of writing they will long remember.

Working with Children in Different Classes and Different Grades

Occasionally, children become inspired to accept new challenges when they have opportunities to take part in different writing workshops. For example, if I confer with a second grader who is the only child attempting poetry in his class, I might suggest he sit in on another second grade in which a poetry course of study happens to be taking place. Then too, I might meet a first grader who is writing a fictional picture book, and I might arrange for some fourth-grade conference partners, ones who have recently completed their own picture book study.

Assigning "For the Good of the School" Pieces

When young children don't seem to be giving writing their all, when they seem to be cranking out any old thing, or feeling everything they produce is good enough, I might challenge such students to accept some "assigned" topics. For example, I might ask young students to write a visitor's guide to all the animals in the school, a welcome letter for new early-childhood students, a lost-and-found inventory, school birthday cards to be duplicated and given to other students on their special days, and so on. (See *Lifetime Guarantees* Chapter 3, "Discovering Real-World Reasons to Write.")

Encouraging a School-Wide Writing Campaign

Early-childhood children frequently write about such topics as their pets, new babies in the families, visits to grandparents, wishes for new toys, and play date experiences. When a child who needs a bigger challenge produces a piece of writing on a popular topic such as these, it makes sense to ask him to put out a call for manuscripts and gather other children's writing about the very same topic. For example, when Andrej shared the piece about his soap collection (see page 15), his teacher might have challenged him to search for other student writing about collections, thereby creating a school-wide anthology. (In essence, Andrej would be creating a new three-ring binder project. See publishing formats in Chapter 10.)

Connecting Writing to Reading

Young children who are particularly fond of certain books can be challenged to take deliberate and specific lessons from them. Jessica was particularly attracted to Ferida Wolff's picture book *A Year for Kiko,* asking to read it on her own after the teacher had read it aloud. This book presents the month-by-month delights of a young child as the seasons change. Her teacher challenged Jessica, a competent but usually uninspired writer, to take lessons from the professional writer and create a parallel picture book. Teacher and child began by listing some of the distinctive elements contained in the book, all of which were new techniques for this second grader. They included writing in third person instead of the usual first person, writing in the present tense instead of the usual past tense, organizing a book into twelve sections, month by month, preparing exactly four sentences for each month's comments, including a surprising element in the fourth line. When Jessica accepted this writing challenge she was at it for several weeks. Although she was kept busy, attempting to meet the demands of the task, the assignment was not busywork. She was learning something new every day.

Following Interests, Inventing New Formats

One of the real joys of teaching writing is inventing new projects and genres that perfectly suit the aspiring writer in front of you. Rather than suggesting familiar formats, ones you have studied and shared with children in the past, you think on your feet, letting the work of students inspire fresh thoughts. It is hoped that children will learn from your demonstrations and begin inventing their own surprising child-size genres.

Figure 6.3

When Darryn's teacher notices that three of the pieces in this first grader's writing folder are poetic tributes to nighttime (see Figures 6.3–6.5), she suggests bigger writing challenges connected to this area of interest. The possibilities include:

- composing additional nighttime poems in order to create an original anthology
- beginning a special bedside journal, writing her thoughts and observations each evening
- turning her finished journal into a gift book for classmates. The book could be published with blank pages in between each of her writings and then duplicated so that each child in the class could be inspired to keep his or her own bedtime book.
- beginning a nonfiction research project, studying the night scenes and sounds in her city environment

Figure 6.4

- inviting family members to join her in keeping a collaborative nighttime journal and periodically sharing contents with classmates
- turning her poetic writing into lullabies for her baby brother
- searching for picture books with similar bedtime themes and attaching her original poems to the inside covers.

Leaving Well-Enough Alone

Occasionally, we are surprised by the very ambitious and seemingly "sophisticated" work that some very young writers produce. Although our job is to teach and to continually help students move toward more fluent, well-designed, and memorably crafted text, we must always remember the age of our students and not ask them to accept challenges they are not ready for. When we look at the writing of very young children, we must resist the urge to turn their texts into the adult version that might pop into our mind's eye. A case in point follows.

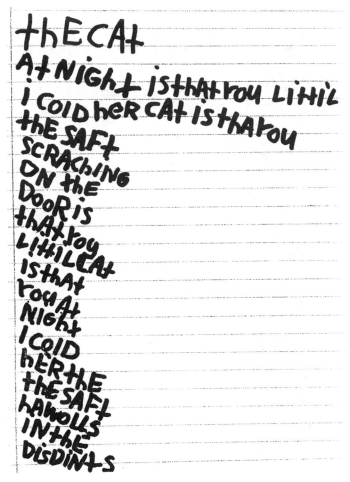

Figure 6.5

Sofia and Gabrielle, toward the end of first grade, collaborated on the piece of fiction appearing as Figure 6.6. For ease of reading, the piece is reprinted on page 181. I took great delight in reading Sofia and Gabrielle's writing. It's clear that they are trying to make sense of the adult world around them. Their writing reminds me what a privilege it is to be around children. We get to see the world through their young eyes.

I was thrilled at the length of the piece and their use of such literary conventions as "Once upon a time" and, "happily ever after." I marveled at their attempts to move the story along through so much dialogue. I was impressed with how the young writers stepped away from the action to talk about Latin dances and a Broadway show tune. I also loved the slip of the tongue, in the cup of "marriage." That kind of content is very rare in the writing of most six-year-olds.

The Man that Lived on the Mountain

Once upon a time a man named Josh sat in his house on the edge of the mountain. And one day he decided to go down the mountain, so he could find a friend. When he went down the mountain he walked and walked until he found a friend. While he was walking he met a beautiful woman who he loved very much and said hi and waved. Do you want to go up to the mountain with me at 6:00 for dinner? O.K. said the lady. We will have hamburgers and French fries and for dessert we will have ice cream and we will have a great time said Josh. The beautiful woman's name was Maria. Oh like the song. What song? The song's My Fair Lady. Oh that song. We can listen to that at my house at 6:00 and we may dance to it how we did in the old days. And we dance all night. O.K. we will dance all night. Which kind of dance should we dance? A Latin dance. O.K. we can dance a Latin dance. What's the Latin dance? It's when you get up and jump and have a great time. We may listen to music. And if you want we can marry. He was embarrassed when he said it. But she said O.K., but when should we marry? Tonight O.K. said Maria. And they went out for dinner and had a great night because it was six o'clock. And then they married. Now let's go to your house. O.K. said Josh You have a beautiful house. I am glad I am with you.

And one day when they were having tea, Maria asked for a nice cup of tea. And Josh said, Do you want a nice cup of marriage? I mean tea. Of course. I would. But we are already married. Oh I forgot. Do you want to get a dog tomorrow? But what if our puppies have babies. We don't have a big enough house. We will get a bigger house, said Josh. But when will we get a bigger house? I don't know when we will get a new house. Hopefully soon said Josh. And why don't we get a house and we need to get groceries. And then they went to sleep. In the morning Maria forgot that she was married. Maria, do you want to get a dog? OK she said tiredly. Then she said What kind of dog? Said Maria. Any kind said Josh. And they went off to get the dog. And they got back with a chiwauhwa. What do we need? Said Maria Hot dogs meat vegetables and dog food of course. And they lived happily . . . ever after.

Figure 6.6

Even though I could think of several ways to help make this a better piece, I kept in mind that these writers were not yet seven years of age. I therefore did not try to instruct them in more realistic concepts of courtship, nor did I tell them that if they are writing about adults they should have a consistent adult point of view. (Adults would probably not choose hamburgers, French fries, and ice cream for a special dinner.) I did not try to slow down their use of time. I did not talk about abrupt transitions. I did not ask them whether they were really referring to the Maria in *West Side Story*.

Instead, I celebrated their attempts at writing a lengthy piece of fiction and simply chose to teach them about the consistent use of "he said" and "she said" as dialogue markers as well as the related use of quotation marks. I am in no hurry to turn early-childhood students into successful romance writers.

Special Share Meetings in the Early-Childhood Workshop

Share meetings, the whole-class gatherings that often end the writing workshop, are prime time to teach all the children, not just the child who is sharing. Teachers should not hesitate to highlight breakthroughs, make suggestions, and even help students begin to carry those suggestions out publicly. Teachers should also feel confident in using their own voices to reread pieces that have been shared too softly. How can we expect genuine and helpful response if students didn't really hear the writing? How can we expect enthusiastic encouragement and advice if classmates were not engaged in the sharing? Teachers can often read student writing aloud in such powerful ways that the author as well as his or her classmates are more likely to hear potential in the work. The following are a few ways that I use share time in an early-childhood workshop to reach more of the children and avoid the often canned and rote responses that lack instructional value.

• After a child has shared, the teacher asks the child to leave the room so as to rehearse helpful responses with classmates. This technique dates back to my very early years with the Teachers College Writing Project, and over the years has never lost its power. Young children love the drama of the author not being able to hear their questions and they benefit from the teacher's advice as to which questions or comments will really help the writer. When the author is invited back into the room, only worthwhile and well-rehearsed questions and comments are made.

• Another way of helping children become more adept at helping a classmate improve their writing is with a "whisper-in-the-ear" share meeting. The children love when I whisper in their ears, actually feeding them helpful questions to ask the author. I might bend down low and whisper in a child's ear, "Ask him why it's so much fun at his grandparents' house," or "Ask her what she might do with this piece of writing, who deserves to read it." Children learn from this modeling and often internalize the kinds of questions that really help writers.

• Young writers need to learn to anticipate the readers' questions. The student who is about to share can be asked, "What questions do you think your classmates will ask you?" The author can then whisper in the teachers' ear and the teacher can record the anticipated questions. Then the share meeting proceeds and at the end the teacher reveals the list of questions the author had expected. Authors learn to be critical readers of their own writing and classmates seem to be especially engaged in these shares.

• Teachers can announce special share criterion. "Today children who have written three pieces on the same topic have been invited to share" or, "Today children who have done something they've never done before have been invited to share."

• Teachers can prepare student work on transparencies to be displayed on the overhead projector, thereby enabling all the children gathered to see the text to be shared. The teacher can mark the places where the author plans to expand, delete, or rearrange. The author can be given the transparency as a record of what he will be doing next.

• Similarly, teachers can enlarge pieces to be shared on a poster printer machine so that all the children can actually see the student's writing. The advantage of displaying this enlarged hard copy is that any cutting and pasting that needs to be done to make room for additional ideas, to rearrange thoughts, or to delete unnecessary lines can be done in public view.

• Teachers can conduct "That reminds me of" shares. In other words, the teacher can select student writing that in some way connects to other texts in the classroom and the teacher can explain her choices. Students are proud that their own work resembles published material and can learn a great deal about topics, writing styles, moods, genres, literary techniques, and so on.

• Teachers can arrange for the former teachers of children who are sharing to be present at the whole-group shares. Students love demonstrating how much they've grown as writers, and new participants often bring fresh insights into classroom shares.

The Reading-Writing Connection

When educators use the expression *reading-writing connection,* they are usually referring to the lessons writers take from the reading that they do. In fact, this *is* the relationship I describe in Chapter 5. Before exploring what that same relationship means for our very youngest writers, I'd like to briefly explore another dimension of the reading-writing connection. Early-childhood classrooms lend themselves particularly well to the kind of instruction that relies upon writing to strengthen your reading ability. First, asking young children to write every day solidifies any of the phonemic understandings they need to become readers. (Phonemic understandings refer to the child's ability to hear component sounds in word.) Attempting to spell words is a much more effective teacher than filling out endless and boring workbook pages on isolated sound-symbol correspondences. The frequent spelling of "high-frequency" words that comes with regular writing opportunities also promotes reading fluency. Then too, asking young children to write makes them approach reading in an intimate way, becoming the insider that Frank Smith has so eloquently described. They look at text with new eyes, noticing things that nonwriters may not have noticed. Writing heightens their awareness to the nuances of text and therefore helps them get more out of these reading experiences. Additionally, children who write regularly and who have been growing as writers understand that reading is not a passive activity. The writer does not give it all away but requires the reader to work to make meaning. (See *Lifetime Guarantees* for additional thoughts on studying students' writing for clues to improve their reading.)

Finally, I'd like to remind readers that the writing young students do can be used to teach reading in early-childhood classmates. In her wonderful book, *The Classroom Interview: A World of Learning,* Paula Rogovin demonstrates how the interviews her first graders conduct and write up become the text for her small-group reading instruction. Likewise, Isabel Beaton binds her kindergartners' original poems into anthologies that become at-home reading materials. Similarly, young writers can deliberately write predictable texts for beginning readers as described in my conference with Matthew on page 172. Then too, there are more unconventional ways that student writing can be used to strengthen reading abilities in an early-childhood classroom. A few of these structures follow.

Word Wall Substitutions

Imagine selecting a simple piece of student writing and displaying it for all to see. After reading it aloud, the teacher can cover over a carefully selected word and ask students to search the word wall for other words that could sensibly replace the hidden word. (Word walls are public postings of words that students have discussed and are expected to become familiar with, recognizing on sight as they read and using as reference to unlock unknown words.) For example, Justin wrote the poem in Figure 6.7 when he was a student in Pam's kindergarten. Pam could present the poem in standard spelling (see below), and then cover the word *eat*, asking for sensible substitutions. Perhaps the classroom word wall contains such words as *dance, sing, walk, write, read,* and so on. The

Figure 6.7

teacher could lead the class in rereading the poem using the alternatives suggested. Such an activity would provide students with practice in rereading their word walls as well as providing a way to honor the author's work. Moreover, teachers would learn a lot about their students based on the words they choose.

Justin's poem in standard spelling is as follows:

Eat
I Love to eat
And eat I shall
I love to eat

Turning Snippets into Shared Reading

Every once in a while, I come across a line or two from a young child's writing that deserves public attention. One day, while browsing some first-grade writing folders, I came across the one-liner that appears in Figure 6.8. This is the kind of line that easily lends itself to playful innovations, eventually becoming engaging shared reading material for the entire class. With the author's permission, I added the lines below to the student's original lyrical thought.

Raise your hand if you went to Disneyland.
Raise your knee if you went to Albany.
Raise your toe if you went to Idaho.
Raise your chin if you went to Michigan.

Figure 6.8

Figure 6.9

Children began orally composing their own such lines, and in fact asked family members to join in on the fun. The resulting chant became popular shared reading material. Young children always seem genuinely motivated to read the work generated by a child in their class and also aspire to create similar text themselves.

Similarly, when a kindergartner wrote the simple line of conversation—"Katy, where are you? Come out to play"—that appears in invented spelling above in Figure 6.9, the teacher could have "published" this text by preparing it in standard spelling and adding a repeating line for every child in the class. (Jorge, where are you? Come out and play. Emily, where are you? Come out and play). What five-year-old wouldn't want to see his or her name in print, decorate the page, and learn to read all those very useful words? Then too, with the author's permission (not very hard to come by), the teacher could have asked each child in the class to compose an answer, thereby creating a predictable text. (Katy, where are you? Come out to play. Sorry I can't, I'm cooking with my mother. Katy where are you? Come out to play. Sorry I can't, I'm playing with my dog.) The class could decide on an appropriate ending. Perhaps little Katy will finally come out to play. Activities like these are not just good for readers, but model possibilities for young writers.

Designing Reading Center Interactions Based on Student Writing

Since stepping away from the Manhattan New School, I have visited many early-childhood reading workshops dependent on the creation of reading centers. In other words, when the teacher pulls a group of students together for needs-driven small-group instruction, the rest of the class rotates from one teacher-designed reading center to another. (At our school, the rest of the class just reads independently when the teacher is working with small groups or conferring one-on-one with students.) The activities created for these centers include such reading tasks as rereading shared reading materials (familiar poems, recipes, songs, big books, etc.), writing in reader-response logs (keeping tabs on the titles of the books they've read and writing a reaction to them), re-creating poems with specially prepared sentence strips (teachers write the lines of poems on separate strips of paper and children arrange them in correct order), listening to books on tape in a listening center and following along with the actual text. (It is hoped that all these center activities promote real reading experiences and not those arts-and-crafts literature extensions that do not ask children to actually read or reread whole texts.) It has occurred to me that teachers who believe in the structure of reading centers could use student writing as part of these interactions. Parent volunteers and student teachers can prepare student writing on tape, as part of sentence strip reconfigurations, or prepared in a special binding that requires written reader response. Of course, student texts must be prepared in standard spelling if they are to be used to strengthen other student's reading abilities.

Using Children's Literature to Lift the Quality of Student Work

On pages 116–127, I describe a collection of literature-based minilessons that I've enjoyed sharing with our older students. I have another shelf of books that I share in our early-childhood writing workshops. Again, students have ample opportunities to listen and respond to these read-alouds before I suggest they take lessons from these potential mentors.

To Inspire Young Writers to Create Concept Books

Many kindergartners spend their writing time drawing and then labeling their pictures. When teachers want to capitalize on their strengths as beginning writers of labels and yet raise the bar a bit, they share a stack of concept books. Instead of producing one page entities, they challenge young writers to create several pages connected to a concept. For example, they might share Michelle Koch's *Just One More,* a very simple presentation of singular and plural, including bold illustrations and labels for leaf and leaves, foot and feet, and child and children. They might also share Jug-Huyn Yoon's *Popposites*, a pop-up book of opposites. Although children will not be able to create such an elaborate multidimensional production, they will be able to write their own book of opposites. They might also borrow ideas from Lisa Grunweld's *Now Soon Later*, a book intended to help young children understand the concept of time. Even kindergartners can create their own version of this book, exploring the concepts of now, soon, and later as they tell about their school days, playtime activities, and dinner, bath, and bedtime rituals.

To Shift Students Away from One-Word Labels

When kindergartners seem ready to shift from writing one-word labels alongside their drawings to writing more informative phrases or sentences, I share Louise Borden's *Caps, Hats, Socks and Mittens: A Book About the Four Seasons*, illustrated by Lillian Hoban, in which the author offers sensory and rhythmic tributes to each season of the year. I prepare in advance one-word labels on small strips of yellow sticky paper. Each label contains the name of a season of the year. I explain to the children, "If Louise had just written these very simple labels, the teacher probably would *not* have chosen to read this book aloud. It just wouldn't have been interesting enough. But Louise wanted to write the kind of book that a teacher *would* choose to read aloud, so she wrote more than that one word next to every picture. For example, instead of simply labeling the illustrations as 'Fall,' she writes about the smells of autumn, what it's like to go back to school, the colors of the leaves changing, and Halloween scenes." I end the lesson by suggesting that if children think they are ready to write like Louise in *Caps, Hats, Socks, and Mittens*, I would be around to help them do it.

(I think it's helpful for teachers to use the phrase, "write like _____ in _____." It reminds children that they are expected to take lessons from the books we read. It also keeps the names of books and authors in the classroom memory bank, so that children are more likely to refer back to these specific books as needed.)

To Remind Children of Their Own Stories

Whenever I read aloud Sally Derby's *My Steps*, I'm prepared for a lot of interruptions. It is the story of a young child who is very attached to her front stoop. Through all the seasons of the year, she reflects on her favorite hangout, eating snacks, meeting with friends, watching neighbors, making up stories, and playing pretend games. Adjoa J. Burrowes' illustrations are as evocative as the words. Perhaps this stoop-sitting book resonates especially with city kids, who inevitably realize how many ideas they have for their own writing. The room fills with lots of, "Me, too! I do that! That's like my friend," leading students to realize that if they write about their everyday pastimes they too can produce the kind of book that will make other children say, "Me, too!"

To Encourage at-Home Writing

Young children can always spot a Marisabina Russo picture book. Her use of color and design are so distinctive. Similar to the main character in *My Steps,* Hannah has a favorite place to play, revealed in the title of the book, *Under the Table*. The child draws on the bottom of the table, completely filling the space with rainbows, flowers, suns, and faces. When her parents discover her wrongdoing, they solve the problem peacefully and respectfully. Hannah receives a big thick pad of paper so her parents can hang up her works of art and Hannah promises never to draw on furniture, clothing, or walls. Whenever I share this book with young children, the conversation invariably shifts to at-home writing. We compile a list of supplies needed, kinds of writing and drawing to do, and safe places to do it. These jottings could of course serve as the basis for a letter home to families about the value of at-home writing.

To Introduce Young Writers to Basic Templates

When our youngest writers are in need of a big challenge in their writing workshop, teachers might suggest such early-childhood projects as writing an alphabet book or a counting book. Children's familiarity with the twenty-six letters and with numbers seem to provide a scaffolding for the new work to come. Many early-childhood teachers create basket collections that demonstrate the wide range of ways that authors have chosen to create alphabet and counting books. For example, Anita Lobel's beautiful picture book *One Lighthouse, One Moon* offers three such safety nets in one. This book is guaranteed inspiration as it contains a simple listlike tribute to the days of the week (listing the color of shoes worn on each day), another for the months of the year (presenting a cat's favorite activity in each), as well as a lyrical counting book (connecting all items to nautical life). In addition to providing these simple templates, teachers can use the book to remind children to pick one umbrella topic to unite all the pages of their books.

Talia and Rachel, a kindergartner and a second grader, coauthored and illustrated the following pages of what they titled "Fall Counting Book."

1-one—When the first leaf hit the ground, it was a sign of fall.

2-two—When two trees turned different colors, it was a sign of fall.

3-three—When three apples hit the ground from a tree, it was a sign of fall.

4-four—When four pumpkins were ripe on their stems, it was a sign of fall.

5-five—When five pinecones were eaten by a squirrel, it was a sign of fall.

6-six—When six acorns were collected by another squirrel, it was a sign of fall.

7-seven—When seven squash were cooked, it was a sign of fall.

8-eight—When eight berries were picked, it was a sign of fall.

9-nine—When nine nuts were blown off a tree, it was a sign of fall.

10-ten—When ten cocoa drops of mine dripped off my cup, it was a sign of winter.

To Encourage Children to Write in a New Way About People They Know Well

When our youngest writers choose to write about people, and they frequently do, they often staple a wad of paper together and title it, "My Family." Each page in their book usually boasts another member of the family, with words such as, "This is my mom. I love my mom. She has curly hair." To add more sparkle to these potential family heirlooms, it is helpful to read aloud such books as Douglas Woods' *What Dads Can't Do*, with illustrations by Doug Cushman, Laura Numeroff's *What Grandmas Do Best* and *What Grandpas Do Best* (companion books bound together), with illustrations by Lynn Munsinger, and Keiko Narahashi's *Two Girls Can*. The authors of all these books present the beloved characters well by describing the specific actions that they take (or don't take, as in the case of *What Dads Can't Do*). How much more we would get to know that mom with the curly hair if we read about how she gently tucks her daughter into bed at night, rushes up and down the aisle of the supermarket, or is able to talk on the telephone while she reads the newspaper and drinks coffee. Even our youngest writers can learn to show the people they write about in action.

To Help Children Select Topics and to Write Fluently About Them

Early-childhood teachers are always encouraging students who are ready to write more fluent texts. They want their children to move beyond one-word labels or one-sentence captions at the bottom of their drawings. One day, I carefully selected a few picture books from Pam's class library, paying careful attention to the titles alone. I pulled off her shelf such books as Anna Grossnickle Hines' *What Joe Saw,* Kim Lewis' *My Friend Harry*, Molly Bang's *One Fall Day*, Jane R. Howard's *When I'm Hungry*, and Laura Krauss Melmed's *I Love You as Much . . .* I suggested that Pam show only the cover of the books to the children, reading the titles aloud and pointing out that each book had many pages and that every page had something to do with the title. The children were then invited to guess what could possibly be on all those pages. In actuality, we were encouraging the children to write list books or attribute books, using broad generic topics. The children guessed that on every page of *What Joe Saw* would be another thing that Joe saw, on every page of *My Friend Harry* would be another piece of information about this person, on every page of *I Love You as Much* would be another kind thing you would say to someone you love, and so on. We encouraged students that day to think about their topics, choosing ones that they could stick to, writing several pages about the one topic they selected. As can be expected in any early-childhood workshop, five-year-old Jacob wrote his own version of "When I'm Hungry." It appears below.

> When I'm hungry, I like to eat.
> When I'm hungry, my tummy growls.
> When I'm hungry, I could eat a whole elephant.
> And then I have dessert!

Once young writers catch on to writing books that have several pages all connected to a title, it's fairly simple to demonstrate the power of an ending that sounds like an ending.

To Spark Conversation About the Powers of a Good Observer

Lily, the main character in Palmyra LoMonaco's *Night Letters*, is a child with a rich imagination and a purple notepad. She imagines that all the creatures in her backyard leave messages for her, which she records in her notepad. Lily is a great observer and has learned to write from other creatures' points of view. She has also made writing part of her evening ritual. Teachers who choose to read aloud this book can inspire lots of talk about writing outside of school, writing about nature, writers needing to be good observers, and the bigger challenge of writing from someone else's point of view.

To Remind Young Writers That They Can Write to Teach Others About Their Areas of Expertise

The young character in Charlotte Zolotow's *Peter and the Pigeons*, with illustrations by Martine Gourbault, cares greatly about pigeons. He knows how they feel, look, and sound. After I read aloud this picture book, I find myself asking the class, "If Peter were not a character in a picture book but a real little boy who attended our school, what topic do you think he would write about during writing workshop?" The answer, of course, is pigeons. I then remind our youngest writers that they too could choose "teaching topics." I suggest that they write to teach others about their areas of expertise. I often follow up by sharing a stack of informational texts written in a variety of basic, accessible nonfiction formats, including alphabet books, question-and-answer books, or attribute books (texts that with each turn of the page list one more attribute—facts, descriptors, or ideas) connected to a topic. These include Blair Drawson's *I Like Hats!*, Philemon Sturges' *I Love Trucks!*, and Olga Litowinsky's *Boats for Bedtime*.

To Help Children Recognize Patterns in Literature

In addition to the very basic alphabet and counting books described above, many of the other books that line the shelves of an early-childhood classroom contain readily recognizable patterns. Teachers select these kinds of books because their often-predictable nature supports children who are just learning to read. These books can also support the child learning to write by providing accessible templates, ones that can become more and more challenging as students move up through the grades. See page 198 for their particular value in grade two.

Providing Early-Childhood Students with Many Reasons to Write

One year, Eve Mutchnick and Layne Hudes, two of our early-childhood teachers, took the *New York Times* best-seller list in nonfiction and showed us how their five- and six-year-olds write in all the formats on the list. These included sportswriting, interviews, letters, and photographic essays. Of course, we're proud when our children write for all the same reasons that the adults in our community write, but a reminder is in order. We are talking about child-size adaptations of these formats. When we encourage variety in an early-childhood writing workshop, we are encouraging variety within the parameters of what is appropriate, meaningful, and realistic for very young children. Our youngest writers are *not* asked to write lengthy footnoted reports; instead we look to child-size genres, ones with appropriate and realistic challenges, supports, and expectations.

Similar thinking applies to social studies inquiry in the early-childhood classroom. We would rather invite our youngest children to study their neighborhood park than the rain forest, outer space travel, or life in colonial times. Some five- and six-year-olds might be curious about these topics, and we can provide simple and satisfactory answers to any questions young children might pose, but we prefer that early-childhood students spend big blocks of time researching the "here and now" topics that allow us to arrange frequent field trips, interviews with experts, firsthand observations, authentic artifact collections, and so on. Just as we are committed to finding topics with appropriate and realistic challenges, supports, and expectations, so too we are ever determined to highlight those genres that enable children to be children.

Encouraging Variety

Ways to encourage variety in primary classrooms include:

• Getting the workshop started in ways that privilege variety (see page 161.)

• Publishing in ways that highlight and encourage variety. For example, teachers might label a collection of blank big books according to desired genres. Teachers would then add individual finished work to ongoing classroom collections. Pam, for example, gathered, sorted, and mounted examples of the more surprising genres her kindergarten students occasionally chose to write. She then invited her students to make beautiful covers for each of three blank books. One was labeled "Poetry," another "Announcements," and a third, "Letters." (Letters are meant to be mailed and so only copies were added to these permanent collections.) Pam also included some real-world artifacts that had meaning for her children, like her student teacher's engagement announcement from *The New York Times*. The books became very popular reading material, as children were eager to read one another's work and the books inspired children to try new formats themselves. Perhaps some children wrote poems, letters, and announcements because they wanted their work included in the class anthologies, but they also wrote in these new formats because they better understood their options and had powerful models. I can easily imagine creating additional collections for Pam's library shelf, perhaps including ones devoted to lists, inventories, and captions attached to family photos. Next year's incoming kindergartners can start the year browsing some very interesting reading material.

• Sharing carefully chosen children's literature in which the main characters write for many reasons in many formats. (See bibliography in Appendix 1.)

• Sharing the portfolio of a child who writes in many formats (see examples from Matthew's folder in Appendix 7.)

• Conferring in ways that promote new formats. I love the look on a five-year-old's face when I look at his writing and announce, "Oh you're taking inventory!" or, "You're the first one in the class to write a caption for a photo" or, "Good for you! Your writing sounds like you're keeping a diary" or, "Let me shake your hand, you're collecting data!" and so on. You can be sure that the next day several more children will be attempting to take inventory, write captions for family photo albums, keep a diary, or collect data. New genres spread quickly in an early-childhood classroom.

• Inviting students to keep tabs on the kinds of writing they're doing. In Karen Ruzzo's second grade, the children fill out a grid to indicate their attempts at new formats. Alongside a sheet of graph paper, Karen lists genre options and the children color in a box for each attempt. In addition to poetry, fiction stories, and nonfiction teaching books, the possibilities included: lists, songs, letters, stories, diary entries, nature journals, recipes, how-to instructions, news announcement, reviews, inventories, interviews, and so on.

• Hosting real-world genre studies in the early-childhood classrooms. Teachers and students can formally study the writing of greeting cards, toasts, how-to instructions, photo album captions, letters to friends who've moved away, party plans, inventories, and so on.

• Inviting children who've discovered a new reason to write or a new way of writing to sit in the Author's Chair and share with the entire class. No doubt, if the young author of the very detailed "Missing Ship" sign in Figure 6.10 or the five-year-old creator of the cartoon bubbles conversation in Figure 6.11 were to share, traces of their stylistic devices would appear in many other students' work. The bubble coming from the airplane in the latter is the pilot announcing arrival in "Rochester!" On the ground is the waiting grandmother asking, "Where's my grandson?" In the former, an object is described in the hopes that it will be identified and returned to its owner. The labeled diagram is followed by these descriptors and instruction:

> Made of styrofoam
> Says x-doom
> If you find it please bring it to room 2-408

• Challenging children to do several pieces of writing, each in a different format, on one topic. For example, the dinosaur lover can write a riddle book, an informational teaching book, a fictional account, a poem, a counting or alphabet book, and a captioned poster about dinosaurs. When completed, the student can share her entire collection with classmates. (See also Darryn's challenge on page 178–180).

Grade Two—What's New?

When students begin attending our school in kindergarten, second grade feels like a turning point. In kindergarten and first grade, we spend a great deal of time making sure that students have joyful attitudes toward becoming writers, take risks as spellers, and write for all the reasons the adults in our community write. When all these elements are in place, we eventually turn our attention to improving the quality of the work. (This was apparent in the conferences with first graders, Luke, Adam, and Matthew, described on pages 171–172). In grade two, especially for children who have been with us since kindergarten, we are able to start the year focusing on lifting the quality of their writing.

Missing Ship

- Made of styRofoam
- Says X Doom
- if you find it please
bring it to room 2-408

Figure 6.10

Figure 6.11

Characteristics of Second-Grade Writers

The following descriptors mark the writing of the second graders I know best, the ones who have been writing regularly for two years and who have been listening to wonderful literature read aloud several times a day.

Second Graders' Writing Folders Contain a Wide Range of Topics and Formats

One year I received a wonderful note from a parent about her daughter's year as a second-grade writer. Leslie's comments began,

> *As I have every year since she started preschool, I just spent the last couple of hours poring over Laura's folders, files, scribbles, drawings, and reports. As I always do, I planned to just glance tonight and really read it later, and as usual I became so absorbed that I read every word on every sheet. I guess it is a function of her age, but this year her work felt compelling.*

She has long written accounts of praying mantis diets and details of the Titanic and her innermost thoughts on everything from her best friends to her grandparents and how she feels feeling grass between her toes . . .

Laura's wide range of interests and her choice of forms to best support those topics indicate to me that Laura has had a very successful second-grade writing experience.

The Writing of Second Graders Maintains the Voice of Childhood

As I've said, I'm not interested in turning children's writing into adult-sounding works of art. I'm delighted when seven-year-olds produce the following kinds of writing.

Annie's picture book titled *Cats Always Play Dress Up*, contains a well-illustrated page for each of these lines:

> Cats love hats.
> Cats love skirts.
> Cats love mittens.
> Cats love earrings.
> Cats love shoes.
> Cats love sunglasses.
> Cats love bows.
> Cats love bracelets.
> Cats love necklaces.
> Cats love to dress up in everything.

Andrej sends me a note, telling me that his teacher enjoyed the following poem.

> **In a Cave**
> In a cave I was scared.
> I lit up a candle.
> I saw a light and my shadow.
> I saw me for the first time.
> I ran out to tell everyone.

Darryn sends me a letter advising me of misconduct:

Dear Shelley,

Kids are writing words on the bathroom walls that are bad influences for kindergarten, 1st grade, and 2nd grade. Since it is Earth Day it would be nice if you could talk to the student council about pollution. I hope all this works out.

Love, Darryn

Stacey writes the following tips for her teacher who has recently moved to Manhattan:

Tips

Watch out for cars.

Don't go out at night because it is scary and somebody can take your pocketbook.

And if you have a dog, don't let it go in the street.

When somebody looks at you and you have a ring on, turn it the other way.

Second Graders Delight in Writing to Move an Audience

In all the above examples, students had real audiences for their writing. In order for students to maintain their interest in writing every day, they need to truly understand what writing is for. Their work cannot simply be stuffed into a cluttered folder. Additionally, second-grade writers are beginning to understand that the conventions attached to punctuation, grammar, spelling, and handwriting help those audiences appreciate their writing and therefore take pride in acquiring the requisite editing skills. Annie's book is read aloud to kindergarten story partners. Andrej's poem is read aloud at a performance of Jacques d'Amboise's National Dance Institute. Darryn's letter is discussed at the next meeting of the student council. Stacey's tips are given to her teacher and the young writer expects them to be taken seriously.

Second Graders Appreciate the Notion That Their Words
Need Not Sound Like Anybody Else's Words

When Matthew shares his short beach story with me, "At the beach I had lots of fun. I love the ocean. I had snacks. I had fun at the beach," I can tell him, "Your words sound like anyone in the class could have written them. Where are the thoughts that only Matthew has?" His revised piece appears below:

At the beach I had lots of fun. I went boogie boarding in the big waves. Sometimes I go bump on the waves like I'm on a roller coaster. I love the ocean so much I don't want to get out. I went in the deep end. I had fun at the beach. I had sliced apples and graham crackers. I found shells. Some shells have snails in them and some don't.

Matthew understood how to add the kind of honest details that make this story uniquely his.

Successful Publications Are Contagious in a Second-Grade Classroom

When Matthew completed his beach story, he needed to find a place in the real world to go public with his work. Will he slip his work into the back of a classroom trade book about the beach and have them read as companions? Will he add these words to a family photo album and start his career as the family archivist, keeping tabs on all the snapshots? Will he begin a childhood scrapbook, pasting this memory into a big blank book, to be added to throughout his elementary school years? Will he start a class anthology of summer memories, putting out a call for manuscripts? Matthew could choose to take part in any of these forms of publishing or invent his own. The added benefit is that any of these ideas will become contagious in a second grade classroom, inspiring other young writers to do likewise. Seven-year-olds seem to delight in doing what their classmates have done. Attempts at riddle books, pop-up books, or original tongue-twisters can spread around an early-childhood classroom quicker than head lice and chicken pox.

Second Grade Is a Prime Time to Ask Young Writers to Take a Slow Look at Texts, Attempting to Do What Their Favorite Writers Have Done

Of course, the choice of text is crucial. If children are writing brief narratives, they can learn to slow down significant parts of the story by studying a picture book such as *Salt Hands* by Jane Aragon. If they want to share informational writing, Seymour Simon's *Book of Trucks* is a model worth studying. (See more on nonfiction writing in Chapter 4 in *Lifetime Guarantees*.) If they want to capture a place they can learn to include telling details from Frane Lessac's *My Little Island*. (See more on writing about a place beginnning on page 258.) If they are interested in writing poetry they can take many lessons from such accessible collections as Marci Ridlon's *Sun Through the Window*. (See pages 300–304 for additional information on second-grade poets.)

Literary Templates Serve Second Graders Particularly Well

As previously noted, in kindergarten and first-grade classrooms, the sky is usually the limit in the writing workshop, with teachers adding as few constraints as possible. Occasionally, teachers might invite their youngest writers to write using a traditional format, such as an alphabet or counting book, a letter or simple poetic form, or teachers might invite an entire class to collaborate on an innovation of a familiar, predictable text. For the most part, however, children draw, write, and share in a mostly open-ended fashion. Teachers are so thrilled that these very young children are writing that they would probably beam with pride if a first grader wrote a story about slipping roaches into his little brother's oatmeal, claiming them to be raisins. Well, perhaps they wouldn't exactly beam with pride. They would need to have some serious conversations, but they would acknowledge that the student understands what it means to choose his own topic and genre.

After more than two years of complete freedom to write whatever pops into their mind, it comes as no surprise that at midyear second graders seem particularly enthusiastic about learning from the books in their classrooms, and in fact, seem very willing to borrow elements from those books. It's as if they've had enough, for the time being, of being on their own and are happy to have a few patterns to follow. The structures, language, and design of these books become templates, providing guidelines for children who want their books to look and sound like books in the library.

The following books can come in very handy for teachers who want to help second graders write a book that has the sound of a book from the class library. Note, whole classes of students are *not* assigned to write versions of these books or to borrow literary elements contained in them. Instead, after reading the books aloud and providing adequate time for response to the texts, second-grade teachers invite children to imagine and orally discuss what kind of writing they *might* do if they chose to attempt to do what these authors had done. Of course, in any one class, a few children might decide to follow through on these ideas. (Note that many children participate orally in playing with the possibilities presented, never choosing to write these ideas down. Even though the elements discussed might not show up in the child's current writing, there is great value in children understanding how authors add literary elements and elegance of design to their writing. This information will serve them well as they continue to grow as writers.)

The topic as well as the design of Jan Slepian's *Emily Just in Time*, with illustrations by Glo Coalson, resonate for seven-year-olds. They easily identify with the young girl who takes pride in growing up but still has trouble spending the night away from home. The author and illustrator present a series of things that Emily couldn't do, but "now she can." Second graders can fill many pages with their own examples of "not-being-able . . . but now I can." Wells wrote the following response to this text. She began by listing all her changing food preferences and ends the piece with a surprising shift.

> When I was little I liked my hotdogs plain, now I like them still cut up, but with ketchup.
> When I was little I did not want to try wonton soup, and then I grew and I tried it and liked it. And now when I go to the Chinese restaurant I order it.
> When I was little I didn't want to try sorbet. Then I tried it and liked it. And now when I go the ice cream shop, I get it.
> I used to not want to go on roller coasters. Then I went on the Kiddie Coaster and I hated it but I did not yell. I never went on a roller coaster again.

Tobi Tobias' picture book *Serendipity,* with illustrations by Peter R. Reynolds, explains the meaning of *serendipity* by providing page after page of child-size examples of the concept, each beginning with the words "Serendipity is when . . ." Second graders can create their own list books presenting other words that they can proudly define for their friends. Second graders suggested such words as *hungry*, *bored*, *excited*, *fortunate* and—true to the spirit of second grade—one student suggested that he could vary this theme by writing, "Gross is when . . ."

Judy Hindley's *The Best Thing About a Puppy*, with illustrations by Patricia Casey, is a classic good news/bad news picture book. The very accessible alternating pattern is very popular with second graders, who readily talk about the pros and cons of such topics as having a new baby in the family, having divorced parents, spending time with a baby-sitter, moving to a bigger apartment, or having their older sibling move out of the house. See Figure 6.12 for Jessica's piece about having friends, in which she used this alternating design and added the requisite closing line, complete with several exclamation points, to make sure her ending sounds like an ending.

Note that, although Jessica's content is not filled with unusually surprising insights about friendship and her style of writing is not spectacularly clever or original, we must remember that she is seven years old and this short, competent piece is worthy of classroom celebration. She worked hard, borrowed a format effectively, shared her thoughts

Jessica Marie Almodovar

The good thing about friends is you can play with them.

The bad thing about friends is that they sometimes says no when you want to play with them.

The good thing about friends is that you can do hand games with them.

The bad thing about friends is that they can hit you and kick you.

The good thing about friends is that they can play tag with you.

The bad thing about friends is that they can get into a fight with you.

The good thing about friends is that they can sing songs together.

But that's what friends are for!!!!

Figure 6.12

honestly, and edited her work successfully. What's more, she beamed with pride at her accomplishment.

Patricia Lauber's *True-or-False Book of Horses* taps into seven-year-olds' desire to teach other people what they consider their own area of expertise as well as their desire to play a friendly "Gotcha!" Each double-page spread in this picture book is headed by a statement about horses followed by the question "True or False?" The author then provides a detailed answer to each question. Seven-year-olds readily accept the challenge of inventing possibly false statements about their areas of interest. The results can be quite humorous when young children choose such topics as babies, homework, mice, catching colds, or playing baseball.

Anni Axworthy's informational "Peephole Books," including *Guess What I Am* and *Guess What I'll Be* also provide a simple riddle-like structure that enables second graders to share their growing areas of expertise. The author offers a series of clues and with the turn of each page the reader discovers the answer. Of course, the actual peephole cutouts, providing the reader with additional visual clues, pose a more sophisticated challenge for second graders, one they often accept with relish.

Second graders seem to love Vera B. Williams' *Stringbeans Trip to the Shining Sea*, a picture book written in postcard format. Seven-year-olds are becoming fluent enough to send significant letters (or e-mails) to people they want to keep in touch with, including neighbors who have moved away, former classmates, and grandparents who retire to warmer climates. Of course, using the letter format to craft a story worth telling poses a greater challenge than simply writing a letter. Some second graders seem ready for the challenge. (See Appendix 1 for a bibliography of picture books written in letter format.)

Win or Lose by How You Choose is one of those interactive books that asks questions of its readers and provides multiple-choice answers. This book, filled with very childlike dilemmas, was written by none other than television's Judge Judy Sheindlin. Most children will have a strong opinion about how to respond to these very realistic situations and some children might be inspired to create their own version of realistic problem scenarios with choice solutions for the reader.

Melinda Long's *When Papa Snores*, with illustrations by Holly Meade, has an alternating pattern—what happens when papa snores, followed by what happens when nana snores, and then back to papa again—which continues until the big ending, when the reader discovers that the grandchild snores as well. In addition to the alternating pattern, this book also is a cumulative tale, with each page repeating the contents of the page before. This additional pattern is a most difficult one for very young children to borrow and usually facilitates their reading more than their writing. (In addition to talking about the patterns in this book, the title alone can inspire some new topic choices. I might tell students that I could write some important and interesting stories from my own childhood titled, "When Mama Sews," or "When Grandma Bakes." I would then invite students to reveal the people about whom they can pick an activity to present well. Of course, I would need to remind children that they need not write their stories with an alternating or cumulative design.)

Many professional writers have published variations of familiar songs and stories and young children can be invited to occasionally do likewise. For example, Will Hillenbrand begins his picture book *Down by the Station* with the familiar lyrics to this popular song. With each turn of the page, the author adds a clever substitution, with the reader meeting a wide range of animals, including pandas, flamingos, and elephants. In addition to the familiar refrain of "puff, puff, toot, toot," the reader adds the sounds of all the animals encountered.

Jill Paton Walsh's *When I Was Little Like You*, with illustrations by Stephen Lambert, is a series of conversations between a child and his grandmother. The child points out something in view (a train, an ice-cream truck, a ship, etc.), and the grandmother reflects on what those things were like when she was a youngster, hence the title, *When I Was Little Like You*. These spoken title words are how the grandmother begins each response. Occasionally, children write the beginnings of such a potentially repetitive text and the teacher need only encourage the child to keep on going. "Good for you," she might say, "you're writing a book like Jill in *When I Was Little Like You*."

Likewise, children can spot the pattern in Ruth Krauss' *You're Just What I Need*, with pictures by Julia Noonan. The mother, spying a child hidden under a blanket, playfully questions, "Can it be a . . . ?" and each time the child responds, "No, No, No." "Imagine," I say to young writers, "an entire book written with a similar question asked over and over again. Can anyone imagine a question that's like the glue that holds a book together? Does anyone think they have the kind of question that would make readers want to keep on turning the page?"

(Whenever children are studying a potential template from literature, it is important to spend a few extra minutes demonstrating how they can use these structures with their own good ideas. For example, when children come up with their own questions after hearing *You're Just What I Need*, I would think through the possibilities of their questions becoming the fulcrum for an entire book and I would do so publicly, orally, and playfully. If the child offers, "How about if I keep asking my mom, 'What should I eat?' Could that turn into a good book with lots of pages?" I would respond by asking, "How would you have that mom answer the question? How would you make the reader want to keep hearing those answers? How would you end the book so it was as good as a book in the library?" If the student had no ideas, I might ask permission to share the kernel idea with classmates and brainstorm possibilities. I might even share my own idea in order to generate more. I would also introduce ways to vary the use of the question. For example, some authors repeat the question but ask it of different people. Some ask it of the same person, but alter the question slightly with each turn of the page. For example, the child can ask his mother, "What shall I eat?" followed by, "What shall I play, wear, sing, read?, etc." Some authors ask the same question of many people and turn the tale into a cumulative one by repeating each respondent's answer with each turn of the page. Then too, I would share additional age-appropriate books that are structured around a repeated question. These would include Charlotte Zolotow's *Do You Know What I'll Do?*, Nancy Van Laan's *When Winter Comes*, and Julie Markes' *Good Thing You're Not an Octopus*!

It's important for children to realize that just because you borrow a pattern from a book does *not* mean that you must borrow the topic of that book. To prevent such limiting connections from happening, I have found it helpful to engage children in lots of the oral play described above, so that children can hear the world of possibilities. Another way for teachers to help children realize that you do not need to use the same or similar topics when you use a similar design is for the teacher to create her own original text based on a literary pattern being studied. In other words, if a book about visiting a grandmother centered on a repeated refrain, I might compose another repeated refrain to shape a book about a new family pet. Then too, it is helpful to collect several published books with similar patterns, ones that clearly demonstrate that you can write about many different things using a similar pattern or structure. For example, Brenda Shannon Yee's *Sand Castle*, with illustrations by Thea Kliros, and Tan Koide's *May We Sleep Here Tonight?* with illustrations by Yasuko Koide, are both picture books in which the continuous arrival of one more person or animal, each repeating a similar request, pushes the plot along. In the first, each new child who approaches the building of a sand castle at the beach adds a new idea to its construction. In the second, each new animal family that arrives at a house in the woods adds to the suspenseful ending of this Goldilocks-like tale. When talking to young children about the similar patterns in the books, I would also ask how they might ever consider using this pattern in their writing. A second grader, for example, might choose to borrow this pattern when she shapes a piece about the guests at her birthday party, the addition of pets to the family menagerie, all the members of the family she calls into her room as part of her bedtime ritual, or all the teachers that entered her classroom on a particularly busy morning. The decision to borrow the elements of design described above, would turn these possibly ordinary accounts into memorable ones with literary quality. They might also open the conversation of adding fictional elements to a "true" story in order to make it sound more like a book in the library. For example, even though only one guest called out, "I can't believe you are seven years old already!" the young author needs to know that it is okay to stretch the truth and make each guest call that out upon their arrival, if it adds to the meaning of the story or enables a clever ending.

The challenge is for teachers to get good at choosing those books that will make seven-year-olds say, "I get it. I know what the author is doing. I can do that. I want to do that." Later, when children arrive at third grade and are asked to carry a writer's notebook, they will once again be faced with a "sky's the limit" world of writing. Their teachers will rarely say, "No, you're not supposed to . . ." or, "No, you are not allowed to . . ." Instead, teachers will invite children to use their writers' notebooks in open-ended and original ways. Students who have played with many different literary shapes and structures seem better prepared to handle these open-ended invitations. They appear confident in tapping into the templates they have internalized, innovating upon them and inventing their own in order to shape significant jottings into publishable formats.

Writer's Notebooks in the Early-Childhood Grades of Kindergarten Through Second Grade Are Generally Unnecessary

Children at those very young ages usually look at the world with wide eyes of wonder. They do find the world a most fascinating place. We have no reason to shift these children into a wide-awake stance. They live wide-awake lives. They notice, question, touch, and are touched by everything.

In Some Circumstances, Second-Grade Teachers Introduce a Modified Version of the Writer's Notebook

For example, teachers might extend an invitation to children who have reached a plateau in their writing, who've become bored with writing, or who somehow have lost that wide-awake stance and have become very conforming and cautious in their writing. They might introduce this tool to the very determined or accomplished writers who clamor to keep on writing in and out of school. They might also suggest a special kind of writer's notebook, one devoted to a particular topic, for the child who has a healthy obsession. I could imagine a second grader keeping a small writer's notebook devoted to such an interest as ballet dancing, coin collecting, or living with a new baby in the family. (These notebooks would be narrow in scope, much the way Karen used the writer's notebook for her second-grade study of New York City described below.)

Sometimes second-grade teachers decide to pull together a small cluster of children at the *end* of second grade to give them a feel for what is ahead in grade three. They might select just a small group of students to begin keeping a writer's notebook. They wouldn't necessarily select the most accomplished writers. They are more likely to invite children who are joyful about their writing, who work independently, and who seem ready to handle a portable tool (children who are reliable enough to bring their notebooks home and return them once again to school). Once this small cluster of children gets going, teachers trust that the use of the notebook will become contagious. Other students will yearn to join in.

Some teachers have also introduced the writer's notebook as a whole-class device for *limited* use in their second grade. One year, Karen Ruzzo wondered about the possibility of using writer's notebooks as a tool to enrich her grade-two New York City research project. During their regular ongoing writing workshop, her second graders used loose sheets of paper, kept together in a folder, to write in a very wide range of genres. They drafted, revised, edited, and published their work regularly. Karen recognized the possibility of using the writer's notebook as a tool to help her second graders closely study New York City.

Karen invited me into her classroom to introduce a simpler version of this writing tool. I explained the idea of everyone having a blank book to record his or her thoughts, learnings, observations, and questions about New York City. I then emptied my pockets and shared with the students all the scruffy slips of paper that I jot down during any one day. The children then helped me sort my own jottings. "If I kept a New York City notebook," I asked, "which of these thoughts would I include?" I couldn't have been more concrete or explicit. The students were quick to tell me that my observations of street scenes and my questions about famous city sights belonged in such a book, but my childhood memory of a family dinner did not, nor did my list of books I've been meaning to read, even though my childhood took place in New York and I do my reading in New York. "Only if it couldn't have happened anywhere else, then you put it in there," one child reasoned, "Other wise you don't."

Karen then invited each child to begin keeping a New York City notebook. Students bought bound blank books in various shapes, colors, and designs. They kept their notebooks in their laps when she read aloud city poems and picture books. They carried their notebooks on field trips. They collected data from the books they read and the people they interviewed. They now had a container for all their city thoughts, observations, questions, clippings, photographs, postcards, maps, and reflections. And just as our older students do, they used their raw material from their notebooks to create very simple publishable work. In this *less* open-ended approach to writer's notebooks, our students did the following kinds of jottings:

Annie writes,

Pigeons
Getting in
People's business.
Pecking away at
Crumbs from the street.
Flying in people's windows.
Making nests on
School roofs!
Pigeons! Pigeons!
They're a mess.

Szilvia writes,

The dump truck crashes
Through the dirt,
While smashing all the garbage.
Its wheels are so glad
To crash and mash up
All the garbage.
I wonder, wonder, why

We have so much garbage?
I know why!
Because people throw away garbage.
The only way not
To have so much garbage is
To make stuff out of it.
Like my grandpa
Who made a flowerpot
Out of a washing machine.

Karen was able to easily help these young writers shape these entries into finished poems.

Other student jottings became content material for classroom keepsakes. Karen created elegant scrapbooks, one for each of the famous sites the children chose to research including the Brooklyn Bridge, Madison Square Garden, the Empire State Building, and the Statue of Liberty. The children who researched each site contributed material to be included in these collaborative scrapbooks, which have the potential to become permanent reference material in Karen's classroom for years to come. These scrapbooks can be added to from year to year and include students' notebook jottings as well as their artwork and souvenirs from site visits. (See also second-grade writing of biographies on page 341 in Chapter 10.)

Heading for Grade Three

Whether or not second graders have been introduced to the writer's notebook in second grade, our entering third graders are eager to add this new tool to their everyday writing life. The notebook has become a third-grade rite of passage, along with studying the recorder, visiting Ellis Island, and getting to have recess on the play street, actually the East Eighty-Second Street gutter that gets closed to traffic during our school lunch hours. Throughout their first three school years, teachers have been nurturing a curious, alert, and interactive way of life. Students have been encouraged to pay attention to their world, responding to their environment with energy, enthusiasm, and strong opinions. Children have been observing ant farms, sketching pussy willows, recording questions about snails, sharing significant personal objects during "show, tell, and teach" time, memorizing dozens of songs and poems, visiting museums, parks, plays, zoos, and apple orchards, writing and reading for a couple of hours each day, and probably participating in over one thousand read-aloud sessions. (My estimations are based on two read-aloud sessions a day, one hundred and eighty days a year for three years, not including any bedtime read-alouds.) The writer's notebook symbolizes our determination to keep that observant, reflective, and literary stance alive as our early-childhood youngsters move through their remaining elementary school years.

RELATED READINGS IN COMPANION VOLUMES

Going Public (Heinemann, 1999) is abbreviated as GP. *Lifetime Guarantees* (Heinemann, 2000) is abbreviated as LG.

Writing workshop basics	**LG:** Ch. 2
The importance of children's literature	**LG:** Ch. 1
Genre studies	**LG:** Ch. 3, Ch. 4, Ch. 5
Using student writing to support reading	**LG:** Ch. 9
Literary templates	**LG:** Ch. 9

CHAPTER 7

Spelling: An Essential Ingredient in the Early-Childhood Writing Workshop

There are always difficulties. You will have to survive them to become a writer. Everyone who writes must survive these horrible problems. They come and go just like writers' block. One of the difficulties is words. You must decide what words to use and how to use them. Another is spelling. If you are a good speller, you don't have to worry about that one . . .

—Annie and Carey, age 8

Key Writing Lessons

1. Early-childhood writing workshops can often be viewed as spelling workshops.
2. There is a wide range of reasons for designing minilessons devoted to spelling.
3. Minilessons can help young writers understand why we bother to record our ideas.
4. Carefully selected literature can promote students' spelling attempts.
5. Teachers can use student writing to demonstrate spelling.
6. Spelling can be taught in writing conferences.
7. Young students can be invited to become spelling researchers.
8. Teachers can design many classroom rituals to promote the study of spelling.
9. Parents must be informed about children's growth as spellers.
10. Spelling must also be taught as we move up in the grades.

SPELLING: AN ESSENTIAL INGREDIENT IN THE EARLY-CHILDHOOD WRITING WORKSHOP

Last year I read a short vignette in the "Metropolitan Diary" section of *The New York Times*. A grandmother spoke of her granddaughter's dismay at having to practice the piano. The seven-year-old asked her mother if she knew what she *really* wanted. Her hint was that the answer began with a *C* and ended with a *T*. After the mother guessed "cat" and "carrot," the child explained that what she really wanted was to "cwit." Obviously, the grandmother was charmed enough with this story to submit it the newspaper. Oh, that all adults were as charmed with their children's early attempts at spelling!

Truth be told, there are many moments when early-childhood workshops can be viewed as spelling workshops. Spelling is often the hot topic in minilessons when teachers begin the writing workshop and then again as they travel the room during writing conferences. When we listen in on young writers at work, they too are frequently puzzling aloud about the spelling of needed words, asking their classmates for help with spelling, or moving about the room searching for the standard spelling of a desired word in environmental print, classroom books, word walls, and the like.

The Teaching of Spelling in Minilessons

There is a wide range of reasons for designing minilessons devoted to spelling. These are summarized below, followed by a few sample lessons.

Teachers can use minilesson time to

- help five-year-old writers understand why putting words on their pages is important. (See minilesson below, "Making Sure Children Know Why We Record Words.")
- encourage children to take risks as spellers. (See minilesson below, "Using Literature to Promote Spelling.")
- show children how to verbally stretch words out to hear more sounds. (Teachers use such metaphors as stretching a rubber band, pulling taffy, spreading out a glob of slime, all the while moving their hands slowly in the air to support the wide expanse.)
- prove to children that adults can read their invented spelling. (Teachers bring in examples of wonderful pieces written in invented spelling and read them aloud to students. Then too, teachers have children spell in front of their peers in order to demonstrate the readability of such attempts. See minilesson below, "Providing Practice Spelling Sessions.")
- teach children how to use classroom charts when their main spelling strategy is sounding words out. (Teachers make sure that children can identify the items used as illustration on classroom alphabet charts. In other words, if a drawing of gloves is included for the letter *G* and children call them mittens, the alphabet chart will not be helpful. Likewise, if children don't know what an igloo is and that is the accompanying illustration for the letter *I*, the chart will not become a

resource for young writers. Teachers also remind children that students' names hanging next to their photographs can support spelling attempts. For example, "If you are trying to write the word *pumpkin*, but aren't sure how to begin, whose name in the class can help you? And where can we find Peter's name?")

- teach children how to use other print resources when attempting standard spelling. (Teachers often remind students that word walls, permanent classroom signs, library collections, books they know, class experience charts, reference sheets of common words, daily agendas, and so on, can all be referred to when students are groping for a word. Teachers need to remind students, however, that these should be referred to only if they remember seeing the word and can quickly spot it. Students should not be looking up every word they need. This will become laborious and take away from fluency and meaning making. "Spell as best you can" remains an important message when children are trying to get their important ideas down.)

- teach young children how to use dictionaries and other classroom supports for checking spelling during editing. (Teachers add this extra step to the editing procedure when their students are ready and appropriate dictionaries are chosen. See Chapter 10, "Editing, Publishing, and Other Ways to Make Parents Smile.")

- point out good spelling attempts by displaying children's work on the overhead projector. (With the author's permission, and after inviting response to his content, the teacher might ask a young writer to talk about the spelling strategies he used to present as complete spellings as possible. For example, the child might reveal that he used familiar words from the word wall, asked a friend, said the word slowly, etc. The teacher might then make additional suggestions as needed.)

Spelling Minilessons Sampler

Making Sure Children Know Why We Record Words

Pam Mayer once asked me to lead her writing workshop because she was looking for new ways to encourage more of her five-year-olds to take risks as spellers. I began their writing workshop by teaching the children to sing "I Know an Old Lady Who Swallowed a Fly." When they were singing the song joyfully and with gusto, I asked how many would like to teach that song to their families at home. Of course many hands went up. "Oh, then we better try writing the words down so we won't forget them." I then took a big can filled with magnetic letters and invited different children to come to the front of the meeting area to take turns recording a word or two from the lyrics. The magnetic letters made it easy for the very young children to work at their spelling without working at their handwriting. The magnetic letters also made it easy for the children to revise their attempts. Most of all they had a reason to write. They wanted to remember the words to the song. They wanted to share those words with their families. That's one of the many reasons you and I write, to help us remember things. I ended my minilesson by reminding the children that they could all do on their own what we had done together. "When Pam and I stop to talk to you about your writing today, we expect to see you spelling the words you need, just as we did together today." That day, as can be expected in an early-childhood classroom, some children continued to write down the words to the new song; most just happily went about whatever drawing and writing popped into their minds.

Using Literature to Promote Spelling

I could have easily enriched the above lesson on the spelling of lyrics by sharing such beautifully produced song books as Marla Frazee's *Hush, Little Baby*, Sarah Weeks' *Crocodile Smile*, or Tom Paxton's *The Marvelous Toy*, inviting students to attempt to do what these authors have done. Then too, we can inspire students to take spelling risks, not by attempting to do what the author has done but by doing what a character in the story has done. For example, one day in order to continue encouraging the non-risk-takers to feel confident in attempting spelling, I read aloud Rosemary Wells' picture book *Bunny Cakes*. In it, young Max makes several trips to the supermarket with his sister's shopping list to which he has added a colorful scribble to represent "Red-Hot Marshmallow Squirters," his favorite cake decoration. The shopkeeper cannot read Max's writing and finally the young bunny decides to draw the squirters and the shopkeeper finally understands his request. "If you were Max," I asked, "what else could you have done to make the shopkeeper understand?" Some students suggested that they would have just spoken up and told the man what they wanted. (Of course, if we believe that bunnies can bake, shop, and write, they should be able to talk.) Others suggested that they would have added the ingredient to the shopping list. I then invited children to attempt to write "Red-Hot Marshmallow Squirters" themselves on their small, individual wipe-off boards. Somehow, even the most reluctant speller becomes more willing when the word is not his own and the surface is not a page in their beloved book. It's as if they're thinking, "I don't really need this word, so it won't matter if I don't get it exactly right." Besides, everyone around the child is attempting the same word. The child has many supports. (See pages 187–191 for other uses of literature in the early childhood writing workshop.)

Using Student Writing to Demonstrate Spelling

More times than might be expected, kindergartners write about people or things that are part of our popular culture, using names or words that appear in newspapers or magazines. On occasion, I ask a young author for permission to use their work to teach some things about spelling to the whole class. (Of course, I choose confident children, ones that would not be devastated to see standard spelling versions of their attempts.) In Figure 7.1 is a young child's attempt at listing some ballplayers on theYankees. I clipped and enlarged the same names in standard spelling from a sports magazine and displayed both lists side by side, announcing, "Sam made a list of ballplayers on the Yankees and I could

Figure 7.1

read all their names. He spelled them just the way five-year-olds spell. Next to it, I have hung a list of these same names that I found in a sports magazine. Here they are spelled the way the grown-ups spell. Let's have Sam read the list to you and then we can talk about what you notice about the different spellings." I would then look at one set of names at a time, the invented spelling version and the standard spelling, encouraging children to notice differences. I would talk about why Sam's inventions made sense and explain why I was able to read them even though they were not the way grown-ups spelled these names. (I might have to point out that names are sometimes filled with surprising spellings because the people come from different countries, where they spoke different languages. See additional spelling lessons using real-world artifacts on page 222.) Here are Sam's ballplayers, in standard spelling:

Bernie Williams
David Cone
Joe Girardi
Paul O'Neill

Cecil Fielder

Andy Pettitte

Derek Jeter

Darryl Strawberry

Mariano Duncan

Providing Practice Spelling Sessions

I once visited with a teacher who began her minilesson by telling the story of her recent honeymoon in Hawaii. At the end of her short presentation, she asked the children, "Of all the words I used to tell my story, which do you think would be hard to spell if I chose to write my story?" Many hands went up, calling out "Hawaii," "honeymoon," "sunbathing," and "hotel reservations." She then proceeded to demonstrate saying each of those words slowly so that she could hear as many of the sounds as possible. Then she called upon individual children to say the words slowly and call out the letters for the sounds they heard as she recorded them on a prominent wipe-off board in the front of the meeting area. Upon looking at the list of honeymoon words, she told the children that they made very good attempts, remarking, "You didn't spell them the way the grown-ups do, but if I were reading a story about a honeymoon in Hawaii, I would know exactly what you were trying to say. You spelled them just the way I expect five- and six-year-olds to spell these hard words." She then called on volunteers to tell their own stories and then encouraged them to do as she had done, asking their classmates, "If I decide to write that story, what words do you think would be hard to spell?" The children then attempted to spell their friends' words, just as they had done with their teacher's. At the end of the minilesson the teacher said, "You are all so good at trying hard words, I can't wait to see what you'll each be writing about today!"

The Teaching of Spelling in Writing Conferences

The most basic of spelling interventions in a writing conference occurs with the child who chooses to attempt no spellings at all. Before encouraging children to stretch words out and choose letters that match the sound of the intended words, teachers have to know if the child is ready to do so. Some children who have not as yet understood sound-symbol relationships are often willing to write strings of random letters. Other children, who *do* understand that letters represent specific sounds, write no letters at all because they sense that they can't do it "correctly," the way the grown-ups do it. Teachers have to encourage these children to take risks and they have to stay long enough to compliment their beginning efforts.

Susie was a kindergartner who chose not to write, even though it was clear that she understood sound-symbol correspondence as she was beginning to read independently. Eve, her kindergarten teacher, explained that Susie was a gifted storyteller, eager to talk through her drawings to anyone who would listen. Her stories indicate that Susie relies on an extensive literary world to make her stories sound like the books she has been read both at home and at school. Unfortunately, Susie sees no reason to write words, explaining that she is always happy to tell people the story that accompanies her drawings.

As five-year-old Susie approached, I spotted a small ragged piece of paper taped to her shirt and a wad of stapled papers under her arm. The torn piece of paper had a little drawing on it. When I asked Susie what was taped to her shirt she answered, "It's a badge, an art badge, cause I'm an artist." My response was, "Oh, you're an artist, so you wear an artist's badge. You know, Susie, I noticed that you drew on your badge but you didn't use words, just like in the books you make. Do you know that if you write the words, 'Artist's badge,' on it, no one would wonder what this paper was all about." We proceeded to remove the slip of paper from her shirt and Susie wrote, "RT BAG."

I then said, "Hey, you're so good at this! I didn't know that you knew all those letters. Now, if I walked in your room and saw that sign I would say, "It says art badge. You must be an artist."

I then made my transition from the badge to the wad of paper under her arm. "You know, Susie," I began, "every time I visit your class you're always very eager to tell me your stories. But one day, I came into your room and you weren't there and I saw the book you're carrying right now and I couldn't remember what it was about. There was only one word on the cover, 'Annie,' so I knew that the book was about a little girl named Annie. There were lots of drawings, but there were no words on the inside pages so I couldn't really remember the story well. So today, I'd like you to begin by telling me the story that goes with these pictures and then I can help you to do just what you did with your art badge, add words to the pictures." As Susie turned the pages of her stapled book, she proceeded to tell me the following story:

Annie the Rag Doll

Once a little girl had lots of dolls, but her favorite was Annie, a rag doll.
    She loved them a lot. And as all girls grow up, she didn't like dolls anymore. And she went to school alone.
    The dolls were very sad, especially Annie. When all the dolls were asleep, she packed a little rose in a bag and went out through a window.
    She went through big, tall buildings, and when it rained she had to climb big tall mountains. Exhausted, she flung herself into a cave, took out her rose and went to sleep.
    The dolls were very sad but especially the little girl. And then when she finished Annie came back.

After celebrating her wonderful literary story, I said to Susie, "You are an artist, but right now I want to help you with the words. And I know that you know how to write words because you wrote Annie and you wrote Art Badge. Would you like a marker or a pencil?"

Susie began saying words quite slowly and wrote the words that appear in Figures 7.2 through 7.4. She continued labeling every page with a very close rendition of the story she so beautifully told.

Figure 7.2

Figure 7.3

It was clear to me that Susie was a child who just needed to be prodded. I knew she could do it and I sensed she would do it, if I gave her a significant reason to bother. Once I established that people wouldn't understand her work if she didn't put words down, she was off and running. I didn't ask whether she wanted to write, but merely gave her a choice of writing instruments. The conversation about her "art badge" served as an effective entrance ramp to get Susie writing.

Unlike Susie, many children do willingly and naturally invent their own spellings of words without much teacher coaxing. Teachers might have different goals for these children during writing conferences, but the teaching of standard spelling can be one of them. Teachers must remember that teaching spelling during a writing conference with very young children is *not* a crime. Teachers *are* allowed to teach, particularly when informing children about "spelling like grown-ups" will improve their risk taking, their attitudes about themselves as writers, their use of writing to accomplish real word purposes and help readers appreciate the important things the writer has to say.

Figure 7.4

Meet Alejandra, a struggling second grader who had been working very hard to learn to read. When I looked over her shoulder, I realized that I couldn't make sense of her text. It appears in Figure 7.5.

When I pulled alongside her, she said, "It's a song my friend taught me." I then realized that Alejandra had written down the words to "Do Re Me" from the *Sound of Music*, beginning, "Doe a deer a female deer." I was in awe of how perfect her recall was. She hadn't missed a word. She used standard spelling for the words she could find on her classroom word wall. Her invented spellings were not consistent, though. When she repeated the same lines, she spelled many of the words differently. I could hear her

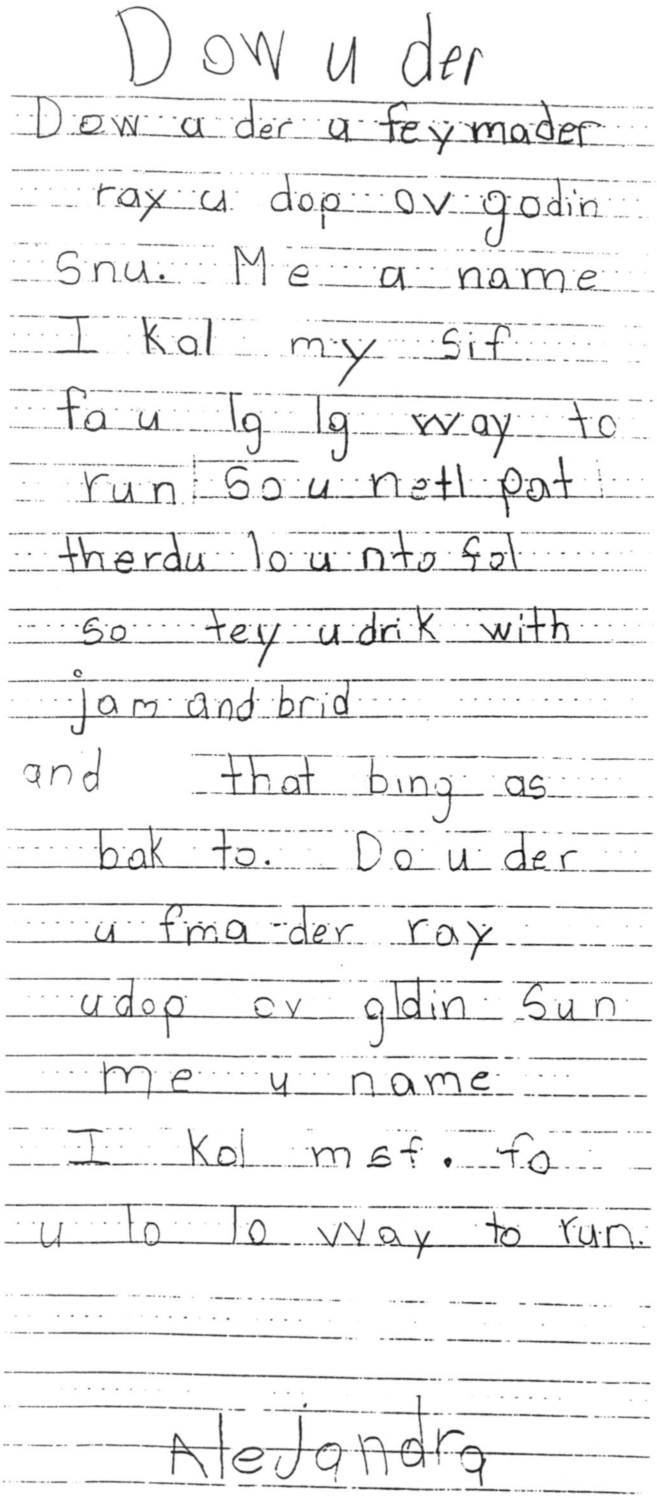

Dow u der

Dow a der a fey mader
rax u dop ov godin
Snu. Me a name
I kal my sif
fa u lg lg way to
run So u netl pat
therdu lo u nto fol
so tey u drik with
jam and brid
and that bing as
bak to. Do u der
u fma der ray
udop ov gldin Sun
me u name
I kal m sf. fo
u lo lo way to run.

Alejandra

Figure 7.5

English mispronunciations. I became aware of all the phonic elements with which she seemed unfamiliar.

Her writing gave me a window into her struggles as a reader. Before I left her side, I asked her if she would like to see how the grown-ups spell these words. She was surprised that they were written so differently. I gave her a complete standard version of the song as reading material so she could practice reading it and teach it to her classmates.

Spelling Researcher Routines

In addition to teaching spelling minilessons and conferring with students about their spelling when necessary, I have invited young children to become spelling researchers once or twice a week. The teaching ideas described below are based on the following beliefs:

- Some children need to perform in community before they are ready to act on their own.
- Some children who *are* aware of sound-symbol correspondences do not attempt to spell words on their own until they watch other confident young spellers.
- Some young writers need a clear image in their mind's eye of children stretching and sounding out words and selecting letters to represent those sounds. They need to watch powerful demonstrations of this slow kind of spelling, done by children, not adults.
- Some children need a great deal of convincing that people can read their invented spellings before they are willing to take marker to paper.

Inventors and Scribes

In Pam's kindergarten, I introduced this spelling research by asking the students if they understood what inventors and scribes do. They were pretty clear about inventors, less sure what scribes did. I then explained that Pam had divided the class into six groups with four or five children in each. Everyone was going to be an inventor, of spelling of course, and that each time we met, one child would be designated as the scribe who does the writing. We then arranged for the clusters to meet in different areas of the room, guaranteeing that they would have enough space to huddle together. Each spelling cluster was given a small experience chart pad and only the scribe was handed a marker. I then invited them to "practice" inventing spellings. The first week I gave them the words, *vanilla, chocolate,* and *strawberry,* one at a time.

Pam, her student teacher, and I visited the clusters, eavesdropping as the children attempted to spell these high-interest words. We gave very little direction, other than, "Help your scribe sound out the words and choose letters for the sounds you hear." On the first round we asked the most proficient speller to serve as scribe, but as the weeks passed all children had a turn. In some groups, the scribe acted as teacher, saying the word slowly over and over again, while other children called out the letters. In some groups the children all pitched in saying the words and suggesting the spelling. In some groups the scribe couldn't resist doing most of the work on her own. We didn't correct any procedures, knowing that each time there was a different scribe different procedures would probably be followed. (Eventually Pam and I became aware of children who did not participate in the spelling attempts and we formed our own spelling clusters. Pam led one and so did I. This structure gave us opportunities to focus our attention on those children who needed to understand sound-symbol relationships as well as those who needed extra help in saying words slowly in order to hear more sounds.)

After a few minutes we collected the chart tablets and assembled the class in the meeting area. I then showed each group's attempt and read the words aloud as they were written. Pam learned a lot about the sounds that were difficult for the children to hear. *Strawberry* was the most difficult spelling. None of the five-year-olds heard the sound of the letter *t* between the *s* and *r*. The children all giggled when I read, "srawberry." We marveled at all the attempts, congratulating each group for spelling just the way five-year-olds do. After discussing the attempts, I showed the children the way the grown-ups spelled these words and invited their comments. I ended this brief spelling work by suggesting that if the children have ice-cream packages in their freezers at home they might look at the spellings on the labels when they are scooping out their desserts.

On my next visit the students attempted to spell *Tamaguchis, Beany Babies*, and *Pokemon*, followed by *hocus pocus, abracadabra*, and *Open Sesame* on my third visit. Each week I continued with very high-interest words, especially ones with lots of consonants and long vowel sounds. Pam and I continued to reflect on their attempts, learning a great deal about early spelling. For example, all the children spelled *Sesame* with only one *S*. A common attempt looked like "SME." We guessed this had something to do with not having a way to hold the place of a short vowel sound yet. When they said the word slowly, they heard the initial *S*, and, not knowing how to record the sound in between the first and second *S*, seemed satisfied with just the one *S*, then went on to record the sound of /m/ and /e/, which they heard so clearly.

Learning to Spell Using Real-World Artifacts

My work with first graders was a bit more challenging and required stacks of real-world artifacts, clipboards, pencils, and a wipe-off board. The children were arranged in pairs of spelling partners. My goals included getting the six-year-olds to continue to take risks as spellers as well as to get them to pay heightened attention to the spelling of environmental print and to talk more about their spelling noticings.

Similar to the work in the kindergarten, I begin these short sessions by inviting children to spell some high-interest words. For example, one day I invited some first graders to write the names of the teachers in our school. Each child worked individually, using a separate clipboard. Students were particularly keen on learning our teachers' last names. (In many schools it would be just as enticing to discover teachers' first names.) I read off a short list including Lorraine Shapiro, Shelley Harwayne, Joan Backer, Sharon Taberski, Joanne Hindley, Pam Mayer, Regina Chiou, Peter Iocona, Carmen Colon, Layne Hudes, Debby Yellin, Eve Mutchnick, and Dawn Harris Martine. Each child attempted to spell these names as best they could. Then I handed out copies of our school's organization sheet and asked the children to get together with their spelling partners and search for the names they spelled and then talk about what surprised them when they saw the grown-up spelling. I eavesdropped as the children discussed their own attempts in relation to the standard spellings. Their comments about their spelling attempts revealed a great deal about their growing theories about conventions of print and their awareness of phonic elements. Several students' attempts follow, in the order of the teachers' names listed above.

<u>Sylvia's</u>	<u>Sergei's</u>	<u>Jonathan's</u>
The Raen Hapro	Lorain shapiro	laraen Shapiero
Sale Royen	Shelly harwain	Shaly horwane
Jon Bacr	Jhone back	Juan back
Harn Tbrbrse	Sharon tuberski	Sharien tabrsky
Joan hdde	Joan hindli	Jouean handley
Pam mayor	pam mayor	Paem mare
MGN hou	Regina choo	raagina hoowe
Pdtr Irknno	peter iyacona	peater iaacounae
Krmen Klan	carmen colone	carmin kaloone
Plaa barr	pala bower	Polaa bawre
Lan Sdeu	Laine hudeis	Laane hooudeeis
Dab elaln	debi yellen	Dabiey walind
Ievf mhnc	eve muchnick	Eve mahnike
Don hrs mrtn	dan harismatin	Douna hars martine

Teachers who collect such data can study it across the class as a whole to appreciate how much phonemic awareness exists as well as to pinpoint phonic elements that are as yet unfamiliar to most six-year-olds. Then too, studying any one child's attempts can help teachers to understand a student's strengths as a speller as well as appreciate their patterns of error. Silvia, a child from Bangladesh, uses the letter *h* to represent the /sh/ sound as in Hapro for Shapiro and Harn for Sharon. She doesn't hear the initial sounds precisely as indicated by the dramatically off-target spelling of "Lorraine" and "Regina" and the surname "Hudes." Sergei, a child from Macedonia, shows much strength as a speller. For example, he consistently uses the /ai/ pattern to create the medial sound wanted in "Lorraine," "Harwayne," and "Layne." Jonathan probably stretches words out so slowly that he adds many extra vowels.

After children wrote all these names, the whole class then reconvened in the meeting area and I listed several attempts at spelling each name on the meeting area wipe-off board. We talked about the attempts that made sound-sense, ones that would read back as the sound of the teachers' names. Below is a list of a more than a dozen ways that students attempted to spell my name. I told the children how I would read these aloud. They starred the ones that read back as /Shelley/.

Hle	Sle	Slle
Shalie	cheley	Shale
Shelly	Sheely	Shalle
Shally	Shlley	Shaellay
Shaly	Sale	Halee

Students talked about what surprised them about "grown-up" spelling. We talked about how names often come from languages other than English and that makes them very difficult. (I do try to pick words that are rich with consonant sounds and long vowels, the sounds that comes easiest and first to young spellers.) Children got to keep individual copies of the organization sheet in a special folder labeled "Real-World Stuff." From that day on, the young children started to pay attention to the spelling of teachers' names when they passed labeled mailboxes and signs on classroom doors.

Other multiple copies of real-world artifacts that I have collected include takeout menus from Italian restaurants (very popular in Manhattan, where kitchens are often too small for very serious cooking). Children love attempting *ravioli, macaroni, meatballs and spaghetti*, television guide pages (children love to attempt the names of popular shows); and street maps of New York City (children are eager to attempt *Broadway* and *Amsterdam, Madison* and *Lexington* Avenues). Sometimes I didn't have actual artifacts to place in students' hands. Instead, I took them on walking tours of the school or the block of the school to research standard spellings. For example, I've asked children to spell all the signs in the school building including, *General Office, Auditorium, Kindergarten, Exit, Boys, Girls, Library*. We then take a tour of the building, comparing our attempts with the posted signs. Children are always surprised that the word *kindergarten* is so long.

I have asked young children to attempt such irresistible words as *Mitsubishi, Toyota, Buick,* and *Chevrolet*. Then we take a walking tour of the neighborhood, clipboards in hand, reading the nameplate of every parked car as we go.

I always choose material that will reappear in children's lives. I want children to find spelling fascinating. I want them to initiate conversations with grown-ups about why words are spelled in certain ways. I want to raise their consciousness to the order of letters in their environment. Children who have attempted to spell *General Office* will pay attention to that sign each time they pass it.

Imagine if I asked adults to spell a very difficult word, one whose meaning they are familiar with, but that has very unfamiliar strings of letters for English-speaking people. For example, I might ask adults to spell *hors d'oeuvres* and then I'd show them the standard spelling in a French cookbook. That night if the grown-ups were to dine out in a restaurant that had a menu section labeled *hors d'oeuvres*, no doubt the adults who had attempted to spell this word would try to remember the order of that French spelling. They would try to hold the spelling features in their visual memory. I would have raised their consciousness to a word in their environment.

Other Spelling Rituals

Inviting students to become spelling researchers is just one of many ways our early-childhood teachers might create enthusiasm for learning to spell. Other moments of attention to spelling apart from the writing workshop include the following:

• The teacher covers the title of a very familiar book at meeting time each morning and invites a child to attempt to write the title. The teacher then reveals the printed title and children compare the student's attempt with the original. Students not only delight in learning to spell, but in recalling titles from the book jacket illustration.

• Teachers sketch high-interest items, or use clippings from magazines, attaching the picture to the outside of a flap of construction paper. Underneath the flap is the standard spelling of the item. For example, the teacher draws a lunchbox, then prints the word *lunchbox* under the flap. The flap is taped onto to a large sheet of paper that is displayed on an easel. All day, children can attempt to spell the hidden word and sign their names next to their attempts. At the end of the day, the teacher very dramatically reveals the adult spelling and children talk about their work. The flaps can eventually be collected and mounted in a bound scrapbook for future reference. Parents can be invited to create additional pictures and hidden flap words.

• Teachers invite students to take part in daily classroom surveys. For example, each morning a large sheet of experience chart paper, mounted on a sturdy chart stand, announces one survey question. If the question of the day reads, "What is your favorite color?" children have opportunities throughout the morning to stop by and write their answers and sign their names. Children chosen to serve as surveyors each day, sort, count, and announce the results. The teacher then talks about the spelling variations, pointing out which ones made sound-sense.

• Teachers play spelling games with high-frequency words that have been added to their word walls. For example, the teacher announces, "I am thinking of a word that has the little word *an* in it and it means a container that food comes in." Students search the word wall looking for possible choices. A child volunteers to write the word from memory without looking at the word wall.

- Teachers invite children to explore the spelling of their classmates' names so that these names can serve as a friendly resource when children are spelling hard words. Children are very quick to learn one another's names and a display of labeled student photographs facilitates students' reading of one another's names. Once students can read one another's names, the names help children read and spell other new words. (See *Going Public*, page 29.)

- Teachers invite children to participate in interactive writing, as described by Fountas and Pinnell in *Interactive Writing: How Language and Literacy Come Together, K–2*. Authors suggest ways for teachers to invite young children to take part in collaborative writing experiences, in order to strengthen their abilities to compose.

- Teachers invite children to participate in spelling explorations as described by Diane Snowball and Faye Bolton in *Spelling K–8: Planning and Teaching*.

Informing Parents

Another essential component to the teaching of spelling in the early-childhood classroom is the education of parents. We don't ever want parents to worry that invented spelling leads to poor habits or that we believe spelling doesn't count or that we don't ever teach standard spelling. We must keep parents informed. Below is a section from a monthly newsletter Pam Mayer sends to the parents of her kindergarten parents. Family members always appreciate the specificity of her information. She writes,

"Take-a-Try" at Spelling

My goal is for children to be fascinated, excited, and curious about print. We recently discussed the fact that adults write *phone* with a *PH* instead of an *F*. We will continue to talk about and explore how words are spelled and which letters are in a word. Some children have noticed that other children's names in the class start with the same sound as theirs. Children love to play with the sound of words. I encourage them to write what they hear as they attempt invented spelling.

Last week we talked about which words might look longer when written on paper, and which words might look shorter. We spelled several words together. I said a word. We then stretched it like a rubber band, saying the word very slowly. The children enthusiastically called out their guesses. I wrote the word using the children's suggestions. We talked about the length of the word. We looked at the way grown-ups spell the word. We wondered about some words, laughed about others. After stretching the words with our mouths, we realized why *wolf* has only four letters and *hippopotamus* has twelve. The children then paired up with a partner. They took a clipboard to a quiet spot in the room to "Take-a-Try" at spelling the word *umbrella*. They said the word slowly to each other and agreed on the spelling. We then met as a group and shared all of the tries. We were fascinated that so many of the partners heard so many of the same letters. We then looked at the conventional spelling of *umbrella*. There were a few surprises for the children.

Pam's note continued with an explanation of the kinds of writing the children were doing and how they were now using writing to label their constructions in the block area.

(See additional information about school-wide newsletters as a means of informing parents on pages 326 and 355.) In addition to corresponding with families, we invite them to observe writing workshops, participate in writing workshops themselves (see *Going Public*, pages 171–176), and read worthwhile and appropriate articles and books. We can also offer important content-rich presentations and create schoolhouse displays that continually educate them about the growth and development of our youngest. (See explanation of an invented spelling workshop on page 341 and description of invented spelling wall displays on page 352 in Chapter 10, "Editing, Publishing, and Other Ways to Make Parents Smile.")

The Teaching of Spelling as We Move Up in the Grades

Parents need to understand that progressive schools that encourage children to write frequently about topics of their own choosing must also care about spelling. The writing process approach and spelling instruction do support one another. If children aren't asked to write, they need not learn how to spell. If children aren't taught to spell, people will not appreciate their writing attempts. Our teachers in second through fifth grade have separate study periods devoted to spelling. Frequently these short sessions take place at the end of morning meeting or as a ritual before the writing workshop. When I visit, teachers and students are engaged in the following kinds of conversations:

- noting common spelling patterns and word parts
- paying heightened attention to certain features as they read
- involving students in gathering words with certain features
- sorting words in order to figure out spelling rules and generalizations
- researching the logic behind spelling variations
- sharing misspellings found in public places
- noting exceptions to expected spellings
- researching unusual word histories and roots
- clustering words belonging to the same family of meaning
- discussing strategies competent spellers use, including memory aids for very troublesome words
- exploring the role of correcting spelling during editing of finished work
- discussing words connected to a topic or theme the class is studying

- comparing spelling issues in the children's first language
- adding commonly used words to their classroom word walls

Our district has long relied on Diane Snowball's expertise in literacy learning, particularly in the area of word study. One year, after listening to Di speak at a principal's conference, I sent the following letter to staff of the Manhattan New School.

November 2, 1998

Dear Friends,

The following are key points from Di Snowball's presentation at last week's principal's conference. I selected those comments that would best push our thinking about our recent word-study concerns. The bulk of her presentation related to the teaching of spelling.

- *Show me their writing and I'll show you what word study they need.*

- *Sounding out does not start from left to right. It's looking for what will help you.*

- *Be explicit. For example, "I've been reading your science notebooks and these are the types of words you are misspelling."*

- *It's crucial to add, "If you know how to spell this word, what other words do you know how to spell?"*

- *You can't look for words with a K sound. K is a letter. There is no K sound. You can make the sound /k/ with the letters cc, k, ch, and qu.*

- *Let the children know what you see in them as spellers. For example, "I notice that you are trying to make use of the sounds you hear. Let's explore those sounds together so we can figure out how that will help you with your reading and writing."*

- *"Word families" refers to meaning. For example, "Play, players, playing, and playful belong to the same word family. This is a meaning strategy."*

- *Using a spelling pattern is a visual strategy. For example, "at, cat, fat, chat, etc."*

- *Some children rely only on sounding out to spell. They also need to rely on sight vocabulary, spelling patterns, structural clues, etc.*

- *Children can be asked to apply what they know about spelling when they work in their writer's notebook, just as you or I don't disregard spelling completely when we write a first draft or jot in a notebook. This does not mean children have to correct notebook jottings. It means we should be expecting them to apply what they are learning about spelling whenever they write. We should be suggesting that children do as we do—if a word happens not to look right, we try it another way. Most adults can't leave a word that doesn't look right. We need to help children to internalize the practice. When we read a child's notebook and we know that they are not thinking about spelling at all, it's more than okay to point out this problem.*

- *We need to ask students why they want to be better spellers. If their answers have to do with passing a spelling test, they are not understanding why we bother to learn to spell.*

(In addition, Di is not sure what spelling tests really accomplish. I'd love to talk more about this. She thinks that time on proofreading is better spent. Are there other ways to make sure that children are studying and holding onto the spellings that they need to learn?)

- *To teach their, they're, and there in a way that children will hold onto these separate spellings, we can ask children to collect examples from their reading and then figure out why the writers chose to spell them the way they did. What did you notice about their choices? (Their is usually followed by a thing, a noun. They're is usually followed by an action word, a verb form.)*

- *Children can hold onto the spellings of to, two, and too, with meaning clues. For example, two is spelled that way because it is related by meaning to twins and twice.*

- *The "Look, Say, Cover, Write, Check, Try Again" method must be done until the spelling is automatic. (Once automatic, these words can be added to a word wall. If necessary, we can also teach children to chunk letters together in order to hold onto the visual image of the word.)*

As Di spoke, I composed the spelling study sheet attached. I was thinking of it for third grade and up as a homework support. I hope it gets some conversation going. Please note my handwritten notes in the margin.

Additional related questions I have included:

Does the search for spelling patterns interrupt the reading, particularly of less than fluent readers?

What do you do with children who cannot spot misspelled words in their own writing?

How can the scope of spelling instruction outlined by Di Snowball and her colleague Faye Bolton in their books inform the work we do?

What other word study issues can we note by reading children's writing?
I hope this is helpful and will spark many conversations.

Love,
Shelley

See the annotated sample study sheet in Figure 7.6, Brian's attempt at the word *school.* Fourth-grade teachers invited children to use these study sheets. Completed student samples—Tahj's attempt at the word *opposite* and Dina's attempt at the word *uncomfortable*—are in Figure 7.7 and 7.8. Haden's attempt at the word *satisfactory* is in Figure 7.9.

(Note: children needed more instruction to understand the worksheet's last two categories, "Words Related to Meaning," and "Words Related to Spelling Features." These were difficult concepts and students needed more demonstrations.) A blank study sheet can be found in Appendix 9.)

(For a thorough explanation of exemplary spelling practice, see *Spelling K–8: Planning and Teaching* by Diane Snowball and Faye Bolton.)

To be selected from their writing

One sheet per word. Depends on their spelling needs, strengths, etc. Children can be asked to do one per night or more.

Name Brian _____   Date October 26, 1998

Would this be a helpful homework sheet? (demonstrated in class first of course)

<u>Spelling Study</u>

This word doesn't look right.   <u>shcool</u>

I tried it another way.   <u>skool</u>

I checked the dictionary
or asked an expert. *(parent, sibling etc if donkeat home)*   *school

asterisk next to correct spelling to remind child to study correct version

I was surprised that
<u>You can make the /sk/ sound</u>
<u>with the letters "sch".</u>

We need to teach children the symbols for distinguishing sounds and letters and help them describe the difference // " ∫∫c.

A trick that will help me remember the spelling of this word
is <u>There is no word "cool"</u>
<u>in school.</u>

Children will not always be able to answer this.

I studied the *correct spelling by using the LOOK, SAY,
COVER, WRITE, CHECK, TRY AGAIN method.

<u>school</u>	<u>school</u>
<u>school</u>	<u>school</u>
<u>school</u>	<u>school</u>

We must remind children to cover the correct spelling attempt. Suggest use of index card.

Other words I can spell because I know how to spell this
word are:

<u>Words related to meaning</u>   <u>Words related to spelling</u>
(word families)   features
<u>schools</u>   <u>schedule</u> pool, fool
<u>schoolhouse</u>   stool, spool

If used as homework, parents will probably offer suggestions

Older students might be probing more sophisticated meaning related words e.g. Scholarly scholastic

We might consider giving a filled out sample sheet as an example.

Figure 7.6

Name _Tahj_   Date _1/27/98_

<u>Spelling Study</u>

This word doesn't look right.   _Oppsit_

I tried it another way.   _Oppsite_

I checked the dictionary
or asked an expert.   * _Opposite_

I was surprised that
There was a "O" in the middle.
_____

A trick that will help me remember the spelling of this word
is _"Op" and like "po" are alike but, they
are the opposite ways. Oppbsite_

I studied the *correct spelling by using the LOOK, SAY,
COVER, WRITE, CHECK, TRY AGAIN method.

Oppbsite   _Oppasite_
Opposite   _Oppasite_
oppssite   _Oppasite_

Other words I can spell because I know how to spell this
word are:

<u>Words related to meaning</u>   <u>Words related to spelling</u>
(word families)   features

_____   ____ ____
_____   ____ ____
_____   ____ ____

Figure 7.7

Name _Dino_   Date _Jan 28, 99_

Spelling Study

This word doesn't look right.   _uncufterbul_

I tried it another way.   _uncomfterbul_

I checked the dictionary
or asked an expert.   *_uncomfortable_

I was surprised that
it had for, and table.
_____
_____

A trick that will help me remember the spelling of this word
is _to put it like this uncomfor, table._
(There is little words in the tag work

I studied the *correct spelling by using the LOOK, SAY,
COVER, WRITE, CHECK, TRY AGAIN method.
Uncomfortable   _____
uncomfortable   _____
uncomfortable   _____

Other words I can spell because I know how to spell this
word are;

Words related to meaning (word families)	Words related to spelling features
Comfortable	_____
Comfort	_____
_____	_____

Figure 7.8

Name Horlon   Date 11/13/98

Spelling Study

This word doesn't look right.   *ba* Satusffaktory

I tried it another way.   Sattasfactury

I checked the dictionary
or asked an expert.   *satisfactory

I was surprised that
there was an or in satisfactory

A trick that will help me remember the spelling of this word
is I ~~know~~ now know the word so I
can think of (satis-fact-ory)
it has factory

I studied the *correct spelling by using the LOOK, SAY,
COVER, WRITE, CHECK, TRY AGAIN method.

Satisfactory   Satisfactory
Satisfactory   Satisfactory
Satisfactory   Satisfactory

Other words I can spell because I know how to spell this
word are: satisfy saturate

Words related to meaning (word families)	Words related to spelling features
Satisfy.	satisfaction
good.	satin
enough.	satisfy

Figure 7.9

Spellers in Literature

Recently, most of the fictional characters I've come across who are concerned about themselves as spellers are those involved in spelling bees. In the children's book by Barney Saltzberg, *Phoebe and the Spelling Bee*, the main character avoids preparing for her classroom spelling bee at all cost. The text is filled with fake stomachaches, fear of embarrassment, and eventually the child's invention of mnemonic and other devices for memorizing correct spellings. In *Missouri School Days*, adapted by Roger Lea McBride, from the Little House Rose Years Books, young Blanche is inconsolable after she mispells *precipice* in the school spelldown. The adult novel *The Bee Season* by Mayla Goldberg is a moving and complicated story of young Eliza, who along with her dysfunctional family, becomes totally obsessed with her participation in a spelling bee. The moving opening page reveals how the school life of this young student has contributed to her low self-esteem. The author writes, "As Eliza stands with the rest of her class, she has already prepared herself for the inevitable descent back into her chair. She has no reason to expect that the outcome of this, her first spelling bee, will differ from the outcome of any other school event seemingly designed to confirm, display, or amplify her mediocrity." How unfortunate that our memories of childhood spelling events are so often attached to fierce yearly competitions. (I can still recall my own disappointment and humiliation at having to leave the auditorium stage after misspelling *moccasin* at my elementary school spelling bee.) How much richer spelling memories will be for those students whose memory banks are filled with honest inquiries, thoughtful discoveries, and many practical applications.

RELATED READINGS IN COMPANION VOLUMES

Going Public (Heinemann, 1999) is abbreviated as GP. *Lifetime Guarantees* (Heinemann, 2000) is abbreviated as LG.

The teaching of minilessons	**LG:** Ch. 2
Literacy rituals	**LG:** Ch. 1
Informing families	**GP:** Ch. 5
	LG: Ch. 8
Discovering spelling needs	**LG:** Ch. 9

CHAPTER 8

THE WRITING WORKSHOP: A PLACE TO EXPERIMENT, IMPROVISE, AND INVENT

*It takes a lot of practice to have great writing. If you are trying to be a better writer, don't worry . . .
Try to find great words like amazing or spectacular, and mix them up, fool with them until it works.
Same type of thing when you put on a dress (if you're a boy you don't have this experience). You have
to fool with the buttons, buckles, zippers, and snaps, until it fits right. You have to go word by word,
button by buckle, step by step, and practice writing long.*

—Annie and Carey, age 8

Key Writing Lessons

1. Writing workshop leaders need a spirit of adventure in order to keep growing professionally.
2. There are many ways to encourage professional talk among teachers of writing.
3. There are many ways for teachers of writing to pursue individual or collaborative inquiries.
4. Teachers of writing need to carefully plan courses of study.
5. Courses of study add energy to our work with young writers.
6. Nonfiction calendars are a rigorous writing project that have potential to become family treasures.
7. Author studies lend themselves to multigrade collaborations.
8. Writing from memories need not result in "memoirs."
9. Students need techniques to capture the essence of a place on paper.
10. Students can appreciate effective similes and metaphors.
11. Teachers need to be choosy about contests.
12. Teachers cannot allow preparation for high-stakes testing to eliminate the energizing possibilities that new genres and projects offer.

THE WRITING WORKSHOP: A PLACE TO EXPERIMENT, IMPROVISE, AND INVENT

After a recent workshop in Ohio, Meredith Melragon, a technology staff developer, slipped me a handwritten quotation, in green ink on a bright yellow index card. I gathered it up with all my notes and overheads, not giving it much heed, until I unpacked my bags back in New York. The colorful card attracted my attention, but the words made an even stronger impression. The quote, attributed to the Native American Siletz tribe, read, "One who learns from one who is learning, drinks from a running stream." The quote spoke to me of professional growth, of staff development, of the need to continuously be learning if we are to be true to the calling of teacher.

I met a principal in California who told me that the problem at her school was that some of her teachers were in private practice. There is no room for private practice in the teaching profession. We need to be continuously learning in the company of our colleagues. In fact, when people ask me what I miss most about not being at the Manhattan New School every day, I have to say that I long for the hours spent with colleagues thinking new thoughts and puzzling about new possibilities in the writing workshop. Of course, I miss the children, their families, and the daily interactions with my colleagues. But most of all, I miss our regular get-togethers, our frequent study groups, in which new ideas were always forming at the table.

Despite their great areas of expertise and myriad professional accomplishments, no one at the Manhattan New School thought they had arrived. No one thought they had all the answers. There was always something big to puzzle over, loose ends to share, questions deserving of our time and attention, and students who challenged our ways of working. There was a spirit of adventure in the teaching of writing that kept us alive and growing professionally. To this day, I can't pick up a book, newspaper, or magazine and not instantly shift into my "I wonder if our students could do that?" mode.

• I read an article about a cowboy poetry gathering in the Southwest and I wonder about similar possibilities in our big city. Would our children and their families be interested in creating restaurant poetry, garment-center poetry, or high-rise apartment living poetry?

• I clip a photo from a Denver newspaper that shows a detective using writing—plotting a timeline—to help solve a crime and I wonder if our students would like to research all the ways the workers and shopkeepers in our community depend on writing to get their jobs done well. What an informative compilation that would be!

• I read plans for a new book about former Yankee pitcher David Cone, to be written by acclaimed baseball writer Roger Angell, and I wonder about designing an effective course of study in sportswriting for student writers. At what age would such a program be appropriate? Which professional writers could our students apprentice themselves to?

• I enjoy an article, a first-person narrative, written by a woman journalist who has just experienced rock climbing for the very first time. I know I will pass it on to the fourth-grade teachers at the Manhattan New School, as each year the fourth graders go rock climbing in Central Park. Should each student be asked to write about the experience?

Would it be an effective way to teach them about quality writing, if they have all had the same powerful experience living through draft one? Would such an assigned topic take away ownership?

• I receive a book lover's page-a-day tear-off calendar and wonder if our students can make their own. Can't all the members of a class get together and recommend 365 books and write brief reviews and background notes on the authors? Can't we get a local printing shop to duplicate and attach the pages? Wouldn't these become popular keep-sakes for students throughout the school? (They would probably would never want to tear out the pages!)

• I come across information about a song format called a *plena* in a curriculum guide about New York City. I learn that this Puerto Rican song style from the 1920s is a sung news account with a set structure for the verse and chorus. I wonder if our students would like to try writing a *periodico cantado*, or sung newspaper articles. I also wonder where I can find recorded *plenas* to serve as a model.

Any time such seed ideas pop into my head I know I need to meet with thoughtful colleagues, ones who will help me think them through, assess their value, connect them to student needs, note their limitations, innovate on their design, connect them to bigger thoughts, and plan for possible implementation. Similarly, my expert colleagues would count on me to help extend their thinking on writing workshop projects, routines, tools, and techniques. It's no surprise then that, above all since leaving the Manhattan New School, I miss the collegial and often informal think tanks that seemed to crop up in every classroom, corridor, and staff meeting.

Maintaining the Researcher's Stance in the Teaching of Writing

There are many ways to push professional talk, including attending conferences together, taking university or district-led courses together, working with staff developers, accompanying one another on visits to other schools, going on weekend retreats, and of course forming book groups around the reading of professional literature. Throughout its decade of existence, the major impetus for growth at the Manhattan New School remains the weekly staff meeting. (See *Lifetime Guarantees* and *Going Public* for details on these after-school get-togethers.)

In my last year at the school, we had shifted the focus of our weekly staff meetings from the teaching of reading to the teaching of writing. We began that year by brainstorming issues that were causing us concern. These had included the following questions:

• What additional ways can we make publishing frequent and stress free?
• What classroom techniques are most likely to enable a well-written text to have an impact on students' writing?

- What classroom rituals and practices help maintain the early-childhood students' inclination to look at the world with wide eyes and wonder?
- How can students' writing give us more clues to their reading lives, particularly for struggling readers? (See *Lifetime Guarantees* pages 318*ff.*)
- How can our conferring practices take full advantage of the scholarly community in which we live?
- What ways of talking about good writing resonate with young children?
- What classroom rituals, structures, and activities promote more risk taking in spelling? (See page 29.)
- What might appropriate rites of passage be in the writing workshop throughout the grades? (See page 221.)
- How might author studies have more impact on students' writing? (See page 248.)
- How can the teaching of spelling be connected to the writing workshop?
- What's all the to-do about interactive writing? Does it fit with the work we're doing and how?
- What are the best ways to introduce new genres? Are there different implications for different-aged students?
- How do we continually lift the quality of students' writing throughout the grades?

No doubt, had I remained at the school, I would have added the question that is at the heart of this book: "How can we tap into the unique attributes of childhood in order to make our writing workshops more appropriate and productive for young writers?"

As a staff, we would then decide on ways to go about answering such questions. Our staff meeting study techniques would include any or all of the following:

- reading and responding to related professional material
- bringing children to our meetings and conferring with them publicly
- watching videotapes of one another at work
- presenting the results of colleagues' visits to one another's rooms or combining classes to coteach a writing workshop
- telling the story of one writer and his body of work and teasing out the implications for many students
- brainstorming new teaching techniques, volunteering to try them out, and sharing the results
- looking at just one piece of student work prepared on an overhead projector and imagining how a conference might go
- reading aloud children's literature and discussing how best to share these with students
- crafting minilessons and rehearsing their presentation with colleagues

- visiting other schools and attending conferences or workshops and sharing our observations notes
- inviting guest speakers with expertise in a selected area of study
- inviting adults to work on their own writing in order to closely understand techniques to be taught to children
- collaborating on teaching plans for new courses of study (See section below, "Taking Time to Plan Courses of Study.")
- presenting a new course of study, workshop tool, or classroom ritual in order to receive feedback from colleagues.

At one time or another, depending on the topic being studied, we have used all of the techniques listed above. More times than not, just one or two of the activities fill the hour-and-a-half time slot reserved for our weekly study sessions.

For example, during our monthlong study of conferring and the possibility of tapping into school-wide resources, classroom teachers took turns showing student work on the overhead projector. At each meeting, two classroom teachers, one from an upper-grade class and one from a lower-grade class, would give the context for a piece of writing and then the teachers gathered would discuss the strengths of the piece. We would then, based on the history of the child provided by the teacher, suggest possible ways to confer with the child in order to lift the quality of the writing. At our next gathering, the classroom teacher would report on how she chose to work with the student and upon the effectiveness of her work.

I once read an article about Supreme Court Justice Ruth Bader Ginsburg, in which the justice was described as someone who likes to look at larger questions through the lens of smaller stories of people's lives. So too, as a staff we like to think through state mandates, district initiatives, and even building policies through the lens of smaller stories of real children's lives. Wislawa Szymborska, the Polish poet and Nobel Prize winner, is quoted as saying, "People get stupid in a wholesale way, but they get wiser in a retail way." Our retail way of getting wiser about the teaching of literacy is to share stories of real children.

We know that looking at any one child's work will help us think through bigger issues in the teaching of writing. We will always ask ourselves, "What are the implications for all the other writers and all the other teachers of writing in this school?"

From Small Suggestions to Well-Developed Practice

Regina Chiou, one of our second-grade teachers, once described my role as that of being the school muse. Nothing makes me happier than to inspire students and teachers, particularly when it comes to writing, my favorite school subject. Teachers frequently took my suggestions to heart and I was particularly delighted when I threw out an idea in passing, and the next time I visited that teacher's room the kernel of an idea had become a well thought out and extended classroom feature. Pam Mayer has always asked her family members to donate flowers along with their weekly turn at snacks. I suggested she ask for the precise names of the flowers, snap their photographs, and create a timeline of labeled photographs. Pretty soon the timeline graced our hallway and parents began sending in background information on each of the flowers. Pam invited students to learn the names of the flowers, study the timeline, read the background facts, and notice patterns and repetitions in flower donations. A simple idea had turned into a literacy feature in Pam's classroom, and the idea began to spread throughout the school.

Taking Time to Plan Courses of Study

I once had the privilege of escorting Courtney Cazden on a visit to elementary and middle school classrooms in both literacy and mathematics. The acclaimed Harvard researcher surprised district educators by noting that classroom talk in mathematics appeared to be richer than classroom talk in literacy. She described the mathematics talk as reaching a crescendo, building up to new learning. She wondered aloud why there wasn't the same momentum in our literature discussions. As a district we began to question whether or not literacy teachers were as clear about the content they wanted to teach as our mathematics teachers appeared to be. This discussion led to a study of the planning involved in literacy courses of study. Taking cues from the work of Grant Wiggins and Jay McTighe in *Understanding by Design*, I designed a course of study on lifting the quality of student writing. I began by asking and answering the four broad questions that appear below. (Of course, each teacher would answer questions differently based on the assessed needs of her students. My answers are based on the students I know best at the Manhattan New School.)

How Do We Define This Course of Study?

It is very helpful for teachers to be clear in their own mind about what they are hoping to accomplish in any focused course of study. For me, a course of study that focuses on lifting the quality of student writing at the elementary level refers to encouraging students to produce writing that is true to the spirit of childhood. I expect to be taken by surprise by children's perspectives, ideas, and opinions. I expect to read texts in many genres that are filled with students' voices. I expect to see students making deliberate moves to lift the quality of their work in an attempt to move an audience. I expect to see the power of my teaching in reference to students making connections from the literature they read to that which they write. I expect to see students growing as writers and for students to acknowledge and take pride in that growth.

What Are Important Understandings for Students?

It's very important for teachers to believe that they have specific content to teach. These might include:

- Writing topics are not limited to big special events, but are contained in every-day happenings.
- There are many formats for shaping writing and we choose the ones that best support our content.
- The point is to attempt to write well, to be able to move an audience.
- Talking with other people can lift the quality of your writing.
- Taking lessons from the literature you read can lift the quality of your writing.

What Classroom Interactions Will Enable
Students to Acquire These Understandings?

In order for students to appreciate that writing topics are not limited to big special events but are contained in the everyday happenings, I might . . .

- share appropriate entries from my own writer's notebook
- read aloud literature that illustrates the power of writing about ordinary things in extraordinary ways, particularly topics connected to the interests of children
- offer specific challenges including capturing moments on neighborhood walks, responding to significant classroom happenings, and inviting students in on the search for literature examples that illustrate this kind of writing

In order for students to appreciate that there are many formats for shaping writing and that we choose the ones that best support our content, I might . . .

- design minilessons in which I present potential writing topics, inviting students to talk through possible formats for shaping these ideas. For example, "I'm planning to shape these several notebook entries about getting braces as an adult into a publishable work. What are my possibilities? A poem? A letter to my dentist? A suggestion brochure for other adults? A tongue-in-cheek editorial?"
- read aloud and invite students to respond to picture books, poems, and magazine articles. Then I might ask, "Can you imagine the author having presented these ideas in any other format? Which ones? Why? Why not?"

In order for students to appreciate that the point is to write well, to be able to move an audience, I might . . .

- create child-size metaphors that demonstrate the difference between just writing and writing well. (The usual dinner versus dinner for company. Getting ready for school versus getting ready for school on school photo day. The way you make your bed most mornings versus the way you make your bed when you want your parents to have more confidence in your ability to take care of your own room.)
- share point-counterpoint writing in order demonstrate the difference between mediocre writing and memorable writing. (Two sight-seeing letters, one bland and one filled with rich detail, two movie reviews, one skimpy, one filled with inspirational lines, etc.)

In order for students to appreciate that talking with other people about your writing can lift the quality of your work, I might . . .

- orchestrate many whole-class shares of work in progress in order to teach specific strategies for improving writing (using telling details, precise language, surprising verbs, eliminating unimportant lines, etc.)
- plan for more frequent individual conferences in order to help students see the strengths and weaknesses in their work

In order for students to take lessons from the literature they are reading, I might . . .

- conduct author studies, requiring students to attempt specific writing challenges
- help students find mentors in the classroom library collections, suggesting that they borrow elements from the writers they appreciate
- provide occasional templates that scaffold students' attempts to try new techniques

How Will We Know That We Are Making a Difference?

In order for students to appreciate their own growth as writers, I might . . .

- ask students to write reflections on their growth as writers
- ask students to prepare point-counterpoint displays of their own writing, highlighting areas of change
- ask parents to comment on students' writing portfolios
- require students to produce several examples in any one genre to facilitate noting specific areas of growth

Adding Special Events to the Writing Workshop

In the remainder of this chapter I will describe several "special events" in the teaching of writing, courses of study that added energy to our work with children and reminded the adults involved how privileged we all were to be working in a school community that honored experimentation, risk taking, and the importance of professional collaboration. Here, rather than presenting the plans, I've included brief descriptions of the classroom procedures. Note however, that as is true of any course of study, teachers need to plan for these projects, taking into account the content they want to teach (the big understandings), the classroom interactions that will help attain the desired understandings, as well as procedures for assessing students' growth. Although every new project requires often time-consuming planning, results are usually worth all the effort. When new formats and ways to excel are periodically being introduced into the writing workshop, many more students can find their niche as writers. Likewise, teachers of writing can also discover their own particular areas of interest and expertise. The following special projects are described in detail below.

- nonfiction countdown calendars
- multigrade author study
- writing from memories
- capturing a place
- appreciating similes and metaphors
- worthwhile contests

Nonfiction Countdown Calendars

One year I invited Joanne Hindley Salch's third-grade class to engage in a long-term project. I began by sharing with the children a stack of calendars I had been collecting. All were theme-related—flowers of Hawaii, Italian cooking, movie classics. The photographs or drawings were labeled or identified briefly on the back page. I explained to the children how I longed for more information when I saw these incredible illustrations. Then I showed them a calendar that satisfied my hunger for information. It was a holiday gift from our science teacher Lisa and was entitled, "Toys We Remember." It had large photographs of such nostalgic toys as Etch a Sketch, Mr Potato Head, Yo-Yos, Silly Putty, Tinker Toys, Ant Farms, Pez, Easy-Bake Ovens, Hotwheels, Slinkies, Monopoly, and Crayola crayons. Of course, there were twelve toys, one for each month of the year, and each was accompanied by a short, snappy commentary. For example, the passage next to a larger-than-life photograph of the Silly Putty label read,

> 1950—Despite scientist's claim that it had no practical applications, Silly Putty has been used by everyone from pilots (as ear plugs) and secretaries (to clean typewriter keys) to athletes (who squeeze it to strengthen their grip), dry cleaners (as a method to remove lint from clothes) and restaurateurs (beats a matchbook for leveling the legs of a wobbly table). It has also found its way into outer space where it was carried aboard Apollo 8 to keep tools fastened down during weightlessness.

After sharing a few of these intriguing passages I explained this ambitious nonfiction writing project to the children. In fact, to make sure they really understood it, I prepared the following handout. (See Appendix 11 for reproducible directions.)

Calendar Project

We will be making very special calendars for 1999. First we will each pick a topic that we care about. We will find 12 subtopics (one for each month) and write short passages for each. Then we will illustrate each one (BIG PROJECT!!). When we are done, we will attach each passage and illustration onto a calendar page. (Your teacher will give you the pages.) Finally we will add a countdown to the year 2000. (So in the box for January 1st we will write 365 days to go!) Remember to choose a topic that you:

- really care about (this will hang on your wall for a whole year)
- can think of 12 subtopics for (see the worksheet attached)
- can illustrate (or use photographs, clippings, etc.)

For example, if I chose "Flowers," I might list the following subtopics:

1. Tulips
2. Roses
3. Lilacs
4. Carnations
5. Daffodils
6. Lilies
7. Peonies
8. Daisies
9. Marigolds
10. Sunflowers
11. Hibiscus
12. Violets

I then distributed a planning sheet, with a fill-in-the-blank title that read as follows (see Appendix 11 for reproducible planning sheet):

My 1999 _____ Calendar

This was followed by a countdown from 1 to 12, with a blank space next to each month of the year.

Joanne and I walked about the room, conferring with children about their choices. We encouraged children to pick topics according to the three criteria listed above and we helped them tease out twelve possible research items. We marveled at the variety of students' interests. Students' topics included jungle animals, birds, dogs, women's changing fashions, sports, vehicles, musical instruments, and perhaps most surprising, English idioms.

Joanne used her writing workshop time over the next two months to help children gather and organize information and craft quality passages. (Yes, this project took two months for many children to complete. Teachers who want students to be able to offer calendars to their families as holiday gifts would do well to begin in late October.) Students also spent time at home as well as time in our nonfiction research room gathering needed information. (See *Lifetime Guarantees* for explanation of this school resource center.)

I periodically stopped in to talk to children about the difference between writing any old thing and writing things you'd be proud to attach your name to and hang on your wall for a year. Children understood that their writing should engage the reader with surprising thoughts and sound true to their own writer's voice. They understood that they needed to choose their language carefully and that every sentence needed to carry new thoughts. Children worked hard to make these the kind of calendars you can't pass by and the kind that you want to save forever.

Joanne had the covers of each calendar laminated and then had the pages attached with spiral bindings. The children couldn't wait to take these very professional publications home.

Sofia's calendar on idioms contained the following twelve subtopics:

Pull your leg

Turn over a new leaf

Costs an arm and a leg

On a shoestring

Mad as a hatter

Need something like a hole in the head

Add fuel to the fire

You're in the dog house

Not my cup of tea

Go fly a kite

If the shoe fits, wear it

Climbing the walls

A sample from this calendar appears in Figure 8.1.

A page from Mia's Calendar of Musical Instruments appears in Figure 8.2.

By providing children with the preprepared calendar pages, with a deliberately narrow space on the left for writing, Joanne was offering a form of template to guide the children and support their efforts. These eight-year-olds were proud to fill this small space, twelve times.

Figure 8.1

Figure 8.2

(I think an equivalent gift calendar can be prepared by our very youngest writers. Imagine asking young children at the beginning of December to comb through their writing folders for their twelve favorite pieces of writing. These can then be assembled into a memorable calendar for families. Their drawings and jottings would form the top half and the preprinted calendar page would form the bottom. Young children could be asked to add any family reminders on appropriate dates.)

Multigrade Author Study

One year, Karen Ruzzo, a grade-two teacher, and Judy Davis, a grade-five teacher, invited me to conduct an author study, working with both their classes at the same time. Just as our students had been reading buddies for many years, it seemed a likely stretch to arrange writing partners between children of differing ages. The procedures were simple and predictable. We would meet in one another's room, crowding both groups of students together, having prearranged working pairs based on students' needs, strengths, and personalities. I would lead the author study by reading a book by the chosen author at each get-together and then I would challenge the young writers to go off and attempt to do some of the highlighted techniques or talents of the author under study. The children could work separately, simply advising one another or collaboratively producing one text in response to the challenge.

I selected Jonathan London as the author (see page 6 for the use of *Puddles,* another of his picture books), because in addition to London being a wonderfully lyrical and prolific writer, I knew that his books would be readily available for the children to borrow from their classroom and public libraries if they wanted to reread and share them with their families. (See Appendix 1 for a listing of his titles.)

At our first gathering, I shared *Like Butter on Pancakes,* the poetic tribute to the early-morning hours on a farm, illustrated by G. Brian Karas. After sharing and chatting about the book I challenged the writing partners to capture a place that they knew well, anchoring it in a specific time of day. (See also pages 258–272 on learning to write with a sense of place.) I also suggested they pay careful attention to their choice of verbs, use repetition carefully, and attempt to tuck in a series of short sentences, all features we lifted from this Jonathan London picture book. A few writing samples appear in Figures 8.3 to 8.5. (Note that the children worked individually on this challenge as they had very

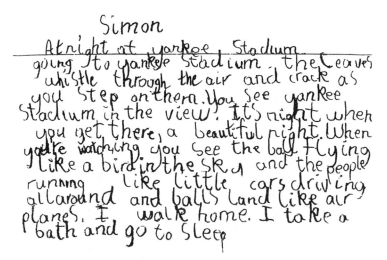

Figure 8.3

[Jessica]

Trick-or-Treating at night in New York.

Trick-or-Treating is so much fun.
The candy crunches.
The pumpkins smile,
The crickets sing.
The owls woooooo.
You fill your bags with lots to eat.

Figure 8.4

Early morning at Church. You
walk through the long corridor unto
the chapel. you sing prayer The
choir burst with music and notes.
The bishop kneels on a cushion and,
leads us in a song. Then communion
starts. you take a cracker and dip it
into wine. After that you take the
hymnal from infront of the pew. My
favorite part has ended.

Figure 8.5

different choices for places that they knew well. Not all children attempted to use all the distinctive features of this text.)

Here are some additional fifth grade examples.

Fifth grader Vickie writes:

Morning Mist in Westchester

The mist tiptoes through the glass and the morning dew upon the flowers is small as a baby's tear. The coffee pot whistles to get my attention while the sunshine flows through my window and stains the French white quilt. The sun casts a ray in my eyes and they sparkle with morning light. I tiptoe down a flight of stairs that leads me into the kitchen. To surprise everyone I make the coffee and sneak a sip, but it's too bitter. I slip on my fluffy Minnie Mouse slippers and go out to pick mint leaves for the mint jelly on toast. I set out into the morning mist in Westchester.

Fifth grader Lauren writes:

Morning Lake

I tiptoe over the cold pebbles, shivering in my bathing suit as the breeze blows over the lake. I glance back at the house making sure I didn't wake anyone up.

Light seeps over the tops of the tallest trees in the east. It burns away the mist that has draped itself over the lake. I sit on a bench that almost leans over into the shallow water. I drag my feet, swinging them back and forth in the cold water. It sends shivers up my arms to the top of my head. I wish I had remembered and brought a sweater along, I mumble to myself.

I unwrap the tarnished rope that anchors the wooden boat to shore. I step in and sit down. I push the paddles into the still water and drift out into the middle of the lake.

I stand up and put my foot on the edge. I lift my arms above my head linking thumbs. My feet push against the cold boat. Suddenly my arms are slicing through water like a knife through butter. I swim in the direction of the sky and burst out of the water. I hold onto the edge of the boat until my breath comes back to me. I then guide the boat toward the shore and my still sleeping house.

Fifth grader Rakheli writes:

Playing in the Playground in the Afternoon Rain

My eyelashes are plastered together with rain. Rain drips off my nose and onto my waiting tongue. Nora's dirty face is streaky from the clean rain water. Our moms left with the car. They don't like the rain. Now that it's just me, Nora, and our bikes. We can play. The light wooden playing equipment is dark from all the rain water it has soaked up. The slides are slippery, so are the sliding poles. Nora runs after me, our wet hair sticking to our cheeks in the humid rainy wind. Our jeans and shirts are soaking wet and heavy. We run around the monkey bars, up the tire ladder, down the cold slide. We pant heavily. Nora calls a "time-out" breathlessly. We hobble toward each other with the wet pebbles that are instead of concrete and sand slipping under us. We lean on each other for support and head for the swings. There are two of them, low to the ground on their own wooden structure. We hobble over to them and notice the puddles in the seats. "I don't want to sit in a puddle," Nora says. "Why not?" I ask, "We're already soaked to the bone." So we sit in the puddly swings and laugh at the squidgy noise we make when we sit down. We sit and cough and pant while the rain stops abruptly. "Now that the rain has stopped, let's go home." "Okay," she says, so we mount our bikes with the sticky seats and ride through deserted wet streets, home to dry clothes, hot chocolate, and a crackling fire.

As is evident, the quality of the work, on a wide range of topics, was high. Students seemed intent on showing one another just how effective their writing could be, valuing one another as coach and audience. Some children, in fact (particularly the older ones), tended to overwrite, trying to impress their partners with unusually lyrical language. Second graders rose to the occasion, thoroughly delighting in doing what the older kids were doing. A fifth grader was just as likely as a second grader to admit that his partner came up with a word or two or had an idea for an ending. The partnerships took on the air of "mutual admiration societies." Older and younger writers learned about the role of audience (perhaps for the first time, they were writing with a very particular and limited audience in mind—their partners), the power of talking through your ideas with a willing listener, and the value of occasionally having a writing assignment with a few constraints.

Throughout the workshops, teachers walked the room (and the corridors—we had to spread out with so many students), stopping to confer with students. We often worked as a trio, talking to one writer or one pair of writers together in order to reflect on our own conferring practice. (This type of study becomes a prime professional development opportunity, with teachers and principal spending time together alongside students.) We also realized that these types of writing challenges became a fairly easy way to get quick finished products to be proud of. The children took about three days to complete these pieces and then it was time to study another Jonathan London book. (The study stretched out over several weeks.) Parents were thrilled to hear of the collaboration, as many children went home talking about this very special project that added new spirit to their writing workshops.

In the weeks ahead, children took lessons from several other Jonathan London picture books, including *I See the Moon and the Moon Sees Me*, a very repetitive, predictable text, illustrated by Peter Fiore (see second-grade Fanny's version of the book, below), *The Candy Store Man*, a lively rap-beat rhyming story of a beloved neighborhood resident (illustrated by Kevin O'Malley), *Hurricane!*, a suspenseful first-person account of a family adventure (illustrated by Henri Sorensen), each book offering different distinctive features to be emulated. Discovering which features to highlight becomes an essential task for teachers who lead this kind of study. Of course, that work begins with selecting an appropriate author, one who students will enjoy reading and will want to emulate and one whose techniques are so distinctive that children will be able to borrow them successfully. Teasing out such features can become a worthwhile activity at a staff meeting. Deciding to do such an author study across grade levels adds another layer of challenge to the work, as the author's work must appeal to and contain lessons for a wide range of writers. (Other writers I might try to study in this way include Charlotte Zolotow, Katherine Lasky, and James Stevenson.)

"*How I Knit*" by Fanny Wyrick-Flax was inspired by Jonathan London's *I See the Moon and the Moon Sees Me*:

> I see the sheep and the sheep sees me.
> "Hello sheep, can I take some wool from you?"
> I see the brush and the brush sees me.
> "Hello brush, can you clean this wool for me?"
> I see the spinning wheel and the spinning wheel sees me.
> "Hello spinning wheel, can you spin this clean wool for me?"
> I see the needles and the needles see me.
> "Hello needles, can you knit this wool for me?"
> I see my sister and my sister sees me.
> "Hi Molly, do you like this sweater from me?"

The final book used in our work together was London's *Dream Weaver*, with illustrations by Rocco Baviera. This poetic picture book tells the tale of a child closely observing a yellow spider. Although I followed the same classroom procedure briefly described above, the teachers decided to publish the students' finished work in a bound book. The following explanation, written by the children, served as an introduction to the collection.

Dear reader,

Over the course of the year, Judy Davis' fifth-grade class and Karen Ruzzo's second-grade class have been participating in a Jonathan London author study designed by our principal, Shelley. The two classes met at either classroom and read a picture book by Jonathan London. Shelley would select a picture book to read aloud to us and then we would discuss the different techniques Jonathan London used that would be good models for us. The two classes met about five times. The kids would buddy up with the children in the opposite grade.

For our final project we went over a picture book called Dream Weaver. *Shelley challenged us to use five different techniques used by the author. They include:*

1. Choosing topics related to nature

2. Using the "you" voice (direct address to reader)

3. Making close observations

4. Using strong, precise, and surprising verbs

5. Writing factual information in a beautiful way (not everyone added a list of facts as Jonathan London did on the last page of Dream Weaver*).*

The writing buddies then went off to write pieces using as many of the five techniques as they could.

In this book you will discover the final and illustrated drafts of our pieces for this last project. We hope you enjoy them as much as we enjoyed writing them.

Sincerely,
The Young Writers of the Manhattan New School

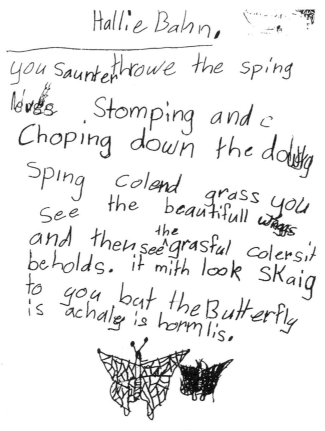

Figure 8.6

The finished products for this challenge were written collaboratively by the fifth graders and their second-grade partners. A few examples are included here.

Hallie, a second grader, and Leily, a fifth grader, wrote separately about butterflies and then combined their efforts. Hallie's draft is in Figure 8.6; Leily's draft is in Figure 8.7. Their combined effort looked like this:

Butterfly Dreams

In the spring, when the daffodils have just risen from the newly seeded earth, you saunter through the newborn flower buds, stomping and chomping. You will see the graceful colors of butterflies. Their wings wiggle, shaking off the winter's dew that has collected during their hibernation. Hundreds of multicolored wings reflect rainbows in the water. They might look scary to you, but a butterfly is harmless. They sit on bright flowers, slurping up nectar with their straw-like tongues. You may not want to touch them, for fear of their glass-like wings shattering. So, instead you watch them—their wings, their tiny black bodies, their colors.

Soon, the frosty winter arrives. The butterflies creep onto trees, flowers and plants. Their bodies slow down and they stay still. Waiting. Once again, the butterfly dreams for spring.

> In the spring, when the daffodils have just risen from the newly seeded earth, ~~butterfly~~ butterflies creep out from the trees. Their wings wiggle, shaking off the winter's dew that has collected from their hibernation. Hundreds of multicolored wings create rainbows over the water. Sunshine sweeps across them, their bodies glittering like sequins. They are so tame, that if you were to hold out your arm, they would sweep on to it in a gust. ~~If you were to follow the stream to where the brightly colored pansy grove is located~~

Figure 8.7

My reaction to the above piece was twofold. First, I felt obliged to share the piece with our science teacher in order to assess the students' understandings about the life of butterflies. Second, I marveled at how they chose to work apart and then together. I wished I had heard their conversations as they decided how to merge their words and add new thoughts along the way.

Jessica, a second grader, and Bari, a fifth grader, combined their efforts to produce the following piece about a cat.

> In the living room of an apartment, in a big building, in a big city, you will see my cat. You will find that she looks like the night sky when white stars glow.
>
> Her bumpy pink tongue feels like pimples on a smooth cheek.
>
> When she sees a mouse she scrunches up and prepares to pounce.
>
> When she walks, you cannot hear her because she is as quiet as the early morning in the country when dew drops spot the grass.
>
> When you pet her you can tell that her pink nose is very wet.
>
> And at night, you will find her asleep on her pillow by the radiator near a window.

Three boys, Sam, a second grader, and Jason and Avi, fifth graders, collaborated on the following piece about a parrot

A Parrot in a Pet Shop

If you walk into a pet shop,
You will see an energetic parrot.
If you say, "Cracker,"
It will say, "Cracker" back to you.

When you look at the parrot's belly,
It's like Picasso's art
Because of the dark layers of color,
The beak of the parrot
Is like a baby elephant's tusk.

Its legs are like walking drumsticks
Playing music.
When you walk out of the pet shop with the parrot,
He says "Cracker,"
And you say, "Cracker" back.

(The older boys were very proud to inform me that the line about Picasso came from seven-year-old Sam.)

It would have been interesting to keep tabs on all the student writers who participated in this author study throughout the remainder of the school year, to note if any of the techniques they were asked to try had become internalized and part of their writer's toolbox, appearing naturally in other works. This added research piece would have added great depth to this author's study.

Writing from Memories

Memoir writing has always struck me as a rather sophisticated act. Today this genre seems more popular than ever. In an article in the *Washington Post*, columnist Jonathan Yardley suggests, "a quarter of a century ago, memoir, or autobiography was a genre practiced and read by relatively few. Most memoirs were written by men and women whose lives had been lived on one public stage or another, notable people about whom we ordinary folk were understandably curious. A few were the work of unknown writers who managed, by sheer force of personality or art or both, to make themselves and their lives interesting to readers who previously had known nothing about them at all. . . . The underlying assumption was that a memoir had to be *earned*, either by the achievements of a lifetime or by the author's literary skills." The article continues with experts exploring the current memoir rage, now calling it the people's genre, with such defining terms as *life review*, *guided autobiography*, and *reminiscences*. I must admit that although I am fifty-three years old and an avid reader of memoirs, I do not feel obliged nor ready to write my own. Nor do I think elementary school children should be asked to write theirs.

(I laughed out loud when I read the introduction to Dave Eggers' memoir, *A Heartbreaking Work of Staggering Genius*. In part, he writes, "Maybe writing about actual events, in the first person, if not from Ireland and before you turn seventy, was Bad.")

I am not interested in asking young children to discover big truths about their lives, reveal significant threads, devise angles for sifting through their life stories, or otherwise make their memories add up. I do believe, however, that children's memories are grist for their writing mills. I just refuse to ask them to use their memories in the service of something so grown-up as crafting their memoirs. Instead, I have come to rely on several less sophisticated yet worthwhile writing projects that depend on children's memories but use them in respectful and realistic ways. A brief listing of them follows:

Annotated Timelines of Their Lives

These can be open-ended, with children listing any significant moments, or they can be more specific, such as a timeline of first-time events, birthday celebrations, moving to new homes or apartments, etc.

Artifact Gallery

Students can bring artifacts or personal treasures from home and write index-card explanations to accompany their choices.

Captioned Photo Albums

Children bring in family photograph albums and write carefully crafted text to sit alongside each snapshot.

"What They Were Thinking" for Children

This project has its roots in the *Sunday Magazine* section of the *New York Times*. The person in a photograph explains what they were thinking at the time the snapshot was taken. Imagine a wall of these insightful explanations lining a classroom. (Cynthia Rylant's poems that accompany Walker Evans' photographs in the collection *Something Permanent* provide a slightly different model of writing in response to photographs.)

Memory Maps

Children are asked to record milestones on maps of their neighborhood, city, state, or country. These would be done in much the way that workers at the Museum of the City of New York have been recording individual stories onto large maps to create a collective history of New Yorkers.

Annotated Cookbooks

Children are asked to record family stories next to favorite family recipes in the margins of well-used family cookbooks.

Baby-Book Updates

Children are invited to update those commercially produced baby books that parents often leave half-finished. Children would need to interview family members to fill out the missing data.

Memory Manuscripts

Children are asked to contribute to specific classroom anthologies. These three-ring binders could be labeled "Playground Memories," "Kindergarten Memories," "Bedtime Rituals," "New Brothers and Sisters," "Learning to Read," "Losing a Tooth," etc. Teachers can also be asked to contribute their own vignettes to add to these growing collections.

Collections of Very Short Stories from Your Life

Eric Carle's autobiographical book is entitled *Flora and Tiger: 19 Very Short Stories from My Life*. Children can do likewise, putting together a collection of the personal narratives they have written over the course of a school year and labeling them as "Very Short Stories from My Life."

Themed Collections of Short Life Stories

If stories chosen are related to one topic—for example, taking care of the family pets—then the collection could be labeled, "Stories from My Life as a Pet Owner." (Over the course of a few years, I wrote leads to "Connecting Readers and Writers with Books," a column in *The New Advocate*, each about my life as a reader and teacher of reading. I could put them all together and label them, "Stories from My Life as a Reader," giving the collection as a gift to my own children.)

Memory Books as Family Keepsakes

Years ago I purchased a little booklet titled, *The Way It Was: Childhood Recollections to Hand Down*, written by Elizabeth Hill and Martha Starr. It is filled with prompts to get the reader to recall childhood memories, including family anecdotes, advice from parents, family rituals, pastimes, etc. Alongside each prompt is plenty of blank space for recording these memories. Despite the prompts and cue words from the authors, I still find the pages hard to fill. I wish I had had it when I was young. Our elementary students can be asked to hold onto their childhoods now, preserving their memories as a family keepsake, one to be saved and passed onto their own children. We can, in fact, create the kind of ongoing books that students fill throughout their elementary years, adding memories as they move up in the grades.

Parent-Child Memories

Children write up vivid memories and ask parents or other family members to comment on them. Work can be published side by side. Parents can also be asked to write companion memory pieces, not mere comments. For example, both child and parent can be asked to write up their own memories of having learned to ride a two-wheeler, received allowance, or attended their first day of school. (Students can interview family members to discover the topics in which they each have strong memories.) Companion pieces can be published side by side.

Growing Up in the 1990s—A Volume of Vignettes

Many of the memories that children choose to record offer a quick glimpse at what it's been like to grow up in the late 1990s. Our New York City children write of playing in the fire hydrant spray, ordering dinners from takeout menus, and teaching their grand-mas about the Internet. These scenes, which can be thought of as vignettes or word-pictures, can be gathered and published in a class magazine each surrounded by the vine leaves and tendril sketches that truly mark a vignette.

Using Memories to Feed Genre Studies

Many of the memories our third through fifth graders record in their writer's notebooks serve as raw material for the poems or picture books they write during their regular writ-ing workshop. Although not labeled as memoirs, the authors are quite proud to shape these memories into finished products within other genre studies. Teachers frequently share work by writers who explain in their author's notes, book jackets, or biographical material how personal memories led them to create the particular work at hand.

Note that although some of the projects described above may appear to be quite simple in nature, I do have high standards for the finished products. Students are asked to craft quality texts and package them in elegant, memorable ways.

Capturing a Place

Children are frequently asked to tell about places. Parents ask children to write and tell them what their sleep-away camp is like. Teachers ask students what it was like to grow up in faraway lands. Grandparents ask children what it's like at their school, their friends' homes, their school trip to the apple orchard, zoo, farm, or museum. With so much prac-tice, one would think children would be accomplished at capturing places in words. Instead, children often shrug their shoulders, saying, "I dunno," or offer the nondescript comment, "It was nice." When our immigrant students write a story that takes place in their homeland we rarely get a picture of that place. Instead, for all its lack of specifics, we can easily imagine that that family dinner in Brazil was occurring in Brooklyn.

When teachers suggest ways to improve the quality of students' writing about a place, they usually tuck the information into a bigger course of study—perhaps one on writing picture books, short stories, or newspaper articles. They suggest ways for stu-dents to make the setting enhance the story, be the setting a town in Serbo-Croatia or a grandmother's kitchen. Here, I am suggesting that learning to write about a place is a significant skill unto itself, and deserving of its own time in the sun. In other words, it need not be tucked into a more important genre study, but big blocks of time can and should be carved out to help young children write exceptionally well about places.

At first, students' attempts at capturing a place they know well could simply be called glimpses, snapshots, or descriptions and mounted alongside photographs of these places. Later they can be asked to turn their newfound skills into travel writing and pub-lished as guidebooks, brochures, newsletter columns, or articles for school magazines. Then too, students' words can be shaped into poems or added as informational text to their social studies inquiries. Writing about a place cuts across so many kinds of writing that when students have strengthened their abilities, this learning can be applied to all the other kind kinds of writing that they do including weaving a sense of place into their personal narratives, fictional tales, and the many kinds of memory writing previously described. In other words, in the beginning we are *not* concerned that young writers add layers of meaning to their writing about a place, to hint at big ideas or somehow use the place symbolically as professional writers might. In the beginning, our goal is for children to understand how to notice the telling details of a place, to capture its essence, to choose words and metaphors that help their readers imagine the place that is in their mind's eye.

(The same kind of thinking can apply to learning to write well about a person. We start with a simple character sketch, before we ask children to craft more elaborate biographies. Then we can ask students to weave what they have learned about "people writing" into all that they do including narratives, short stories, or essays.)

If I were to carve out several weeks for elementary students to focus their attention on writing well about places, I would begin by surrounding children with the works of professional writers who have written well about their current hometown or geographic area. I would then invite children to learn from these selected mentors, by writing thoughtfully about their own school, neighborhood, or city, places they know well. I would then invite them to take what they had learned in their community and write well about places of their own personal choosing. More specific plans would include the following preparations and classroom interactions.

Consult Professional Resources

I always begin a new course of study by reading up on the topic. To learn what it takes to write eloquently about a place, I might reread selected chapters from William Zinsser's *On Writing Well*, Ralph Fletcher's *What a Writer Needs,* Don Graves' *Investigate Non-Fiction,* and Don Murray's *Read to Write.* I'd sift through these wonderful texts for ideas that would be appropriate for the age of my students. Then I'd think through ways to share that information that would make sense for my particular students. For example, Zinsser warns about the use of "syrupy words and groaning platitudes." I might interpret that thought in the following way in a minilesson with my third graders. "If you are writing about your grandmother's kitchen and you say it is 'pretty as a picture,' those words won't hold much meaning for your readers. Those words, 'pretty as a picture,' are used so often that people aren't really touched by them. Remember the reader will be moved when you describe something in a surprising way. How about saying something like, "Grandma's kitchen could be on the cover of a Mother's Day card? Do you think most readers would pay attention to that?"

Zinsser also suggests the use of "details that are significant, . . . ones that do useful work." If I were planning to work with third graders, I might very well read Zinsser's exact words to the children. I think they could understand the following: "We don't want him (the writer) to describe every ride at Disneyland, or tell us that the Grand Canyon is awesome, or that Venice has canals. If one of the rides at Disneyland got stuck, or if somebody fell into the awesome Grand Canyon, *that* would be worth hearing about." Then, I'd give concrete examples pertaining to our city. I'd ask, "Which detail is more helpful to the reader, does more useful work—'New York is crowded,' or 'Crossing the street at lunchtime on Broadway, you can barely see the sidewalk when you look down'? Which is more helpful, 'New York has many tall buildings,' or 'If you want to see all of our sky-scrapers, your neck will hurt from looking up so much when you walk down the street'?"

In *Read to Write*, Don Murray reveals how writers develop a sense of place by offer-ing his own running commentary on dozens of literature selections. His thoughts, intended for an adult audience, can be quite helpful for the elementary teacher willing to sift through the ideas, deciding which can and should be redesigned for children. For example, he comments on the value of weaving in local dialects, statistics, bits of history, and the "artful selection" of details in order to develop a sense of place. Certainly, our young students can be shown child-appropriate examples of these techniques.

Of course, I'd record any notes I take or teaching ideas I design in a special note-book marked, "Writing About Places." Having these ideas in one central location will make it easier to return to them as needed and to share them with interested colleagues. I would also ask colleagues to join me in designing "kid-friendly" minilessons based on professional reading. These minilessons will be taught throughout this course of study.

Consult Children's Literature in Which the Locale Is Powerfully Presented

In addition to collecting well-written nonfiction books about our hometown, I would gather fictional picture books in which the author captured the essence of the place. For New York City youngsters, these might include such picture books as the following:

> *Amy Elizabeth Explores Bloomingdale's* by E. L. Konigsburg
>
> *Subway Sparrow* by Leyla Torres
>
> *What Zeesie Saw on Delancey Street* by Elsa Okon Raels (illustrated by Marjorie Princeman)
>
> *Harlem: A Poem* by Walter Dean Myers
>
> *The Garden of Happiness* by Erika Tamar
>
> *Mama Provi and the Pot of Rice* by Sylvia Rosa-Casanova (illustrated by Robert Roth).
>
> *Around Town* by Chris Sontpiet (see page 124)
>
> *When a City Leans Against a Sky* by Alan A. De Fina
>
> *Stone Bench in an Empty Park,* selected by Paul Janeczko
>
> *Louis the Fish* and *Hey, Al,* picture books by Arthur Yorinks and Richard Egielski
>
> *Nana's Birthday Party* by Amy Hest (illustrated by Amy Schwartz)
>
> *Busybody Nora* by Johanna Hurwitz

Read Nonfiction Texts Aloud, Inviting Response to the Content and Technique

For example, Shirley Climo's *City! San Francisco* is an informational text divided into seven chapters including a street map of the city and a chapter titled, "A Pocketful of Facts." The book begins with an intriguing lead that reads, "What's high in the middle, low at the edges, and washed by water on three sides?" (The subsequent leads are just as appealing to young readers.) Children need to know that accomplished authors of informational texts always attempt to engage their readers. The text is studded with quotes, memorable stories, Spanish words, song lyrics, historical facts, and even explanations of how some neighborhoods got their names. (I learned that Nob Hill comes from the word *nabob*, a rich person.) The book also contains an author's note, maps, captioned photographs, and an index. Jennifer Owings Dewey's *Antarctic Journal: Four Months at the Bottom of the World* is another nonfiction text that presents several different formats for young writers to attempt. These include sketches, photographs, journal entries, and letters home.

You might also consider studying several nonfiction books dealing with the same setting in order to demonstrate various styles of writing. In addition, you might discover additional tools used to convey information including glossaries, timelines, graphs, subheadings, and so on. Ask students to share their preferences and the various techniques used by the authors.

Read Aloud Fictional Material Set in the Locale and Allow Time for Response

It might help to ask such questions as, "Could this same story have happened somewhere else? How would the story have had to change if it took place other than in New York City?" Then reread, asking children to note lines that prove that these authors really know this city. Children might develop a chart listing the following elements:

How do authors create a sense of place?
The authors include the names of real places and streets.
The authors include occasional words in the languages heard in this city.
The authors mention specific foods, customs, and music that are popular in this city.
The authors have the people do things that this city's residents do.
The authors compare things in our city to other places to show how unique our city is.

Invite Children and Families in on the Search for Hometown Materials

Encourage participants to seek out a variety of formats, including poems, nonfiction articles, informational books, brochures, travel guides, and magazines.

Gather Texts About Other Settings

I would continue my read-aloud sessions with picture books that are about places unfamiliar to my students, but that effectively develop a sense of place. Once again I would ask children to note how the author helps readers get to know these places well. (I would also ask students to wonder how the illustrator adds to the sense of place.) I would encourage students, as they read independently, to search for writers who capture places effectively.

All of the picture books in the list below give a strong sense of place.

Sayonara Mrs. Kackleman by Maira Kalman (Japan)
The Roses in My Carpets by Rukhsana Khan and illustrated by Ronald Himler (Afghanistan)

Somewhere in Africa by Ingrid Mennen and Niki Daly, illustrated by Nicolaas Maritz (an African City)

Bigmama's by Donald Crews (a farm in Cottondale)

Snowed In by Barbara M. Lucas, illustrated by Catherine Stock (Wyoming range in the early 1900s)

I Have Heard of a Land by Joyce Carol Thomas, illustrated by Floyd Cooper (Oklahoma Territory)

A Little Prairie House, adapted from *The Little House Books* by Laura Ingalls Wilder, illustrated by Renee Graef (prairie land)

The Beach Before Breakfast by Maxine Kumin, illustrated by Leonard Weisgard (beach life)

Silver Morning by Susan Pearson, illustrated by David Christiana (foggy woods)

Island Summer by Catherine Stock (an island village in summertime)

The following elements might be added to the chart described on page 261.

The authors mention plants and animals that live in these places.

The authors refer to the kinds of houses that are really in these places.

The authors include the right kind of clothing for these places.

The authors mention the pastimes of the people who live in these places.

The authors mention the kinds of jobs that are unique to these places.

The authors gives authentic names to characters in these places.

The authors weave in unusual expressions that are used in these places.

Engage Children in Activities Directed at Capturing the Feel of Their Town or City

When I attended the Whole Language Umbrella Conference in Nashville, Tennessee, I picked up a newspaper contest entitled, "You're so Nashville if . . ." Residents sent in very telling (often brutally honest or sarcastic) details about life in the city. I can easily imagine our students (probably grade three and higher) being eager to respond to, "You're so New York if . . ." They'd probably think you're so New York if you pass the Empire State Building and don't even look up, you can travel the subways without a map, or you know the names of the carved lions that sit in front of the 42nd Street library (Patience and Fortitude). Perhaps their teachers would probably think you are so New York if you know how to get discount tickets for Broadway shows, order from different takeout menus every night of the week, and are able to hail a taxicab even in the rain. It might be fun to hang a graffiti board on a corridor wall asking members of the school community to add their own responses to, "You're so _____ if . . ." Children would certainly get the feel for the details that capture their town or city. Other playful activities might include browsing the local newspaper for events that cause the reader to say, "It could only happen here!" Have students explain their responses. Have students keep a running list of "Very _____ Sights and Sounds" (filling in their own hometown).

Provide "Point-Counterpoint" Examples

Over the years, I have invited many students, together with their families and teachers, to my home for a summer barbecue. Occasionally, a child will write me a thank-you note after the visit. (Most just stop me in the hallway to extend their thank-yous.) After second-grade Joseph's visit he sent me the very detailed thank-you that appears in Figure 8.8. He let me know exactly what he appreciated.

It is effective to show Joseph's response to visiting my home next to a bare-bones one, the kind that simply reads, "Thanks for letting me visit. I liked your house and your food too."

(See *Lasting Impressions* for further elaboration of point-counterpoint examples, pages 129–132. See *Lifetime Guarantees*, Figure 2.7, for an example of a well-written travel postcard that can be effectively shared next to a meagerly written one.)

Invite Family Members to Tell the Story of Their Homelands

Ask children to take notes on the family members' presentations. After the guest speaker has left, ask students to imagine writing about this place. What information would you

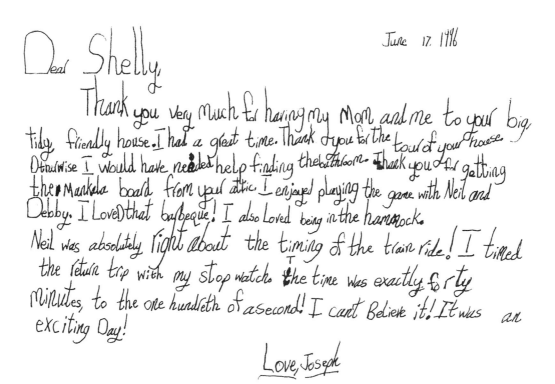

Figure 8.8

include? Which details really helped you to get a sense of this place? What additional information would you need?

Help Children Understand That Important Places Need Not Be Found on a Map

Read aloud poems from such a collection as Charlotte Huck's *Secret Places,* letting students know that they too can write about such places as a chair house they've built, a hideout in a tree, or a friend's house.

Record Your Responses to Your Environs and Share These with Your Students

On page 39 I include a page from the dialogue journal I kept with one early-childhood student. That kind of writing, my reflections about driving to work in the early morning hours, is filled with New York City observations. It is that kind of writing that I would be sure to share with children who are attempting to capture places they care about. Teachers should avoid asking children to do things they are not willing to do themselves. In fact, throughout the school day teachers can demonstrate when their location gives them reason to pause. (In New York City, teachers can marvel at scenes out the window, the incredible noises from the street, and even the driving and parking hassles they endured on their way to work.)

Ask Children to Categorize Books in the Class Library by Locale

Writers and books could be grouped in the following categories:

> Big-city writing
>
> Desert books
>
> Mountain tales
>
> Ocean/beach stories
>
> Faraway lands
>
> Small-town events

Browsing might help children discover potential mentor writers and desirable formats for writing about a place or writing with a sense of place.

(See also pages 373–374 in *Lifetime Guarantees* for helpful poetic template for English-language learners writing about their home country.)

Conduct Minilessons Based on the Information Learned from Professional Books and Children's Literature

These would include the charted elements listed on pages 261 and 262, as well as the information gathered from reading the experts: William Zinsser's advice on writing with important detail and surprising language; Ralph Fletcher's advice on using your five senses to gather data on your locale (*What a Writer Needs*); Don Graves' suggestions for becoming a great observer (*Investigate Nonfiction*); Don Murray's advice on the power of the precise detail (*Read to Write*).

Teach Children About the Power of Metaphor in Capturing a Sense of Place

An additional minilesson topic would be the use of metaphor in capturing a place. My daughter called me one night to share a line she had heard on the HBO program *Sex and the City*. One of the characters was describing Staten Island, the borough my daughter grew up in. The character said, "Staten Island is like a quaint European country—bad American music and everyone smokes." According to my daughter the comparison worked, although I felt obliged to defend my smoke-free weekend retreat, ofttimes filled with the voices of Billy Joel, Frank Sinatra, and Barbara Streisand. I must admit, however, that a well-crafted metaphor can certainly help readers get the feel of an unfamiliar place. The use of metaphor has become so important in my teaching life that I describe its power in a separate section beginning on page 273.

Assign Writing Challenges Based on the Literary Elements Students Have Studied

Edward Sorrel dedicates his picture book *The Saturday Kid*, written in collaboration with Cheryl Carlesimo, to "The New York City of my childhood." Writing tasks that require children to pay close attention to their immediate surroundings will provide our students with rich memory banks filled with the cities of their childhoods.

Students might be asked to capture such familiar places as:

their school neighborhood

their classroom

the common areas of the school—auditorium, cafeteria, playground

their favorite setting in their apartment

a place where they spend a lot of time waiting, relaxing, or playing

a relatives' home

a tourist site they have visited frequently

the supermarket their family frequents

a summer hangout

their bedroom on a Sunday morning (See also teaching in response to Jonathan London's *Like Butter on Pancakes* on page 248.)

Some children might be so pleased with the result of these challenges, they will want to work them into such formats as picture books, letters to relatives, poetic odes, and so on. (At one of our middle school–high school complexes, the Upper Lab School, eighth graders compiled a collection of writing about the best of New York City, including such surprising topics as the Best Place to People Watch in New York, the Best View of the New York Skyline, the Best 24-Hour Breakfast Shop, and the Best French Fries in New York. Teachers had their work, cleverly entitled *Coring the Apple*, beautifully bound and published by Chapbooks.com.)

(See also *Lifetime Guarantees* for information on photographic essays—pages 154–156—and street image poetry—page 187.)

Invite Writers to Share Work in Progress

In addition to minilessons, children can learn a great deal about lifting the quality of their writing by listening to the work of others as well as suggestions given to other young writers. For example, if seven-year-old Lauren had shared the narrative that appears in Figure 8.9, perhaps the author would have been asked the questions that follow.

- What made the hikes so beautiful?
- What kind of flowers grow in that town?
- Can you say more about the lake and the woods?
- What kind of rocks did you rest on?

During that share meeting, the teacher could have pointed out to all the children how adding specific details would help the reader really picture this setting.

(Of course, seven-year-olds would have also asked how she felt when she was lost in the dark woods, how come her cat knew where to find her, what she did with the bouquets, and why she called the story "My Country House" when it's really about the woods, not the house.)

Invite Writers to Share Completed Writing

When Rafe was in grade two he wrote a lengthy piece about having lived in the Middle East. His article appeared in a student-published school literary magazine, *Kids Write On*. In part he writes,

> Jerusalem is not that far away from Egypt. So let me tell you about Egypt. Egypt used to be a very rich country about 1800 years ago. It had pharaohs as rulers, and they were buried in tombs when they died. King Tut was not one of the most famous kings of Egypt. He started as a nine-year old pharaoh and his wife was seven when they got married. They could have been at our school! King Tut would be in fourth grade and his wife in second grade! . . .
>
> I went to the Pyramids of ancient Egypt. They were fun. The one we went to in the morning wasn't that fun because we went there on horseback and I fell off my horse because it started to gallop. I didn't really get hurt when I fell off. The reason I really didn't like the pyramid was because it was full of old tracks to move stones around the pyramids, not ancient tracks, but for workers who were there only fifty years ago. There was a lot of junk there, and if you looked at the ground you could tell that there had been a lot of horses there, if you know what I mean . . .

When Rafe reads his words aloud to the class, all his classmates can benefit from thinking about how much this article sounds like the classmate they know. It is filled with the voice of a second grader. He did some original thinking about what he was learning and included some surprising details.

page (1)

Every Year I go to a
country house. Last year I
went to Old Chatam. I
went on beautiful hikes.
    I picked flowers and
I made the flowers into
bouquets. I swam in the
lake and I got lost
in the woods. When I
was quite far from home I
saw some rocks so I took
a rest and I fell asleep.

page (2)

When I woke up it
was dark. Then I heard
a sound in the bushes.
AND OUT POPPED
my cat Meow Meow and he
showed me the way home!!!

Figure 8.9

Invite Students to Reread Their Earlier Writing and Revise Based on What They Have Learned About Place

Once children have produced effective descriptions of places, they will be ready to look back at old pieces of writing in which they neglected to develop a sense of place. They will now have an opportunity to apply what they have been learning. At this point your minilessons should suggest the many roles that setting can play in a personal narrative, short story, or chapter book. Once again, I find myself referring to professional reading. For example, in *What a Writer Needs*, Ralph Fletcher suggests several ways that the description of the setting can be useful to a writer, including serving as an introduction to a story and as a way to develop the characters in the story. For example, in the piece below, the fourth-grade author Robert, an English-language learner, could have begun the piece by giving the reader a feel for his homeland, Malta. Additionally, an elaborated setting would help the reader appreciate why his grandfather so loved that field and how hard he worked.

> My grandpa's field had all sorts of stuff like big red apples, tomatoes, big juicy watermelons, pears and some other vegetables. In this field our grandpa left us a space to run around except we didn't like going there and neither did my grandpa because the farm right next to the field it had pigs in puddles of mud, cows, sheep, rabbits, horses, chickens and some donkeys.
>
> Sometimes my grandpa got mad when we took fruits. He then told us that they were not ready to take but he told us that in one day or two that they were ready to take. But one day he got sick and the doctor said he had to sell the field so he did. Now we couldn't get fruits to make a picnic or work with our grandpa in the field. Now I pass by the field when I'm in Malta and it turned to dust but still when I go to a picnic I remember the days when we took fruit without his permission and when we talked about what we were going to do when we grow up. Sometimes he said if he could stand the smell he would live there. He never got his wish and he never said his wish will come true. His other wish was for the smell of the animals will go away but that wish will never came true.

Fifth-grade Jiva can share the finished piece in Figure 8.10, and her classmates can help her decide if the Bulgarian setting needs to play a bigger role. If Jiva's classmates had been studying a sense of place when she wrote this, perhaps their conversation would have touched on the following issues:

- Is it important that this story took place in Bulgaria? If it is, how can you help the reader feel your country?
- What details can you add that would be important to the story?
- Would the doll be particularly Bulgarian, if it came from the storage closet in your grandparents' home?
- Does the reader need to know more about what it is like on a hot summer day in Bulgaria, so we can better understand what it was like to be rummaging in a storage closet and finding such a treasure?

The Magical Doll

If my grandfather had taken a photograph of me that hot summer day in Bulgaria, I would have told you the story of how I was rummaging through the storage closet when I stumbled upon something magical.

The doll was just sitting there wrapped in a silky dress full of flowers. It looked like a field. Her hair was dark like the sky on a clear night and her eyes sparkled at me like countless stars. "That was your mother's doll, said my grandma and smiled when she saw me hugging it.

The part the photograph would probably leave out is this. After I happily danced around and went into my room, I immediately began playing with her. Suddenly I heard a terrible ripping sound and as I saw the dress split in two. The sound of it ripped my heart. I touched the dress, feeling the loose threads tickling my fingers like summer grass. Then suddenly I let the doll go and ran out crying.

Figure 8.10

Create an Across-the-Grades Celebration

As principal I took great pride in displaying across-the-grades collections of children's writing. (See publishing ideas in Chapter 10.) I can easily imagine a wall of writing that begins with kindergartners and stretches right on through the grades to our fifth-grade graduating seniors, with each and every piece being about life in our city. (Tourist post-cards would make the perfect bulletin board border!) The accompanying figures show the potential for such a dramatic wall. Note how the authors prove that they know their turf and can therefore write with honesty, specificity, and accuracy.

Figures 8.11–8.14 are a collection of writings by five-year-old Marcellino, a New York enthusiast. In Figure 8.11 Marcellino writes about the buses he takes up First Avenue. He includes the logo MTA, our Metropolitan Transit Authority, as well as the actual routes of the buses, the M15 and the M23. In Figure 8.12 Marcellino writes about Yankee Stadium, announcing that the Yankees are playing the team from Atlanta. In Figure 8.13 Marcellino writes of his love for autumn in New York. And in Figure 8.14 he writes about his favorite street, First Avenue.

Figure 8.11

First grader Sydney, a Broadway theater buff, wrote the piece in Figure 8.15.

Each year, Paula Rogovin's first-grade class researches a construction site. Figure 8.16 is an invitation they sent to me announcing a "topping-off" party, celebrating the completion of the infrastructure of a building whose progress they'd been following.

Fifth-grade Chelsea compiled the following list of what makes for a true New Yorker, crediting her classmates with a few of these beliefs.

The True New Yorker

The true New Yorker knows to ignore people who are shouting.

The true New Yorker knows that "Don't Walk" signs usually blink from ten to fourteen times, so it's safe to take your time.

The true New Yorker knows that you don't need a watch, the time can be seen in most shops.

The true New Yorker knows what's in and what's not.

The true New Yorker knows when trick-or-treating, not to eat any bags of candy that are already open.

The true New Yorker knows not to step in yellow snow.

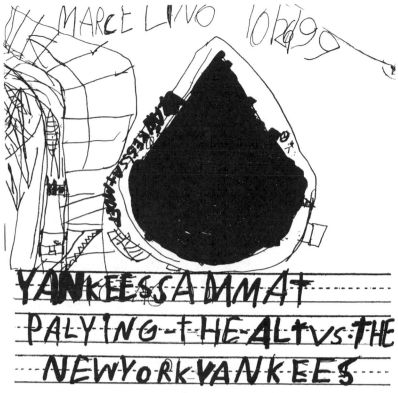

Figure 8.12

The true New Yorker knows how to bargain, and where to find them.
The true New Yorker knows where the best bagels are.
The true New Yorker knows that rush hour is all afternoon.
The true New Yorker knows to bring air freshener in taxis.
The true New Yorker knows where the best restaurants are.
The true New Yorker knows when to leave town.

Another example comes from Juliana, a fifth grader who wrote the city-sight poem that appears in Figure 8.17. (See also Kate's poem about Vermont on pages 136–137.)

Put Children's Work to Real-World Uses

Young writers will keep on writing long after we ask them to, if they witness how their words can make a difference in the world, can move an audience, or otherwise be treated as meaningful contributions to the world of literature.

These last several years, Karen Ernst has led a writing and sketching project with students in one of our Chinatown schools. Her fourth graders from Westport, Connecticut, and our students from Dr. Sun Yet Sen Intermediate School in Manhattan have been corresponding with one another by creating handmade postcards, detailing in

Figure 8.13

words and pictures their respective lives and neighborhoods. I can't imagine a more meaningful way to make new friends, learn about other people's lives, and strengthen abilities to communicate. Perhaps these three criteria need to be applied to more of the writing projects we design so that they carry the likelihood of making a difference in children's lives.

Other possible ways for students to reach real audiences include mailing their memorable "place-pieces" to local newspapers, chambers of commerce, and embassies. Of course, children might simply choose to turn these pieces into nostalgic gifts for family members or shape them into letters to send to family members that are far away.

Figure 8.14

Appreciating Similes and Metaphors

Teachers of writing frequently carve out courses of study for their students. These units usually focus on genres—poetry, picture books, informational texts, and the like. Learning to write about a place or learning to write about people cuts across all of these writing formats. Similarly, such seemingly narrow units of study as the use of dialogue, precise verbs, or in this case similes and metaphors can have a very dramatic effect on children's writing. Although a study of one aspect of language use, in this case figurative language, appears to be just a tiny sliver from the world of big ideas that are shared in a writing workshop, shining the light on such a small, yet significant way of using language will be well worth the effort. If taught in powerful and engaging ways, children

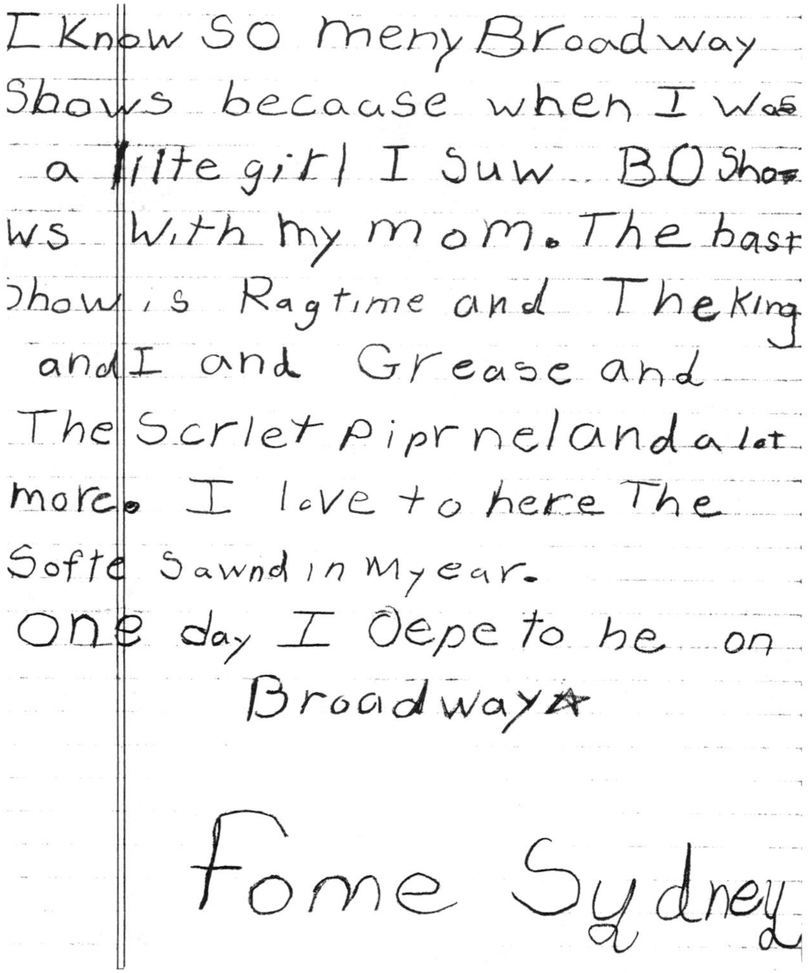

I Know SO meny Broadway
Shows because when I was
a lilte girl I Suw BO Shows
with my mom. The bast
Show is Ragtime and The King
and I and Grease and
The Scrlet Piprnel and a lot
more. I love to here The
Softe Sawnd in My ear.
One day I Oepe to he on
Broadway↑

Fome Sydney

Figure 8.15

will continue referring to similes and metaphors throughout the school year and throughout their writing lives. Students won't be able to resist sharing a well-turned phrase they've discovered while reading, eavesdropping on conversations, or working at their writer's desk.

Many years ago I heard Garth Boomer say that the great theorists in English education are the metaphor makers. And of course, we need only think of Frank Smith's literacy club, Donald Graves' cha-cha-cha curriculum, and Nancie Atwell's dining room table to know just how right the late Australian educator was.

As a principal and now as a superintendent, I continue to put my trust in the power of a great metaphor not only to develop theory but to enhance practice. I have long been awed when I walk into classrooms and hear a teacher make her meaning clear by inventing a metaphor or simile that her young students understand instantly. One teacher I

Dear Shelley, You are invited to the topping-
off party. We are all gowing. I don't know if you
wont to go. But if you wat to go it is att
12:00 noon   86 sh beatwen 2 and 3 on thursday

Figure 8.16

Lady on the Street
She has wild eyes and
nobody trusts her.
She wears stinking clothes
and nobody approaches her.
She lives on garbage and
near garbage cans and
nobody likes her.
When her warm blanketed arms
needed someone to hold, nobody
was there.
When her voice needed to be
heard, nobody listened.
When her tears needed a
dam, nobody could build it.
When she died, nobody would
    say their last good
      byes.

by Julianna Tobak.

Figure 8.17

know asks her children to "pretzel up" when they are sitting on the rug. (They immediately fold their legs and sit on their bottoms.) Another tells her kindergartners that reading strategies are power tools that they can turn to when they are stuck. (They know she is talking about using picture cues, listening for patterns, or skipping words and reading on.) A third suggests her struggling writers ask for a "charrette" to help them through their writing pieces. (*Charrette* is an architectural term referring to asking for help from other architects.)

Today I spend a great deal of time listening to administrators, and once again I am fascinated by those who make their meaning clear via the clever use of language. Daria Rigney, a new principal determined to lift the spirits as well as the academic abilities of her struggling children, inspires all members of the school community by her lyrical use of language. I hear her suggest to her staff, "We need kids to know that we expect them to grow out of their word walls and into new word-solving issues that replace the old ones. Kids always notice when their sneakers get too tight or their pants too short and know this evidence is a surefire assessment of their growth." She refers to children's choice of easy books to read as "Pastina," comfort food. She describes her own role as principal with these words: "I can't help but feel an affinity with the adventurer who, having taken on a dangerous and important mission and humbled by the explorations that preceded her, treads gingerly around the obstacles that abound and struggles to remain true to her vision of a new land."

Jacqui Getz, the new principal of the Manhattan New School, spoke eloquently at her first graduation. She cleverly referred to the graduates' social studies inquiries. In part she said, "All of your families have been so much luckier than I have been; they've known you all for a long time. I've only known you for a year, but I think I know some important things about you from these last ten months. I know you have smiles as long as the Oregon Trail and hearts as big as the Great Plains. I know that you have the curiosity of Lewis and Clark and the courage of the Pioneers. I know that you have an appreciation of beauty like the Plains Indians and dignity equal to that of the Rocky Mountains." As she spoke, I wondered about the creative process that led her to such comments.

It's no surprise, then, that I have allowed my own personal fascination with the use of figurative language as an effective communication tool to become part of my work with children. Shakespeare, in *Love's Labour's Lost*, writes, "They have been at a great feast of languages, and stolen the scraps." I want to be able to say that our students have been at the great feast of language every day that they are at school, and have not stolen scraps but have dined on the juiciest bits, tastiest morsels, and the most sumptuous delicacies. (All teachers should feel free to bring their particular language interests into their writing workshops. Students will not only learn the content, they will benefit from being around a passionate learner.)

The following classroom interactions pave the way for children to appreciate other people's use of similes and metaphors and to begin relying upon them themselves. At the elementary level, these courses of study need only last a week or two.

Modeling Figurative Language

I am a great collector of strong images, knowing that someday these could become metaphor for a hazy or difficult concept I am trying to convey or as a means of adding energy to otherwise flat writing. Throughout this book, the reader might have noticed that I clung to the teaching of writing like a kindergartner clinging to her parents on the first day of school, that I believe that children belong in the Little League of writing not in Yankee Stadium, that children often need training wheels when they begin to write, and that writer's notebooks can be thought of as friendly playgrounds in which young writers can stretch their skills.

Just recently, I met with a group of new teachers who were using their writing workshops to cover social studies and science curriculum, prepare children for the written tasks in standardized tests, and satisfy the required genres in standards-based portfolios. I suggested that they take a look at the soup recipes in any cookbook. Recipes for most soups including minestrone, vichyssoise, and lobster bisque all require the chef to begin with basic stock. Basic stock has become my metaphor for the good old-fashioned, regularly scheduled writing workshop. You need basic stock before you can go on to more specialized writing tasks. (Note that I do not think of mandated writing assignments as gourmet treats. Metaphors only go so far.) First, children need to feel at home picking topics, receiving feedback, making reading-writing connections, revising their texts, and so on, before they try to write in specialized formats. Mind you, I understand new teachers' urgent desires to cover curriculum, fill mandated portfolios, and help children get ready for tests, but I also know that those tasks become so much easier to accomplish when children have found their stride as writers.

Metaphors come in handy when working with children as well as with adults. I visited a classroom where the children had been taught to use substitutes for the word *said.* Unfortunately, the use of such words as *whispered, exclaimed, responded,* and *queried* was so out of control that it was hard to find the word *said* in any students' writing. They seemed to be on a campaign to "put said to bed," and their writing was suffering. The frequency of their alternative words was so distracting, the reader hardly noticed the written dialogue. I referred to the metaphor mentioned in the letter to teachers on pages 107–108. I asked the children if they had ever been on an elevator with a person who was wearing too much perfume or cologne. "We really only appreciate a hint of the aroma, we don't want to drown in it. Just like perfume," I suggested, "you need to use these special words carefully and sparingly so as not to overwhelm and distract the reader."

In *Lasting Impressions,* I note that after chatting with children about how different hurried weekday breakfasts are as compared to more leisurely and elaborate Sunday morning breakfasts, I continually reminded students who were working toward publication to give it their all and write with a Sunday-morning-breakfast feel.

In *Lifetime Guarantees* (page 305), I include a list of metaphors that I used to convey to students who were passive readers the need to become active. These included reading as if they were playing Go Fish strategically, being like Curious George and not being passive couch potatoes.

Teachers who use metaphors to teach are not only facilitating the teaching-learning exchange, they are serving as model fluent-language users. They should feel confident inventing their own metaphors, being creative with language.

Sharing Quality Literature

Whenever teachers read aloud to children, they should be fussy about the literature they choose. Whether they are sharing poetry or prose, reading from newspapers or nonfiction texts, they can be on the lookout for the memorable figurative phrase. Lines can be recorded on a classroom chart for future reference. In Sharon Creech's picture book *Fishing in the Air*, a parent serves as an effective language model. As the young child accompanies his father on a journey, the father points out the street lamps that are "glowing like tiny moons all in a row," the trees that "look like tall green soldiers standing at attention," and the birds singing songs "like little angels." In Marsha Wilson Chall's beautifully written *Sugarbush Spring*, a tale of tapping maple syrup, the young narrator announces, "I find two holes in a maple, one on each side, like front and back belly buttons." What child wouldn't understand that?

Designing Appropriate Minilessons

As with any course of study, it pays to read up on your topic. While browsing a *Similes Dictionary* put together by Elyse and Mike Sommer, I discovered a list of suggestions for writers interested in crafting their own. The authors write, "Surprise readers or listeners with comparisons that go beyond the obvious. Appeal to all the senses. Consider clichés as sources of inspiration and adaptation. Practice moderation." Not only does this text provide suggestions worth sharing with young writers, it provides thousands of examples of similes written by very accomplished authors. I can easily imagine sharing the ones below with children.

> Nadine Gordimer—"Bracelets seemed to grow up her arms like creeping plants."
>
> William Faulkner—"Behind the glasses his eyes looked like little bicycle wheels at dizzy speed."
>
> Michael Denham—"Busy as an oven at Christmas."
>
> W. P. Kinsella—"Baseball games are like snowflakes and fingerprints, no two are ever the same."
>
> Marge Piercy—"A building long and low like a loaf of bread."
>
> Martin Cruz Smith—"[You were] so silent it was like playing with a snowman."
>
> William Shakespeare—"Cold as if I had swallowed snowballs."
>
> Mary Hedin—"Gruff as a Billy-goat."
>
> H. G. Wells—"Difficult as an elephant trying to pick up a pea."
>
> Willa Cather—"Small pointed teeth like a squirrel's."
>
> Rumer Godden—"Thin as chop-sticks."
>
> Henrik Ibsen—"Snug as the yolk in an egg."

After enjoying these, I might invite children to orally invent some of their own. How might *you* let the reader know someone or something was busy (or thin, snug, difficult, cold, or silent)?

Inviting Children in on the Search

Just as in any genre study, it makes sense to invite children and their families in on the search for additional examples. With metaphors and similes, children can include what they hear, not just what they read. Perhaps their grandma always says, "My pancakes are light as a feather." Or their grandfather says, "I'm as hungry as a bear." Or their brother always complains, "I have butterflies in my stomach." These familiar sayings can be charted and labeled, "Very Familiar Sayings (Clichés)," and then contrasted with the more surprising ones they discover in the works of their favorite writers. Students can also follow the Sommers' advice listed above and let clichés inspire them to think new thoughts. Would their family members ever consider saying, "My pancakes are as light as the air we breathe," "I'm as hungry as a shipwrecked survivor," or "I have fireflies dancing all over my stomach"?

Creating Original Collections

Students can be asked to contribute to a class scrapbook of similes and metaphors from literature, a sort of student version of the Sommers' dictionary, listing the quote, author, as well as the title of the text in which the quote was found. Additionally, students can continue to record any language they want to savor, including figurative language, in their writer's notebook, or they can create individual collections.

Rereading Finished Work

After studying the power of a well-turned simile or metaphor, students will discover many places in their writing in which they could have used figurative language. Students usually spot places where feelings and descriptions could have been conveyed in stronger ways. However, teachers need to be on the lookout for too many figurative phrases added to any one piece, or ones that don't ring true. If teachers aren't willing to be honest with students about weak usage, they will be sorry they ever brought the topic up. (Teachers will be reading about "pillows soft as marshmallows" and "children as happy as Santa jumping for joy.") Students need to know what George Orwell knew. He advised, "Never use a metaphor or simile that you are used to seeing in print." Students need to be encouraged to look at things in new ways in order to surprise the reader with their fresh insights.

Highlighting Children's Figurative Language

Several years ago, I recall my nephew finishing a bowl of cereal at the kitchen table. The milk was all gone and just a soggy mound of cornflakes remained. Jonathan looked at me and said, "Oh, Aunt Shelley, it's a lonely little island." Thankfully I didn't just say, "Come on now, just hurry with the breakfast dishes!" Instead I responded, "What an incredible way to describe it." Throughout the school day, especially, it seems, when their eyes fill with wonder during science class, children do say remarkable things, without even trying to be literary. Our job is to call attention to the power of their words so that they understand what moves an audience.

As students move through the school day, they too will discover similes and metaphors in their reading materials as well as in the conversations of their teachers, administrators, and friends. For the duration of this short study, teachers can create a simple closing-of-the-day ritual, "Who has a simile or metaphor to share?" Conversations surrounding words shared can by prompted by such questions as; "What did the person mean? Was it effective? How else could he have said it? Was it original or clichéd?" Teachers will be surprised, once students' figurative language antennae are out, how many examples students come across. (Be prepared for children to use similes as put-downs—slow as a _____, dumb as a _____, fat as a _____. Such use will lead to a totally different and necessary classroom conversation!)

Sharing Effective Language

When teachers spot insightful uses of similes or metaphors in children's writing, the authors can be invited to sit in the Author's Chair and share their writing. The examples from student writers shown here would be worthy of celebration. The kindergartners in Isabel's class were asked to do close observations on specially prepared paper, with a space for sketching and a space for writing. Their work appears in Figures 8.18–8.20.

Figure 8.18

Figure 8.19

Five-year-old Remy wrote in Figure 8.18:

The popcorn comes, comes out fast. The popcorn comes out like a volcano. The popcorn is popping fast. Popcorn is yummy. I love popcorn.

Five-year-old Grace described the same popcorn maker in Figure 8.19 above.

Grace brought the popcorn maker and we made popcorn. It was good. It looked like a waterfall.

Doris wrote about pussywillows in Figure 8.20.

The pussywillows are so tall that I feel like an ant.

When I was out sick, Josh sent me the rhyming get-well greeting that appears in Figure 8.21. Angelina, a fifth grader, made the following figurative observation:

The sun dips into the ocean like a cookie into milk.

Name Doris   Date March

Project Pusewillos

The Pusewillos are so tall that i feel
Like an Ant

Observations

Figure 8.20

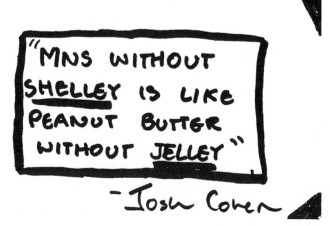

"MNS WITHOUT
SHELLEY IS LIKE
PEANUT BUTTER
WITHOUT JELLEY"

—Josh Cohen

Figure 8.21

Elena wrote:

Writing is like slowing down, taking a breath. Writing is like for some grown-ups like drinking cappuccino. For some it's like having a baby. Sometimes life is like writing. (See original of this piece on page 319 in *Lifetime Guarantees*.)

When I announced my departure as principal of the Manhattan New School, many children wrote to me. Among their emotional and gracious comments were the following:

The school won't be the same without you. You're like the school's right arm . . . As you know, a person is disabled without a right arm.
—Emmy

We shall miss you because you are like the mother and we and the school are like growing trees. You water us and let us grow . . .
—Haden

Manhattan New School was like a sidewalk that's safe and assuring. Now is the time for us both to look both ways and cross cautiously to the other side.
—Mia, a graduating senior

These students needn't have worried. They now know they are in Jacqui Getz's capable and loving hands.

When I reread the last three projects I described, I can't help but imagine a long-term course combining these studies. I would begin with asking fourth or fifth graders to do some of the memory writing described, then we'd add a strong sense of place to those memories, and finally we'd revisit the pieces with a knowledge of metaphor and simile. Now, those would be finished products worthy of a gala celebration. (I can envision a workshop for teachers titled, "Memories, Manhattan, and Metaphor: Teaching Rich Content in the Upper-Grade Writing Workshop.")

Other Learnings Attached to Figurative Language Study

Children who are made aware of just how effective the right turn of phrase can be are not just learning to improve their writing, but their speaking and reading abilities as well. It will come as no surprise to young connoisseurs of figurative language that public speakers often use metaphors to enhance their messages. I trust that our students who have attempted to use figurative language in their own writing will understand and marvel at powerful metaphors and similes when they encounter them in their reading and listening. Are we raising children who will grow to appreciate the use of language demonstrated in the examples that follow?

• Joe Leiberman, during his campaign for vice president, used an agricultural metaphor to explain his position on the creation of new jobs in America. He commented, "Government can turn the earth and provide some nutrients, but it's the private sector that comes along and plants the seeds and nurtures the crops."

- The first black president of an Ivy League university, Ruth Simmons of Brown, explained her interest in behind-the-scenes, nitty-gritty work as follows: "It's like cleaning. Some people clean just enough so that what you see looks good. I clean so that you can move the chair out of the way and not find dust bunnies under it."

- Thomas Sobol, the former Commissioner of Education in New York State, when talking about the misuses of standardized testing said, "I would be less interested in rewarding people who get the standardized scores to rise a few points, and more interested in rewarding people who find better ways to assess progress. No more prizes for measuring rain; prizes only for building arks."

Worthwhile Contests

We tend to downplay competitive activities in our school and therefore steer clear of the many contests that come our way. I usually discard contest announcements in order not to clutter teachers' busy lives with pressures from outside our community. One year, however, we received an announcement that was simply too good to pass up. The contest called for narratives titled "My Family, My City." Fourth-grade students were asked to tell the long or short histories of their families in New York City, the challenges they may have faced, and their hopes for the future. We all agreed that the topic was a perfect match for our community. After all, the heart of our curriculum is to help children see the richness of their lives. And for us that often means helping them appreciate the city we live in. We also acknowledge each child's immigration story. (That includes acknowledging that some families did not immigrate but are of Native American ancestry, and some family histories can be traced to slaves who did not come to our country on their own free will.) Telling the story of how your family came to be in New York has become a third-grade rite of passage. So the contest topic was just right for us, but the prize was even more so. The grand-prize winners, one fourth grader from each of the five boroughs, would have the honor of pushing the button that signals the lowering of the New Year's Eve ball in Times Square. How could we resist entering? There were teachers on staff who wished they were eligible for the contest. Imagine this once-in-a-lifetime opportunity. Imagine our delight when Dominique Miller, one of our fourth graders, won and served as the Manhattan representative. Her winning essay appears below.

> My family moved from South Carolina to New York City for a better life. A long time ago, black people were treated very poorly in the South. My great-great-great-grandmother was a beautiful black woman but because her husband was white she had to hide in the house while my great-great-great-grandfather worked across town cutting hair at a barbershop. If the town would have found out that he had a black wife, both of them could have been killed.
>
> In New York City you see different kinds of people: white, black, Spanish, Asian and many others. Unfortunately, even today there is still racism, but it's much much better than slavery.
>
> My great-great-grandmother had to scrub the floors of white families and clean houses. When she came to New York she was still a domestic worker but things were eas-

ier. She was able to send my grandmother to New York University and my grandmother was one of the first blacks to graduate. Being in New York, my grandmother was able to get a higher education.

I'm glad my great-great-grandparents moved North because look how well I'm doing and the opportunities ahead of me.

Dominique not only got to lower the ball, she was also interviewed at press conferences, appeared on all the local television news shows as well as on the cover of all our major daily newspapers, where excerpts from her essay were reprinted, rode in a limousine to a New Year's Eve bash at an elegant hotel, and attended a New Year's Day celebration with the mayor. But Dominique alone was not the winner. Our entire school community felt like winners. Students were quick to congratulate her, make her cards and banners, and read and post all related newspaper articles. And of course, her essay became reading material for every student in the school. When Dominique pressed that button, she had over five hundred little hands with her in spirit. You can be sure many more children in our neighborhood stayed up later than usual to welcome in 1998. You can also be sure students continue to ask me if there are any more worthwhile contests to enter.

Other Arenas for Experimenting, Improvising, and Inventing

One afternoon while traveling home on the subway, I couldn't help but notice a man selling whistles. He wore a thick garland of whistles around his neck, each shiny noise-maker threaded through a colorful rope. It wasn't this underground vendor's appearance that caught my eye, but rather the rhymes he was chanting that resounded loudly throughout the crowded subway car. If memory serves correct, he sang of everyone who needs a whistle, including, "hawkers, stalkers, gawkers, and New Yawkers, screechers, preachers, teachers, all creatures, vegetarians, Palestinians, octogenarians, electricians, comedians, and so on." I was so taken with this outgoing, charismatic whistle-seller, I talked to him about how cleverly he played with words. "You should visit our schools," I finally added. "The children would love to hear your sales pitch." "No," he replied, "They wouldn't be interested in what I do." Of course they would! Children are interested in anything that has purpose and real-world payoff, particularly if it is something engaging, surprising, and connected to their childhood interests.

The writing workshop is a perfect place to push the literacy envelope. I have a long list of *F* words that I'd love to study, including *fiction, fables, fairy tales, folktales, feature articles,* and *food writing*. Introducing a writing format that you've never studied before guarantees a freshness in your approach. Teachers' preparations fill with hitherto untapped literature selections and professional reading materials, as well as curiosity about students' response to the format selected. Children also love new challenges, proud to assess their growth as they attempt things that they have never tried before.

Children are as proud of their firsts in the writing workshops as they are about their firsts in the playground or gymnasium. They will long remember their first newspaper article, lullaby, or travel brochure.

Today, with so many high-stakes pressures surrounding them, teachers need to maintain their sense of ownership and creativity and not become swallowed up by outsiders' agendas. Yes, we must prepare our children to do the kind of writing that helps them pass the required standardized tests, but we must maintain control of the amount of time we devote to such preparations, never allowing test preparations to become the mainstay of our teaching lives. We cannot allow the movement toward standardization of teaching to eliminate energizing possibilities.

Then too, when standardized testing requires specific genres, we must hold to the theory that when life gives you lemons you make lemonade. In New York City, for example, fourth-grade students are required to write responses to literature, informational reports, narrative accounts, and narrative procedures. Teachers here need to approach these genres with gusto, searching for the best literature examples and the finest teaching techniques, along the way discovering real-world uses for these formats so that the writing children do is not merely geared to their doing well on an upcoming exam or filling a required portfolio, but to their doing well in *life*. In other words, responses to literature can be published school-wide as summer reading recommendations; personal narrative accounts can be presented as family gifts; procedural writing can shared with younger students, inviting them to carry out directions; and informational accounts can be put to many significant school and community uses. (These uses are detailed in *Lifetime Guarantees*, on pages 142–146). Just as the grain of salt starts out as an irritant in the life of an oyster and becomes a beautiful pearl, mandated genre studies have the potential to do good work in the world.

RELATED READINGS IN COMPANION VOLUMES

Going Public (Heinemann, 1999) is abbreviated as GP. *Lifetime Guarantees* (Heinemann, 2000) is abbreviated as LG.

Professional development for teachers	**GP**: Ch. 7
	LG: Ch. 7
Nonfiction study	**LG**: Ch. 4
Multigrade moments	**GP**: Ch. 4
Templates for writing about a place	**LG**: Ch. 10
Metaphors for readers	**LG**: Ch. 9
High-stakes testing	**GP**: Ch. 1, Ch. 6
	LG: Ch. 9

CHAPTER 9

FOCUSING ON PARTICULAR GENRES: POETRY

A thought is in my head
And I draw it out
And put it on the paper.
Sometimes I put it on the paper with paint
And sometimes with markers
And sometimes with words
Just like poems.

—Sarah, age 5

Key Writing Lessons

1. Taking a fresh look at traditional genres can serve to lift the spirits of students and teachers.
2. Kindergartners who are immersed in poetry, song, and chants often announce that they are writing poems.
3. First graders can create poems in response to favorite words as well as literature excerpts.
4. Second graders appreciate poetic templates.
5. Third graders can be taught to discover poetry-shaped ideas in the pages of their writer's notebooks.
6. Third graders can benefit from the visits of published poets.
7. Conferring strengthens students' attempts at writing poetry.
8. Fourth graders appear ready to closely examine published poems and establish mentor relationships with favorite poets.
9. Fifth graders can begin to read about the art of writing poetry.
10. Adult members of the school community who write poems themselves can become important mentors for children attempting to write poems.
11. Although not everything students call poetry may deserve that label, young people do have unique strengths that facilitate their abilities to create poems.

Each summer, our literacy staff developers help teachers plan their extended-year programs, summer classes for children who need extra time to strengthen their growing abilities as readers. At a recent gathering, we brainstormed ways to make these intense six weeks feel different from the teaching that, for one reason or another, had not sufficiently supported the students during the regular school year. My favorite suggestion for reenergizing instruction, at the upper-elementary school level, involved devoting the entire six weeks to a total immersion in one genre. Suggestions included reading and writing such formats as plays (you get to perform them for real audiences), mysteries (you get to solve them and challenge a friend to do likewise), or tall tales (you get to practice your storytelling abilities and impress your friends with your "whoppers").

Of course, students need not be in summer school programs for teachers to feel the need to lift everyone's spirits, including their own, by introducing a genre to read and write. Throughout the school year, in addition to designing entirely new genre studies, teachers should also feel comfortable in rethinking the ways they approach the most traditional genres. Taking a fresh look at familiar genres might include reading new professional texts, working with different colleagues, or changing the literature used as models. Whatever the energy source, teachers are guaranteed a receptive audience if they plan carefully (see "Taking Time to Plan Courses of Study" on page 241), present the genre study with gusto, and provide students with inspiration, information, and ample time to do their best work. Of course, students also need real reasons to do their best, which mandates that publication and celebration be attached to any formal whole-class genre study.

The teaching of particular genres does take place throughout the grades and children seem to delight in the change of pace that any focused study brings. Instead of writing in any format that suits their content, children are asked to try their hands at genres that their teachers have placed center stage. These invitations to attempt specific formats are often filled with surprises, as the community discovers writers whose areas of expertise may have otherwise gone unnoticed. In other words, you never know who will be the finest poet, journalist, songwriter, picture book creator, and so on.

The teachers I know best devote bigger and bigger blocks of time to the close study of carefully selected genres as students move up in the elementary grades. For example, a kindergarten teacher might spend a few days highlighting such simple formats as birthday cards, photo album captions, or signs. A first-grade teacher might choose to spend two weeks on the writing of how-to books. A second-grade teacher might spend three weeks on a study of letter writing. A third-grade teacher might choose to set aside one month for the writing of predictable picture books to be given to the students' kindergarten book buddies. A fourth-grade teacher might spend six weeks on the study of informational articles to be added to the science library. A fifth-grade teacher may focus on journalism throughout the school year in order that students produce a school newspaper.

Zooming in on Poetry

Many genres reappear year after year, challenging children to become more and more accomplished as they grow as writers, building on earlier understandings. Imagine a senior class hallway display showing letters, or poems, or informational articles written by the same children as they moved from one grade to the next. When staffs decide that some genres are worth introducing over several years, it would be helpful for teachers to pull together to articulate how to build on one another's teaching and to decide on realistic expectations connected to genres. In other words, what new understandings about poetry would teachers add as children move from grade to grade? How would you expect first-grade poets to differ from fifth-grade ones?

Leily Kleinbard, a graduate of our school and a wonderful writer, informed me that her surname (klein-bard) means "little poet." The pages that follow are filled with glimpses into the work of little poets as they move throughout the grades.

Doing What Comes Naturally: Writing Poetry in Kindergarten

Kindergarten children are so immersed in poetry via the songs they sing, verses they recite, hand-clapping games they chant, and simple poetic texts they read that they often announce they are writing poems. Sometimes their attempts have little connection to poetry as we know it, but most early-childhood teachers have a hard time informing five-year-olds that the work they have called "poetry" doesn't qualify technically. Instead, most are very accepting of students' attempts, proudly announcing, "You are very fine beginning poets." When children really do make poetic breakthroughs, teachers highlight the poetic elements and the student poets become poetry teachers for one another. When poetry fever spreads in a kindergarten, students' work often fills with language play, repetition, honest thoughts, and strong feelings. With a little help from a caring grown-up coach, the youngsters can shape their words to look and sound more like genuine poetry.

Each year, Isabel Beaton and her friend Doris Levy, an accomplished teacher of poetry, publish a kindergarten anthology titled, "Poetry Every Day, Everyday Poetry." The students' poems get typed, illustrated, duplicated, and bound into a beautiful anthology, destined to become bedtime reading material for the entire family. Not only do the children's poems become prime at-home reading material, the short verses are also put to good classroom uses.

Sofia's poem "The Meal," which appears below, can easily be enlarged and used as shared reading material for the entire class. The poet can even be asked to illustrate the enlarged text to provide extra supports for her beginning-to-read classmates. Nothing can compare to a five-year-old's drawing of such delicacies as spaghetti, ice-cream cones, pancakes, and soup with carrots and noodles.

The Meal

Spaghetti! Spaghetti!
Spaghetti with sauce.

Spaghetti! Spaghetti!
Spaghetti with meatballs.

Ice Cream! Ice Cream!
Ice-cream cone.

Ice cream! Ice Cream!
Ice cream with sprinkles.

Pancakes! Pancakes!
Pancakes with syrup.

Pancakes! Pancakes!
Pancakes with butter.

Soup! Soup!
Soup with carrots.

Soup! Soup!
Soup with noodles.

I can easily imagine kindergartners reciting the poem written by Diana (see Figure 9.1), a five-year-old in Eve Mutchnick's class, each time a classmate celebrates a birthday.

To be 6 I love it
To be 5 I love it
To be 4 I love it
To be 3 I love it
To be 2 I love it
To be 1 I love it
But now I am six
I'm 6
I'm 6

Kindergartners would probably have a lot to say in response to classmates' poems that follow. The first, "Very Cold," was written by five-year-old Chelsea. Would class-

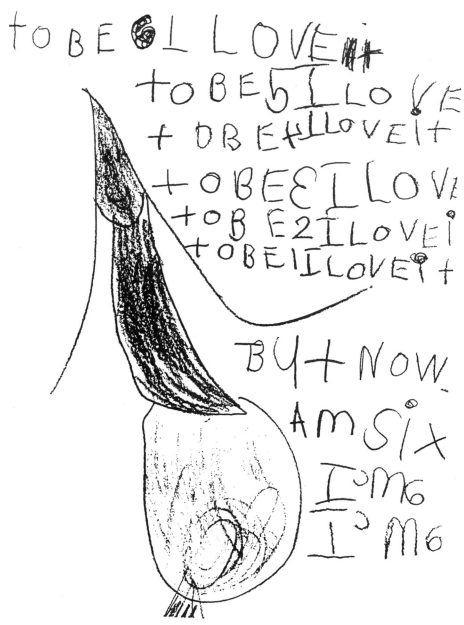

Figure 9.1

mates understand what Chelsea means? Would they agree or disagree? Would they have their own stories to tell in response to Chelsea's thoughts? Similarly, would they identify with Sasha's ambivalent stance in "Undecided"?

Very Cold

I'm
So Cold
I
Wonder why
I
Can
Warm
Everybody
But I
Can't warm
Up me.

Undecided

Oh n-o-o-o. Oh n-o-o-o.
Oh yes!!! Oh yes!!!
Well . . . . maybe.

These Are a Few of Our Favorite Things: Writing Poetry in Grade One

Our first graders continue to take pride in announcing they are poets. Haden wrote the following when she was six years old.

New Shoes

When I am getting
new shoes,
I like to have
sparkles on them.
I want to have
diamonds and pearls
on them.
Purple violets on my shoes
and little bows on them.

Perhaps my favorite invitation to first-grade poetry is Darryn's poem titled "I Did For You" (see Figure 9.2).

In order to encourage more students to attempt poetry writing, early-childhood teachers sometimes offer minipoetry courses of study, inviting all youngsters to try their

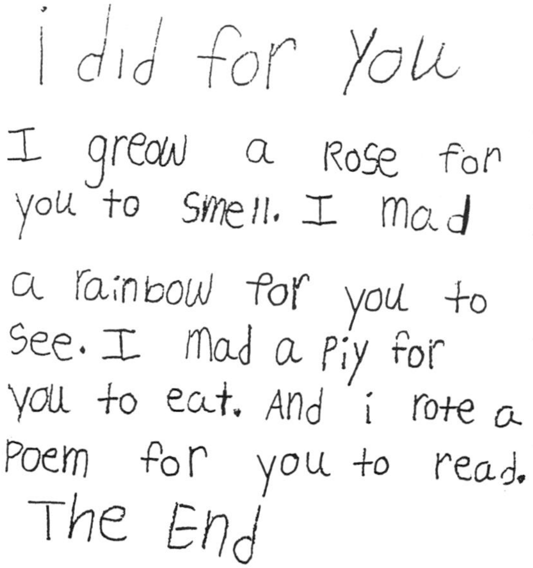

i did for you

I grew a Rose for
you to smell. I mad

a rainbow for you to
See. I mad a piy for
you to eat. And i rote a
Poem for you to read.
The End

Figure 9.2

hands at writing poetry. In *Lifetime Guarantees* (pages 190–191), I note that formal
poetry courses of study include the following:

- surrounding students with a wide range of poems and reading them aloud over
  and over again
- providing structures for students to save and savor favorite poems
- providing students with a rich toolbox of poetry techniques
- encouraging students to establish mentor relationships with favorite poets
- setting aside ample time for performance and celebration of poems

All these suggestions work well in early-childhood writing workshops. Alongside
these general structures, teachers often add activities exclusively designed for early-
childhood classrooms. For example, during the first few weeks of school one year, Layne
Hudes hung an intriguing sign on the door to her first-grade classroom. It read, "Come
in and ask us about our favorite words." Who could resist? Anyone who entered was
given a walking tour of the classroom to see each child's favorite word, selected and illustrated by these budding readers. The children quickly learned twenty-five new sight
words, as they were eager to remember their friends' favorite words. They remembered
them as easily as they read the words *Little Mermaid* and *101 Dalmatians* off each other's
lunchboxes. Several weeks later, Layne wondered if these words weren't kernel ideas for
poems. I agreed. After all, favorite words would probably have strong images and feel-

ings attached to them. It sounded like an easy invitation to craft poems with very young children.

I met with the students after choosing my own favorite words. I began with a few of my favorite things—antiques, baseball, and my mom's cooking. I talked to the children about the strong images I had in my mind's eye when I thought of these words and the strong feelings associated with these things. Believing in the power of demonstration, I proceeded to craft the following poems in front of the students. Note, I allowed students to watch all the false starts, cross-outs, and changes of mind as I drafted and continually reread and reworked my poems. Eventually, I completed the simple poems below, intended for my very young audience

Antiques

Old, worn-out, crumbly

Sometimes chipped
Sometimes stained
Sometimes wobbly

People ask me why I love
That old rocking chair
That old picture frame
That old wooden cabinet

I tell them
Someday I'll be old
and I'll want people
To take good care of me.

Mom's Cooking

Holiday smells lead me to the kitchen.

I watch mom's hands struggle to
lift the heavy golden turkey.

I watch mom's hands squash lumps of
sweet potatoes.

I watch mom's hands
chop ruby-red cranberries.

I taste Thanksgiving.

Baseball

The Yankees make me smile.
I close my eyes
And hug their
Pitchers
Catchers
Batters
Coaches
And especially their fans.

Especially my family
Their wildest fans.

The six-year-olds had much to say in response to these poems. What first grader doesn't have an opinion about old things, holiday meals, and their favorite sports and teams? I then led the children in a discussion of the ways of writing I deliberately chose in order to turn my thoughts into poetry. We listed such basics as:

• the need to pick topics that you had strong feelings about. (I explained how much I care about baseball, antiques, and my mom's cooking. I asked children to share the strong feelings that were attached to their favorite words.)

• clear images to help turn those feelings into lines of poetry. (I closed my eyes and described the pictures in my mind's eye when I thought of antiques, baseball, or my mom's cooking. I asked children to do the same, encouraging them to be specific.)

• the careful choice of words. (I chose the words *struggle*, *chop*, and *squash* because I wanted the readers to picture exactly what my mom was doing. I reminded children to fill their poems with actions that are packed with information, not just "so-so" actions. I reminded them that *cook* is a so-so word, *sizzle*, *roast*, and *barbecue* are stellar, million-dollar words. Similarly, I suggested that *walk* is a so-so word but *jog*, *skip*, and *hop* are richer words.)

• saying things in new ways. (Instead of saying I "like" their pitchers, catchers, and batters, I wrote I "hug" them even though I really didn't hug them. I thought the word *hug* would be surprising and make people understand how much I care for my team. Instead of saying I taste the dinner or the turkey and the trimmings, I simply wrote I taste Thanksgiving. I thought that would be a surprising way of saying the same thing. I suggested to the children that when I read their poems I would tell them what surprised me.)

• including close observations. (I really tried to use an imaginary zoom lens in my camera when I thought about my mother cooking in her kitchen. I suggested that whatever their topic, children try to do likewise.)

• including sensory details. (I tried to make the reader feel and see those old pieces of furniture. I tried to make the reader see, touch, taste, and smell Thanksgiving dinner. I asked children how would they put *my* senses to work when they wrote poems about their bikes, brothers, and baby blankets.)

• the repetition of certain lines and phrases. (I asked the children how many times I said, "I watch mom's hands" or used the word *sometimes* in the poem about antiques. I suggested that poets often repeat important words or lines because they want the reader to really understand what they mean. Repeated words also make the poem seem musical, like the words to a song. I told the children I would help them decide if they should repeat certain words.)

• choosing words with the right sounds. (I wrote the poems right in front of the children, demonstrating how I continually read the lines aloud, discarding words that simply didn't sound right. The children heard me say such comments as, "Those words aren't easy to say together, so I better change them," or "I love the sound of the two *r*'s in ruby-red, so I'll keep those words."

• the shaping of lines into a poetry look. (After showing the children the shape of many published poems, I wrote my words on separate yellow sticky papers so that I could continually move them around, making them look more and more like poems, with distinctive line breaks and white spaces.)

The children also noticed that some of my poems contained short lists of words and some had surprises in the endings. I suggested that these are choices poets can make, but that not every poem needed to have any of these elements, just as not every poem has to rhyme.

Then the children went off to craft their own poems that were inspired by their favorite words. First-grader Shayla began with the word *cake* and crafted the poem below (original is in Figure 9.3).

Cake

I love cake
I like the way the white frosting comes around
your face
I love cake
One day I will wish upon a star
I will wish for cake.
I could do without pizza for a month.
But I couldn't go without
Cake
Cake
Cake

Literature as Inspiration for First-Grade Poets

On another occasion, Lorraine invited me to work with her first-grade writers. She noticed that her students often made rather broad and bland statements when they

Figure 9.3

wrote poems. In order to remind them to get closer to the truth and say things no one else would probably say, I relied on Lilian Moore's collection, *I Never Did That Before*, a book filled with simple verses that speak to very young children. I read the entire collection aloud because the topics included such six-year-old conversation starters as getting new sneakers, outgrowing clothes, biting into a pickle, mixing paint colors, taking a walk with your grandfather, and learning to skip. We then talked about what made these read-alouds poems. Not surprisingly, we listed the same basics described earlier. I then invited the children to write their own poems.

Katie's first poetry draft read:

Figure 9.3 (*continued*)

My Cat

My cat is black,
My cat is fun.
My cat is nice.

When I conferred with Katie, I pushed her to reveal strong images, close observations, and surprising thoughts. I encouraged her to share the little truths about her cat by asking such questions as, "What can you say about your cat that probably no one else in the whole world could say? What are things about your cat that you pay attention to and probably no one else does? What things about your cat makes you smile?" She then revised her poem as follows:

My Cat

My cat is black,
   Like he is in the dark.
My cat is fun.
   When I hold him, his eyes curl.
My cat is nice,
   When I pet him, he doesn't scratch.
He just puts his body against me.

But when I don't pet him,
He just walks . . . away.

(See additional first-grade poetry conference with Luke, on page 171.)
      Other poems written in response to the Moore collection appear below.

Kittens

Kittens are cute
My mom wants a kitten soon
But not yet
But soon
Very soon
So do I
Want a kitten
But first
We have to
Get rid of our allergies

—Maia

Drums

When I play my drums
I get rhythms.
It's like I am in a big earthquake
Sometimes.

—Kadlif

Lean on Me: Writing Poetry in Grade Two

Second grade seems to be the beginning age for falling in love with specific poets and
their poems in order to take writing lessons from them. We often see seven-year-olds

becoming self-conscious about their own poetry, much the way they become overly critical about their ability to draw. They start to sense that there is a right way to do things and hesitate to invent totally original ways. It's not surprising at this grade level to see children latch onto templates, appealing models and mentors, as described previously (see pages 198–203). Seven-year-olds seem to thrive on studying just a few great poems and find security in borrowing the techniques and structures from accomplished poets.

Since Karen Ruzzo, one of our second-grade teachers, is always on the lookout for accessible poems for her seven-year-olds, I was eager to share with her and her students *Sol a Sol*, a collection of bilingual poems put together by Lori Marie Carlson. Many of the poems contained in this anthology have such distinctive forms, young children can easily attempt to do what these poets have done. (These include "The Wind Bragging," "Chocolate," and "Mama.") Karen's students were particularly influenced by Lori Marie Carlson's "My Grandmother." It reads:

> My grandmother
>   is a honey-colored woman
>   warm as the sand
>   on her tropical island
>
> My grandmother is a tall straight woman
>   swaying like the palms
>   on her tropical island
>
> My grandmother
>   is a talking woman
>   chattering like the green parrots
>   on her tropical island
>
> My grandmother
>   sweet sugarcane woman
>   I love her so.

This one poem contained several important lessons for seven-year-old poets. After hearing it, many of the children tried to:

- write about a person they cared about
- use a repeating refrain
- make interesting comparisons
- add a little twist to their endings

In response to this poem and borrowing several of this poet's techniques, Alexis wrote the poem that appears in Figure 9.4.

My Cat

My cat
is a calico cat
colorful like the blanket
on my bed

My cat
is a cuddily cat
soft as the pillows
on my bed

My cat
is a playful cat
as fun as the stuffed animals
on my bed

My cat
sweet as sugar
I love my cat.   By Alexis

Figure 9.4

In addition to containing poetic techniques that young writers could notice, name, and borrow, the topics throughout this collection resonated for our young writers. They include such popular childhood issues as eating chocolate, riding a bicycle, and having bedtime rituals.

I also selected poems from Pat Mora's *Confetti: Poems for Children*, a collection filled with poems particularly suited to second-grade poets. Young writers noted how poets effectively use the following elements:

- lists
- repeated refrains
- questions
- words of other languages
- sensory details

This Big Sky, also by Pat Mora, contains many poems for older students, but two were particularly strong models for second graders. In "Noche," the poet creates a long list of repetitive descriptors to present the nighttime. Similarly, in "Mountain Silhouette" the poet shares the image of a rock formation through a list of surprising sensory details.

Seven-year-old students also took to Toby Speed's *Water Voices*, a collection of poetic riddles illustrated by Julie Downing. Each of the poems contains a lyrical description of differing water formations including ocean spray, mud puddles, and bedtime baths. Children were eager to borrow the poet's use of the following techniques:

- use of direct address
- the introductory phrase "When you . . . "
- long lists of lyrical actions
- the repeated use of, "Who am I?"
- the solution to the riddle
- follow-up line containing an appropriate short invitation or warning

These qualities come to life in all of the poems written by second graders appearing below.

> When the sun peeks through the trees
> And you're buttering your pancakes,
> Pouring orange juice into your glass,
> And watching the dew evaporate from blades of grass,
> I watch you from the top of a plant
> Outside your misty morning.
> Who Am I?
>
> I am grasshopper. Watch me hop.
>
>   — Sam

When you wear sleeveless tops and Capri pants,
And go to the park to get out of the blazing house,
And you buy a popsicle from the dinging truck
And it starts dripping on the ground after only seconds,
And you run around staying far from the burning slides
So that you don't burn your legs.
A fireman opens me
And I spray ice cold water from my body
While children run around me.
Who Am I?

I am fire hydrant. Come get wet.

—Maxine

When you come home from school
And you don't feel like doing your homework,
And something really exciting has happened in school,
I sit in the closet all locked up
Waiting to hear about your day.
You run to me, unlock me,
And fill my pages with secrets.
Who Am I?

I am diary . . . DO NOT TOUCH!!!

—Brooke

When frost nips your nose
And trees are frozen still,
When squirrels scurry to their small caves
Knowing there's no food for them to find.
I stand looking down at you with my raisin eyes.
My body was rolled and molded into three balls.
If the burning hot sun stays out too long,
I will vanish into a puddle.
Who Am I?

I am snowman. Come and build a friend for me.

—Andy

Making the Leap: Writing Poetry in Grade Three

In third grade, when most students are introduced to the notion of keeping a writer's notebook, it's again no surprise that children often discover poetry-shaped ideas in their writer's notebooks. After all, teachers at this grade level rely heavily on poetry to help children understand the notion of gathering fleeting thoughts, capturing touching moments, and recalling strong images and memories. (See pages 61–67 for a complete description of poetry and the writer's notebook. This section includes several third-grade poems gently shaped from short notebook entries. Read Billy's poem about a cloud in the night sky, Gina's thoughts about her papa, and Alexei's comments about his brother on page 67. In addition, in Appendix 1 there is a bibliography of particularly helpful anthologies that provide inspirational "entry-like" poems.)

Third Graders Learn from Visiting Poets

Over the years, several published poets visited our classrooms, including Rebecca Dotlich, David Harrison, Georgia Heard, Allan A. DeFina, Ralph Fletcher, and Donald Graves. Not only did children learn about poetry writing from their visits, but under the guidance of a masterful teacher, children learned a great deal from the preparations for the visits. (Louise Borden's picture book *The Day Eddie Met the Author* is a must-read before an author's visit.) Pat Werner's third graders spent days preparing for the visit of Rebecca Dotlich. After the visit, I sent Pat a thank-you note that summarized many of the festivities. In part, it read,

> *I must begin by acknowledging how wonderful that visit was and thanking and applauding you for all that went into that exquisite time in your classroom. The children were so well-prepared and eloquent about reading, writing, and celebrating poetry in their lives. The room was so beautiful and the corridors and stairwells leading all the way up to your classroom in the penthouse were so well adorned with the poet's work that it was no surprise the poet felt like such an honored guest. The bouquet of flowers, the mural of favorite lines, the children's memorization of so many of her poems, and their genuine requests for her autograph, no doubt, made her feel like "Queen for a Day."*

Whether or not poets make school visits, children can become intimate with any favorite poet's body of work. Such activities as those alluded to above, including memorization of poems, turning favorite lines into murals, and lining the walls with enlarged and illustrated copies of the poet's work, will certainly help young writers take lessons from the poets they admire. (See *Lifetime Guarantees*, page 150, for notes taken by student during poet's visit.)

Poet Allan A. De Fina visited our school and in addition to sharing his wonderful poems with our students, he also offered writing advice. He told the children about his "Yes!" book, what our students would refer to as a writer's notebook. He explained that he always carries this blank book and when he gets a great idea he calls out "Yes!" and records his thoughts. He also revealed that he posts the drafts of his poems on his refrigerator door to be sure he visits them frequently. Above all, Allan demonstrated his devotion to poetry and joyously read aloud from his collection, *When a City Leans Against the Sky*. The poems are powerful models for city children, helping them to realize that everything in their environment is grist for the mill. Our students loved his choice of topics, including poems about subways, fire escapes, and taxicabs, and they were particularly taken by his ability to say things in fresh ways. Children who had studied similes and metaphors were particularly impressed with the poet's fresh way of thinking about things. Allan's taxicabs were "Yellow fireflies, that flicker and flash." On a snowy day, "A solitary taxi cab, opens a zipper up the avenue." And the cat sitting on a windowsill is "a fire escape princess."

Yet another way to learn from visiting poets is to invite them to respond to students' work. The wonderful poet Janet Wong has been doing just that, at Sun Yat Sen Intermediate School in our district. In addition to sharing her powerful poems, Janet helps English-language-learning students shape their thoughts into poetry. The students read their words aloud and Janet publicly writes their words down for all to see, selecting, honing, and rearranging thoughts, all the while explaining her choices. When she returns to the West Coast our lucky students are able to e-mail their poems to her and continue to get response.

Conferring to Strengthen the Poems of Third Graders

While visiting Joanne's third-grade workshop, Rakheli, a very sophisticated writer, asked me for a conference. I was sitting with two students who were not as yet fluent readers. When Rakheli said she needed help in shaping her entry into a poem, I asked if I could write the words publicly on a wipe-off board. My objective was twofold. First, I know that shaping a poem by deciding on line breaks and white space requires hearing and seeing the words. (I've often thought that I'd like to manufacture large blank magnetic word strips, so that children could write a word on each one and then easily arrange and rearrange their words until satisfied with the look and sound of their poem.) Secondly, I sensed that the two young girls I had been working with would profit from this shared reading experience. I would be writing the words on a wipe-off board as Rakheli read them aloud to me. Her classmates were naturally interested in hearing an original poem written by a friend. "Help us turn her words into a poem," I suggested. As it turned out, Rakheli needed very little help. She read her text aloud, chunking the words in the way she wanted them read. I served as scribe, writing the phrases exactly as the poet requested. The young readers listened intently the entire time. Except for a few decisions about line breaks and word choices, Rakheli's finished poem was remarkably close to the original page in her writer's notebook. It reads:

Binocular View

I pick up the pair of binoculars
that rest on the window sill.
I peer far out into the distance
farther than I can see with bare eyes.
I see four buildings
all alike.
I name them the Quadruplet Towers.
Then I look again through that odd pair of glasses.
I see a lighthouse
with the sun setting beside it.
It reminds me
of a picture book
about New England.
It reminds me of a cranberry field,
with a girl stooping over
to pick a basketful of cranberries.
Those cranberries look
so sour and delicious.
They are so red,
ready to burst,
waiting for grandma's homemade sauce.
How do binoculars make you see so much?
They are so powerful.
They make you think
And write,
not only see.

The poet's classmates who gathered around the wipe-off board not only learned about reading from watching our interchange, they also learned about writing from an accomplished poet. Joanne has much to be proud of in her third-grade writer's workshop.

Similarly, in the following school year, I urged children to gather round when Emmy, another of Joanne's third-grade students, asked for a writing conference to smooth out the rough edges of a poem she had written about her brother. Joanne's students had recently studied Cynthia Rylant's picture book *Night in the Country*, and were challenged to borrow some of the author's techniques. Rylant's phrasing and repetition show up in this honest commentary on her brother. Once again, I took the role of scribe, recording the phrases as she read them. Then the poet was able to take a good hard look at her word choice, line breaks, and white space and her classmate/onlookers were able

My Brother
by Emmy Rush

There is no life
so hard, so annoying
as life with my brother.
He gets to wake up
an hour later then me.
    Annoying morning.

He teases me
when I come home.
    Hard afternoon.

He gets to go out with friends
for dinner.
    Bad evening.

But there is
one good thing
about my brother.
He makes me
want to grow up.
    And be 26.

Figure 9.5

to participate in and learn from this very public conference. Emmy tightened the poem as I wrote her words down and the final draft appears in Figure 9.5.

Tricia, too, was attempting to write a poem. She shared the following notebook page:

I Wish I Had

I wish I had soft hair like my friend Jessica.
I wish I had green, blue, hazel eyes.
I wish I had a dog.
I wish I had money.
I wish I had lipstick.
I wish I had friends.
I wish I had gold.
I wish I had new shoes
I wish I had all of these things.

Tricia and I spoke about her wishes. Writing teachers can't ignore the important feelings children reveal in their seemingly simple sentences. Why does she feel that she has no friends (especially when she includes her friend Jessica in the poem)? Why does she want to look different? Why is she so concerned about money? Then too, our job is to help them lift the quality of their writing. How could I help her write a stronger poem? I began by telling her that the first line really touched me. Wishing she had soft hair like her friend Jessica's gave me a very strong image. I asked if she had strong images to go with her other wishes. Tricia began to talk and I made a polite exit, suggesting she record those newly presented images. Tricia returned with the beginning of a new poem in her writer's notebook.

I wish I had a dog, a dog with neat black spots.
I wish I had lipstick, coco lipstick.
I wish I had gold, sparkling gold.
I wish I had earrings, shiny silver earrings.
I wish I had hair, soft hair like my best friend Jessica.

Not all students see the power of poetry on their own. Some need a little prodding. One day, Joanne suggested I confer with Tahj, an eight-year-old who wasn't being very productive during writing workshop and in fact was spending time creating a cover and a table of contents for his own Goosebumps book, a book he lacked energy for ever really writing. I began our conference by skimming his writer's notebook, all the while asking Tahj to narrate the contents. When we got to the page that simply said, "Haden is a sweet and kind girl," Tahj's beautiful face beamed a million-dollar smile. I knew I

was on to something. I challenged Tahj to say more about this classmate that he cared so much about. In fact, I suggested he be the first one in his third-grade class to write an ode. Tahj's "Ode to Haden" follows:

> Haden's polite.
> When she does
> something wrong
> she says, "Sorry."
>
> Haden's nice.
> When people say
> something bad to her
> she doesn't get into
> an argument.
>
> Haden's gentle.
> When she reads
> to her little sister,
> she reads slowly.
>
> Haden's kind.
> When people fall,
> she asks,
> "Are you okay?"
>
> Haden's sweet.
> When she has snack,
> she shares with her friends
> without them even asking.
>
> Haden is a polite, nice, gentle,
> kind and sweet little girl.

Writing like Tahj's is important in a school community. Tahj made Haden feel wonderful. He proudly shared the poem with all his teachers as well as with all of Haden's teachers, kindergarten right on up the grades. Everyone was proud of this young writer, and proud of Haden for being such a good member of our school community. Writing odes to members of a school community can easily become contagious, but it's a fever that you don't mind spreading. Children can write easily about people that they know well, filling their tributes with authentic, accurate bits of information. The bigger payoff is the contribution such writing makes to the social tone of the school. How wonderful it is for people to pay compliments and tributes to the people they care about. The ode can

become a very important school genre. (See additional school genres in *Lifetime Guarantees*, pages 104–105.)

Going Deeper: Writing Poetry in Grade Four

In grades four you are likely to see more formal whole-class courses of study in the writing of poetry. When David invited me into his fourth-grade classroom to begin a poetry course of study, we began by filling the room with stacks of poetry anthologies. The children were given lots of time to read poems, including their daily reading workshop as well as part of their nightly reading assignments. They were asked to copy the poems they loved and write what they appreciated in the poem—what made them envious. (They copied each poem on the left-hand side of a folded sheet of paper and on the right-hand side, they jotted notes about any distinctive poetic features they admired.) I placed their copied poems as well as their comments on transparencies and began each writing workshop by sharing their choices. I was very demanding in regard to the precision of the handwritten copies of the selected poems. Students understood that every word, line break, punctuation mark, and white space added to the author's meaning. Miscopied poems did not ring true and did not honor the author's intention. In fact, less than perfect copies served to highlight the importance of every decision a poet makes.

Students spent many days closely examining published poems. Once they seemed at ease talking about other people's poems, they were invited to craft their own. Some children began by searching their writer's notebooks for poetry-shaped ideas. Others wrote fresh images in the hopes that these would lead to poems. Still others began by attempting to craft poems straight away on the next blank pages of their writer's notebooks. Students discovered that poems could grow from strong images, feelings, or words.

Similar to our work with published poems, I placed students' work on transparencies and the whole class listened to the poem read aloud by the poet, commenting on strengths as well as weaknesses.

Classmates always noted strengths first, modeling their ideas on such often-heard teacher comments as the following:

- "Oh, that part really rings true. I know exactly what you mean."
- "I never heard anyone say that in such a way. Good for you!"
- "I can't believe you noticed such a small thing."
- "I wonder if anyone else in the world has ever written a poem about ___."
- "Those words that you chose to repeat really hold your poem together."
- "I was so surprised to see such seemingly unconnected ideas together in one poem."
- "Your way of describing makes me feel like I've never seen a _____ before."

- "How did you ever think of using the word ____ in this poem? It is so surprising and at the same time a simply, perfect fit."
- "Your writing reminds me of the poet _____. Have you been reading her poems?"
- "Your title is not just a label, it really adds meaning to the poem."
- "Your ending makes me want to read the entire poem again. I like when that happens."
- "When I read your poem in my mind, I couldn't wait to read it aloud."
- "Your poem is like music. I could really sing your words aloud."
- "Your poem has the feel of a very special kind of poetry, called ____. Would you like to study more poems like that?"
- "I loved the way you wrote your poem from a ____'s point of view. It showed that you really understood how a ____ would feel."
- The way you spaced your words and lines really adds to the meaning of your poem."
- "I think this is the first time you spoke directly to your reader when you wrote a poem. How did you decide to talk to the 'you' who was reading your work?"
- "I love the line, _____, so much that I am going to copy it into my own writer's notebook so that I can save it."

After offering compliments to the poet, students suggested areas needing improvement. As a class, we invented our own ways of describing problematic elements and we discussed the necessity of making suggestions in gracious and respectful ways. Children became very good at pointing out the following kinds of weaknesses in their own poems and those of their peers:

- lazy words (The poet didn't work hard enough in choosing precise or surprising words.)
- blurry images (The poet left too much to the reader's imagination and didn't motivate readers to make pictures in their mind's eye.)
- bit of blah, blah, blah (The poet went on and on with lines that do not build the meaning of the poem.)
- too much sugar (The poet relied on too many flowery adjectives and gushy sentiments.)
- easily tongue-tied (The sound of the words and/or their arrangements are awkward to say aloud.)
- seasick feeling (The poet needs to add a satisfying shape to the poem. Right now the reader gets dizzy from reading the poem.)

Following are a few representative poems written by fourth graders.

Clouds

They get piggy backs from gallant glorious breezes.
They float, fly above the world.
They move as slowly as turtles, but never stop.
Big balls of fur is what they look like.
There's a camel.
There's a rabbit.
There's a chimpanzee.
Different shapes.
Different sizes.
Everywhere, anywhere.
Big fluffy balls of fluff.

—Nicholas

My Mom Cooking Dinner

Every night there
In the kitchen
There she is
Cooking
Pots and pans
Steaming
Carrots, broccoli
And peas
Boiling for tonight's
Soup special.
You can never know
What will be on the stove.
The powdered cheese melts
To a flowing glob
Of creamy sauce
On the macaroni
Every night there she is cooking
luscious, lumpcious
Deliciously, delightful dinners
For our hungry family
My mom cooks, cooks, cooks
And cooks.

—Jennifer

Wisconsin

In a little city called Milwaukee,
At the edge of Wisconsin,
There was a house.
Steam puffed
Out of the chimney.
Snow fell lightly
on the ground.
The kettle whispered
and fogged the window.
Then I made pictures.
Daylight fell and
I heard my grandparents
Say goodnight.

—Rosie

I usually don't find student poems about poetry very appealing. (Their attempts frequently suggest that the students simply couldn't think of a significant topic and so they expediently chose poetry.) The following are two exceptions. Both are written by fourth graders who were really wild about the reading and writing of poetry.

Using Post-its While Reading Poems

As you stick me
On that wonderful page
Lying flat
Upon my back
SQUASH!
You shut the book.
I'm lettuce
In a sandwich,
You open the book
to share
what you have found,
that amazing sentence
you never
thought of . . .

—Szilvia

The Beauty of Poetry

Poetry.
A small baby wren
Fragile
In danger of being broken
Or lost.
Poetry.
Traveling inside of itself.
Waiting for somebody
To scratch the disguise
And discover it
The beauty of poetry.
Poetry.
A still, cool surface
Of a glassy mirror of water
The moonlight and clouds
Reflecting all of it
The perfect fairyland.
Waiting
For a fish
To come up
And break the surface
Of the dream
Of poetry.

—Madeline

In Sharon Hill's grade-four class, each student selects a mentor poet. The children are not merely falling in love with *one* poem that will provide a scaffold for their writing, as second graders often do. Instead, they study a favorite poet's body of work, taking lessons from an author's signature poetic devices. Each child is expected to study techniques closely and use their notebook as a place to experiment with these specific techniques. All the while, they are developing the critical ears and eyes that will enable them to decide when a specific technique will help them create the effect they desire. They become very conscious of choosing the right form to support their content. They also benefit from sharing their work with others and learning from their peers who have studied the work of other professional poets.

Reaching Out: Writing Poetry in Grade Five

Fifth graders seem very ready to extend their knowledge about crafting poems. After all, they have been writing poems since kindergarten, with the help of *well-versed* teachers (pun intended). They can now sift through their richer, deeper notebook entries and produce poems layered with meaning. They can try more sophisticated techniques and work harder on revisions. They have studied the work of many poets and now seem ready to develop their own unique style, innovating on all they have learned from others. They can even begin to read about the art of poetry on their own. They can read guidebooks intended for students, such as *Poetry from A to Z: A Guide for Young Writers* compiled by Paul B. Janeczko and *A Crow Doesn't Need a Shadow: A Guide to Writing Poetry from Nature* by Lorraine Ferra. They can also read excerpts from such invaluable professional resources as *For the Good of the Earth and Sun* and *Awakening the Heart* by Georgia Heard, books written with a teacher audience in mind. Ten-year-old poets can read chapters from these books and form study groups or reader-response groups to share their discoveries. In other words, interested fifth graders can choose such books to read during their reading workshop book clubs. After all, they do qualify as worthy nonfiction reading matter and purposeful talk is guaranteed as the students readily put their growing knowledge to use during their writing workshops.

Often, especially toward the end of the school year, when I read the poems of our fifth graders, I take comfort in knowing that they are ready to move on to the bigger challenges of middle school. Their poetry reveals that they have become more reflective about their school and family lives and have begun to pay close attention to the world apart from their school and family. Their poems also remind me just how important our chosen profession is. We have taught our children to look at the world with new eyes, to tell the truth, and to care about the words they use to do that telling.

Below is a poem written by a fifth grader in Judy Davis' writing workshop. (Judy and Sharon Hill are currently collaborating on a book detailing their upper-grade writing workshops, to be published by Heinemann in the next school year.)

Gentle Dad

Dad came in from work
  the other day
and sat on the couch.
I'd been waiting all day.
  He calls my name.
He takes off his shirt
And says, "Dirty clothes."
I love the smell of his working shirt.
I hold it in my hands, gently
So I don't lose the smell of my dad.

As soon as I've had enough of his smell in me,
I place it softly in the hamper.

—Joey Djelevic

The following poem was written by a fifth grader in Amber Krantz' class at P.S. 41, another elementary school in our district. The poem, written by Alana Perino in response to a news story about a young child being accidentally shot by a classmate, was sent to the governor of our state.

Dear Governor Pataki,

She didn't get to see herself graduate
from middle school
or see her mother shed tears of joy.

She didn't get to see herself win
the science fair
or watch as her homemade volcano
started to flood with baking soda and
other ingredients.

She didn't get to see her dog have
six baby puppies
or watch them as they grew up and old.

She didn't get to see her college
or meet her new roommate.

She didn't get to see her new job
or watch herself make a difference in the company.

She didn't get to meet her husband
or watch him become a father.

She didn't get to help her baby
learn how to walk
or help her with her homework.

She didn't get to see the day
when she became an aunt
or a grandmother

Just because of a gun.
Just because a boy pulled
the trigger.

Just because the bullet
hit her in the neck
Just because the boy's
uncle taught him how
to use it
Just because of a gun.

And to think she was only six, only six. . . .

Respectfully yours,

Alana Perino

When Principals Are Willing to Write Poems

Throughout the books I have written about my work at the Manhattan New School (*Going Public, Lifetime Guarantees,* and the one in your hands), I have tucked in examples of poems I have written for or about school events and experiences. I am not so foolish as to consider myself an accomplished poet. I know that I don't have any of the literary gifts that the poets I admire do. Even though I have read many great books on the teaching and writing of poetry, I have never formally studied the technical aspects of writing poetry. But I do write poems with gusto and I do have the nerve to let them be heard in the school. And that's where their power lies.

I think the people in my professional community think it's more than okay to have a principal who writes occasional poems, even if they are mediocre ones. I know my poems could become much better. But truth be told, they are good enough right now for the purposes for which they are intended. I don't claim to be a great poet. I don't ever intend to publish a collection of poems. I simply take delight in writing poems, and that's a worthwhile demonstration for my school community.

I think, in fact, that I'm a rather good model, because most people think, "I can do that." In fact, they probably think, "I can do better than that." The folks at school probably learn more from my pleasure than from my products, and that's okay with me. Besides, I don't ask children to do anything I won't do myself. The old saying, "It takes one to know one," can be tweaked to read, "It takes knowing one to become one." It takes knowing a passionate poet for children to become enthusiastic poets themselves.

Chelsea, in first grade, wrote the poem appearing in Figure 9.6. In this piece, Chelsea was not talking about her ability to spell when she suggested that she is not a good writer of poetry. Somehow she believed that she did not have the very special tools and talents that poets have. When I read Chelsea's comments about writing poetry, I thought she demonstrated that she already knew a great deal about writing poetry. She chose a topic with deep meaning for her. She used a comforting repetition of lines. She

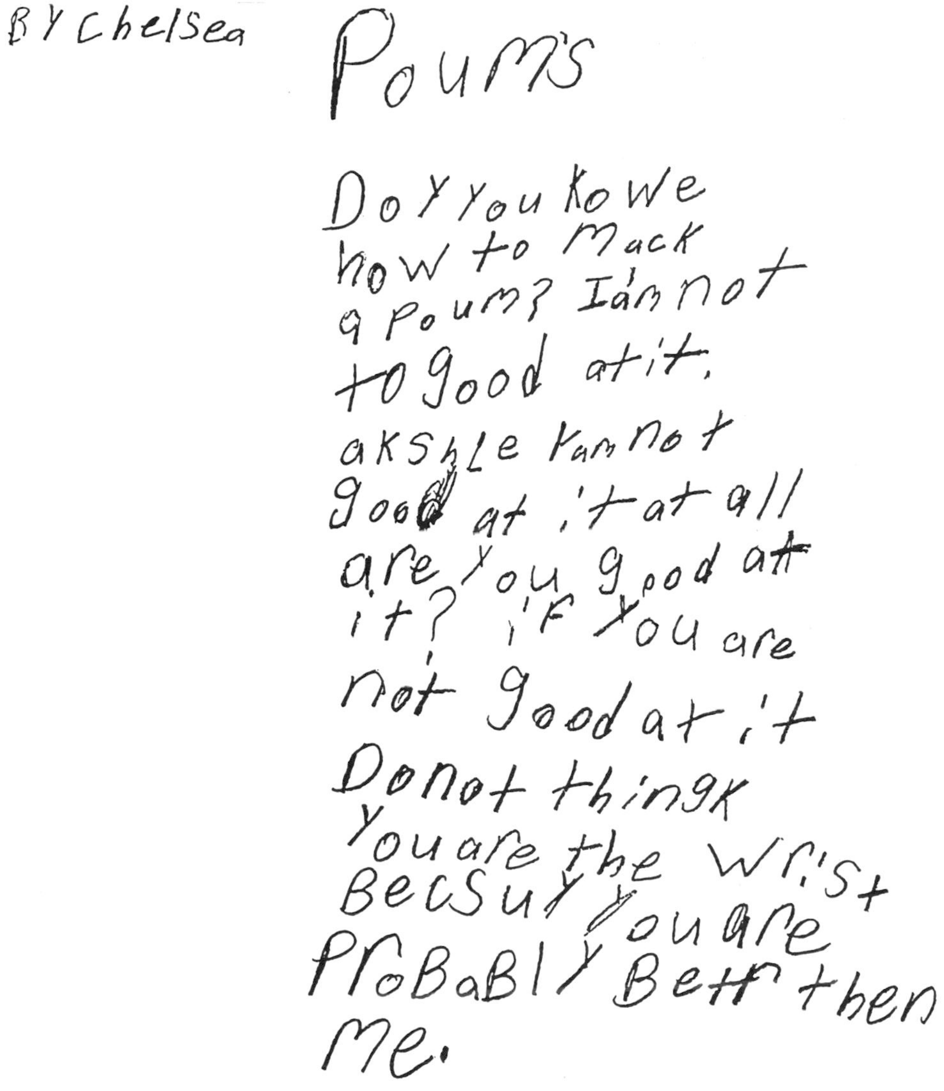

BY Chelsea

Poums

Do y you kowe
how to mack
a poum? I am not
to good at it,
akshle I am not
good at it at all
are you good at
it? if you are
not good at it
Do not thingk
You are the wrist
Becsuy you are
ProBaBly Bett then
Me.

Figure 9.6

began to shape her words to look like a poem. She has an ending that sounds like an ending. Perhaps with a little information about line breaks, Chelsea could publish a poem that any first grader would be proud of.

Don't get me wrong. I am not a pushover when it comes to young children writing poetry. As I stated previously, I don't consider everything they say or write to be poetry. I have no problem suggesting that young poets need appropriate information about the craft of poetry. But I do keep in mind that we are *not* a community of professional poets. Above all, I want students to feel comfortable writing poetry and to be confident about a few basic ways to make their poems the best they can be. Similarly, too, I don't want teachers to be afraid to invite the young writers in their class to attempt poetry because they lack confidence in their own abilities as poets. The Australian stance of "having a go" suits me fine when it comes to experimenting with poetic form. As soon as we become too self-conscious, we start to think like Chelsea does and none of us will "actually be good at it at all."

When principals (and teachers, student teachers, community members, and volunteers) are willing to write a few poems, they will have created a well to draw upon when they teach youngsters to write poetry. In previous books, I have included the following poems:

"Tribute to Teaching" (*Going Public*, page 85)

"School Rules" (*Going Public*, page 112)

"What Really Matters" (*Going Public*, page 241)

"September, 1952" (*Going Public*, page 183)

"You and Me" (*Lifetime Guarantees*, pages 300–301)

Another, "Mashed Potatoes," appears on page 122 of this volume.

As I look back on these half dozen poems, I realize that I can easily share with young poets some of the ways poets get ideas for poems by simply revealing the sources for my own. I don't have to consult any books on poetry about issues of topic choice because I have my own strategies to share. They can't be wrong, because they have worked for me.

"Tribute to Teaching" began by watching the morning news. I was so struck by all the bad things happening in the world that I left for work with a sense of urgency.

"School Rules" began with a refrain in my head. I was watching children play in the schoolyard when one child began play fighting in a not so playful way. The child was actually pretending to choke another classmate. I happened to call out, "There's no choking. There's joking, but no choking." By the end of the recess hour I had made up several more rhyming rules, and by the end of the day I had an almost complete list jotted down. (When I show the completed poem, students are quick to notice that I have chosen to leave out the original phrase, "No choking, just joking." I explain that I substituted poking for choking because choking is just too severe an act.)

"What Really Matters" came to me when I was daydreaming at a conference. I couldn't concentrate on the speaker's presentation and began thinking that I would prefer to be at work, especially at the lunchtime hour on an early summer day. That's when my office window is wide open and my office comes alive with the "stuff" from outdoors. The bureaucratic meeting contrasted strongly with the sensual delights of my little office. I realized that the meeting was as lackluster as some of the administrative mail I receive.

"September, 1952" originated as an entry in my writer's notebook. Since we began this school, I have been digging to discover my own memories of elementary school and writing to flesh out these rather sketchy images. Oh how I wish I had been asked to keep a writer's notebook back then. Oh how I wish someone had suggested that I save my notebooks forever.

"You and Me" was written for a particular group of children at school. I had been working with these youngsters on the value of knowing spelling patterns in order to attack new words. I had been impressed by the preponderance of short rhyming phrases in Christine Loomis' engaging picture book *In the Diner* and wondered if I could create a very simple book by playing with words and sketching illustrations that added meaning and support for these struggling readers.

"Mashed Potatoes," was written in response to an exercise I assigned myself. I attempted to write a piece borrowing techniques learned from Ruth Brown in the picture book *Toad* described on page 122. I'm not sure why I chose to do so in poetic form and I am not sure where the idea of mashed potatoes came from. I suppose I wanted my demonstration to be as far away as possible from the idea of a septic toad. I was worried that students when they attempted the exercise would think they must write about slimy creatures in order to borrow the literary techniques contained in the book.

Children, too, can learn to write poems when they are touched by some news, have a refrain in their head, reflect on a daydream, capture memories, emulate a writer, and play with language. And they so appreciate learning from a real live "poet."

I can use the drafts of these poems to demonstrate revisions and what propels them. I can show students all the work that went into making my meaning clear, creating strong images, selecting just the right words, eliminating insignificant phrases and shaping the design. I can show students how reading aloud over and over was an essential act and how my ears cued me into needed revisions.

I can be honest when I confer with students on their own poetry drafts because I've been where they are. I've struggled with all the same issues they face. I can also suggest poets they might establish mentor relationships with, because I am a reader of poetry.

Childhood Poets

Poetry begins in the childhood years. Although I don't swoon every time a child brings me writing he has labeled as poetry, I do believe that children have several strengths that facilitate their ability to wax poetic. They are awed by things and not afraid to stare. They notice everything, paying attention to the tiniest of details. They love to play with language and they do so without ever being asked. They say things in surprising, memorable ways. They have strong feelings and are not afraid to show them. They love music and take to rhythm, rhyme, and repetition as easily as a fashion designer takes to window shopping in Paris. Teachers need to tap into children's love of poetry and capitalize on these natural poetic strengths.

RELATED READINGS IN COMPANION VOLUMES

Going Public (Heinemann, 1999) is abbreviated as GP. *Lifetime Guarantees* (Heinemann, 2000) is abbreviated as LG.

Genre study	**LG**: Ch. 3, Ch. 4, Ch. 5
Poetry for adults	**GP**: Ch. 5
Poetry and school social tone	**GP**: Ch. 4
	LG: Ch. 5
Poetry and the celebration of names	**GP**: Ch. 2
Poetry and principals	**GP**: Ch. 2
	LG: Ch. 5, Ch. 7
Poetry to honor teachers	**GP**: Ch. 3
Poetry rituals	**LG**: Ch. 5
Poetry across the curriculum	**GP**: Ch. 2
	LG: Ch. 5
Creating poetry-friendly schools	**LG**: Ch. 5
Poetry and the teaching of reading	**LG**: Ch. 5, Ch. 9
Poetry and the teaching of writing	**GP**: Ch. 5
	LG: Ch. 5

EDITING, PUBLISHING, AND OTHER WAYS TO MAKE PARENTS SMILE

Make sure you don't use the same words too often, because it will cause your writing to be a bit dull, as if it is repeating over and over again. Words have a way of sneaking out onto paper without "permission," and once it gets there it will keep coming. The way to prevent that is to have a good vocabulary. Dictionaries are very useful for this, so are books. You have to use words that pop your mind. You have to choose your own pop-mind words, we can't help you. If you use pop-mind your writing will be much more interesting. People will love reading what you write. If you aren't pop-mindistic, they won't even stop by . . . It's actually very hard to publish your writing, and if I were you, I would wait 'til you're grown-up.

—Carey and Annie, age 8

Key Writing Lessons

1. Teachers must take pride in their students' growing expertise in the conventions of written language.
2. Publishing students' edited work is a major way of keeping parents informed about the work we do.
3. There are many ways that teachers can address such editing concerns as the use of correct punctuation, grammar, spelling, and legible handwriting.
4. Publishing techniques need to be simplified and woven into the everyday life of a school.
5. Putting students' writing to real-world uses can be viewed as a significant means of publishing.
6. There are many ways to inform parents about the teaching of writing.
7. Workshops can provide parents with helpful information on a variety of writing topics.
8. Bulletin boards can serve to inspire and inform family members.
9. Newsletters intended for parents should contain useful information.
10. Parents learn most when they are invited into our writing workshops.

I must admit, there were many very early morning hours when I did walk the empty building with a tiny jar of correction fluid in hand. I have a very hard time with walls adorned with sloppy work. I do correct spelling, remove unnecessary apostrophes, and make grammatical changes. Except for the work of our very young writers, I expect published work to be legible and technically accurate. We do care about punctuation, grammar, handwriting, and spelling. We never say, "Spelling doesn't count." Of course it does. Not too long ago, I was watching a news program and the words "Heroin Bus Driver," flashed across the screen. I was all set to hear the tragic story of a drug addict who crashed his school bus. Instead, it was a celebratory report about a woman who had saved children's lives. Of course the title should have been "Heroine Bus Driver." We can't rely on spell-check to do our editing. (My spell-check, in fact, changes the word *headlice* to *headline* each time I write it, and unfortunately I used to write it several times a year. Oh that I could make headlice disappear with the press of a delete button!)

As much as I love the sketch in Figure 10.1, I don't think it's okay for this child not to know that she should have used the word *you're* and the word *whole*. I don't think it's okay for the *y* in the first word of the sentence not to be capitalized, and for the *b* and *p* in the words *best principal* in the middle of the sentence to be capitalized. I would also like this young writer to take care in spelling names precisely. I spell my name Shelley, not Shelly.

Figure 10.1

An Explanation of the Chapter Title

As a teacher, principal, and as superintendent, I care about the conventions of written language, and I am not alone. All the writing teachers I know best take pride in their students' growing expertise in the conventions of written language. Additionally, family members are particularly concerned that their children learn to do things inside of school that they will be expected to do outside of school. These include such language basics as using correct spelling, grammar, and punctuation, and having legible handwriting. I have chosen to combine the teaching of editing with a discussion of the importance of publishing, as the two go hand in hand. Young writers readily understand the importance of editing when they go public with their work. They understand that their readers will never appreciate their meaning if they can't read the work in the way it was intended.

Perhaps more surprisingly, I have chosen to include a discussion of parents' role in the teaching of writing within this same chapter. My reason is simple. I have come to appreciate that publishing students' edited work is a major way of informing parents about the work we do. Parents who read, hear, perform, and respond to students' published writing come to appreciate the writing workshop and the process approach to teaching writing. They realize that students are doing more than we ever thought possible. They are moved to laughter and to tears by their children's ideas and their abilities to convey these ideas well. They realize that skills *are* being taught in ways that make human sense. In other ways, parents can become our best supporters and allies in our attempts to invite students to become committed and accomplished writers.

The Teaching of Editing

Editing becomes the frosting on the cake, the final things we do to make our work as effective as possible for our readers. Just as the baker who creates a cake from scratch takes pride in adding butter-cream roses atop chocolate swirls, students must learn to delight in knowing how to add the important touches of correct spelling, grammar, and punctuation. (See Chapter 7 for information on the teaching of spelling.) Students must even become critical of their handwriting, choice of paper, and quality of any illustrations that accompany the work that bears their names. Lily Woo, a principal in Chinatown, tells me that even her youngest students see their handwriting as a means of presenting themselves to the world and therefore work very hard at forming beautiful letters.

Students need to know that we value editing, and so do their family members. In order to help parents fully understand our concerns for the conventions of print, I sent the following letter home. Note how hard it was for me to separate the teaching of editing from the issues of having real reasons to write and issues of publishing students' work.

Dear families,

Over the years we have come to understand that punctuation is for the reader. So too, is handwriting, grammar, and spelling. After all, if no one is going to read our writing, there is no real reason to make it readable or more presentable. But when we publish our writing for all to see we want to do our best and help the reader in as many ways as we can to appreciate what we have to say.

Even beginning this letter with the expected "Dear families," followed by a comma, surrounded by white space, and even skipping a line before beginning my thoughts to you, the reader, are deliberate moves to aid you as a reader of my letter.

So what does all this mean for our students? Punctuation, handwriting, grammar, spelling, and all the conventions of different modes of writing are also for our children's readers. When young writers publish their work, when they send their work out into the real world, and receive real-world feedback, they begin to value punctuation, grammar, handwriting, and standard spelling. As teachers of writing we are obligated to provide real occasions for children's writing to do good work in the world. Children need to write every day, to publish frequently, and to learn the skills of editing as they go along.

For our very young writers, these real occasions might include making signs for the classroom and corridors, sending letters to family and friends, posting announcements, labeling classroom supplies or photos in an album, or their own artwork. Young children might also prepare lists, jot thank-you notes, take surveys, prepare how-to instructions, recall the words to songs or compose original ones. Eventually our young children are writing the kinds of poems and stories that can be added to the classroom library and shared by the teacher at read-aloud time. (Of course, much of the above might easily and naturally take place at home as well as at school.)

For our very youngest writers, editing can mean leaving spaces between the words, saying words slower in order to hear and then record more sounds, adding final punctuation marks, improving the formation of letters, using appropriate capital letters, writing on lined paper, and then moving toward standard spelling.

As children move up in the grades we continue to encourage them to do the kinds of writing that get the business of living done. We expect to see them crafting petitions, letters to the editor, toasts, surveys, informational brochures, inventories, speeches, letters of request and complaint, as well as thank-you notes. Alongside all this our students are also composing and publishing picture books, personal essays, poems, interviews, articles, reports, and so on.

Editing of course becomes more elaborate and sophisticated as we move up through the grades. Before our students rush to print out their finished pieces on the word processor, we talk about punctuation and paragraphs, choice of words and grammatical decisions, the conventions of different genres, and all the issues connected to standard spelling. Our students understand why we bother to study such things. We must, if we want people to appreciate how interesting we are.

And then we must guarantee that the work of our older students receives real-world feedback just as the work of our youngest children does. It's not surprising to see our students performing their texts, mailing their work for real reasons to real people, adding their work to class libraries or to school or class anthologies, offering their work as gifts, entering contests, or publishing their work in the school newsletter.

Yes, we care about process, but we want our products to shine as well. Please don't hesitate to drop me a line if you have further questions about the teaching of editing.

I closed this letter by sharing several well-edited samples of student writing.

When parents visit classrooms, they can expect to stumble upon the following editing interactions:

- teachers teaching editing skills based on assessed needs during whole-class minilessons
- teachers suggesting ways for students to proofread their own writing
- teachers showing student work on the overhead projector in order to point out editing needs and/or analyze editing attempts
- teachers pointing out elements of punctuation and grammatical concerns by displaying their own writing as well as published texts on the overhead projector
- teachers creating editing checklists with students (These serve as reminders whenever students are proofreading completed work—see sample Editing/Publishing Checklist in Appendix 8.)
- teachers updating editing checklists as the year goes on (In other words, as different editing skills are mastered, the checklist necessarily changes.)
- teachers responding to students' editing attempts on editing checklist forms (See Appendix 8.)
- teachers offering specific handwriting practice for students in need
- teachers meeting individually with students for editing conferences based on assessed needs
- teachers reminding students to edit their work throughout the day, not just during writing workshop
- teachers discussing editing with family members during portfolio meetings
- students teaching one another during peer editing (See checklist column for friend in sample editing checklist in Appendix 8.)
- teachers working collaboratively with curriculum specialists to articulate editing expectations (In other words, when children write science lab reports, prepare Spanish dictionaries, compose titles for their works of art, recall the words to songs they are studying, or record instructions for playing soccer, the classroom specialists should hold children to the same editing standards as do their teachers of writing.)
- teachers teaching spelling strategies as described in Chapter 7

Publishing in the Life of a School

While visiting a fifth-grade classroom recently, I asked a student why his teacher had asked him to keep a writer's notebook. He responded, "It has to do with authorization. You know, she wants us to be authors." Publishing as well has to do with "authorization," helping children become authors. It is the gift that keeps on giving. The more children publish, the more they want to keep on writing and writing well.

One year, in order to discover if our students could be encouraged to publish more frequently, I asked the staff to respond to the following questions:

- Describe your publishing procedures. Are they consistent throughout the year? Are they the same for all children?
- How often do your students generally publish? How many pieces a month? A year?
- Do you have any whole-class publishing events, requirements, and projects?
- What genres have been published this year in your class?
- What are the main obstacles to more frequent publishing?
- What school-wide resources or structures would facilitate more publishing?
- Do your students have access to real-world publishing opportunities?
- Do you and your students have opportunities to read or listen to the published works of other students in our school? How can we make this occur more frequently?

The teachers' comments in response to this questionnaire helped me to realize that some people's images of publishing had too many time-consuming trappings attached to them. In *Lifetime Guarantees*, I note, "We need to continually simplify the notion of publishing, taking away the extravaganza feel by creating everyday containers for going public with student work." (p. 108) In other words, we need to think through simple, elegant ways to publish that do not burden already overextended teachers.

As a student teacher in our school, Meredith Davis led a group of third graders in a production of *The Wizard of Oz*. This young actress-turned-teacher understood drama, but she also understood the needs of children. Every girl in the class got to be Dorothy, every boy had a turn at being the Wizard. Right in front of the audience, the children traded places, slipping off and on the distinguishing hat, apron, or cape. The frequent and visible changes in cast were part of the magic of this very polished yet childlike production. When it comes to the publication of student writing, polished yet childlike adds to the magic.

Earlier in this book, I talk about early-childhood teachers who add a simple strip of bright masking tape to bind a young writer's masterpiece, and classmates toast the "published" author. Not all publishing need be this simple, but if we are to expect frequent publishing, teachers need to have uncomplicated ways for children to feel accomplished and celebrated. Julie, a former Manhattan New School teacher, sets up miniature wooden easels, intended for the display of photographs or works of art, all around the countertops of her classroom. Her first graders publish by placing their finished work on these simple stands. Pat Werner, as noted in *Lifetime Guarantees*, uses Lucite menu stands, clear on both sides, as centerpieces for the round tables in her room. Wherever you sit, you can read student work that has been slipped into both sides of these holders. Recently at the

Manhattan New School, students have made their works of nonfiction available to all members of the community, by placing them on the computers that sit outside their classrooms. Simply by scrolling down the screen, you can learn about prairie life, Native Americans, and Colonial America. The reading material is so irresistible that it takes a long time to walk the halls of the school.

For me, publishing has less to do with choosing fancy fonts, creating elaborate covers, and adding work to portfolios, and more to do with going public in very real ways. Publishing means finding places in the world for our students' writing to touch many audiences and to do good work. There needs to be many ways to make publishing less of an intrusive special event. The last thing busy teachers need is to stop all their regular work to engage in a publishing extravaganza. I prefer publishing techniques that are woven simply into everyday life, and those that require the help of grown-ups who are *not* busy classroom teachers.

Publishing Techniques Woven into Everyday Life

Student Guest Speakers at Writing Workshops

It's not uncommon at our school to invite accomplished student writers to teach minilessons in different classrooms, using their own powerful work as inspiration. I've often watched the faces of students listening to another child take their teacher's place during the writing workshop minilesson. They seem to be a bit awe-struck, wondering if they too can learn to write so well.

Student Performances of Original Work

I can think of no better reason to interrupt students' regularly scheduled work than to provide opportunities to watch schoolmates perform. In addition to music, art, drama, and dance performances, students need to meet regularly to listen to one another read their finished works aloud. It's everyone's job in a school community to *kvell* (Yiddish for "beam with pride").

In fact, if all members of the school community knew that the last Friday morning of the month was a time to meet for a whole-school share, many children would write toward the occasion. Maybe some adults would as well. Large schools or schools that prefer more intimate gatherings might get together in smaller clusters during the last week of the month. In our school, I could easily imagine a few kindergarten and first graders being asked to step up to the microphone, on the last Monday morning of the month, to read aloud their words to all the other children in their grades. Then on Tuesday morning the second graders would share, and so on, right up to the fifth graders on Friday morning. I know how I would spend my mornings during the last week of each month. I would also invite children from different grade levels to occasionally sit in on grade performances not their own so that third graders, for example, would get to hear what is being written in the fourth and fifth grades.

Three-Ring Binder Projects

One day, I was talking to some sixth-grade girls about their homelands of Bulgaria and Serbo-Croatia. "What is it you miss most?" I asked. Aside from their family and friends, they missed the taste of bread, the kind that could not be found in New York City. That conversation resulted in a school-wide campaign. The girls plastered our walls with such "manuscript-wanted" signs as that appearing in Figure 10.2.

The resulting anthology, collected in a three-ring binder, can be added to for many years to come. I can easily imagine setting up an entire shelf for similar ones, in one of our reading rooms, each devoted to a topic that frequently rises to the surface in our students' notebook jottings. There could be one devoted to "First Impressions of New York

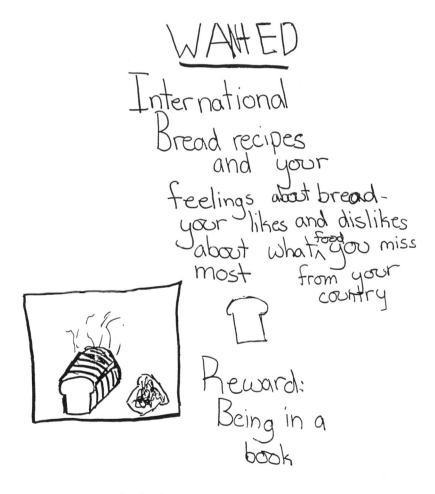

Figure 10.2

City," "Central Park Memories," or "Snowy City Days." (See page 336 for additional ideas on calling for manuscripts.)

Years ago I read a book titled *River Reflections*. The editor, Verne Huser, arranged a remarkable and varied collection of writings about rivers by such notable writers as William Faulkner, Washington Irving, and Wallace Stegner. I wonder how many times since the publication of the book the editor discovered just one more river writing he would have liked to have included. Three-ring binder projects afford us the luxury of never being complete, of having no carved-in-stone due dates, and the editor's torch can be passed from one graduating senior to an upcoming one.

Coffee House Readings

There is a great coffeehouse just two blocks from our school. It's called D.T.U.T., standing for Downtown, Uptown. It's filled with lots of overstuffed wing chairs, ornately carved Victorian couches, odd-shaped coffee tables, and dimly lit reading lamps. It's a perfect setting for informal readings of poetry or prose. I imagine taking over the place, the last Thursday of the month from three to four in the afternoons. Teachers would attend when they are able. Parents would be responsible for buying snacks for their own children. (Hot cocoa in lieu of coffee available.) Students would be responsible for selecting their own pieces to read aloud. I learned a long time ago that good ideas come a dime a dozen in schools. The really important question is, "Who is going to parent those good ideas?" I like this coffeehouse structure because it adds no extra burden to anyone's busy life. Parents in any community can be asked to scout for such places as ice-cream parlors, bookstores, or libraries that would be willing and able to host young author readings.

Student Work in School Library Collections

As previously noted, we have small reading rooms scattered throughout the building. What could be easier than to label baskets "Student Work," and place appropriate pieces in our poetry, fiction, and nonfiction reading rooms? The same can be done in all classroom libraries. It saddens me that copies of student work are not kept permanently in school settings. When children leave a classroom in June, so does most of their writing. Having simple structures for copying, laminating, categorizing, and displaying student work will guarantee student literary legacies, long after they graduate.

Neighborhood Displays

Our local restaurants, bagel shops, and bookstores often display student artwork. They could just as easily display student writing. When Paula Rogovin's first graders researched the construction of a neighborhood high-rise apartment building, they became so popular with the workers that the management corporation created a Plexiglas gallery surrounding their work site and displayed the students' poetry and art. Gina, a sixth grader in Judy Davis' class, wrote the letter in Figure 10.3 to our local Barnes and Noble bookstore.

Gina's poster, shown in Figure 10.4, contained the following drawing and vignette.

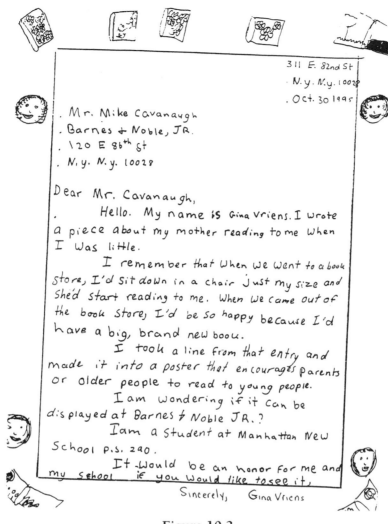

311 E. 82nd St
· N.y. N.y. 10028
· Oct. 30 1995

· Mr. Mike Cavanaugh
· Barnes + Noble, JR.
· 120 E 86th St
· N.y. N.y. 10028

Dear Mr. Cavanaugh,
·   Hello. My name is Gina Vriens. I wrote
a piece about my mother reading to me when
I was little.
        I remember that When we went to a book
store, I'd sit down in a chair just my size and
she'd start reading to me. When we came out of
the book store, I'd be so happy because I'd
have a big, brand new book.
        I took a line from that entry and
made it into a poster that encourages parents
or older people to read to young people.
        I am wondering if it can be
displayed at Barnes + Noble JR.?
        I am a student at Manhattan New
School P.S. 240.
        It would be an honor for me and
my school if you would like to see it,
                Sincerely, Gina Vriens

Figure 10.3

Figure 10.4

Read to Your Child

I sit on the couch with my mom. I'm all snuggled up with my long shirt pulled over my knees. My legs are mountains on her lap. My head rests on her shoulder and I'm looking over at the pictures in the book.

Her soft, kind voice makes the characters my friends. In my head, I play with them.

I begin to watch her brown curly hair. Her freckles look like chocolate sprinkles on her face. I play with her crinkled soft hands and make streams with her skin.

My eyes start to weaken and the words go far off. She closes the book and say, "Time for bed."

Poems about derricks, forklifts, and cranes belong at construction sites; posters about reading belong in bookstores. We need to see our entire neighborhood as a forum for student work. All it would take is one parent volunteer to make appropriate matches between student writing and neighborhood sites. I can easily imagine teachers handing over a poem about pizza, an ode to libraries, or a how-to book about playing with Legos, to our own matchmaking parent, and then walking the neighborhood to see our student's work in real-world settings. (See more in *Lifetime Guarantees*, Chapter 3, "Discovering Real-World Reasons to Write.")

Regular Correspondence

If I had my very own class, I'd probably add a very surprising item to a beginning of the year supply list. I'd ask for a real pen-pal for every student. I'd ask every student to find one person who would be interested in beginning a once a month correspondence. Each month, my students would be expected to write a fully composed and worthy letter, to be addressed, stamped, and mailed. The person chosen would not be a next door neighbor, or a sister who shares the writer's bedroom, but a person that the child might naturally write to. The friend or relative would make the commitment to write back once a month as well. I would set aside monthly time to share the story of these correspondences. Writing regular letters seems like an important way to make your writing public. (See *Lifetime Guarantees*, Chapter 3, "Discovering Real-World Reasons to Write.")

Web-Site Publishing

Over the years, we have been awakened to the limitless possibilities for using high technology in our school community. Our students work appears on our Web site (www.mns.csd2.k12.ny.us), and children e-mail their polished work to faraway friends and family. In the evenings, they even e-mail rough drafts to one another for response and friendly advice. (See Condon and McGuffee's *Real ePublishing, REALLY PUBLISHING!: How to Create Digital Books by and for All Ages* for more sophisticated technological publishing of student work.)

Feature Columns in the School Newspaper

In the hectic life of most schools, it's too easy for students to publish too few pieces each year. For many students, it helps to have a few ongoing publishing rituals and some predictable red-letter due dates marked on calendars. These would guarantee the monthly publication of additional pieces of student work. For example, I can easily imagine asking fourth graders to be in charge of such regular newspaper monthly features as interviews of school personnel, reviews of recommended books, or a description of an art project taking place in the school along with instructions for replicating.

Designated Writing Areas

In the main reception area of our school we have a bright red easel. This stand serves as a perfect place to display student work. One year, Judy Davis and her fifth graders laid claim to this public space and a group of roving student reporters began wandering the school looking for a hot topic to report on. Each month they took a series of digital photographs, and then published them along with a photographic essay that provided commentary on the selected scenes. Over the years, the bright red easel served as a backdrop to essays about such common school occurrences as performance of poetry, read-aloud time, and the use of mathematics manipulatives. Showcases, bulletin boards, podiums, and the like can be assigned to different classes, with the expectation that students will adorn them with published writing.

Box-Frame Galleries

Every classroom in our school has a carpeted meeting area, often bordered with overstuffed bookcases, couches, rocking chairs, and an occasional beanbag chair. The message is clear: A great deal of reading takes place in this room. So too, the message needs to be clear that a great deal of writing takes place in this room. When you enter Sharon Taberski's second-grade classroom you'll find a special desk filled with letter-writing equipment, including baskets of stationery and writing instruments, set off by a reading lamp. If we want students to write, we must give them the right tools. If we want students to publish, we must also give them the right tools. When Judy Davis moved to our school she brought cartons of Lucite box frames in all shapes and sizes. She hung them throughout her third-floor living space and fills them during the year with her students' best work. What could be simpler than borrowing Judy's idea and hanging two or three Lucite box frames low down on the wall outside *everyone's* classroom and asking students from each class to change the contents periodically? The boxes can be filled with published poems, vignettes, personal essays, and so on.

File-Cabinet Publishing

David Besancon, a fourth-grade teacher at the Manhattan New School, brightly painted a small old file cabinet. Inside it, he stores copies of completed student work on five-by-seven-inch index cards and organizes them by genre. His collection is cumulative, so students can read work written by students in previous years. Students not only read and study the pieces contained, they also long to have their best work entered into this very permanent collection.

Slightly *More Elaborate Publishing*

A few additional publishing possibilities follow. These demand a bit more preparation, time, and areas of expertise. Therefore, they should only be attempted occasionally so that publishing never becomes a headache for the busy teacher and an unpleasant, stressful activity for students.

Literary Anthologies

School-wide publications are another means of enabling children to get to know one another's work. Students can learn a great deal by merely reading, responding, and discussing the best work put forth by children throughout the school. After spending time with the work of their peers, it's not uncommon for children to say, "I want to learn to write like _____." (People involved in the standards movement need to focus more on practices such as these that help children see high-quality work produced in their own communities.) Collecting, editing, typing, proofreading, organizing, and duplicating written work can be quite time-consuming, however, for busy educators. Students, with the help of a parent or two, assumed responsibility at the Manhattan New School. See Figure 10.5 for fourth-grade Carey's call for manuscripts for the literary magazine *Kids Write On*.

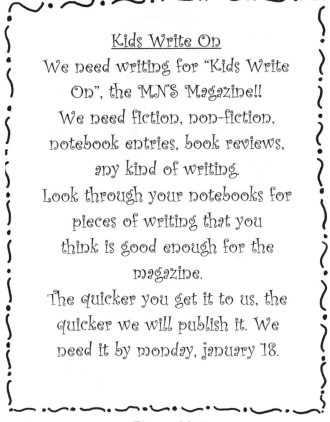

Figure 10.5

In addition, each edition of a school-wide anthology can become a resource pack for teachers preparing assessment-driven minilessons. Any staff member (including the principal) who is knowledgeable about quality writing offers to edit and annotate the school literary magazine. The annotator adds a few words alongside each piece, highlighting the qualities of good writing that each piece demonstrates. The collection then serves as an in-house minilesson resource pack for teachers. The extra payoff is that all the authors are available for guest appearances. The role of annotator can rotate among staff members and eventually be handed over to capable students.

Bookmaking

Teachers of writing are always interested in attending bookmaking workshops. They long to be able to package their students' best work in beautifully bound, unusually shaped fabric-covered booklets. Unfortunately, bookmaking usually takes up a great deal of class time. One way to cut down on the class time is to involve the art teacher and include bookmaking as part of the children's art instruction. Another way is to encourage active and artistic parents to take bookmaking workshops. After all, many of those homemade books become family heirlooms. Who better to collect all those scraps of

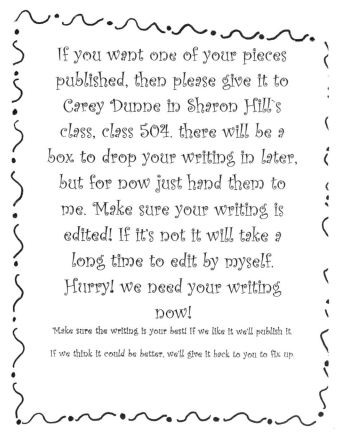

If you want one of your pieces published, then please give it to Carey Dunne in Sharon Hill's class, class 504. there will be a box to drop your writing in later, but for now just hand them to me. Make sure your writing is edited! If it's not it will take a long time to edit by myself. Hurry! we need your writing now!

Make sure the writing is your best! If we like it we'll publish it.

If we think it could be better, we'll give it back to you to fix up.

Figure 10.5 (*continued*)

fabrics and clever fasteners than parents of young children? Then too, if just one teacher takes the time to learn bookmaking and shares the techniques with the oldest students, they in turn can share bookmaking possibilities with other classes. Janet Williams, a British teacher on a Fulbright exchange, taught at the Manhattan New School for two years. As an expert at bookmaking, she left an indelible mark on what it means to publish your best work. Throughout the school, students are making accordion-folded books, books with intricate flaps, and books with shapes that support their content.

Inquiry Studies

When students are immersed in a content study, they usual brim with information to share. These inquiry studies lend themselves particularly well to the publication of many formats. Second graders in Keri Zurlini's class at P.S. 183 studied rocks and crystals and published an anthology cleverly entitled "Get Ready to Rock." It was filled with a question-answer section, followed by an experiment write-up, a trip narration, a glossary, an index, a list of resources, and even a recipe for rock candy. At P.S. 234 in Tribeca, early-childhood students who study snails share their understandings by recording observations, keeping snail journals, writing care manuals, labeling diagrams, and preparing recounts of snail experiences. When Manhattan New School received a grant to study nutrition, students and teachers throughout the grades complied an anthology entitled "Food for Thought: Yummy Writing by Kids, for Kids." The magazine was filled with feature articles, recipes, book reviews, poems, restaurant reviews, and food-related puzzles and mazes. The collection also contained childhood food memories crafted by teachers.

Fourth-grade Rachel's commentary on her vegetarian lifestyle appears below.

> I was born a vegetarian. I stopped drinking milk when I was a toddler. I refused to eat chicken, even though my grandma tried to make me.
>
> While other people eat animals at camp, I eat veggieburgers. When I go to McDonalds with some friends, I eat only French fries. When I go to restaurants with my grandparents, I eat pasta or pizza.
>
> I'm in control of what I eat, and refuse to eat dead animals.
>
> Cereal, pasta, and grains (for example, rice wheat, oatmeal), are all excellent sources of protein and calcium.
>
> Other parents teach their kids that animals should be eaten, however, my parents taught me that they should be loved.
>
> Some people don't understand me. That's okay, but I wish they would understand that animals have feelings too. Would you like to be someone's dinner?
>
> I love being vegetarian; it makes me feel proud. I wish that everyone had this feeling.

Kindergarten teacher Isabel Beaton wrote a memory of her grandmother's kitchen. Her words, "Nothing was ever done. Everything was always doing," apply as well to Isabel's collaborative classroom. She writes:

> My grandmother's kitchen was such a simple kitchen . . . not too many pots . . . not too many pans. She had one wooden spoon, one sharp knife, and a special glass with just the right rim for cutting ravioli. Most of all, that kitchen had an air of expecting people, people

to cook with, people to chat with, people to eat with, and babies to hold. Life in that kitchen was enormously collaborative. Nothing was ever done. Everything was always doing.

The cooking in that kitchen was so simple. A three-year-old tore the lettuce; a four-year-old made meatballs. So many hands in every meal.

The climactic event of each year was the cutting of the tomatoes. 14 bushels of plum tomatoes from the Hunts Point Market, basil from the garden and my grandmother, my mother and various aunts and cousins sweltering in the basement kitchen in 98 degree August heat as the bottles were sterilizing.

The youngest of us turned the crank of the machine that chopped up the tomatoes. The air tasted of tomatoes and basil. Lunch each day was tomato salad. Grandma's creation of sliced plum tomatoes, basil, lettuce, and chunks of Italian bread drizzled with oil and garlic. And we could see the jars of tomato sauce that promised another year.

Additional Publishing Possibilities

My favorite way of publishing student writing is to use that writing to enrich and improve the quality of life in a school. When five-year-olds list suggested snacks for parent donations outside their classroom doors or hang welcome signs, they are going public with their words. So too, when older students distribute writing such as that appearing in Figures 10.6 and 10.7, they are going public with their words. The first is Claire and Sofia's lending library notice; the second are excerpts from an English-language-learners' guide to the Manhattan New School, prepared by students with the

Looking for a book that's neither in the classroom nor at your house? Just go to us, at Claire and Sofia's Library, because we have most of the books that you don't. Tell us the name of the book, we'll go home, see if we have it, and if we do, (which is likely) we'll bring it back to school the next day. You can keep the book for a week.

Buy a Library card for the low price of only $1.00! 15 cents a book, (if you don't want a card) and only 15 cents a day overdue.

Figure 10.6

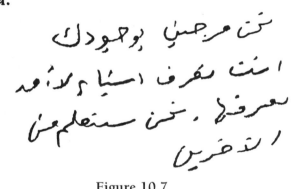

Leaving the room

The first English word you should learn is "bathroom." When you want to go to the bathroom, you ask your teacher to leave the room. When you want to get a drink, you say, "Can I please go drink water?"

НАПУСКАНЕ НА СТАЯТА.
Първата английска дума, която трябва да научиш е тоалетна. Когато искаш да отидеш до тоалетната, поискай разрешение от учителя да напуснеш стаята. Когато си жаден казваш на учителя: „Мога ли да отида да пия вода?"

We are glad you're here. You know things nobody else does. We will learn from each other.

Figure 10.7

help of Constance Foland, their special English-language teacher. Translations are in Bulgarian and Arabic.

There are, of course, many additional ways for teachers to simplify their publishing routines. The reader is advised to revisit the description of labeled blank big books for early-childhood students as described on page 192 ("Publishing in ways that highlight and encourage variety"). Similarly, Paula Rogovin's method for conducting classroom interviews results in regularly published writing as briefly described in *Going Public* (page 24) and fully explained in her book, *The Classroom Interview: A World of Learning*, and her video, *The Classroom Interview in Action*. Many options for publishing student work are described in *Lifetime Guarantees* (nonfiction writing on pages 142–146, "A Commitment to Putting Students' Nonfiction Writing to Good Use," poetry suggestions on pages 186–188, and parent-produced classroom newsletter publishing on page 122). Students will also be eager to publish when an occasional contest is offered as described on page 284, "Worthwhile Contests."

Informing Families About the Teaching of Writing

In both companion volumes, *Going Public* (Chapter 5, "Reaching Out to Families"), and *Lifetime Guarantees* (Chapter 8, "Informing Families About the Teaching of Reading"), I suggest ways to keep family members informed about school happenings and curriculum priorities. All strategies apply to the teaching of writing. These include sending home captioned photo albums of children at work (or even videotapes), involving families in curriculum-related surveys (tell us how you use writing in your everyday life), and sending home copies of class journals (day-to-day recordings of key happenings and big learnings).

There are however some techniques that are particularly well suited to helping parents appreciate and support the teaching of writing. For example, publishing student work, as previously described, and making sure that copies are sent to families is in itself a means of communicating with parents. They get to see the finished products and those finished products often receive the royal treatment. They adorn refrigerators, become part of holiday greetings, become wrapped as gifts and stored as family keepsakes.

Likewise, when we invite family members to join author's celebrations, they usually are in awe of the work that young people can accomplish. Karen Ruzzo's second graders wrote biographies of famous people and then invited family members in to tour their classroom gallery. Family members walked from one beautifully designed storyboard to another, learning about such diverse folks as Jessie Owens, Amelia Earhart, Harriet Tubman, Beatrix Potter, Boris Yelstin, Laura Ingalls Wilder, Jackie Robinson, Ben Franklin, and William H. Johnson. (See photograph on page 128 in *Lifetime Guarantees* and page 324 in this book.)

Similarly, parents of both kindergartners and third graders beamed with pride when book buddy pairs read aloud from original poetry anthologies, and parents of fifth graders delighted in watching their children read aloud original picture books they had written with first graders in mind.

There are many other ways to communicate with parents about the teaching of writing. Many of these activities help family members understand process as well as appreciate product. For example, in *Going Public* I describe in detail how I hosted a parent writing workshop in order that parents understand firsthand what it means to select an important topic, then draft, revise, edit, and publish your work. Other activities that help parents understand the writing process approach include offering content-rich teaching-of-writing parent meetings and workshops, rethinking school bulletin boards as a source of parent education, and sending home significant parent newsletters pertaining to the teaching of writing. A fuller discussion of each of these strategies follows.

Content-Rich Teaching-of-Writing Parent Meetings

A Workshop on Invented Spelling for Parents of Our Youngest Writers

Parents of very young students always appreciate a special workshop devoted to invented spelling. I usually advertise these as, "Learning to Read Your Child's Invented Spellings."

I begin by explaining to parents why it's usually easy for teachers to understand their children's attempts. Their spellings are fairly predictable. I then go through such common young writer's spelling strategies as:

- using only the first letter of each word, so that ILS might stand for "I love school," and then ILVSL might stand for the same when the child has learned to add final consonant sounds

- adding vowels, beginning with the long vowel sounds because they are easier to associate with the sound of the name of the letter

- using the letter *H* for the sound of /ch/ because the name of the letter has that sound in it

- using the letter *Y* for the sound of /w/, again because the sound of the name of the letter makes the needed sound

- using single letters for whole words, such as *R* for *are*, *U* for *you*, and *B* for *be*

- repeating letters in a word several times because the child kept saying the word over and over again slowly, so they recorded the repeated sounds time and again

- using the letter *A* often for the sound of /e/ because the child is matching the feel of the articulation in his mouth to the name of the letter that is articulated in the same way (When you say the medial vowel sound in the word *bed*, your tongue and lips are in the same position they would be in to say the name of the letter *A*, therefore many children sounding the word out slowly use an *A* instead of an *E*. This thinking explains many young writers' early attempts at vowel sounds, ones that are often referred to as "short" vowels.)

After sharing a few of these insider understandings, I invite family members to read pieces of early writing. Parents leave delighted that they can make more sense of their child's early attempts and eager to see more writing using invented spelling. It is also helpful to distribute parent-friendly journal articles on invented spelling and/or show professional videos devoted to the topic.

A Workshop on Helping Students Use Their Writer's Notebook at Home

I am frequently asked by parents of upper-grade students how parents can help when their children say that they have nothing to write about and they are expected to write in their writer's notebook each evening. I address this issue at regular PTA meetings and have prepared the following handout for parents and family members. After reading and discussing the following suggestions, I ask parents to imagine how their students might utilize any of these prompts. I then ask if the prompts would inspire them to write as well.

When Your Children Say That They Have Nothing to Write About

You might suggest that they take advantage of "at-home" inspiration:

1. Look around the room. Are there objects that have stories, feelings, or memories attached to them (e.g. photographs, paintings, books, or pieces of furniture)? Let your mind go on a journey to discover why those objects call out to you.

2. Share your old writing entries with a member of the family. Does your conversation push you to add new thoughts or ask questions of your old entries? (Do you still feel that way? Do you now have new thoughts? Can you connect these thoughts with something important a family member said?)

3. Browse the old books in your bedroom. Do they inspire new thoughts, ideas, memories, or stories? Do they push you to ask questions?

4. Look through your family photo album with a member of your family. What new stories do you have to tell? What surprises you? What questions are you asking?

5. Browse the newspaper with a member of the family. What newspaper articles, captions, headlines, or photographs make you think new thoughts?

6. Check out a hidden "junk" box you keep. Why can't you throw those things away? What thoughts are attached to them?

7. Use old or outgrown clothing in the same way. What items are you attached to? Do you know why?

8. Stare out your favorite window. Why is that view important to you?

9. Let your senses capture the feel of your home. What are the important smells, textures, sights, sounds, tastes that represent home to you?

10. Do some close observing of someone or something important to you (your cat, dog, baby sister, grandfather, a plant, a sculpture). Capture the object or person or animal on paper. Think about your feelings attached to your choice.

Rethink Bulletin Boards as a Source of Inspiration and Education

The Principal's Gallery

There is a fairly long bulletin board hanging in our main floor corridor. I have designated this space as my very own publishing gallery. As principal, I don't have just one grade level to highlight. Instead, I use this space to create displays of writing across the grades. This space has become an easy way for me to take an active role in publishing. From time to time, I put out a call for student work from specified genres, including poetry, letters, nonfiction, personal memories, and so on. Teachers send me appropriate student work and I take on the responsibility of proofreading, mounting, and displaying the student's writing. I label the board according to the genre collected, perhaps calling the display "Poetry Across the Grades." No one busy teacher has to fill this bulletin board. Instead, it represents the work of students from every grade.

Although I totally believe that students should not write for bulletin boards alone, I am committed to having significant bulletin board displays, ones that make a difference in the life of a school. This principals' gallery serves several important purposes. First, it provides a place for students' work to be read by a wider audience, not just members of one class or one grade. (School bulletin boards are usually hung too high for young children to read one another's work. Low benches, strategically placed, serve as sturdy step-stools enabling younger and/or shorter students to read their friends' work.) I've learned from our fifth-grade teachers to add a blank index card and a dangling pen to invite reader response, thus enabling the bulletin board to become a source of feedback for writers. Hanging a photo of the writer alongside also encourages readers to spot the writers and offer comments and compliments in person.

Secondly, readers can read the wall from left to right and, at any one point in time during the year, read letters written by five-year-olds on up through letters written by eleven-year-olds. They can see how their content, spelling, sense of audience, topics, handwriting, and fluency grow over time. We have come to expect that poems written by fifth graders will be different from poems written by second graders and those written by kindergartners. This wall has proven to be a good conversation starter. It also helps parents understand where we are headed.

I have on occasion varied these collections across the grades, and rather than calling for genre, put out a call for topics that seem to appear across the grades. Imagine a board labeled, "Writing About Grandparents Throughout the Grades," or "Writing About Pets Throughout the Grades," or "Writing About Moving Throughout the Grades." Or "Writing About Learning English Throughout the Grades." These topics were not assigned but were discovered in our children's folders and notebooks because these issues are common to our children and appear naturally in their writing. The board displays work in many genres all dealing with these child-size issues. The board becomes an anthology on a wall. When pieces are taken down to make room for a new collection, the pieces can form the beginnings of a new three-ring binder collection. (This wall can be enriched by posting the book jackets of professionally published picture books that deal with the same topics. Students, parents, and teachers can pitch in adding favorite books about grandparents, pets, moving to new schools, etc. These titles can form the beginnings of important bibliographies for classroom collections.)

Then and Now Boards

Another way to collect writing from across the grades is to scrounge cumulative portfolios looking for early writing samples from when current upper-grade students were in kindergarten and first grade. (I've also asked students to bring in early pieces of work they have been saving at home.) I mount these on a bulletin board labeled, "Then and Now." This very public invitation puts out a call for students to hang a current piece of writing alongside their early attempts. Students as well as adults appreciate the incredible growth over time. Children can't believe they used to spell, draw, and form letters in such primitive fashion. Parents have proof positive that children will not be inventing spelling when they walk down the graduation aisle. (Then and now photographs add just the right finishing touches to this display. See photograph of the display on page 2

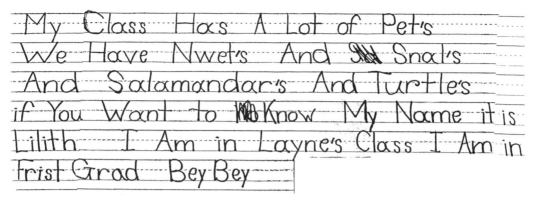

My Class Has A Lot of Pet's
We Have Nwet's And Snal's
And Salamandar's And Turtles
if You Want to Know My Name it is
Lilith   I Am in Layne's Class I Am in
frist Grad Bey Bey

Figure 10.8

of *Lifetime Guarantees*.) The following paired pieces show students' growth over five years. Lilith's first-grade piece about class pets is in Figure 10.8. Here is Lilith's poem, written in fifth grade:

Beautiful

Beautiful are the sun's rays
in the early morning
when they spread across the sky
like melting butter on bread.

Beautiful is the sea at night
when the waves sparkle
like diamonds
embedded in black velvet.

Beautiful is the snow
like a thin layer
of powdery sugar
covering the city.

Beautiful are the first swallows
as they swoop down
upon the gray winter
bringing spring
riding on their wings.

Figure 10.9 contains Ivan's random strings of letters done in kindergarten. Below is Ivan's fifth-grade narrative.

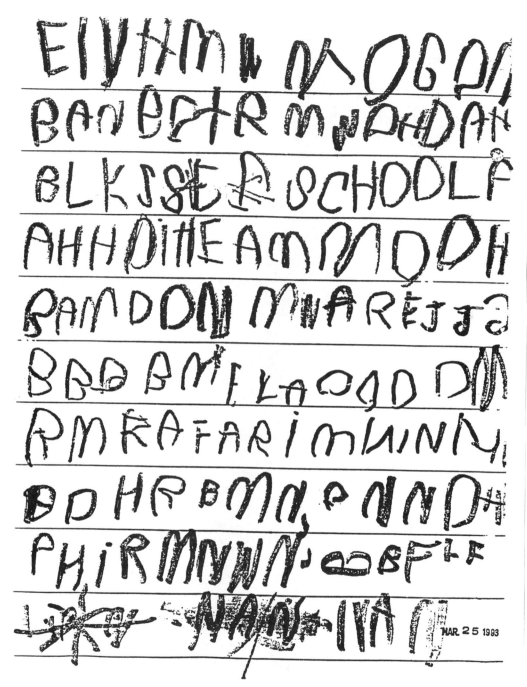

Figure 10.9

Krispy Kreme

I can smell the fresh aroma of heated up glazed doughnuts from outside the store. When I see the Krispy Kreme sign I can't wait to skedaddle inside. I see bunches of different people, especially policemen, all staggered up in lines, just to get one or two chocolate covered, green-and-red sprinkles all-over and absolutely delicious doughnuts.

"Oh! I have to get one doughnut. I don't care if I skip Lopez the policeman or get handcuffed. I just want one!"

I set my target on the chocolate glazed doughnuts, that are neatly arranged in a rectangle of 6 or 8 doughnuts on the gray counter. I can hear the machine chinking with each sale. I sneak past Lopez and quickly buy my doughnut. I run out of the store like I'm in a marathon holding my doughnut like the Olympic torch. As I leave, I hear Lopez shrieking, "Hey! You skipped me kid!"

I don't pay any attention to him, even if he is 5'11" and weighs 353 pounds. Once I'm on the street I don't just eat the doughnut, I demolish it. I stuff it in my mouth all in just one bite. Everyone stares at me. I am oblivious. As I savor the delicious taste, all I can say is MMMMMM!!!

Call for Manuscripts

On occasion, I do put out a call for manuscripts, inviting children to write about issues I think would spark important conversations, promote reading, inspire writing, build relationships, or solve community problems. For example, I once sent a note to teachers asking if any students wanted to write about a character from their reading that they thought would make a good member of our school community and to explain why. The results not only gave us a mirror into what the children thought of as good citizens, but also served as a wall of recommendations to other readers. (Hanging the book jacket for each title mentioned added a finishing touch.)

Principals or teachers of writing need not fear taking away ownership as these invitations to write are voluntary ones. Besides, the ends justify the means as many community-building or academic-supporting fringe benefits are often attached to these assignments.

I always try to offer the kind of invitations that other members of the school community would be interested in reading. As often as possible, I ask students to accompany their writing with an appropriate photograph. Most invitations prove irresistible to parents, resulting in family members collaborating on the responses.

Other calls for manuscript include:

- Explain the history of your name (see *Going Public* pages 30–31).
- Write about a photograph of yourself reading at home (see *Lifetime Guarantees*, pages 279–280).
- Share an area of expertise not connected to school (*Lifetime Guarantees*, pages 132–133).
- Write about your favorite season of the year for reading (*Lifetime Guarantees*, pages 12–13).

- Write about family writing traditions (holiday letters, tooth fairy messages, lunchbox notes, etc.).

- Interview family members about the elementary schools they attended. Compare theirs to ours.

- Try to capture in words your trip to school each morning.

- Describe your favorite school lunch. Compare it to your favorite at-home lunch.

- List your top-ten New York City sites. Explain your choices.

- What would you change about our city if you could?

(See *Lifetime Guarantees* pages 282–283 for additional bulletin board ideas related to reading and ways to involve parents in these displays.)

Old Faces from the 1950s, New Voices from Fifth Grade

Sometimes I must admit that when I am called upon to cover classes I have a very clear ulterior motive in mind. I have an idea for a great bulletin board display and simply need a group of youngsters to help me make it happen. For example, I once set out to spoof old basal reader pages. I had found several classic pages from those Dick, Jane, and Sally readers. I envisioned a clever bulletin board display, using the old illustrations from the fifties and our students' writing from the nineties. The board was labeled, "Old Faces from the Fifties, New Voices from the Fifth Grade." (Believe it or not, I keep a little sketch pad filled with ideas for functional, informative, entertaining, or community building bulletin boards.)

I asked the fifth-grade teachers for a little time with their students. I read aloud several pages and the students could not believe that children were once asked to read this drivel. They couldn't believe grown-ups had written such text. I then challenged them to create a wall of interesting writing to accompany each illustration from the readers and I told them we would use their writing to show their families how much things have improved over the years. These are some of the students' responses. Next to an illustration of Dick, Jane, and Sally in a rowboat, watching their dog Spot jump out, Zach wrote the poem in Figure 10.10. Zach's poetic thoughts were much more powerful than the original "Oh, Oh," said Dick. "See Spot go."

Next to an illustration of Father batting a baseball toward Dick, Jane, and their dog Spot, Donna wrote this little vignette:

The little kid throws the ball up. Its many colors dance in the sky, making the kid laugh. He catches it and throws it again. It sails up, past the trees and houses, then falls down.

The kid throws it once more, but this time it doesn't return to him. It bounces over the fence and is caught by a dog. The dog plays with it. The moves of the dog make the boy laugh. When it is returned to him, the boy cries because the ball is spoiled. It is no longer new. He puts it on a shelf, never playing with it again. For fear the dog will get it and never return it. To this day, it still rests on the same shelf.

River of Life   by   Zach medress
As   the   boat   sails   away
You   will   begin
the   adventure   of life;
through   water
your   first   job;
through   leaves
You   fall   in   love,
through   branches
You   get   married;
through   rocks
You   have   Kids;
down   a   waterfall
You   will   finally   die,

Figure 10.10

These words were a strong contrast to the original ones that contained a great deal of, "See the red ball go. See it go up, up, up."

A few teachers on staff worried about this display. They thought visitors might get the wrong idea. Perhaps visitors would think we use basal readers or that we rely on story starters, instead of letting our children choose their own topics. "Not to worry," I suggested. "As soon as parents read the children's writing they will understand. They will dramatically see the differences in the texts and they will understand the point we are making. They will understand how lucky we are to be teaching reading and writing today." Bulletin boards can be used wisely to help parents understand our work.

(See also the article "Top Ten Bulletin Boards that Teach" in *Teaching Pre-k-8* May, 2000.)

Name That Tune

I want parents to read invented spelling and walk away smiling, proud of their youngest writers' attempts and confident that the children will grow as spellers. Bulletin board displays come in very handy in reaching these objectives. My experiences with Alejandra

da yo me say daaayo day liyt Com man i wont go hom. hay mister tall man tall me bnana day liyt Com man me wont to go hom.

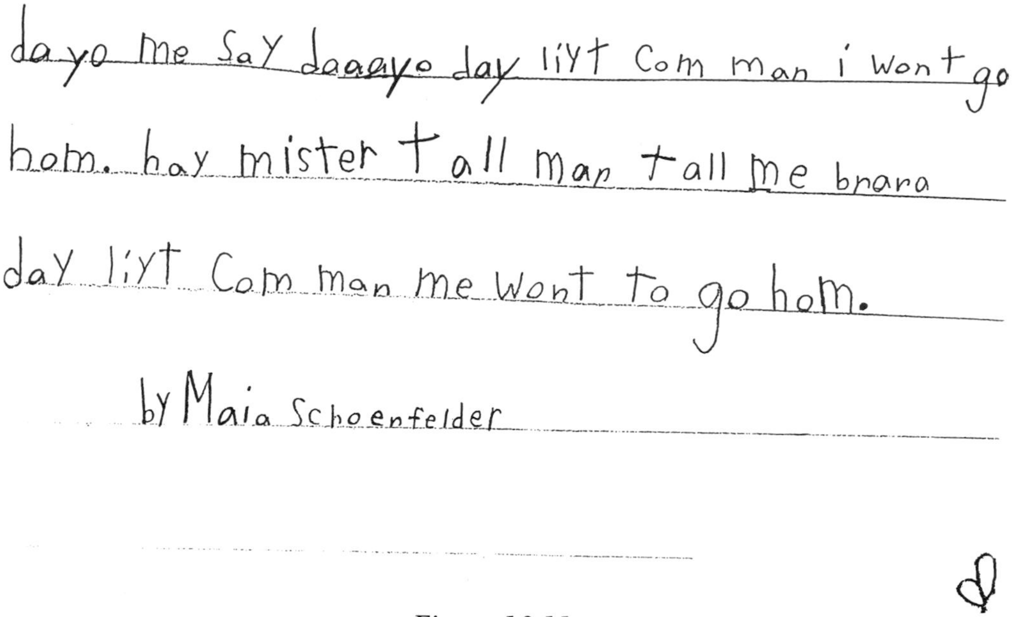

by Maia Schoenfelder

Figure 10.11

recording the words to "Doe a deer" (page 220), and Pam's children trying to record the words to "I Know an Old Lady who Swallowed a Fly" (page 212), inspired me to create a very public song wall. I invited kindergartners and first graders to write down the words to the songs they knew best and then hung their attempts on a bulletin board labeled "Name That Tune." I added a small placard in the corner, explaining that these were not edited lyrics but very early attempts. The titles of the songs were printed in standard spelling and hidden under colorful flaps. Parents walked away smiling and singing, and so did our older students. Maia, a six-year old, would make Harry Belafonte proud (Figure 10.11):

> Dayo me say dayo. Day light come and I want to go
> home. Hey mister tally man, tally banana
> Day light come and I want to go home.

Another first grader, Justin, sings the song of the working coal miner (Figure 10.12):

> 16 tons what do you
> get? You get another day
> older and deeper in debt
> St. Peter don't you call
> me cause I can't go
> I owe my soul to the
> company store. I was born one

Justin

16 tuns wudoo u

get u get a nuther day

older and deeper in det

Sat peeder dote u koll

my kus I kant go

I o my sol to the

Kirpny geer I wis her I

morning wen the  sun

didit shin I pikt up my

shuvl and went to the mines

I lodide 16 tuns uv

numbers 9 sol the

old bos yeld wel blel

my sol dut dut dut dut dutdududa

Figure 10.12

Morning when the sun
Didn't shine, I picked up my
Shovel and went to the mines
I loaded 16 tons of
Number 9 coal, the
Old boss yelled "well bless
My soul," dut dut dut dut dut dut duh.

Invented Spelling: Workshop on a Wall

Prior to parent-teacher conferences one fall, I anticipated the new kindergarten parents' concerns about invented spelling and met their inquiries head on. I asked for samples of children's work, mounted them carefully on colorful construction paper, and posted a little flap next to each. The board was labeled, "In the Beginning—Our Youngest Writer's Earliest Attempts at Spelling Words." An explanatory note followed that suggested "Kindergarten students write about trips, toys, animals, family members, make-believe moments, and . . . Lift the flaps to read the standard spellings and some explanations." Under each flap, the teacher prepared a transcription of the writing in standard spelling and I wrote a possible explanation of the child's spelling strategies.

If you lifted the flap next to the drawing in Figure 10.13, labeled "RBO," you'd see the following explanation:

Figure 10.13

Young writers often begin with labels.
They write one word to describe their drawing.
RBO are the clearest sounds heard in rainbow.
Consonants usually appear before vowels.
Long vowels, those that match with the name of the letter,
    usually appear before short vowels, sounds that do not
    match with the name of the letter.

If you lifted the flap next to the drawing in Figure 10.14, with the words, "MY MOMZ FRD HAD A BAB," you'd see the following explanation.

This writer has learned to write announcements.
    "My" is written in standard spelling. It is probably a sight word by now.
    "MOMZ" is written just how the young writer Hadley hears the word. The last sound does match with the sound of the letter Z.
    "FRD" is written in consonants only, a very common strategy for young writers. The sound of N is difficult to hear. The short vowel sounds are even more difficult to determine.

Figure 10.14

"HAD" happens to be the first three letters in the writer's name and so is an especially easy word for her to recall. "A" is a perfect match and oh so easy to remember.

"BAB" The writer hears the initial consonant B. She also hears the A in this word because it is what has long been known as the long sound of the vowel, or in other words, the sound matches with the name of the letter. The writer probably has no Y or I or E at the end of the word because the name of the letter B appears to have the long sound of the letter E built in. We say the name of the letter as if we were saying the word bee.

If you lifted the flap next to the drawing and caption, "Ths is a Frllorr and gras and sun and skai" (Figure 10.15), you'd find the following explanation:

This writer has moved from labels to captions. Her writing is very close to standard spelling.

Frllorr as flower reveals a possible overuse of sounding words out slowly. The writer stretches the words and adds extra letters because she is holding the sounds so long.

She has learned to space between words and is very aware of separate words.

My colleagues called this display a workshop on a wall, and indeed, it did deliver an abundance of information.

Figure 10.15

Send Home Significant Parent Newsletters

Parents always appreciate when we devote school newsletter space to the real specifics of curriculum. I trust that even without teacher education coursework, family members can understand the specifics of what we are hoping to accomplish, if we present the information in noncondescending ways, free of professional jargon. The following are excerpts from a letter I sent home to families in order that they understand my conference guidelines in the teaching of writing and how they can best support our efforts at home.

> *Dear families,*
>
> *Sometimes when I have a spur of the moment request to teach a class, I grab a stack of new books that I'm anxious to read aloud. I also keep a folder of newspaper articles that I think will be particularly engaging for our students. I've also been known to "cover" classes by teaching the children how to play a new word game. More times than not, however, I simply say to my colleagues, "I'll do writing." Even though each classroom has its own ways of working, I feel pretty much at home in any of the writing workshops in our school. You see, I bring to my role as principal many years experience as a teacher of writing and as a staff developer in the teaching of writing. Along with many of the teachers in this school, I have spent a good part of my professional life researching the teaching of reading and writing. It comes as no surprise then, that I frequently find myself saying, "I'll do writing."*

I then briefly explained the four questions I ask myself: "Do the children feel good about writing? Do they take risks? Do they understand what writing is for? Do they have strategies to improve their work?" (See Chapter 4, "Responding to Student Writing.") I continue by suggesting how family members can support each of these areas. I begin with making children feel good about themselves as writers. I note:

> *So what does all this mean for children writing at home with an interested parent, grandparent, baby-sitter, or neighbor at their side? Just as we do in school, family members can begin by making children feel good about themselves as writers and designing ways to help students take their writing seriously outside of school. A good way to start is by marveling at your children's efforts. Even if your five-year-old brings you a random string of letters, you must appreciate their work. Family members also need to remember how important drawing is to young writers. It is not surprising for very young children to think of themselves as authors even if they have never put a letter on their work. Then, too, family members can help by answering children's questions about how print works. Don't hesitate to tell children how to spell your dog's name, why our school is sometimes called M.N.S., or how come crackers doesn't start with a k and city doesn't start with an s. When that big day arrives and your children realize the connection between letters of the alphabet and the sounds of words, you need to respond with joyous tribute much the way we got excited when our children uttered their first words, so too we must celebrate when our children write their first tooth fairy note, post that first sign on their bedroom door, or offer to write captions for the family photo album, even if their spelling is more inventive than we ever thought possible. Remember, when you were a student you were probably never asked to write in the early grades. Our students are doing more with writing, at an earlier age, than we ever thought possible.*

Then too, family members need to encourage older children to share their writing. (Our youngest children usually need no encouragement.) And when older children do share, we need to respond to the content, not simply the form. In other words, we need to resist the urge to make corrections before we respond to their ideas. (Children will stop sharing important topics if they only receive comments on their handwriting, spelling, and punctuation.) Family members also need to appreciate how important the writer's notebook becomes to our older students. Notebooks need to be kept in safe, private, and predictable places so that they are readily accessible to students. Serious writers never know when they might need to do some jotting. Students also need to be encouraged to carry their notebooks with them when they travel, sit in waiting rooms, or visit museums, parks, or playgrounds. They also need to be encouraged to respond to books, movies, newscasts, or musical performances in their writer's notebook. Students also need to know that when they come to the end of their writer's notebook, a new one will be provided.

For all our students, no matter their ages, family members can help by carving out space and time and by providing the necessary supplies to enable children to take their writing seriously at home. Then too, family members can take a major role in honoring finished work by proudly posting student poems and stories on the refrigerator door, or better yet sending them as gifts to friends and relatives.

I then made suggestions for at-home risk taking in writing. I write:

Next we need to explore ways to encourage children to take risks as writers. Spelling is probably the greatest area of concern at home. When your young children asks, "How do you spell ____?" perhaps the first response needs to be, "Why don't you give it a try and spell it as best you can?" You might encourage your child to say the word slowly, stretching it out to hear more of the sounds. Afterward, I often find myself saying, "Good for you! That's exactly how five-year-olds spell that word." Sometimes, depending on the child, the occasion, and the word, I might ask, "Would you like to see how the grown-ups spell that word?" With children who are more than just beginning writers, you might first commend them for taking a chance on spelling difficult words. Then you might invite your children to reread their entire work, asking them to point out the words that just don't look right. Spelling is so dependent on visual memory, that we must encourage children to pay attention to the look of words. When older students spot a word that doesn't look right, their teachers often suggest they try it another way. The same suggestion can be made at home. Don't hesitate to eventually provide your child with the standard spelling, especially when they are editing a finished work. If other people are going to appreciate a student's work, they have to be able to read it. Legible handwriting, correct grammar, punctuation, and spelling are always important to the reader.

Next I wrote to the parents about variety, and encouraging children to write for real reasons.

We also want our students to write for many reasons, in many genres, for many different audiences. Family members can be especially helpful in this regard. Let your children know all the reasons you write. Show them your lists, letters, signs, notes, forms, songs, invitations, announcements, etc. Encourage children to do the kind of real writing that gets the business of living done. For example, you might ask your children to write their own party invitations, shopping lists, absence notes, or letters to friends who have moved away. And when you and your children discover new reasons to write, do share these discoveries with their classmates and teachers. New kinds of writing can be contagious at school. In fact, if you do a particular kind of writing for your work or leisure time, don't hesitate to arrange a visit to our writing workshops to share your work with students. We love to spread the wealth.

Finally, I wrote to family members about ways to support children who are trying to become better writers. I wrote:

The best way for folks at home to support students' efforts to become better writers is to continue to read aloud wonderful books, and every once in a while, particularly when you are rereading a book, to stop and talk naturally about the parts you love and explore why. (I suggest this for rereading times, because I wouldn't want read-aloud moments to be turned into little lessons about good writing. Readers should always enjoy a book in its entirety, paying attention to the meaning of the text, not isolating bits and pieces.) Sometimes I find myself reading to children and the words sound so wonderful, I can't help but stop and savor them, pointing out to the young listeners, "I just love this line. I love the way the writer put these words together. What wonderful words the writer chose. How great these words sound together."

And there are so many wonderful writers to suggest for reading aloud. Some of my favorites for children include Cynthia Rylant, Eloise Greenfield, Gary Soto, Kathryn Lasky, Paul Fleischman, Eve Bunting, Mem Fox, Rosemary Wells, Langston Hughes, Jane Yolen, Patricia Polacco, Charlotte Zolotow, E. B. White, Katherine Paterson, and Patricia MacLachlan.

I end my letter by suggesting parents join in on the fun. I write:

Perhaps the greatest writing gift of all would be for family members to occasionally work on writing pieces collaboratively with their children. I can easily imagine parents illustrating the text of picture books written by their children or children illustrating picture books composed by their parents. I can imagine family members translating student writing into their first languages and mailing them to relatives back home. I can imagine parents and children collaborating on an anthology of family stories. I can imagine parents and children working together on a travel diary, a baby book about the new arrival in the family, a collection of favorite family recipes, or keeping a journal together on a new garden, a renovation project, or a family pet. I can also imagine family members keeping their own writer's notebook and sharing their jottings regularly with their children.

The last bit of advice is perhaps the most important. I write:

Whatever role you decide you play in your child's writing life, please remember that we value writing as nourishment, as a way of living a richer, more wide-awake life, and as such, we work hard to never attach drudgery, stress, or punishment to the teaching of writing. Don't hesitate to write me a note if you have more specific questions.

(See *Going Public*, Appendix 13, for Handwriting Letter to Families." See *Lifetime Guarantees*, pages 93–94, for a letter to families regarding invented spelling, and pages 261–263 and Appendix 4 of that text for information about content-rich newsletters. See also page 327 in this text for a letter to families regarding punctuation.)

Keep Parents Smiling

Over many years, I have discovered that the easiest way to make parents smile is to invite them into our writing workshops. Family members always take great pride in watching their children discover important things to say and listening to their children share their ideas with voice, clarity, and confidence. This chapter began with the importance of teaching the conventions of print. It ends with a pitch for the unconventional—that is, with a plea to think out of the box, extending bold invitations for family members to become active participants in their children's writing lives.

RELATED READINGS IN COMPANION VOLUMES

Going Public (Heinemann, 1999) is abbreviated as GP. *Lifetime Guarantees* (Heinemann, 2000) is abbreviated as LG.

Learning conventions of print	**LG:** Ch. 9
Putting nonfiction writing to good use	**LG:** Ch. 4
Using poetry to enrich school life	**LG:** Ch. 5
Publishing in authentic ways	**LG:** Ch. 3
Reaching out to families	**GP:** Ch. 5
	LG: Ch. 8
Bulletin board ideas	**GP:** Ch. 2
	LG: Ch. 1, Ch. 4, Ch. 8

CONCLUSION

In 1858 Charles Dickens wrote, "It is one of my rules in life not to believe a man who may happen to tell me that he feels no interest in children." Certainly for those of us involved in the education of children, such a possibility does not exist. Our interest in children is most likely what brought us to our chosen careers. Our interest in children's writing further suggests that we must remain in awe of all that pertains to the world of childhood.

In *The Old Curiosity Shop*, Dickens reveals his fascination with childhood and with the need to protect the innocence and imagination that so defines what it means to be very young. He writes, "It always grieves me to contemplate the initiation of children into ways of life when they are scarcely more than infants. It checks their confidence and simplicity—two of the best qualities that Heaven gives them—and demands that they share our sorrows before they are capable of entering into our enjoyments." It is my hope that this book has served to remind its readers that children who write are different from adults who write, and need to be treated accordingly.

We must always remember that these are the people who can turn an empty cardboard box into a clubhouse with a secret password for admission, easily start conversations in elevators with complete strangers, skip down the street, laugh at the silliest jokes, sing out loud in the playground, swing endlessly around a subway pole, joyfully sink their hands into mud pies, send Valentines with no inhibitions, eat dripping ice-cream cones with gusto, chew gum and take delight when the bubbles stick to their faces, revel in painting sparkly cat faces onto their own, and wear outrageous costumes as they walk down the street. Passersby don't think any of this unusual, because children are different from adults. It's true outside of school; it must be true inside of school. Our writing workshops should reflect and pay tribute to this unique and all-too-short period of our students' lives.

APPENDICES

1. Bibliography
   Favorite Poetry Collections
   Poetry Anthologies That Support Notebook Writing
   Picture Books That Inspire Notebook Writing
   Informational Texts That Inspire Notebook Keeping
   Professional Books That Highlight the Needs of Childhood
   Picture Books Containing Characters Who Write
   Picture Books Written in Letter Format
   Picture Books About Being an Author or Illustrator
   Autobiographical Works by Children's Authors
   Biographical Material About Children's Authors
   Biographical Material About Authors Written in Child-Friendly Formats
   Children's Writers on Writing
   Picture Books That Support Teaching About Crafting Techniques
   Professional Books That Support Teachers Learning to Confer
   Professional Books That Support Teachers Learning Crafting Techniques
   Professional Books That Inspire Teachers to Work on Their Own Writing
   Professional Books That Explore the Reading-Writing Connection
   Professional Books That Introduce Teachers to the Writing Workshop
   Books for a Jonathan London Author Study
2. Worksheet on School-Wide Rites of Passage in the Teaching of Writing
3. Questionnaire on Carving Out Time for a Regularly Scheduled Writing Workshop
4. Worksheet on Implications for Broad Goals
5. Joanne Hindley Salch's Worksheet for Learning from Conferences
6. Conference Practice Sheets—Our Youngest Writers
7. Matthew's Writing Folder—Illustrating Variety of First-Grade Genres
8. Editing/Publishing Checklist
9. Blank Spelling Study Sheet
10. Professional Development Scenarios in the Teaching of Writing
11. Calendar Project Directions and Planning Sheets

APPENDIX 1: BIBLIOGRAPHY

Favorite Poetry Collections

Carlson, Lori Marie (ed.). 1998. *Sol a Sol*. Illustrated by Emily Lisker. New York: Henry Holt.

Cullinan, Bernice (ed.). 1996. *A Jar Full of Tiny Stars*. Illustrated by Andi MacLeod. Urbana, IL: NCTE.

De Fina, Allan A. 1997. *When a City Leans Against the Sky*. Illustrated by Ken Condon. Honesdale, PA: Boyds Mills Press.

Dotlich, Rebecca Kai. 1998. *Lemonade Sun and Other Poems*. Honesdale, PA: Boyds Mills Press.

Farber, Norma, and Myra Cohn Livingston (eds.). 1987. *These Small Stones*. New York: Harper & Row.

George, Kristine O'Connell. 1997. *The Great Frog Race and Other Poems*. New York: Clarion.

George, Kristine O'Connell. 1998. *Old Elm Speaks: Tree Poems*. Illustrated by Kate Kiesler. New York: Clarion.

George, Kristine O'Connell, 1999. *Little Dog Poems*. Illustrated by June Otani. New York: Clarion.

Giovanni, Nikki. 1987. *Spin a Soft Black Song*. Illustrated by George Martins. New York: Hill and Wang/Farrar, Straus and Giroux.

Glaser, Isabel Joshlin (ed.). 1995. *Dreams of Glory: Poems Starring Girls*. Illustrations by Pat Lowery Collins. New York: Atheneum.

Graves, Donald. 1996. *Baseball, Snakes, and Summer Squash: Poems About Growing Up*. Illustrated by Paul Birling. Honesdale, PA: Boyds Mills Press.

Gunning, Monica. 1999. *Not a Copper Penny in Me House: Poems from the Caribbean*. Illustrated by Frane Lessac. Honesdale, PA: Boyds Mills Press.

Hopkins, Lee Bennett (ed.). 2000. *My America: A Poetry Atlas of the United States*. Illustrated by Stephen Alcorn. New York: Simon & Schuster.

Huck, Charlotte (ed.). 1993. *Secret Places*. Illustrated by Lindsay Barrett George. New York: William Morrow.

Janeczko, Paul B. (ed.). 1994. *Poetry from A to Z: A Guide for Young Writers*. New York: Simon & Schuster.

Janeczko, Paul B. (ed.). 1999. *Very Best (Almost) Friends*. Illustrated by Christine Davenier. Cambridge, MA: Candlewick Press.

Janeczko, Paul B. (ed.). 2001. *Dirty Laundry Pile: Poems in Different Voices*. Illustrated by Melissa Sweet. New York: HarperCollins.

Levy, Constance. 1996. *When Whales Exhale*. Illustrated by Judy Labrasca. New York: Margaret McElderry/Simon and Schuster.

Levy, Constance, 1991. *I'm Going to Pet a Worm Today*. Illustrated by Ronald Himler. New York: Margaret K. McElderry Books.

APPENDIX 1 *continued*

Liatos, Sandra Olson. 1997. *Bicycle Riding and Other Poems*. Illustrated by Karen Dugan. Honesdale, PA: Boyds Mills Press.

Lyne, Sandford. 1996. *Ten-Second Rainshowers: Poems by Young People*. Illustrated by Virginia Halstead. New York: Simon & Schuster.

Mavor, Sally (ed.). 1997. *You and Me: Poems of Friendship*. New York: Orchard Books.

Michaelson, Richard. 1996. *Animals That Ought to Be: Poems About Imaginary Pets*. Illustrated by Leonard Baskin. New York: Simon & Schuster.

Moore, Lilian. 1995. *I Never Did That Before*. Illustrated by Lillian Hoban. New York: Atheneum.

Medina, Jane. 1999. *My Name Is Jorge: On Both Sides of the River*. Illustrated by Fabricio Vanden Broeck. Honesdale, PA: Boyds Mills Press.

Mora, Pat. 1999. *Confetti: Poems for Children*. Illustrated by Enrique O. Sanchez. New York: Lee & Low.

Mora, Pat. 1998. *This Big Sky*. Illustrated by Steve Jenkins. New York: Scholastic.

Morrison, Lillian. 1992. *Whistling the Morning In*. Illustrated by Joel Cook. Honesdale, PA: Boyds Mills.

Nye, Naomi (ed.). 1996. *This Same Sky: A Collection of Poems from Around the World*. New York: Four Winds Press.

Nye, Naomi (ed.). *Salting the Ocean: 100 Poems by Young Poets*. Illustrated by Ashley Bryan. New York: Greenwillow.

Ridlon, Marci. 1996. *Sun Through the Window: Poems for Children*. Honesdale, PA: Boyds Mills Press.

Rosen, Michael J. (ed.). 1996. *Food Fight: Poets Join the Fight Against Hunger with Poems to Favorite Foods*. New York: Harcourt Brace.

Schertle, Alice. 1995. *Advice for a Frog*. Illustrated by Norman Green. New York: Lothrop, Lee & Shepard.

Schertle, Alice. 1999. *A Lucky Thing*. Illustrated by Wendell Minor. San Diego, CA: Harcourt Brace.

Shaw, Alison (ed.). 1995. *Until I Saw the Sea: A Collection of Seashore Poems*. New York: Henry Holt.

Steele, Susanna, and Morag Styles (eds.). 1990. *Mother Gave a Shout: Poems by Women and Girls*. Volcano, CA: Volcano Press.

Soto, Gary. 1995. *Canto Familiar*. San Diego, CA: Harcourt Brace.

Soto, Gary, 1992. *Neighborhood Odes*. New York: Scholastic.

Speed, Toby. 1998. *Water Voices*. Illustrated by Julie Downing, New York: G.P. Putnam's Sons.

Swanson, Susan Marie. 1997. *Getting Used to the Dark: 26 Night Poems*. Illustrated by Peter Catalanotto. New York: DK Publishing.

Weil, Zaro. 1992. *Mud, Moon and Me*. Boston: Houghton Mifflin.

Wong, Janet. 2000. *Night Garden: Poems from the World of Dreams*. Illustrated by Julie Paschkis. New York: McEldery Books.

See *Lifetime Guarantees* for additional poetry recommendations including collections related to the school experience (page 167), favorite general anthologies, (page 171), as well as poems about reading (page 189), poems about writing (page 192), and poems about poetry (page 192).

Poetry Anthologies That Support Notebook Writing

Fletcher, Ralph. 1997. *Ordinary Things: Poems from a Walk in Early Spring*. Illustrated by Walter Lyon Krudop. New York: Atheneum.

Greenfield, Eloise. 1988. *Nathaniel Talking*. Illustrated by Jan Spivey Gilchrist. New York: Black Butterfly Children's Books.

Grimes, Nikki. 1978. *Something on My Mind*. Illustrated by Tom Feelings. New York: Dial.

Little, Jean. 1986. *Hey World, Here I Am!* Illustrations by Sue Truesdell. New York: Harper & Row.

Margolis, Richard. 1969. *Only the Moon and Me*. Illustrated with photographs by Marcia Kay Keegan. New York: J.B. Lippincott.

Margolis, Richard. 1984. *Secrets of a Small Brother*. Illustrated by Donald Carrick. New York: Macmillan.

Rosen, Michael. 1983. *Quick, Let's Get Out of Here*. Illustrated by Quentin Blake. London: Puffin Books.

Stevenson, James. 1998. *Popcorn*. New York: Greenwillow.

Stevenson, James, 1999. *Candycorn*. New York: Greenwillow.

Stevenson, James. 1999. *Sweetcorn*. New York: Greenwillow.

Stevenson, James. 2000. *Cornflakes*. New York: Greenwillow.

Turner, Ann. 1986. *Street Talk*. Illustrated by Catherine Stock. Boston: Houghton Mifflin.

Turner, Ann. 2001. *In the Heart*. Illustrated by Salley Mavor. New York: HarperCollins.

Picture Books That Inspire Notebook Writing

Kraus, Ruth. 1954. *I'll Be You and You Be Me*. Illustrated by Maurice Sendak. New York: HarperCollins.

Oakley, Graham. 1987. *The Diary of a Church Mouse*. New York: Atheneum.

Wilson, Beth. 1990. *Jenny*. New York: Macmillan.

Zolotow, Charlotte. 1992. *Snippets*. Illustrated by Melissa Sweet. New York: William Morrow.

Zolotow, Charlotte. 1976. *It's Not Fair*. Illustrated by William Pene du Bois. New York: Harper & Row.

Informational Texts That Inspire Notebook Keeping

Daniel, Alan, Lea Daniel, and Jim Penner. 1998. *Letters from the Sea.* Bothell, WA: The Wright Group.

Dewey, Jennifer, Owings. 2001. *Antarctic Journal: Four Months at the Bottom of the World.* New York: HarperCollins.

Brenner, Barbara. 1970. *A Snake Lover's Diary.* New York: Harper & Row.

George, Jean Craighead. *Look to the North: A Wolf Pup Diary.* Illustrated by Lucia Washburn. New York: HarperCollins.

Heinrich, Bernd. Adapted by Alice Calaprice. 1990. *An Owl in the House: A Naturalist's Diary.* Boston: Little, Brown and Company.

Krupinski, Loretta. 1995. *Bluewater Journal: The Voyage of the Sea Tiger.* New York: HarperCollins.

Krupinski, Loretta. 1997. *Into the Woods: A Woodland Scrapbook.* New York: HarperCollins.

Lyons, Mary E., and Muriel M. Branch. 2000. *Dear Ellen Bee: A Civil War Scrapbook of Two Union Spies.* New York: Simon & Schuster.

Mathis, Sharon Bell. 1997. *Running Girl: The Diary of Ebonee Rose.* New York: Harcourt Press.

Murphy, Stuart J. 2000. *Pepper's Journal: A Kitten's First Year.* New York: HarperCollins.

Roop, Peter, and Connie. 2000. *Good-Bye for Today: The Diary of a Young Girl at Sea.* Illustrated by Thomas B. Allen. New York: Atheneum.

Roth, Susan L. 1990. *Marco Polo: His Notebook.* New York: Doubleday.

Yolen, Jane, and Heidi Elisabet Yolen Stemple. 1999. *The Mary Celeste: An Unsolved Mystery from History.* Illustrated by Roger Roth. New York: Simon & Schuster.

Yolen, Jane, and Heidi Elisabet Yolen Stemple. 2001. *The Wolf Girls: An Unsolved Mystery from History.* Illustrated by Roger Roth. New York: Simon & Schuster.

Professional Books That Highlight the Needs of Childhood

Dragan, Pat. 2001. *Literacy from Day One.* Portsmouth, NH: Heinemann.

Dyson, Anne Hass. 1997. *Writing Superheroes: Contemporary Childhood, Popular Culture, and Classroom Literacy.* New York: Teachers College Press.

Evans, Janet (ed.). 2001. *Writing in the Elementary Classroom: Reconsideration.* Portsmouth, NH: Heinemann.

Glover, Mary Kenner. 1997. *Making Schools by Hand.* Urbana, IL: NCTE.

Glover, Mary Kenner, and Beth Giacalone. 2001. *Surprising Destinations: A Guide to Essential Learning in Early Childhood.* Portsmouth, NH: Heinemann.

Hudson-Ross, Sally, Linda Miller, Cleary, and Maria Casey (eds.). 1993. *Children's Voices: Children Talk About Literacy.* Portsmouth, NH: Heinemann.

Lindfors, Judith Wells. 1999. *Children's Inquiry: Using Language to Make Sense of the World*. Urbana, IL: NCTE.

Lewis, Richard. 1998. *Living by Wonder: The Imaginative Life of Childhood*. New York: Touchstone Center Publications/Parabola Books.

Matens, Prisca. 1996. *I Already Know How to Read: A Child's View of Literacy*. Portsmouth, NH: Heinemann.

Michel, Pamela A. 1994. *The Child's View of Reading: Understandings for Teachers and Parents*. Boston, MA: Allyn and Bacon.

Newkirk, Thomas. 1989. *More Than Stories: The Range of Children's Writing*. Portsmouth, NH: Heinemann.

Owocki, Gretchen. 1999. *Literacy Through Play*. Portsmouth, NH: Heinemann.

Owocki, Gretchen. 2000. *Make Way for Literacy: Teaching the Way Young Children Learn*. Portsmouth, NH: Heinemann.

Taylor, Denny. 1993. *From the Child's Point of View*. Portsmouth, NH: Heinemann.

Picture Books Containing Characters Who Write

Baylor, Byrd. 1986. *I'm in Charge of Celebrations*. New York: Charles Scribner.

Carr, Jan. 1996. *The Nature of the Beast*. Illustrated by G. Brian Karas. New York: William Morrow.

Gregory, Valiska. 1999. *A Valentine for Norman Noggs*. Illustrated by Marsha Winborn, New York: HarperCollins.

Hest, Amy. 1995. *How to Get Famous in Brooklyn*. Illustrated by Linda Dalal Sawaya. New York: Simon & Schuster.

Gottleib, Dale. 1991. *My Stories by Hildy Calpurnia*. New York: Knopf.

Hopkinson, Deborah. 2001. *Fannie in the Kitchen*. Illustrated by Nancy Carpenter. New York: Atheneum.

Moss, Marissa. 1995. *Amelia's Notebook*. Berkeley, CA: Tricycle.

Moss, Marissa. 1999. *Emma's Journal: The Story of a Colonial Girl*. Orlando, FL: Harcourt, Brace & Company.

Murphy, Shirley Rousseau. 1974. *Poor Jenny, Bright as a Penny*. New York: Viking Penguin.

Schotter, Ronni. 1997. *Nothing Ever Happens on 90th Street*. Illustrated by Krysten Brooker. New York: Orchard Books.

Spinelli, Eileen. 1991. *Somebody Loves You, Mr. Hatch*. Illustrated by Paul Yalowitz, New York: Aladdin.

See related titles in *Lifetime Guarantees* (page 107), and *Lasting Impressions: Weaving Literature into the Writing Workshop*.

Picture Books Written in Letter Format

Ahlberg, Janet, and Allan Ahlberg. 1995. *The Jolly Postman*. London: William Heinemann Ltd.

Allan-Meyer, Kathleen. 1995. *I Have a Friend*. New York: Barron's.

Anholt, Laurence. 1995. *The Magpie Song*. Illustrated by Dan Williams. Boston: Houghton Mifflin.

Asch, Frank. 1992. *Dear Brother*. New York: Scholastic.

Brisson, Pat. 1989. *Your Best Friend Kate*. New York: Bradbury Press.

Brisson, Pat. 1990. *Kate Heads West*. New York: Bradbury Press.

Cleary, Beverly. 1984. *Dear Mr. Henshaw*. New York: HarperCollins.

George, Jean Craighead. 1993. *Dear Rebecca, Winter Is Here*. New York: HarperCollins.

George, Lindsay Barrett. 1999. *Around the World: Who's Been Here?* New York: Greenwillow.

Hobbie, Holly. 1997. *Toot and Puddle*. New York: Little, Brown and Company.

James, Simon. 1991. *Dear Mr. Blueberry*. New York: Simon & Schuster.

Olson, Mary W. 2000. *Nice Try, Tooth Fairy*. Illustrated by Katherine Tillotson. New York: Simon & Schuster.

Pomerantz, Charlotte. 2000. *The Birthday Letters*. Illustrated by JoAnn Adinolfi. New York: Greenwillow.

Schick, Eleanor. 1996. *My Navajo Sister*. New York: Simon & Schuster.

Stewart, Sarah. 1997. *The Gardener*. New York: Farrar, Straus, Giroux.

Swanson, Susan Marie. 1998. *Letter to the Lake*. Illustrated by Peter Catalanotto. New York: DK Publishing.

Willard, Nancy. 1997. *The Magic Cornfield*. New York: Harcourt Brace.

Williams, Vera B., and Jennifer Williams. 1988. *Stringbeans Trip to the Shining Sea*. New York: William Morrow.

Picture Books About Being an Author or Illustrator

Borden, Louise. 2001. *The Day Eddie Met the Author*. Illustrated by Adam Gustavson. New York: Simon & Schuster.

Christelow, Eileen. 1995. *What Do Authors Do?* New York: Clarion.

Christelow, Eileen. 1999. *What Do Illustrators Do?* New York: Clarion.

Cobb, Vicki. 1989. *Writing It Down*. Illustrated by Marylin Hafner. New York: Lippincott.

Goffsein, M. B. 1984. *A Writer*. New York: Harper & Row.

Krensky, Stephen. 1996. *Breaking into Print: Before and After the Invention of the Printing Press*. Illustrated by Bonnie Christiansen. New York: Little Brown and Company.

Lester, Helen. 1997. *Author: A True Story*. Boston: Houghton Mifflin.

Pinkwater, Daniel. 1993. *Author's Day*. New York: Simon & Schuster.

Voyages of Discovery. 1996. *The History of Making Books*. New York: Scholastic.

Willard, Nancy. 1995. *Gutenberg's Gift: A Book Lover's Pop-up Book*. Illustrated by Brian Leister. New York: Harcourt Brace & Company.

Autobiographical Works by Children's Authors

Aardema, Verna. 1993. *A Bookworm Who Hatched*. New York: Richard C. Owen, Publisher, Inc.

Bauer, Marion Dane. 1995. *A Writer's Story: From Life to Fiction*. New York: Houghton Mifflin Company.

Bulla, Clyde. 1985. *A Grain of Wheat: A Writer Begins*. Boston: David R. Godine.

Byars, Betsy. 1991. *The Moon and I*. New York: Julian Messner.

Carle, Eric. 1997. *Flora and Tiger: 19 Very Short Stories from My Life*. New York: Philomel.

Cleary, Beverly. 1988. *A Girl from Yamhill: A Memoir*. New York: William Morrow and Company, Inc.

Cleary, Beverly. 1995. *My Own Two Feet: A Memoir*. New York: Morrow Junior Books.

Cole, Joanna, with Wendy Saul. 1996. *On the Bus with Joanna Cole: A Creative Autobiography*. Portsmouth, NH: Heinemann.

Cormier, Robert. 1991. *I Have Words to Spend: Reflections of a Small Town Editor*. New York: Delacorte Press.

Dahl, Roald. 1984. *Boy: Tales of Childhood*. New York: Farrar, Straus & Giroux.

Dahl, Roald. 1986. *Going Solo*. New York: Farrar, Straus & Giroux.

Dahl, Roald. 1994. *My Year*. Illustrated by Quentin Blake. New York: Viking Penguin.

Dewey, Jennifer Owings. 1995. *Cowgirl Dreams: A Western Childhood*. Honesdale, PA: Boyds Mills Press.

Fleischman, Sid. 1996. *The Abracadabra Kid: A Writer's Life*. New York: Beech Tree.

Fox, Mem. 1990. *Mem's the Word*. Australia: Penguin Books.

Fritz, Jean. 1982. *Homesick: My Own Story*. New York: G.P. Putnam's Sons.

Fritz, Jean. 1993. *Surprising Myself*. New York: Richard C. Owen Publishers, Inc.

Godden, Rumer. 1987. *A Time to Dance, No Time to Weep*. London: Macmillan.

Greenfield, Eloise, and Lessie Jones Little. 1979. *Childtimes: A Three-Generation Memoir*. New York: Thomas Y. Crowell.

Hopkins, Lee Bennett. 1993. *The Writing Bug*. New York: Richard C. Owen Publishers.

Hopkins, Lee Bennett. 1995. *Been to Yesterdays: Poems of a Life*. Illustrated by Charlene Rendeiro. Honesdale, PA: Boyds Mills.

Hopkins, Lee Bennett (ed.). 1995. *Pauses: Autobiographical Reflections of 101 Creators of Children's Books*. New York: HarperCollins.

Joyce, William. 1997, *The World of William Joyce Scrapbook*. New York: HarperCollins.

L'Engle, Madeleine. 1972. *A Circle of Quiet*. New York: Farrar, Straus & Giroux.

Little, Jean. 1990. *Stars Come out Within*. New York: Viking.

Little, Jean. 1991. *Little by Little: A Writer's Education*. New York: Viking Kestrel.

Marcus, Leonard S. 2000. *Author Talk*. New York: Simon & Schuster Books for Young Readers.

Martin, Rafe. 1992. *A Storyteller's Story*. New York: Richard C. Owen Publishers, Inc.

Meltzer, Milton. 1988. *Starting from Home: A Writer's Beginnings*. New York: Puffin Books.

Myers, Walter Dean. 2001. *Bad Boy: A Memoir*. New York: HarperCollins.

Naylor, Phyllis Reynolds. 2001. *How I Came to Be a Writer*, revised edition. New York: Aladdin Paperbacks.

Peck, Richard. 1991. *Anonymously Yours*. New York: Beech Tree Books.

Peet, Bill. 1898. *Bill Peet: An Autobiography*. New York: Scholastic.

Stine, R. L., as told to Joe Arthur. 1997. *It Came from Ohio: My Life as a Writer*. New York: Scholastic.

Rylant, Cynthia. 1984. *Waiting to Waltz: A Childhood*. New York: Simon and Schuster.

Rylant, Cynthia. 1989. *But I'll Be Back Again*. New York: Beech Tree Books.

Rylant, Cynthia. 1992. *Best Wishes*. New York: Richard C. Owen Publishers, Inc.

Uchida, Yoshiko. 1991. *The Invisible Thread*. New York: Beech Tree Books.

Vogel, Ilse-Margret. 1993. *Bad Times, Good Friends*. San Diego: Harcourt Brace Jovanovich.

Yep, Laurence. 1991. *The Lost Garden*. New York: Beech Tree Books.

Yolen, Jane. 1992. *A Letter from Phoenix Farm*. New York: Richard C. Owen, Publisher, Inc.

Students will also benefit from hearing the life stories of prominent illustrators of children's books including those in Harper & Row's *Self-Portrait Collection* that contains autobiographies by Trina Schart Hyman, Margot Zemach, and Erik Blegvad, Ted Lewin's *Touch and Go: Travels of a Children's Book Illustrator* (Lothrop, Lee & Shepard, 1999), Pat Cummings' *Talking with Artists*, Volumes 1–3, Clarion Books, and Beverly Gherman's *Norman Rockwell: Storyteller with a Brush* (Atheneum, 2000).

Many wonderful autobiographical sketches of authors of books for young adults are contained in Don Gallo's *Speaking for Ourselves* and *Speaking for Ourselves, Too* published by NCTE. Likewise, the Laurel-Leaf library contains biographical material on several acclaimed authors for older students.

Teachers of elementary-age students will also gain from reading and rereading the following classic memoirs, written by accomplished authors of adult material: Russell Baker's *Growing Up* (Congdon & Weed, 1982), Annie Dillard's *The Writing Life* (Harper & Row, 1989), *An American Childhood* (Harper & Row, 1987), Robert MacNeil's *Word-struck* (Viking Penguin, 1989), and Eudora Welty's *One Writer's Beginnings* (Warner Books, 1983).

Biographical Material About Children's Authors

Aldis, Dorothy. 1987. *Nothing Is Impossible: The Story of Beatrix Potter*. Peter Smith.

Anderson, William. 1992. *Laura Ingalls Wilder: A Biography*. New York: HarperCollins.

Becker R. Margot, with Ann M. Martin. 1993. *Ann M. Martin: The Story of the Author of the Babysitter's Club*. New York: Scholastic Biography.

Copeland, Jeffrey S. 1993. *Speaking of Poets: Interviews with Poets Who Write for Children and Young Adults*. Urbana, IL: NCTE.

Ehrlich, Amy (ed.). 1996. *When I Was Your Age: Original Stories About Growing Up*. Cambridge, MA: Candlewick Press.

Engel, Dean and Florence B. Freedman. 1995. *Ezra Jack Keats: A Biography with Illustrations*. New York: Silver Moon Press.

Gherman, Beverly. 1992. *E.B. White: Some Writer!* New York: Atheneum.

Graham, Paula W. 1999. *Speaking of Journals: Children's Book Writers Talk About Their Diaries, Notebooks and Sketchbooks*. Honesdale, PA: Boyds Mills.

Kamen, Gloria. 1990. *Edward Lear: King of Nonsense*. New York: Atheneum.

Kovacs, Deborah, and James Preller. 1991. *Meet the Authors and Illustrators—Volume One*. New York: Scholastic Reference Library.

Marcus, Leonard S. 1999. *Margaret Wise Brown: Awakened by the Moon*. New York: Quill/HarperCollins.

Ohanian, Susan. 2001. *Books Day by Day: Anniversaries, Anecdotes, and Activities*. Portsmouth, NH: Heinemann.

Rylant, Cynthia. 1996. *Margaret, Frank and Andy: Three Writers' Stories*. Orlando, FL: Harcourt Brace & Company.

Silvey, Anita (ed.). 1995. *Children's Books and their Creators*. New York: Houghton Mifflin.

Stine, Megan. 1992. *The Story of Laura Ingalls Wilder, Pioneer Girl*. New York: Dell Yearling.

Wallner, Alexandra. 1995. *Beatrix Potter*. New York: Holiday House.

Biographical Material About Authors Written in Child-Friendly Formats

Aliki. 1999. *William Shakespeare & the Globe*. New York: HarperCollins.

Bedard, Michael. 1992. *Emily*. Illustrated by Barbara Cooney. New York: Doubleday.

Loewen, Nancy. 1994. *Walt Whitman*. Mankato, MN: Creative Editions.

Osofsky, Audrey. 1996. *Free to Dream: The Making of a Poet: Langston Hughes*. New York: Lothrop, Lee & Shepard.

Pettit, Jayne. 1996. *Maya Angelou: Journey of the Heart*. New York: Dutton.

Reef, Catherine. 1996. *John Steinbeck*. New York: Clarion.

Spires, Elizabeth. 1999. *The Mouse of Amherst*. Illustrated by Claire A. Nivola. New York: Farrar, Straus & Giroux.

Stanley, Diane, and Peter Vennema. 1992. *Bard of Avon: The Story of William Shakespeare*. New York: William Morrow.

Stanley, Diane, and Peter Vennema. 1993. *Charles Dickens: The Man Who Had Great Expectations*. New York: William Morrow.

Ross, Stewart. 1997. *Charlotte Bronte and Jane Eyre*. Illustrated by Robert Van Nutt. New York: Viking.

Walker, Alice. 1974. *Langston Hughes, American Poet*. New York: Thomas Crowell.

Children's Writers on Writing

Aiken, Joan. 1999. *The Way to Write for Children*. New York: St. Martin's Press.

Cassedy, Sylvia. 1979. *In Your Own Words: A Beginner's Guide to Writing*. New York: Thomas Crowell.

Cooper, Susan. 1996. *Dreams and Wishes: Essays on Writing for Children*. New York: Simon & Schuster.

Hunter, Mollie. 1975. *Talent Is Not Enough: On Writing for Children*. New York: Harper & Row.

Hunter, Mollie. 1992. *The Pied Piper Syndrome and Other Essays*. New York: HarperCollins.

Jackson, Jacqueline. 1974. *Turn Not Pale, Beloved Snail: A Book About Writing Among Other Things*. Boston: Little, Brown.

Nixon, Joan Lowery. 1988. *If You Were a Writer*. New York: Four Winds Press.

Paterson, Katherine. 1985. *A Sense of Wonder: On Reading and Writing Books for Children*. New York: Penguin.

Yolen, Jane. 1973. *Writing Books for Children*. Boston: The Writer, Inc.

Picture Books That Support Teaching About Crafting Techniques

Aliki. 1996. *Those Summers*. New York: HarperCollins.

Creech, Sharon. 2000. *Fishing in the Air*. Illustrated by Chris Raschka. New York: Harper-Collins.

Lasky, Katherine. 1979. *My Island Grandma*. New York: Frederick Warne.

Pearson, Susan. 1998. *Silver Morning*. Illustrated by David Christiana. Orlando, FL: Harcourt Brace & Company.

Pochocki, Ethel. 1993. *Wildflower Tea*. Illustrated by Roger Essley. New York: Simon & Schuster.

Stock, Catherine. 1999. *Island Summer*. Illustrated by David Christiana. New York: Lothrop, Lee & Shepard.

Thomas, Meredith. 1998. *Rainbows of the Sea*. Photographs by Adrian Lander. New York: Mondo.

Zolotow, Charlotte. 1993. *Peter and the Pigeons*. Illustrated by Martine Gourbault. New York: Greenwillow.

See also those described in Chapter 5, "Reading to Inform Your Writing."

Professional Books That Support Teachers Learning to Confer

Anderson, Carl. 2000. *How's It Going?: A Practical Guide to Conferring with Student Writers*. Portsmouth, NH: Heinemann.

Atwell, Nancie. 1998. *In The Middle*. Second ed. Portsmouth, NH: Heinemann.

Graves, Donald. 1994. *A Fresh Look at Writing*. Portsmouth, NH: Heinemann.

Hindley, Joanne. 1996. *In the Company of Children*. York, ME: Stenhouse.

Kaufman, Douglas. 2000. *Conference & Conversations: Listening to the Literate Classroom*. Portsmouth, NH: Heinemann.

Murray, Don. 1968. *A Writer Teaches Writing*. Boston: Houghton Mifflin.

Professional Books That Support Teachers Learning Crafting Techniques

Fletcher, Ralph. 1993. *What a Writer Needs*. Portsmouth, NH: Heinemann.

Fletcher, Ralph, and JoAnn Portaluppi. *Nonfiction Craft Lessons: Teaching Information Writing K–8*. York, ME: Stenhouse

Fletcher, Ralph, and Portaluppi, JoAnn. 1998. *Craft Lessons: Teaching Writing K–8*. York, ME: Stenhouse.

Murray, Donald. 1982. *Learning by Teaching: Selected Articles on Writing and Teaching*. Montclair, NJ: Boynton/Cook.

Ray, Katie Wood. 1999. *Wondrous Words*. Urbana, IL: NCTE.

Zinsser, William. 1976. *On Writing Well: An Informal Guide to Writing Non-Fiction*. New York: Harper & Row.

Professional Books That Inspire Teachers to Work on Their Own Writing

Fletcher, Ralph. 1996. *Breathing In Breathing Out: Keeping a Writer's Notebook*. Portsmouth, NH: Heinemann.

Graves, Don. 1990. The Reading Writing Teacher's Companion Series, *Discover Your Own Literacy*. Portsmouth, NH: Heinemann.

Heard, Georgia. 1995. *Writing Toward Home*. Portsmouth, NH: Heinemann.

Le Guin, Ursula K. 1998. *Steering the Craft*. Portland, OR: The Eighth Mountain Press.

Murray, Donald. 1996. *Crafting a Life: In Essay, Story, Poem*. Portsmouth, NH: Heinemann.

Wooldridge, Susan Goldsmith. 1996. *poemcrazy: freeing your life with words*. New York: Three Rivers Press.

Professional Books That Explore the Reading-Writing Connection

Carr Chappell, Janine. 1999. *A Child Went Forth: Reflective Teaching with Young Readers & Writers*. Portsmouth, NH: Heinemann.

Hansen, Jane. 2001. *When Writers Read,* 2nd ed. Portsmouth, NH: Heinemann.

Harwayne, Shelley. 1992. *Lasting Impressions: Weaving Literature into the Writing Workshop*. Portsmouth, NH: Heinemann.

Jenkins, Carol Brenna. 1999. *The Allure of Author: Author Studies in the Elementary Classroom*. Portsmouth, NH: Heinemann.

Murray, Donald. 1986. *Read to Write: A Writing Process Reader*. New York: Holt, Rinehart, Winston.

Professional Books That Introduce Teachers to the Writing Workshop

Fletcher, Ralph, and JoAnn Portaluppi. 2001. *Writing Workshop: The Essential Guide*. Portsmouth, NH: Heinemann.

Hindley, Joanne. 1996. *In the Company of Children*. York, ME: Stenhouse.

Ray, Katie Wood, with Lester Laminack. 2001. *The Writing Workshop: Working Through the Hard Parts (And They're All Hard Parts)*. Urbana, IL: NCTE.

Rogovin, Paula. 2001. *The Research Workshop: Bring the World into Your Classroom*. Portsmouth, NH: Heinemann.

Books for a Jonathan London Author Study

Ali, Child of the Desert. 1997. Illustrated by Ted Lewin. New York: Lothrop, Lee, & Shepard.

At the Edge of the Forest. 1998. Illustrated by Barbara Firth. Cambridge, MA: Candlewick Press.

The Candy Store Man. 1998. Illustrated by Kevin O'Malley. New York: Lothrop, Lee & Shepard.

Confor's Egg. 1999. Illustrated by James Chafee. San Francisco: Chronicle Books.

Crunch Munch. 2001. Illustrated by Michael Rex. New York: Harcourt.

Dream Weaver. 1998. Illustrated by Rocco Baviera. New York: Harcourt Brace.

The Eyes of Grey Wolf. 1993. Illustrated by Jon Van Zyle. San Francisco: Chronicle Books.

Froggy Eats Out. 2001. Illustrated by Frank Remkiewicz. New York: Viking.

Froggy Gets Dressed. 1997. Illustrated by Frank Remkiewicz. New York: Viking/Puffin.

Froggy Goes to School. 1998. Illustrated by Frank Remkiewicz. New York: Viking/Puffin.

Froggy Learns to Swim. 1997. Illustrated by Frank Remkiewicz. New York: Viking/Puffin.

Froggy's First Kiss. 1998. Illustrated by Frank Remkiewicz. New York: Viking/Puffin.

Hip Cat. 1996. Illustrated by Woodleigh Hubbard. San Francisco: Chronicle Books.

Honey Paw and Lightfoot. 1995. Illustrated by Jon Van Zyle. San Francisco: Chronicle Books.

Hurricane! 1998. Illustrated by Henri Sorensen. New York: Lothrop, Lee & Shepard.

I See the Moon and the Moon Sees Me. 1996. Illustrated by Peter Fiore. New York: Puffin.

Into This Night We Are Rising. 1993. Illustrated by G. Brian Karas. New York: Viking.

Let the Lynx Come In. 1996. Illustrated by Patrick Benson. Cambridge, MA: Candlewick Press.

Let's Go, Froggy! 1994. Illustrated by Frank Remkiewicz. New York: Viking/Puffin.

Like Butter on Pancakes. 1995. Illustrated by G. Brian Karas. New York: Viking.

Little Red Monkey. 1997. Illustrated by Frank Remkiewicz. New York: Dutton.

Phantom of the Prairie: Year of the Black-Footed Ferret. 1998. Illustrated by Barbara Bash. San Francisco: The Sierra Club.

Puddles. 1997. Illustrated by G. Brian Karas. New York: Viking.

Sun Dance Water Dance. 2001. Illustrated by Greg Couch. New York: Dutton.

White Water. 2001. Illustrated by Jill Kastner. New York: Viking.

Worksheet on School-Wide
Rites of Passage in the Teaching of Writing

	Tools	Genre	Publishing	Involvement	Family Rituals	Author Studies
K						
1						
2						
3						
4						
5						

Questionnaire on Carving Out Time for a
Regularly Scheduled Writing Workshop

1. Is there anything you're spending time on that can be eliminated (e.g., busywork, non-assessment-driven assignments, or any rituals, structures, or activities that have outlived their usefulness or effectiveness)?

2. Is there anything you're doing that can be done in less time (by using more effective management techniques, explicit instruction instead of eliciting from students or quickening your overall pace)?

3. Are there units of study, topics, or subjects that need not be worked on, on a daily or weekly basis? In other words, can you chunk your time and devote longer blocks to one thing while holding off on another and then alternating these subjects?

4. How many minutes a day are you spending on transitions? If too many, how can you learn to streamline these moments? How can your colleagues help?

5. How much time is taken up with behavioral issues (e.g., disciplining a student, whole-class discussions concerning affective issues, anticipating controversies)? If too much time is taken up in this arena, whom can you turn to for help?

6. Are there ways to make the opening and closing half-hours of the day more instructionally valuable?

7. Are there school-wide specials, events, or interruptions that you'd like to see revised or eliminated?

8. Have you addressed the issue of allocating time with your staff developer?

9. Do you have a colleague who seems to make better use of time? Have you had time to observe that teacher and discuss the issue?

10. Would guidance in planning and scheduling your day and your week be beneficial?

11. When you are able to carve out sufficient time to run a regularly scheduled writing workshop, what additional support would you need (e.g, staff development, workshops, professional literature, inter-visitations, etc.)?

12. How much time are you currently spending on writing?

Worksheet on Implications for Broad Goals

Broad Goals	Launching	Mini-lessons	Conferring	Courses of Study	Sharing	Publishing	Involving Families	School-Wide Supports
Feeling good about themselves as writers								
Taking risks as writers								
Writing for many reasons								
Lifting the quality of the writing								

Joanne Hindley Salch's Worksheet
for Learning from Conferences

conf. #	1	2	3	4	5	6
The teacher . . .						
utilizes the history of the writer/reader						
uses examples or metaphors to clarify meaning						
acknowledges what the child does well						
sets a clear goal/task for the child						
teaches the reader/writer, not the reading or the writing (can they use what they learned again?)						
uses self as an example						
The child . . .						
has voice (ownership) in the conference						
is held accountable to do something specific after the conference						
has a clear sense of what to go off and do						

Joanne Hindley Salch's worksheet

APPENDIX 6

Conference Practice Sheets—Our Youngest Writers

The following pieces of writing, each accompanied by brief background blurbs on the young writers, are intended to be used similarly to the story of Joseph that appears on pages 8–9. After reading the material, teachers can be asked the following two questions:

What would your goal be for each of these writers?

How might this goal inform what you say in a conference?

1. Raquel is an enthusiastic writer. Each day she draws a member of her family and then writes a one- or two-word label alongside the pictures. She usually whips off three or four pieces during each writing hour. When her teacher asks her to read this piece, she confidently says, "Black hair. My mom bought a rubber band for my hair."

2. Michael is one of the few children in the class that works on the same piece of writing for several days. He draws slowly and colors in his drawings methodically. He gets frustrated when his teacher asks him to share because he often forgets what he wrote. In this piece, all he can read is "Dad" and his own name.

3

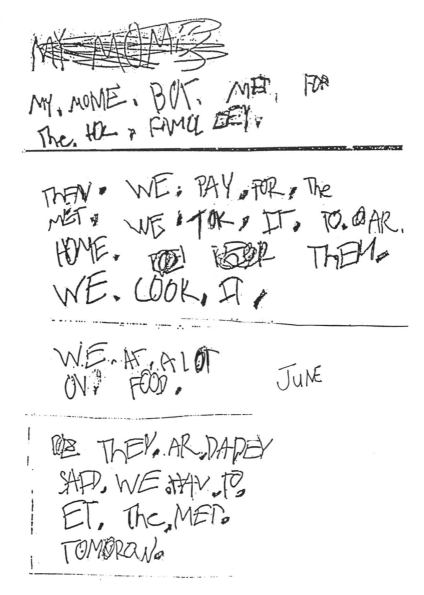

3. June always selects pre-prepared blank draft books from the paper supply. If there were ten pages stapled together, she would fill them eagerly. Each of the sections in her writing appeared on a separate page. All her books record what happened in her family on the previous day. They are always written in the past tense. She rarely draws. June is also a confident reader. Eric Carle and Rosemary Wells are her favorite authors. Her teacher recently taught a minilesson to the whole class about placing periods at the end of sentences.

4

Jennifer

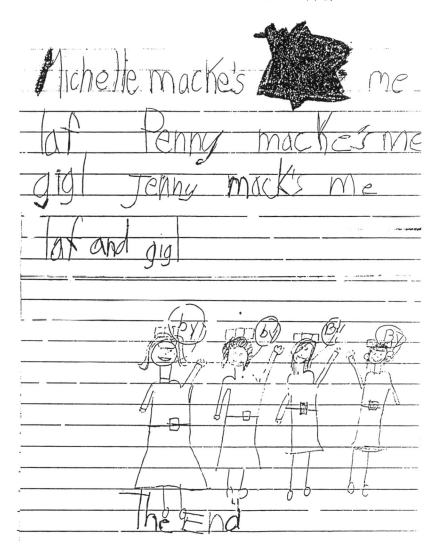

Michelle macke's ~~ me

laf   Penny macke's me

gigl   Jenny mack's me

laf and gigl

The End

4. Jennifer is very popular during writing time. Classmates view her as a great artist and accomplished speller. She has recently begun to write first and then illustrate her text at the bottom of her paper. She rarely stays on a piece for more than a day. In fact, she often finishes her work in ten minutes and spends the remaining workshop time helping friends or reading in the class library. She prefers nursery rhymes, alphabet books, and riddle books.

6

Sam

MM NDEFLOFLI

5. For several weeks, Sam has been filling his pages with apparent random letter strings. When asked to read his work back, he responded without even looking at the text. He said, "It says the family is in the house." Sam appears to be quite pleased with his work.

**Matthew's Writing Folder—Illustrating Variety
of First-Grade Genres**

I found a mape this mape
leaes onder grond I digx and digx
and digx until I find a
sekerit. clus all the clus
look like this

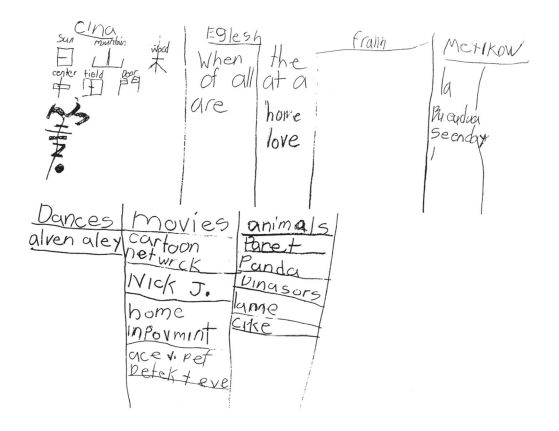

1. Minarels and maker
2. Metal detekter
3. mail holder
4. Dog Pet
5. Scienc books
6. Clekehens
7. fossils
8. sutcase weele
9. art sepliys
10.
11.

12.
13.
14.
15.

16.
17.
18.
19.

(pond life)

tertels preteckt there selfs with
there shells. Some tertels live
dry land. And some tertels live i
the water.

Some snacks eat frogs. Some are
poyseninis. And some are not. Some s
are wiyde. And some are not.

Birds
Some have loge lages. And some hav
shorters lags.

all jellyfish have bones.

In Spring

My tooth is loose in April
spring a day for birth
Animels are born, flowers grow,
Kids mack friends and play spring games

soker

books

what do You like the mows to do

| |

Sciene

| | |

lab

| |

other

Money

| |

sports

| | |

food

Jobe

| | |

art

| | | | |

When I have a computer
and desk, I am going to
tipe fish facks and go online
to scienc and work. artd I have
to do alot of work. I will learn
untel I become a gronup and mak
and sale. Then I'm done and go
home and visit my cetgren.
I eat and sleep. and go back
to work.

non ficshen

When I was wakin
to school I saw a
sine it had 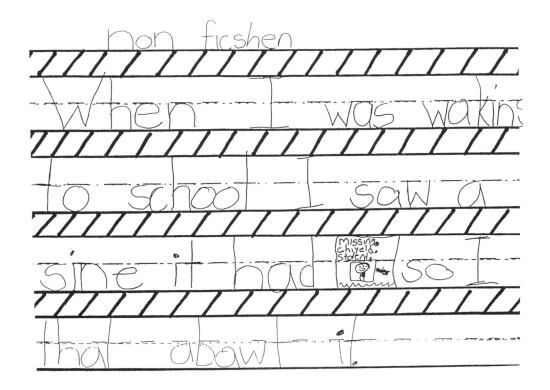 so I
that abowt it.

Editing/Publishing Checklist

NAME _____ DATE _____

TITLE _____ GENRE _____

STUDENT

THINGS I MUST REMEMBER TO <u>DO WHEN I EDIT</u>

TEACHER'S NOTES

YOUR STRENGTHS AS AN <u>EDITOR</u>

	WRITER √	PEER EDITOR √
SPELLING		
Check for words that don't look right.	❏	❏
Try them in other ways.	❏	❏
Check in dictionary or ask an expert speller.	❏	❏
PUNCTUATION		
Check for periods.	❏	❏
Check for capital letters.	❏	❏
Check for question marks.	❏	❏
Check for quotation marks.	❏	❏
Check for use of commas.	❏	❏
OTHER EDITING CONCERNS		
Check for indenting of paragraphs.	❏	❏
Check for use of verb tense.	❏	❏
Check for legible handwriting.	❏	❏
Check for appropriate spacing.	❏	❏
_____	❏	❏
_____	❏	❏
_____	❏	❏
_____	❏	❏

1. _____
2. _____
3. _____
4. _____
5. _____

SEE ME FOR AN EDITING
CONFERENCE ABOUT:
<u>YOUR AREAS TO WORK ON</u>

1. _____
2. _____
3. _____
4. _____
5. _____

<u>Circle Yes or No</u>

I have reedited my work after our editing conference.	Yes	No
The teacher has checked my final edit.	Yes	No
I am ready to publish this piece.	Yes	No
I would like to use the computer.	Yes	No
I would like to hand copy.	Yes	No
I would like to illustrate.	Yes	No

I would like to give it to _____.
I would like to send it to _____.
I would like to display it _____ (location).
I would like to keep it _____ (location).

CONCERNS, QUESTIONS, OR OBSERVATIONS ABOUT
<u>EDITING/PUBLISHING</u>

_____
_____
_____

Blank Spelling Study Sheet

Name _____ Date _____

This word doesn't look right. _____

I tried it another way. _____

I checked the dictionary or asked an expert. *_____

I was surprised that _____

_____

_____

A trick that will help me remember the spelling of this word is _____

_____

I studied the *correct spelling by using the LOOK, SAY, COVER, WRITE, CHECK, TRY AGAIN method.

_____	_____
_____	_____
_____	_____

Other words I can spell because I know how to spell this word are:

Words related to meaning (word families)	Words related to spelling features
_____	_____
_____	_____
_____	_____

APPENDIX 10

Professional Development Scenarios in the Teaching of Writing

1. Your colleague has just hung a new bulletin board. The wall outside her classroom is filled with well-written letters about neighborhood concerns. You realize that the letters are addressed to make-believe neighbors. What would you like to say to your colleague? How would you say it in a way that she can hear it?

2. Your colleague proudly shows you a batch of recent student writing. You notice that the pages are filled with overwritten passages that bring to mind sappy Hallmark card inscriptions. In other words, the teacher puts a premium on flowery adjectives and adverbs, clichéd similes, and distracting "put said to bed" type verbs. What do you think she needs to learn? How and when would you choose to inform her practice?

3. When you visit with your colleague during writing workshop you notice that she gets frustrated because so many children are demanding her attention at once. She is in the midst of a poetry course of study and all the children seem to need help with line breaks at the same time. What might you suggest?

4. An inexperienced teacher, at a grade level you are unfamiliar with, asks **you** for help in creating a nonfiction writing course of study. Where would you begin?

5. Colleagues are complaining that preparing children for the fourth-grade writing test as well as the genre requirements for the new standards portfolios are taking up all their writing workshop time. You are worried that they might be losing the joyful spirit that once was attached to the teaching of writing. What can you do about it?

6. You visit your colleague during his writing workshop and realize that his minilesson is not effective because he is teaching too many things at once and the children are confused. They really don't know what to do when they return to their seats from the meeting area. How would you coach your colleague and offer the kind of suggestions that would help him tomorrow?

7. Your colleague really doesn't believe that her children have significant life experiences to write about. She therefore insists on assigning very specific topics. How might you help her to see that there is a better way?

8. One teacher has had great success in helping children write short skits related to the social studies they are exploring. Another teacher on the same grade level decides to do likewise and in addition to hanging up a beautiful display of the students' work, decides to invite classes to the auditorium to watch the children perform their work. In some very real way, the first teacher is upset that the second teacher borrowed her idea and in fact took it further. Would you intervene? What might you do?

9. You notice that your colleague takes away ownership when she confers. She actually rewrites occasional sentences on a student's draft paper in order to lift the quality of the work. What might you say?

10. The volume in your colleague's classroom is so loud that you can barely hear the children when they share their writing. In addition, you can hardly concentrate on the conferring you were intending to model because the children seem to be in constant motion during the workshop. Your colleague doesn't seem to notice that there exists what you consider a chaotic atmosphere. How would you proceed?

11. You have invited a few colleagues into your room to observe your writing workshop. While you are conducting your minilesson, carefully prepared for this demonstration, you realize that your colleagues are chatting with one another, browsing through your library shelves, and reading your bulletin boards. You're feeling disappointed. What would you do?

12. You're leading a lunchtime meeting on introducing writer's notebooks to third graders. Some teachers begin to talk negatively about students, complaining that the children will probably lose their notebooks, their handwriting and spelling are so poor that no one will be able to read their writing, and the children seem so passive they probably will not have a thing to write about. How would you handle this gathering?

13. You want to organize a writing celebration in the school, but don't want to disenfranchise teachers who have not been paying much attention to the teaching of writing. You're afraid their contributions will pale in comparison to the teachers who have made the teaching of writing a priority. How would you proceed?

14. You want money for books to support the teachers who attend your writing network meetings. Who would you go to? What would you say?

15. Parents are concerned that the use of invented spelling in the early childhood classrooms will lead to bad habits. The principal has asked you to speak at the next PTA meeting. You've agreed to present. What would you say?

16. Teachers in second grade like to teach the writing of how-to books. They are surprised to discover that the new teachers in grade one are doing a course of study on writing how-to books and they request that the staff comes up with an agreed upon list of set genres assigned to each grade. How would you respond?

Calendar Project Directions and Planning Sheets

We will be making very special calendars for 200___. First we will each pick a topic that we care about. We will find *12* subtopics (one for each month) and write short passages for each. Then we will illustrate each one (BIG PROJECT!!). When we are done, we will attach each passage and illustration onto a calendar page. (Your teacher will give you the pages.) Finally we will add a countdown to the year 200___. (So in the box for January 1st we will write in the corner—365 days to go!) Remember to choose a topic that you

1. care about
2. can think of 12 subtopics for
3. can illustrate

For example, if I choose:

Flowers

1. Tulips	5. Daffodils	9. Marigolds
2. Roses	6. Lillies	10. Sunflowers
3. Lilacs	7. Peonies	11. Hibiscus
4. Carnations	8. Daisies	12. Violets

Name _____

Planning Sheet

My 200___ "_____" Calendar

1. January _____
2. February _____
3. March _____
4. April _____
5. May _____
6. June _____
7. July _____
8. August _____
9. September _____
10. October _____
11. November _____
12. December _____

INDEX

A

Ackerman, Diane, 67
Adults
    memories of, comparing with children's memories, 257
Aldis, Dorothy, 62
Alliteration, 121–22
Alphabet books, as writing structure, 189
Amelia's Notebook (Moss), 122–23
Amoore, Susannah, 119–20
Animals/pets, writing about, 68
Anthologies/collections
    of kindergarten poetry, 290–93
    from other schools, sharing, 152
    of poetry, 204–6, 363–65
    of student writings, 336–37
Apprenticeship relationships, 105–6, 114. *See also* Mentoring relationships; Models
Armadillos Sleep in Dugouts : and Other Places Animals Live (Ryan and DeGroat), 120
Around Town (Soentpiet), 124
Assessment-driven instruction, 85, 256
    reading-writing connections, 113–28
Attention, encouraging. *See also* Details, adding to writing
    awareness of surroundings, 116
    writing notebooks for, 43
Attitudes about writing. *See* Writing conferences
Atwell, Nancie, 3
Audience response, as impetus for good writing, 171–72, 242
    among second graders, 197
    writing for younger audiences, 38
Author studies
    Jonathan London example, 248–55
    memories, childhood, 383
Authors' visits, 305–6
Awakening the Heart (Heard), 316
Axworthy, Anni, 201

B

Ballpark (Cooper), 124
Bang, Molly, 190
Bauer, Marion Dane, 118
The Bee Season (Goldberg), 234
Beaton, Isabel, 290–93
Beatrix Potter (Wallner), 134
Beginning writers
    challenging, 176–77
    concept books and, 187
    descriptive/sensory language use, 165–66
    details, adding to writing, 164–65
    finishing, teaching about, 163
    multiword labels, 188
    pattern recognition, 191–92
    practice sheets for writing conferences, 388–92
    reading-writing connections, 177, 183–91
    real-world uses, demonstrating, 161, 165
    realistic goals for, 3–4
    respecting individuality of, 162
    setting realistic goals for, 3–4, 179–81
    share meetings, 179–81
    sharing writing with friends, 163
    spelling minilessons, 162–63
    surprise, adding to writing, 166–67
    teaching others, 191
    template structures, 189
    topics for, choosing, 177–79, 189–90
    variety, encouraging, 192–93
    verb usage studies, 166
    writing at home, 188–89
    writing materials, introducing, 162
    writing materials, providing variety of, 166
    writing routines, establishing, 164
Behaviors, childhood, as basis for writing workshops, 28–29
Besancon, David, letter to fourth grade class, 142–45

The Best Thing About a Puppy (Hindley and Casey), 199
The Big Brown Box (Russo), 14
Blood on the Forehead, What I Know About Writing (Kerr), 134
Bodies of work, studying, 315
Bolton, Faye, 229
Bookmaking, 337–38
Books, matching children with, 127–28
Boomer, Garth, 140
Bootman, Colin, 123
Borden, Louise, 5, 188, 305
Box-frame galleries, 335
Brennan, Neil, 130
Bridges, Margaret Parks, 137
Brooks, Kevin, 120
Brown, Ruth, 121–22
Browne, Philippa-Alys, 120
Bulletin boards, using creatively, 343–49
Bunting, Eve, 135
Burleigh, Robert, 119
Burrowes, Adjoa J., 188

C
Cadnum, Michael, 119
Caines, Jeannette, 120
Calendar project, 244–47
    planning sheet for, 398
The Candy Store Man (London and O'Malley), 251
Caps, Hats, Socks and Mittens: A Book About the Four Seasons (Borden and Hoban), 188
Carle, Eric, 257
Carlson, Lori Marie, 301
Catalanatto, Peter, 119
Cazden, Courtney, 241
Chall, Marsha Wilson, 118, 278
Childhood behaviors, writing about
    acting independently, 34–36
    collecting/collections, 28–29
    friendships/relationships with siblings and older children, 37–39
    having an advantage over adults, 33–34
    rites of passage, 29–33
    pretending, 23–28
Childhood needs, professional books about, 368
Childhood, unique attributes/viewpoint of
    appreciating, tapping into, 3–7, 12–13, 239–40, 318–21, 359
    as basis for notebook writing, 53–56
    emphasizing in writing workshops, 39
    in second grade, 196–97
    and poetry, 321

writing to preserve memories of, 10–11
Children's literature
    about New York City, list of, 260
    about non-city places, list of, 262
    about spelling, 234
    authors of, autobiographical works by, 369–70
    authors of, biographical works about, 371–72
    with characters who write, 367
    genre studies using, 149–50
    as inspiration for poetry, 293–300
    as model for place-based writing projects, 260
    as model for quality writing, 186–87
    as model for using figurative language, 278
Chiou, Regina, 240
Christmas House (Turner), 123
Ciardi, John, 67
City! San Francisco (Climo), 260–61
Classroom/school environments
    fostering mutual trust and respect in, 86
    interactive nature of, 85, 242–43
    supplies and materials in, 84
    writing supports/materials in, 84–85, 166
Clements, Andrew, 121
Click, Clack, Moo: Cows That Type (Cronin and Lewin), 121
Clifton, Lucille, 64
Climo, Shirley, 260
Coalson, Glo, 199
Coffee house readings, 332
Collections, of things
    as writing topic, 13, 15, 28–29
    using figurative language to describe, 279
Common topics, events
    similes/metaphors for, 279–80
    writing about in interesting ways, 118–19
Competitions, useful contests, 284–85
Concept books, 187
Conference guidelines, 87–88, 380
Conferring, professional books that support, 373. *See also* Professional development
Confetti: Poems for Children (Mora), 303
Cookbooks, annotated, as writing structure, 256
Cooper, Elisha, 124
Correspondence, letter writing, as publishing technique, 334
Counting books, as writing structure, 189
Country/foreign homes, writing about, 68
Course of study-driven reading-writing connections, 149–50
Crafting techniques
    helping students understand, 135–38

picture books that illustrate, 372
professional books that discuss, 373
Creech, Sharon, 278
Critiquing writing, importance of, 140–45. *See also*
Feedback
Crocodile Smile (Weeks), 213
Cronin, Doreen, 121
Cross-grade special projects, 37, 37–39
author studies, 248–55
genre studies, 37–38
mentoring of younger writers, 105–6
place-based writing projects, 269–73
*A Crow Doesn't Need a Shadow: A Guide to Writing Poetry
from Nature* (Ferra), 316
Cushman, Doug, 189

D

Daddy Played Music for the Cows (Weight and Sorensen),
123
Davis Judy, 75, 106, 135, 248
The Day Eddie Met the Author (Borden), 305
De Fina, Allan, class visit by, 305–6
DeGroat, Diane, 120
Demonstrations, of writing notebooks, 45, 50, 305–6. *See
also* Models, modeling; Teachers, roles of
Descriptive language, encouraging use of, 165–66
Details, using and appreciating, 120, 164–65, 259–60
encouraging observation, 117
in place-based writing, 262–63
Dewey, Jennifer Owings, 125
Dialogue journals, 58–61
Diana, Maybe (Dragonwagon), 137
Dicken, Charles, 359
"Distinguished teachers," 138–39
Do You Know What I'll Do? (Zolotow), 202
Doney, Todd L. W., 127
Dotlich, Rebecca, visit by, 305
Down by the Station (Hillenbrand), 201
Downing, Julie, 303
Drafts, realistic expectations, 78
Dragonwagon, Crescent, 137
Dreams, encouraging sharing of, 17–19
Ducky (Bunting and Wisniewski), 135

E

Early-childhood writing workshops
choosing topics, 164–67, 177–79, 189–90
encouraging observation, 190
encouraging pattern recognition, 191–92
encouraging variety, 192–93
encouraging writing to teach others, 191

goals of, 167–70, 173–76, 179–81
"good-for-the-school" challenges, 176
handling different rates of learning, 176
minilessons about materials and writing process,
162–64
minilessons about writing quality, 164–67
questions to ask during, 171
reading-writing connections, 177, 183–91
schoolwide writing campaigns, 177
share meetings, 182–83
spelling minilessons, 211–12
using template structures, 189
Editing/publishing checklist form, 402
Editing, teaching about, 326–28
Effective language, sharing, 279–80, 280–83
Eggers, Dave, 256
Emig, Janet, 3
Emily Just in Time (Slepian and Coalson), 199
Ernst, Karen, 271
Evaluations, individual, lessons for the whole school in,
240
Evans, Lezlie, 137
Experimentation, importance of encouraging, 237–38
Exploding Ants: Amazing Facts About How Animals Adapt
(Settel), 125

F

Faces Only a Mother Could Love (Dewey), 125
Families/parents. *See* Parents/families
Fantasy life, as impetus for writing, 17–19, 23–28
Favorite books, rewriting, 145–46
Feature columns, in school newspaper, 334–35
Fedden, Mary, 119–20
Feedback, importance of, 140–45, 148
finding lessons for the whole school in, 240
teaching conference basics, 83–86
Ferra, Lorraine, 316
Fiday, Beverly and David, 136
Fifth grade, fifth graders
author studies, 248–55
poetry studies, 316–17
realistic goals for, 75–78
rites of passage during, 31–32
Figurative language, adding to earlier writings, 279
Figurative language studies
modeling, 116–17, 120, 277–78
real-world examples, 278–80, 280–84
rewriting earlier works to include, 279
similes and metaphors, 273–76
File-cabinet publishing, 335
Finishing pieces, teaching about, 163

Fiore, Peter, 251
First grade, first graders
    example writing folder, 385–93
    poetry studies, 293–300
    rites of passage during, 31
    writing activities, 45
First-person narratives. *See* Personal narratives
Fishing in the Air (Creech), 278
Fletcher, Ralph, 117, 259
Flora and Tiger: 19 Very Short Stories from My Life (Carle),
    257
Foreign homelands, collecting stories/memories about,
    263–64
Formats, varieties of. *See also* Genres; Templates, supports
    appeal of, to second graders, 201
    helping students understand, 242
    introducing new formats, 129–31
    letter format picture books, 370
Fourth grade, fourth graders
    poetry studies, 311–16
    realistic goals for, 71–74
    rites of passage during, 31–32
    writing samples from, 68–70
Frazee, Marla, 213
Friends, sharing writing with, 163

G
Galleries, box-frame, 335
Garcia, Stephanie, 129
Garland, Sherry, 120
Genre studies, 149–50
    poetry, 290–321
    using memories for, 258
    in writing notebooks, 71–77
George, Kristine O'Connell, 127
Getz, Jacqui, 283
Ginsburg, Ruth Bader, 240
Goals, implications of (worksheet form), 378
Goldberg, Mayla, 234
For the Good of the Earth and Sun (Heard), 316
"Good-for-the-school" challenges, 176
Good Old Days (Greenfield), 137
Good Thing You're Not an Octopus! (Markes), 202
Good writing. *See* Writing quality, improving
Goodman, Yetta, 39
Graham, Paula W., 10
Grammatical challenges, 136–37. *See also* Verb choices
Grassby, Donna, 130
Gravers, Don, 259
Graves, Donald, 3
The Great Frog Race and Other Poems (George and
    Kiesler), 127

Greenfield, Eloise, 137
Groups, learning in, 221–22
Growth, as writers
    helping students evaluate, 243
    including in expectations, 48
Grunweld, Lisa, 187
Guess What I Am (Axworthy), 201
Guided autobiographies, 255–58

H
Hall displays, using writing notebooks in, 77
Harwayne, Shelley, poetry by, 319–20
Heard, Georgia, 316
A Heartbreaking Work of Staggering Genius (Eggers), 256
Henderson, Kathy, 124
Hest, Amy, 122–23
Hey, Little Ant (Hoose, Hoose and Tilley), 130
Hill, Sharon, 315
Hillenbrand, Will, 201
Hindley, Judy, 199
Hines, Anna Grossnickle, 190
Hoban, Lillian, 188
Home at Last: A Song of Migration (Sayre), 121
Home countries, writing about, 68
Home, writing at, 56–58, 188–89
Hoops (Burleigh), 118–19
Hoose, Phillip and Hannah, 130
How to Get Famous in Brooklyn (Hest), 122–23
Howard, Jane R., 190
Hurricane! (London and Sorensen), 251
Hush, Little Baby (Grazee), 213

I
I Love You As Much. . . (Melmed), 190
I Never Did That Before (Moore), 298
"I Never Hear" (Aldis), 62
I See the Moon and the Moon Sees Me (London and Fiore),
    251–52
"If I Were In Charge of the World. . . " (Viorst), 138
If I Were Queen of the World (Hiatt and Graham), 137
If I Were the Wind (Evans), 137
If I Were Your Father (Bridges and Denton), 137
If I Were Your Mother (Bridges and Denton), 137
"If It Were My Birthday" (Weil), 137–38
If You Were Born a Kitten (Bauer), 118
Illustrations, as impetus for writing, 124, 162
Illustrators, professional, picture books about, 371
Imagination, encouraging use of, 17–19, 23–28, 116–17
In the Company of Children (Salch), 66
Independent moments, children's appreciation of, 34–36
Individual voice, helping students find, 47–48, 197
Individuals, treating students as, 85, 168–70

Information Ecologies: Using Technology with Heart (Nardi and O'Day), 4
Informational texts, as writing inspiration, 367
Inquiry studies, 338–39
Interests, students'
    elevating into projects, 16–17
    encouraging writing/talking about, 12–15
Invented spelling. *See also* Spelling minilessons
    bulletin board displays of, 349–52
    teaching parents about, 341–42
    workshop on a wall, 352–54
Investigate Non-Fiction (Graves), 259
The Invisible Ladder (Rosenberg), 134–35

J

Janeczko, Paul, 129, 316
January Rides the Wind: A Book of Months (Otten and Doney), 127
Journal keeping
    paired dialogue journals, 39
    as tool for preserving memories, 10–12
Just One More (Koch), 187

K

Kangaroos Have Joeys (Browne), 120
Karas, G. Brian, 248–51
Kerr, M. E., 134
"Kid-watching", 39
Kiesler, Kate, 117, 127
Kindergarten, kindergarteners
    poetry studies, 290–93
    rites of passage during, 31
    writing activities, 45
Klein, Doris, 152
Klein, Judi, 152
Kliros, Thea, 203
Koch, Michele, 187
Koide, Tan and Yasuko, 203
Krantz, Amber, 317
Krauss, Ruth, 202
Krementz, Jill, 43
Krensky, Stephen, 116–17
Kurtz, Jane, 130

L

Labels, multi-word, as writing structure, 188
Lambert, Stephen, 202
Language, appreciating, 117–18
    newspaper language, 132–34
    poetic/sensory language, 120–22
    specialized vocabularies, 120
Language, appreciation of, sharing, 117–18, 279–80

Lasky, Kathryn, 123–24, 251
Learning by Teaching: Selected Articles on Writing and Teaching (Murray), 152
Learning process, respecting, 85
Letter format picture books, 368
Letter to the Lake (Swanson and Catalanotto), 119
Letters, correspondence
    as inspiration for writing, 58–61
    as tool for preserving memories, 11–12
Levy, Doris, 290–93
Lewin, Betsy, 117, 121
Lewis, Kim, 190
Library collections
    including student work in, 332
    sorting books in, based on place, 264
Life stories, suggested formats for, 255–58
Like Butter on Pancakes (Karas), 248
Lionni, Leo, 13
Listening, importance of, 85, 140
Literacy teachers, planning needs, 241–43
Literary anthologies, 336–37
Literary magazines, sharing among schools, 152
Literature, children's. *See* Children's literature
Little, Jean, 64
Livingston, Myra Cohn, 64, 127
Local materials, helping students find, 261
LoMonoco, Palmyra, 190
London, Jonathan, 6
    author studies of, 248–52, 383
Long, Melinda, 201
"Look Up!" (Turner), 43
The Lost and Found House (Cadnum), 119

M

Making things, as writing topic, 13–14
Manuscripts, calls for, 344–47
Margolies, Richard, 64
Markes, Julie, 202
The Marvelous Toy (Paxton), 213
Materials, writing, introducing new writers to, 162
May We Sleep Here Tonight? (Koide and Koide), 203
Mayer, Pam, 23, 241
McBride, Lee, 234
Meade, Holly, 201
Meier, Deborah, 3
Melmed, Laura Krauss, 190
Memories, childhood
    encouraging writing about, 120, 255–58
    writing as way of preserving, 10–11, 119
Memory books, 257
Memory manuscripts, 257
Memory maps, 256

Mentoring relationships, 148. *See also* Models, modeling
  apprenticeships, 105–6, 114
  partnering older with younger students, 37–39
Metaphor, teaching about, 118, 265, 273–76
Missouri School Days (McBride), 234
Models, modeling. *See also* Mentoring relationships
  children's literature as, 198
  of figurative language, 277–78
  teachers' writings as, 45, 50, 167, 373
  during writing workshops, 50
Moore, Lilian, 298
Mora, Pat, 303
"Morning Strangers", 63–64
Moss, Marissa, 122–23
Motivating good writing, 8–9
Motley the Cat (Amoore and Fedden), 119–20
Multigrade projects. *See* Cross-grade special projects
Multiword labels, encouraging use of, 188
Munsinger, Lynn, 189
Murphy, Stuart J., 129
Murray, Don, 152, 259
My Bunny and Me (George), 137
My Father's Boat (Garland), 120
My Father's Hands (Ryder), 117
My Friend Harry (Lewis), 190
In My Mama's Kitchen (Nolen and Bootman), 123
My Steps (Derby and Burrowes), 188
My Teacher's Secret Life (Krensky), 116

N
"Name That Tune" invented spelling project, 349–52
Naming the Cat (Pringle and Potter), 119
Narahashi, Keiko, 189
Nardi, Bonnie, 4
Nature's Paintbrush: The Patterns and Colors Around You
    (Stockdale), 124–25
Needs-based minilessons, 115–27
Neighborhood displays, 332
New York City, children's books about, 260
Newspapers
  examples of quality writing in, 132–34
  as source of inspiration/subject matter, 131–32, 135
Night in the Country (Rylant), 307
Night Letters (LoMonaco), 190
Night Sounds, Morning Colors (Wells), 117
Nocturn (Yolen), 118
Nolen, Jerdine, 123
Non-local place settings, 261–62
Nonfiction read-alouds, 260
Noonan, Julia, 202
  Notebooks, writing. *See* Writing

Nothing Ever Happens on 90th Street (Schotter), 116–17
Now-and-then bulletin boards, 344–47
Now Soon Later (Grunweld), 187
Numeroff, Laura, 189

O
Observation, as writing tool, 117, 190–91
O'Day, Vicki, 4
"Old Voices from the Fifties" project, 348–49
O'Malley, Kevin, 251
One Fall Day (Bangs), 190
Only the Moon and Me (Margolies), 64
Ordinary topics, making engaging, 118–19
Otten, Charlotte F., 127

P
Paired dialogue journals, 39
Paley, Grace, 67
Parent workshops
  on invented spellings, 341–42
  on using writing notebooks at home, 342–43
Parents/families
  bulletin boards for, 348–52
  informing about students' work, 326
  informing about writing program, 327, 341, 355–58
  inviting to writing workshops, 358
  involving in searches for figurative language, 279
  involving in spelling minilessons, 226–27
  parent newsletters, 355–58
Partnering. *See* Mentoring relationships
Pasten, Linda, 134–35
The Pattaconk Brook (Stevenson), 116
Pattern recognition
  distinguishing from topic imitation, 203
  encouraging in beginning writers, 191–92
  and template books, 199–202
Paxton, Tom, 213
"Peephole Book" series (Axworthy), 201
Pepper's Journal: A Kittens First Year (Murphy and
    Winborn), 129
Performances/public speaking, as publishing techniques,
    330
Personal narratives
  encouraging beginning writers to write, 188
  firsthand experiences, 53–56, 120
  introducing, 120
  structures/formats for, 122–24, 255–58
Personification, introducing, 127
Personal voice, encouraging, 47–48, 197
Pets, writing about, 119–20
Phoebe and the Spelling Bee (Saltzberg), 234

Photography-based projects, 129, 256
Picture books, lists of
    with characters who write, 367
    that inspire notebook writing, 365
    that teach about crafting techniques, 372
    about writers and illustrators, 368
    written in letter format, 368
Pictures of Home (Thompson), 130
A Pinky Is a Baby Mouse and other Baby Animal Names
    (Ryan and deGroat), 120
Place-based writing projects, 68, 258–59
    capturing details, 262–63
    children's literature as model, 260
    collecting oral stories, 263
    cross-grade special projects, 269–70
    nonfiction read-alouds, 260
    point-counterpoint techniques, 263
    professional resources for, 259–60
    real world uses for, 271–72
    sharing works in progress, 266
    simile/metaphor studies, 265
    writing challenges, 265–66
Plagiarism, 131, 148
Playfulness, encouraging, 19–20
Poetic language, encouraging appreciation/use of,
    116–17, 120
Poetry
    course of study, 149
    finding appropriate poems, 65
    grammatical challenges in, 137–38
    importance of, to professional writers, 67
    as model to encourage writing, 61–67
Poetry collections, lists of
    anthologies that support notebook writing, 365
    favorites, 204–6, 363–65
Poetry from A to Z: A Guide for Young Writers (Janeczko),
    316
Poetry studies
    fifth grade, 316–17
    first grade, 293–300
    fourth grade, 311–16
    kindergarten, 290–93
    second grade, 300–304
    shaping poems, 306–7
    third grade, 305–11
Pond Year (Lasky), 123–24
Popposites (Yoon), 187
Potter, Katherine, 119
Pretending, fantasy, encouraging, 17–19, 23–28,
    116–17
Prewriting activities, 3

Principal's Gallery, 343–44
Principals, poetry writing by, 318–21
Pringle, Laurence, 119
Problem-solving, encouraging varieties of approaches to,
    84–85
Professional development activities
    brainstorming sessions, 238–39
    exploring links between reading and writing, 373
    planning courses of study, 241–43
    scenarios for the teaching of writing, 396–97
Professional development books
    on crafting techniques, 372
    on learning to confer, 373
    on needs of childhood, 366
    as writing inspiration, 373
    on writing workshops, 374
Projects, special
    cross-grade special projects, 37
    long-term writing studies, 114
    memory-based writing projects, 255–58
    place-based writing projects, 258–73
Publishing, reasons for, 328–29
Publishing techniques, 330
    bookmaking, 337–38
    box-frame galleries, 335
    calls for manuscripts, 347–48
    coffee house readings, 332
    designated writing areas, 335
    for early writers, 329–35, 394
    feature newspaper columns, 334–35
    file-cabinet publishing, 335
    inquiry studies, 338–39
    literary anthologies, 335
    neighborhood displays, 332
    performances of work, 330
    regular correspondence, 334
    for second grade writers, 197–98
    student guest speakers, 330
    student works in library collections, 332
    three-ring binder projects, 331–32
    Web-site publishing, 334
Puddles Challenge, responses to, 8–9
Puddles (London), 6

R
Re-reading books and writings, 127
Read-alouds, 52–53, 260–61
    during share meetings, 182–83
Read to Write (Murray), 259–60
Reading centers, allowing interaction with writing center
    activities, 186–87

Reading material, choosing, 127–28. *See also* Children's literature
Reading-partner collaborations, 39, 113
Reading-writing connections
   assessment-driven, 113–28
   with beginning writers, 183–91
   course of study-driven, 114
   professional books that discuss, 374
   student-driven, 114
   text-driven, 128–45
   using with beginning readers, 177
Readings, public, as publishing technique, 330, 332
Real-world items, as spelling models, 222–25
Real-world responses, to writing notebooks, 79
Real-world uses for writing, 91, 124
   emphasizing/demonstrating, 121, 283–84
   place-based writing, 271–72
   publishing opportunities, 339–40
Recording information. *See* Research, information gather
Reluctant writers, encouraging, 309–10. *See also* Beginning writers
Reminiscences, as writing structure, 255–58
Rereading/revising earlier material, 279
Research, information gathering
   encouraging a researcher's stance, 50–51
   expanding tools for, 117
   finding local materials, 261
   inventors and scribes, 221–
   as means of improving writing, 171–72
   using real-world artifacts, 222–25
Respect, mutual
   encouraging children to show, 84
   fostering in the classroom environment, 85–86
   showing towards youngest writers, 162
Revising
   limiting amount of, 49
   reshaping, 171–72
   rewriting pieces written when younger, 268
Reynolds, Peter R., 199
Rhythm and rhyme, studies using, 119–20
Ridlon, Marci, 62
Risk-taking, in writing, encouraging, 88–91
Rites of passage
   as source of writing topics, 29–33
   rting writing notebooks, 43–44
   w heet for, 376
River F   lly, River Wild (K   and Brennan), 130
Roberts, N   131
Rogovin, Paula,   0
Rosenberg, Liz, 134–35
Russo, Marisabina, 14, 188

Ruzzo, Karen, 204–6, 248, 301
Ryan, Pam Munoz, 120
Ryder, Joanne, 117
Rylant, Cynthia, 307

S
Sadis, Renay, 129
Salch, Joanne Hindley, 11, 34, 63, 65–67
   comments on writing conferences, 95–96, 100
   worksheet for writing conferences, 379
Saltzberg, Barney, 234
Sand Castle (Yee and Kliros), 203
The Saturday Kid (Sorrel and Carlesimo), 265
Sayre, April Pulley, 121
School newspaper, feature columns, 334–35
Schoolwide writing campaigns, 177
Schotter, Roni, 116
A Seaside Alphabet (Grassby and Tooke), 130
Second graders, second grade writing workshops
   author studies with fifth graders, 248–55
   developing individual voices, 196–97
   poetry studies, 300–304
   publication tools, 197–98
   range of interests and formats, 195–96
   rites of passage, 31
   template structures, 198–203
   use of literature as incentive, model, 198
   using modified writer's notebooks, 204–6
   writing activities, 45
   writing to affect audience, 197
Second-language learners, writing conference transcript, 98–101
Sensory language, 122
   eliciting in beginning writers, 166
   narratives using, 120
Serendipity (Tobias and Reynolds), 199
Share meetings, 182–83
Sheindlin, Judy, 201
Siblings
   writing about, 11
   writing for, 38–39
Simile, introducing, 118, 273–76
Similes Dictionary (Sommer and Sommer), 278–79
Sixth grader, writing conference transcript, 92–98
Sled on Boston Common (Borden), 5
Slepian, Jan, 199
Smith, Frank, 67
Snapshots from the Wedding (Soto and Garcia), 129
Snippets, expanding into shared reading, 185–86
Snowball, Diane, 228–29
Soentpiet, Chris K., 124

Sol a Sol (Carlson), 301
Sommer, Elyse and Mike, 278–79
Sontag, Susan, 43
Sorensen, Henri, 123, 251
Sorrel, Edward, 265
Soto, Gary, 129
Sounds, encouraging appreciation of, 119. *See also*
    Alliteration; Poetic language
Speaking of Journals (Graham), 10
Speed, Toby, 303
Spelling, invented
    accepting, 142, 162
    helping beginning writers with, 170
    workshops on for parents, 341–42
Spelling K-8: Planning and Teaching (Snowball and Bolton),
    229
Spelling minilessons
    for beginning writers, 211–13
    children's books about spelling, 234
    inventors and scribes, 221–22
    in older grades, 227–33
    practice spelling sessions, 215
    spelling fears, overcoming, 116
    spelling research activities, 215–25
    spelling study sheets, 230–33, 395
    tools for improving, 162–63
    using literature as a model, 213
    using student writing as model, 213–15
    during writing workshops, 225–26
Standardized testing, creative approaches to requirements
    of, 286
Stevenson, James, 116, 251
Stockdale, Susan, 124–25
Stone Bench in an Empty Park (Janeczko and Silberman),
    129
Stringbeans Trip to Shining Sea (Williams), 201
Structures, for writing, 36–37. *See also* Formats, varieties
    of; Genres; Templates, supports
Student-driven reading-writing connections, 146–49
Student writing, spelling minilessons using, 213–15
Sugarbush Spring (Chall), 118, 278
Supplies, abundant, need for, 84
Supports, for writing. *See* Templates, supports
Surprises, in writing
    communicating personal vision, 121
    encouraging, 142, 166–67
Swanson, Susan Marie, 119

T
Teacher demonstrations. *See* Models, modeling
Teacher training activities, 85–86

listening to professional writers, 150
pairing writing by students with writing by
    professionals, 152–54
reading literary publications, 152
recognizing good writing, 150–51
treating student writing as literature, 154
Teachers, role of
    during assessment-driven instruction, 114–16
    choosing appropriate reading materials, 127–28
    in fostering beginning writers, 174–75
    as model, 140–45, 148, 166–67, 264
    need for flexibility, 121
    as writers, 380
    during writing conferences, 106–9, 168
Templates, supports
    for beginning writers, 36–37, 189
    popularity of among second graders, 198–203
Temple, Charles, 119
Text-driven reading-writing connections, 113–28
    autobiographical material, 134–35
    crafting techniques, 135–38
    formats, introducing, 129–31
    grammatical challenges, 136–37
    newspapers as resources for, 131–34
    works by students for, 138–45
"The Irresistible Urge to Make Things" (Lionni), 13
Third grade, third graders
    poetry studies, 305–11
    realistic goals for, 48, 70–71
    rites of passage during, 31
    writing conference with, transcript from, 101–3
    writing notebooks, 43–44, 206
Thompson, Colin, 129
Three-ring binder projects, 330
Tilley, Debbie, 130
Time to Go (Fiday and Fiday), 136
Time, uninterrupted
    for teaching conferences, 85
    for writing in writing notebooks, 79
    for writing workshops, 385
Timelines, life stories, 256
Titles, learning to appreciate, 124–25, 142
Toad (Brown), 122
Tobias, Tobi, 199
Tolstoy, Leo, 7–8
Tooke, Susan, 130
Topics, for writing
    allowing children to choose, 3
    for beginning writers, 162
    using children's interests as, 12–17
    tools for finding, 124

Train (Temple), 119
Trifon, Linda, 6
True-or-False Book (Lauber), 200
Turner, Ann, 43, 123
Twilight Comes Twice (Fletcher and Kiesler), 117
Two Girls Can (Munsinger and Narahashi), 189

U
Under the Table (Russo), 188
Usis, Amy, 138–40

V
Van Laan, Nancy, 202
Variety, encouraging in beginning writers, 191–92
Verb choices, introducing students to, 127, 166, 248
Viorst, Judith, 138
Vision, personal, communicating through writing, 121
Vocabularies, specialized, introducing, 120

W
Walk a Green Path (Lewin), 117
Wallner, Alexandra, 134
Walsh, Jill Paton, 202
"Watching Things" (Ridlon), 62
Water Voices (Speed and Downing), 303
Web-site publishing, 334
Weeks, Sarah, 213
Weidt, Maryann, 123
Weil, Zaro, 137–38
Well-informed teachers, importance of, 85–86
Wells, Rosemary, 117
Werner, Pat, 305
What a Writer Needs (Fletcher), 259
What Dads Can't Do (Woods and Cushman), 189
What Grandmas Do Best (Numeroff), 189
What Grandpas Do Best (Numeroff), 189
What I'll Remember When I Am A Grown-Up (Willner-Pardo), 44
What Joe Saw (Hines), 190
"What Were They Thinking" project, 256
When a City Leans Against the Sky (De Fina), 306
When I Was Little Like You (Walsh and Lambert), 202
When I'm Hungry (Howard), 190
When Papa Snores (Long, Meade), 201
When Winter Comes (Van Laan), 202
Whole-group shares, 182–83
Whole-school activities, 38
William and the Good Old Days (Greenfield), 137
Williams, Vera, 201
Willner-Pardo, Gina, 44
Win or Lose by How You Chose (Sheindlin), 201
Winborn, Marsha, 129

Window Wishing (Caines and Brooks), 120
Wisniewski, David, 121, 134–35, 311–16
Wolff, Ferida, 177
Wong, Janet, 306
Woods, Douglas, 189
Word sounds, 121–22
Word wall substitutions, 184–85
Words. *See* Language, appreciating
Workshop on a wall, invented spelling, 352–54
Workshop (Clements and Wisniewski), 121
Workshops, with family members
    on invented spellings, 341–42
    on using the writer's notebook at home, 342–43
The Writer's Desk (Krementz), 43
Writers, of children's books
    autobiographical works by, 369–71
    biographical works about, 371
    books about writing, 372
    picture books about, 368–69
    practice books, 148
    on writing process, 140, 150
Writers, young. *See* Beginning writers
Writing areas, 334–35
Writing buddies, 37
Writing conferences
    with beginning writers, 167–69
    children's options during, 84
    encouraging writing risk-taking, 88–91
    errors to avoid during, 106
    guidelines for, 87–92
    identifying feelings about writing, 88
    materials and supplies for, 84
    practice sheets, 380–84
    as reason for writing, 191
    routines during, 83
    spelling minilessons, 215–21
    supportive school structures and beliefs, 84
    tips for successful partnering, 86, 106–9
    transcripts from, 92–106
    well-informed teachers, importance of, 85–86
    worksheet for (Salch), 3791
Writing materials, for beginning writers, 166
Writing notebooks
    adding to quality of drafts, 78
    appreciating value of, 122–23
    changing focus of as child grows, 78
    demonstrations of, 45, 50, 305–6
    as dialogue journals, 58–61
    in early-childhood grades, 204–6
    fostering enthusiasm for writing using, 43–46
    genres for, 78
    helping students appreciate value of, 116, 122–23

initial goals/expectations for, 45–46
introducing students to, 43–45
personal narratives, 53–56, 68–70
personal voice, developing, 47–48, 197
poetry, 61–67
read-alouds of contents of, 52–53
real-world response to, 79
scientific observations in, 50–51
setting realistic goals for, 46–50, 70–77
time for, making, 79
writing at home in, 56–58, 342–43
Writing process, books about, 376
Writing, purpose of, clarifying student's understanding of, 91
Writing quality, improving
discussing/identifying good writing, 140–42, 150–54, 242–43
literature studies for, 186–87, 278
minilessons about, 164–67
poetry studies for, 62
sharing and, 152
tools for, 91–92
Writing, responses to, helping students understand, 91
Writing, real-world uses for, 121, 124
demonstrating to beginning writers, 165
emphasizing with beginning writers, 169–70
teaching others, 191
Writing strategies, enlarging, 116–17
On Writing Well (Zinsser), 259
Writing workshops. *See also* Writing conferences
across-grade activities, 38
calendar project, 244–47

child-selected topics, 8–9
creativity and experimentation during, 12–13, 19–20, 237–38, 285–86
defining content of, 241–43
editing minilessons, 326–28
evaluating success of, 9
figurative language, lessons about, 273–84
inviting parents/family members to, 358
making time for, 377
memory-based writing projects, 255–58
motivating factors, 8–9
place-based writing projects, 258–59
professional books that discuss, 374
providing supports/writing models, 36–37
routines in, 84
spelling minilessons during, 225–26
student guest speakers, 330
topics for, 5–7
with young children, skills needed for. *See also* Early-childhood writing workshops

Y
A Year for Kiko (Wolff), 177
A Year in the City (Henderson and Howard), 124
Yee, Brenda Shannon, 203
Yolen, Jane, 118
Yoon, Jug-Huyn, 187
You're Just What I Need (Krauss and Noonan), 202

Z
Zinsser, William, 259
Zolotow, Charlotte, 202, 251